Domestic Violence and the Law
in Colonial and Postcolonial Africa

To Kathleen —
a colleague
and friend
— Emily

NEW AFRICAN HISTORIES SERIES

Series editors: Jean Allman and Allen Isaacman

David William Cohen and E. S. Atieno Odhiambo, *The Risks of Knowledge: Investigations into the Death of the Hon. Minister John Robert Ouko in Kenya, 1990*

Belinda Bozzoli, *Theatres of Struggle and the End of Apartheid*

Gary Kynoch, *We Are Fighting the World: A History of Marashea Gangs in South Africa, 1947–1999*

Stephanie Newell, *The Forger's Tale: The Search for Odeziaku*

Jacob A. Tropp, *Natures of Colonial Change: Environmental Relations in the Making of the Transkei*

Jan Bender Shetler, *Imagining Serengeti: A History of Landscape Memory in Tanzania from Earliest Times to the Present*

Cheikh Anta Babou, *Fighting the Greater Jihad: Amadu Bamba and the Founding of the Muridiyya of Senegal, 1853–1913*

Marc Epprecht, *Heterosexual Africa? The History of an Idea from the Age of Exploration to the Age of AIDS*

Marissa J. Moorman, *Intonations: A Social History of Music and Nation in Luanda, Angola, from 1945 to Recent Times*

Karen E. Flint, *Healing Traditions: African Medicine, Cultural Exchange, and Competition in South Africa, 1820–1948*

Derek R. Peterson and Giacomo Macola, editors, *Recasting the Past: History Writing and Political Work in Modern Africa*

Moses Ochonu, *Colonial Meltdown: Northern Nigeria in the Great Depression*

Emily Burrill, Richard Roberts, and Elizabeth Thornberry, editors, *Domestic Violence and the Law in Colonial and Postcolonial Africa*

Domestic Violence and the Law in Colonial and Postcolonial Africa

Edited by Emily Burrill, Richard Roberts, and Elizabeth Thornberry

OHIO UNIVERSITY PRESS
ATHENS

Ohio University Press, Athens, Ohio 45701
www.ohioswallow.com
© 2010 by Ohio University Press
All rights reserved

Printed in the United States of America
Ohio University Press books are printed on acid-free paper ⊗ ™

17 16 15 14 13 12 11 10   5 4 3 2 1

Library of Congress Cataloging-in-Publication Data

Domestic violence and the law in colonial and postcolonial Africa / edited by Emily
Burrill, Richard Roberts, and Elizabeth Thornberry.
    p. cm. — (New African histories series)
Includes bibliographical references and index.
    ISBN 978-0-8214-1928-1 (hc : alk. paper) — ISBN 978-0-8214-1929-8 (pb : alk. paper)
— ISBN 978-0-8214-4345-3 (electronic)
    1. Family violence—Africa—History. 2. Family violence—Law and legislation—
Africa—History. 3. Justice, Administration of—Africa—History. 4. Colonies—
Africa—History. I. Burrill, Emily. II. Roberts, Richard L., 1949– III. Thornberry,
Elizabeth.
    HV6626.23.A35D66 2010
    362.82'92096—dc22

                    2010017441

Contents

Preface

Domestic violence is fraught and complex, as a lived experience and a social and historical unit of analysis. From conference to published volume, this project has been deeply influenced by spirited and engaging discussions with colleagues regarding our use of the term *domestic violence*—that is, why we use the term *domestic violence* and not *sexual violence, gender-based violence,* or *household violence.* In their chapters, Codou Bop and Pamela Scully both make impassioned arguments for using *gender-based violence* as the appropriate analytical category.

Here, we use the term *domestic violence* to indicate overwhelmingly controlling and punitive behavior—whether physical, psychological, or emotional—directed by one member of a household toward another as a means of establishing dominance. Such punitive actions very often take the form of gender-based violence, but not always. "Domestic," in this sense, indicates a realm of shared living space oriented around relationships within households. Given the range of complex African residential patterns, living spaces were often gendered, often contained several generations, and consisted of kin as well as dependents of various kinds. We recognize domestic space and household relationships as processual and linked to larger social relationships and movements rather than part of a binary relationship that pits the private against the public. Using the term *domestic* allows us to talk about kin-based violence, marriage-based violence, gender-based violence, as well as violence between patrons and clients who shared the same domestic space.

Domestic violence, as a legal and criminal category and a cause for social activism, is often associated with European and North American contexts that center on the nuclear family. Our use of the term is also tied to a tradition and recent history of legal and political liberalism; however, the chapters that follow reveal the ways in which domestic space and domestic relationships take on different meanings in African contexts that extend the boundaries of family obligation, kinship, and dependency. Therefore, we use the term *domestic violence* recognizing the potential limitations of the term as a unit of analysis but with the expectation that it will provoke further discussion and research.

As the chapters in this volume demonstrate, African histories of domestic violence demand that scholars and activists refine our terms and analyses and that we pay attention to the historical legacies of contemporary problems.

This volume began as the Symposium on Law, Colonialism, and Domestic Violence in Africa and in Comparative Perspective held at the Stanford Humanities Center in April 2007. Each of the three editors had been conducting research on issues relating to marriage, domestic violence, and sexual violence using colonial court records. We felt that the topic was rich enough to bring together a group of scholars working on the general topic of domestic violence to share their findings and to spark further research and debate. The papers presented at the conference exceeded our expectations and congealed around a set of issues relating both to the domestic space as a site of violence in Africa and the mutually reinforcing interests of researchers working on historical and contemporary aspects of domestic violence. For their participation in the original symposium we thank especially Wayne Dooling, history, School of Oriental and African Studies, University of London; Prinisha Badassy, history, University of KwaZulu-Natal; Robert Gordon, anthropology, University of Vermont; Helen Moffett, University of Cape Town; and Leslye Obiora and Zelda Harris, School of Law, University of Arizona. We regret that given the constraints of publication, we were unable to include all of the excellent papers presented at the symposium. We are grateful to Raising Voices, a Kampala-based NGO, for permission to use the image that appears on the cover. Since 1999, Raising Voices has been tirelessly working to prevent domestic violence and to educate both women and men about the harmful effects of domestic violence not only on households but on the wider communities as well. This image was originally used in one of Raising Voices' teaching aids. We also express our thanks to the Center for African Studies, the Department of History, the Stanford Humanities Center Law and History Workshop, and the Division of International and Comparative Areas Studies, all at Stanford University, for their support of this project. Richard Roberts is especially grateful to the Mericos Foundation, which funded his yearlong fellowship at the Stanford Humanities Center as the Donald Andrews Whittier Fellow.

Emily Burrill
University of North Carolina at Chapel Hill

Richard Roberts
Stanford University

Elizabeth Thornberry
Stanford University

Domestic Violence and the Law
in Colonial and Postcolonial Africa

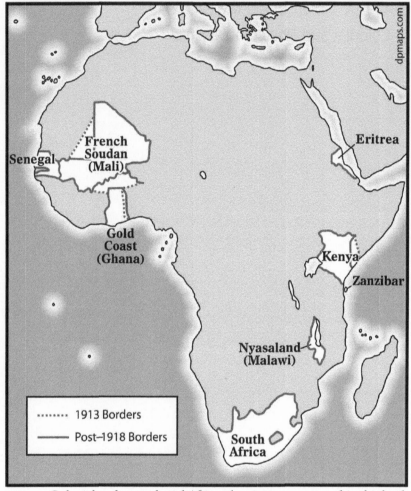

MAP 1. Colonial and postcolonial Africa, showing areas covered in this book

Domestic Violence and the Law in Africa

EMILY BURRILL, RICHARD ROBERTS, AND ELIZABETH THORNBERRY

SINCE THE 1990S we have seen an explosion of public attention paid to domestic violence within Africa. New pressure groups have formed, new laws have passed, and new names have been given to old kinds of violence. From People against Women Abuse in South Africa to Raising Voices in Uganda to Women in the Law and Development in Ghana, African men and women have organized—albeit with varied success—to push the issue onto national and international political agendas. Domestic violence itself, however, is not a recent phenomenon in Africa, nor are struggles against it. Given the importance of ideas of family and kinship in many African political systems, it is not surprising that families themselves have often been the site of violent coercion. This volume uncovers the history of domestic violence in Africa and illuminates the challenges faced by contemporary attempts to end domestic violence. By bringing together activists, legal scholars, anthropologists, and historians, this volume puts into conversation disciplinary approaches to the problem of domestic violence and thus provides enhanced perspectives on the complexities of domestic violence and efforts to address it.

The history of domestic violence in Africa comprises two interwoven narratives. The first describes changes in the experience of violence within the family, helping us understand why the form and prevalence of family-based violence changed over time in particular communities. However, we also recognize that the *idea* of domestic violence as a category of analysis is not a universal phenomenon. Rather, as Linda Gordon writes, the "modern history of family violence is not the story of changing responses to a constant problem, but, in large part, of redefinition of the problem itself."[1] A second narrative thus tracks the changing definitions of the "problem" of domestic violence. The essays in this volume form an argument for the need to understand the changing definitions of domestic violence in order to understand the persistence of these acts of violence and for the need for legal definitions and solutions.

It is fitting, then, to start with a definition of our own. In recent years, acts once called domestic violence have increasingly been relabeled by both activists and academics. The terms *gender-based violence, violence against women,* and *intimate partner violence* are most commonly used to describe violence committed by men against their partners. These terms have the merit of drawing our attention to the gendered nature of such violence, and of challenging characterizations of such violence as a private matter rather than a public concern.[2] Many of the chapters in this volume, however, are concerned with the production and perpetuation of precisely such a conception. In many parts of colonial and postcolonial Africa, legal responses to violence within the family differed from responses to other kinds of violence. Violence that was understood as domestic was often punished less harshly, if at all. By retaining the term *domestic violence* we wish to emphasize the importance of such an understanding to the histories under examination.

We therefore define domestic violence broadly, to include all acts of violence which are seen by those who inflict, endure, or regulate them as being justified by a familial relationship. By using this definition, we also wish to draw attention to the connections between violence committed by men against women and other forms of violence that are justified through the institutions and ideologies of kinship and family. Violence between parents and children, violence between co-wives in polygynous marriages, and even—as Katherine Luongo demonstrates in her chapter—violence against suspected witches were all shaped by such ideologies.

This volume brings together perspectives on the problem of domestic violence in Africa from historians, anthropologists, activists, and legal scholars. The first and second parts of the volume are devoted to analyses of domestic violence under colonialism, and the third part focuses on the contemporary period. Taken together, the contributors to this volume demonstrate how changes in the colonial past set in motion structures of domination that persist into the present. They also draw attention to the ongoing struggles within Africa to change these systems of domination. African states are signatories to all the major international conventions protecting women from discrimination and against violence as basic human rights but often with reservations that deflect and delay the application of these rights. This volume links these reservations to colonial legal regimes that privileged the maintenance of custom over women's desires to escape violent relationships.

All of the chapters in this volume focus on some aspect of the law, a focus that stems from the importance given to legal reform in recent efforts to combat domestic violence in Africa. Several essays in the second part examine shifts in the law around domestic violence during colonialism, and essays in the third part of this volume evaluate postcolonial efforts at legal reform. Other contributors use court records to find traces of domestic violence; and still others show how some Africans used the courts to challenge violent partners; whereas other contributors demonstrate how the law was changed to prevent women from using the courts to escape domestic violence. Taken together, their research demonstrates that, while law has shaped the history of domestic violence in fundamental ways, domestic violence nonetheless persists. Legal practice both shapes and is shaped by larger public understandings of domestic violence.

Although legal reform remains integral to efforts to reduce violence within households, the history of domestic violence in African legal systems reveals the difficulties facing current reformers. At the same time, several of the essays contained in this volume find in domestic violence a window into the ways that Africans and colonial administrators have given meaning to the major social changes of the nineteenth and twentieth centuries. The intellectual and social history of domestic violence illuminates the challenges faced by those in charge of African legal systems—whether colonial administrators, traditional leaders, or postcolonial African judges—as they struggled to regulate societies in states of change. Attempts to eradicate, or simply to regulate, domestic violence sparked debates about the proper relationship between law, culture, and gender relations as well as the contents of African custom. These debates continue to be central problems in many African legal systems.

This introductory essay locates the essays that follow in several frameworks. In addition to legal history, we discuss the place of domestic violence in the history of the family as well as contemporary debates about the interaction between international human rights theory and local cultures. An understanding of these contexts helps illuminate not only the chapters in this volume but also the predicament of current struggles against domestic violence in Africa.

EXPLAINING DOMESTIC VIOLENCE

In 2005, the World Health Organization conducted a global survey of the prevalence of intimate partner violence, one subset of domestic violence. We have drawn the accompanying table of categories of intimate partner violence from the WHO study and an earlier UN report; they are equally useful for thinking about the broader range of domestic violence referred to in this book.

The WHO 2005 study found that between 15 percent and 71 percent of the ever-partnered women respondents had experienced some form of physical or sexual violence in their lifetime. The lowest rate was found in an urban Japanese setting and the highest rate in a rural province of Ethiopia. The

TABLE 1 Categories of Intimate Partner Violence,
UN 1989 Report and WHO 2005 Study

Physical Violence	slapping and throwing something, pushing or shoving, pinching, pulling a woman's hair, hitting, choking, clubbing, kicking, dragging, burning, throwing acid or boiling water, threatening or actually using a weapon
Sexual Violence	being forced to have sexual intercourse when the female partner did not want to because she was afraid of what her partner might do, was forced to do something sexual that she found degrading or humiliating, specific attacks on the breasts or genitals
Emotional Violence	being insulted or made to feel bad about herself, being belittled or humiliated in front of others, being scared by the male perpetrator by the way the male partner looked at her, by yelling, by smashing things, by having the male partner threaten to hurt someone she cared about, harassment, degrading comments, threatening with divorce or intentions of taking another wife
Controlling Behavior	being kept from seeing friends, being restricted from seeing her family of birth, by the male partner insisting on knowing where she is at all times, by ignoring her or treating her with indifference, by getting angry if she spoke to another man, by being suspicious that she was unfaithful, and by demanding that she ask his permission before seeking health care for herself, isolation, deprivation of physical and economic resources, restricting access to family income, excessive possessiveness

Source: UN, Center for Social Development and Humanitarian Affairs, *Violence against Women in the Family* (New York: Center for Social Development and Humanitarian Affairs, 1989), 13–14; *World Health Organization Multi-country Study on Women's Health and Domestic Violence against Women: Initial Results on Relevance, Health Outcomes and Women's Responses* (2005), 14.

wide variation in these findings suggests that intimate partner violence is not an unchanging human propensity but rather produced by historically contingent factors including colonialism, poverty, cultural beliefs, and barriers to education.

Explanations of this variation move from theories that seek the origin of abuse in individualized causes to those that seek to explain the problem within broader structural and cultural contexts.[3] The earliest theories fell within a medical paradigm, described domestic violence as pathological, and focused on individual household deviance. More recent research has rejected the model of individual deviance but noted the importance of individual-level risk factors such as personal history of violence, economic deprivation, and substance abuse. At the level of the family, resource theories posit that decision-making power in the household derives from the "value" of resources that each person brings to the relationship. Family systems theory seeks to understand individuals within their interconnected family roles; the most sophisticated versions of this model see household members constantly jockeying and renegotiating control in the family, with domestic violence as a strategy employed by the household head to enforce his culturally sanctioned control over family members and dependents.[4] Proponents of social learning theory, which finds support in studies of child abuse, have described violence as a social statement learned from role models in the family or community.[5] Also at the community scale, social disorganization theory describes domestic violence as resulting from the weakness of people's ties to the communities in which they live.[6] On the broadest scale, feminist theories focusing on patriarchy as a form of domination locate the causes of domestic violence at the level of whole societies whose institutions and culture reinforce the power of men over women.[7] Although such theories concentrate on violence between male and female intimate partners, they employ models of power within the family that can be extended to other forms of violence, particularly violence committed by older family members against younger ones. Recent research has begun to integrate these levels of causation into "ecological" models that account for the interplay between them.[8]

AFRICAN FAMILY HISTORIES

To understand the changing role played by violence within African families, we must start by looking to the broader history of the family. Historically, in Africa as elsewhere, family structures have shown substantial variability. The normative family structure in contemporary Euro-American culture—a nuclear family made up of a husband, wife, and their children—is actually a relatively recent variant of much more complex configurations of kin and dependents. The pioneering debates in comparative family history centered on changes in family structure as a result of the process of industrialization in Europe and North America.[9] A central question driving this research was the question of when and how the "modern" family emerged.

By contrast, despite a strong interest in social history, family history has not gained much traction among Africanists. There is a paradox here, since Africa was an important site for the development of anthropological theses on kinship. In a world where kinship so deeply shaped social relations, it would seem that evidence about "families" should be readily available. However, very little work resembling what European and American students of the family have achieved has been conducted in Africa. With a few exceptions (white settler

South Africa,[10] Portuguese census and parish records,[11] a handful of Amharic and Arabic family histories or *tarikhs*[12]), historians of Africa do not have the necessary data to trace subtle patterns of change in fertility and mortality over time, as has been done in Europe and North America.

Even where sources are available, however, Africanists must confront the very notion of the family as the unit of analysis. The family form that lies at the heart of the great debates in family history may not be appropriate to the great variety of family systems that characterize Africa's past and present.[13] Indeed, recent research by Naomi Todamor suggests that the "nuclear" (or "proto-nuclear") family as the nominal unit for family history may not be as meaningful as originally thought in Europe.[14] Todamor argues that the eighteenth-century English "family" was a flexible unit, composed of a vast cast of individuals who lived and interacted in a household. Included in this unit might be spouses, children, other relations, servants, apprentices, boarders, and sojourners. Thus, she suggests that the household is the more useful and accurate unit of analysis.[15]

The concept of the household, if used carelessly, can also obscure important dynamics. Jane Guyer has warned social scientists working in Africa against taking the family household as a basic unit of analysis lest this focus elide power struggles within households, whether between older and younger generations or between husbands and wives.[16] Historians of domestic violence must conceptualize the household as a site for negotiations between numerous actors who are tied together by kinship—real or fictive—rather than a cohesive unit.

Some of these dynamics have been highlighted in the work of Jack Goody, whose research in northern Ghana suggested that African families do not fit the European template or even the broader concept of household. Rather, the complexity of African households should be interpreted in terms of the intersecting units of production (those who worked together), of consumption (those who ate together), of reproduction (those who generated descendants together), and of coresidence (those who lived together).[17] Goody's work permits us to conceptualize the diverse spatial and gender dimensions of African polygynous households, which may have included several wives, each with her own unit of reproduction and residence. In this volume, Cati Coe in particular examines the extended nature of the household in the Gold Coast through the lens of rape cases of debt pawns and adopted kin.

Flexible definitions of domestic units and diachronic approaches have led to the examination of the "family as a process" that "translates the impact of large structural changes to its own sphere."[18] The idea of the family as a process within the context of changing societies echoes the ecological model of family violence, which seeks to integrate large- and small-scale causes of

MAP 2. West Africa

family violence. It also recalls a paradigmatic debate on social history.[19] We can, following the lead of Charles Tilly, study the household as an institution that changed as a result of the development of the colonial and postcolonial state and the emergence of industrial and global capitalism. Alternatively, as David Cohen advocates, we can examine the household as it translates wider processes of change through its interior architecture, mediating these pressures and interpreting them through categories and processes of adaptation that have emerged over centuries of experimentation. Both approaches to social history share the assumption that households are not static and that all households interact with other institutions and processes of change.

The forces that shaped household dynamics in Africa include the slave trade, conversion to Islam and Christianity, the redefinition of ideas of "custom" and "tradition" under colonial rule, new colonial legal systems, the end of slavery, male labor migration and the resulting feminization of poverty in rural areas, the emergence of new forms of property and new means of accumulation in the colonial and postcolonial economies, urbanization, and the HIV/AIDS pandemic. Space does not permit more than a cursory discussion of the impact of these forces, but family history in Africa must be attentive to them and to their persistent legacies.[20] The slave trade deepened the commoditization of rights in persons. The tendency to retain female slaves in Africa while exporting men consolidated ideologies of patriarchy.[21] As Europeans scrambled to claim African territories as colonies in the late nineteenth century, they used antislavery rhetoric as part of their civilizing missions and set in motion conditions that led to the end of slavery within Africa.[22] In areas where slavery was a widespread institution, the end of slavery ushered in profound changes in household organizations whether or not slaves left their masters.[23] Where slaves remained with or close to their former masters, new ideologies and practices of dependency emerged. Masters whose slaves left them turned to their households to make up for this labor shortage. Those slaves who left their masters needed to establish their own households and often struggled to succeed.[24] The end of slavery was exactly the kind of pressure on households that exacerbated struggles over obligations, reciprocity, and power and resulted in incidences of domestic violence, as Marie Rodet and Emily Burrill and Richard Roberts discuss in their chapters.

In the twentieth century, the rise of industrial capitalism and cash-crop farming led to widespread labor migration by men and major transformations in the households that they left behind. The absence of adult men resulted in increased agricultural labor for women and children, leading some women to increase their reliance on sisters and female friends for survival.[25] The face of rural poverty became increasingly female, and migration also increased women's vulnerability to diseases such as tuberculosis and HIV that were carried by men returning from work.[26] Large-scale migration toward urban centers accelerated after World War II, leading to the formation of new types of households in urban settings. To cope with the struggles of urban life, many city dwellers adopted bilateral descent systems that allowed them to claim assistance from a wider pool of kin.[27]

Meanwhile, successful urban dwellers often sought to "shrink" kinship relations in order to control new forms of accumulation.[28] Such a shrinkage of kinship obligations was linked to cycles of the domestic group, as urban residents nurtured kinship connections in rural areas in anticipation of their eventual burials or as safety nets for retirement or respite from the chaos of urban life.[29] In her chapter, Codou Bop points to these processes in the creation of the "modern Senegalese family" as the site of domestic violence that occurs in the absence of restraint from wider kinship groups. Data from the WHO 2005 study show that the prevalence of intimate-partner violence is usually higher in rural provinces than in urban centers of the same country. The only African nation in the survey that included both rural and urban sites was Tanzania, where 56 percent of rural women experienced physical or sexual violence by an intimate partner compared to 41.3 percent of urban women.[30] This finding suggests the importance of historical investigation into the processes of urbanization for understanding contemporary patterns of domestic violence.

Set against the backdrop of these broad changes are three nested structural processes that shaped domestic violence during the colonial and postcolonial periods. The first is the insertion of the household into the broader structure of colonial domination. Colonial governments sought to collect revenue from Africans to pay for colonialism. Colonial taxation systems in colonial Africa exhibited a characteristic paradox: as in Europe, the household head was normally responsible for payment, but tax regimes also reflected the desires of colonial administrators to remake individuals and the family.[31] Thus, the characteristic British "hut" tax was intended to discourage polygyny by taxing men on their "extra" wives, while tax policy in the Belgian Congo was designed to bolster the birth rate.[32] In French West Africa, by contrast, the household head owed a simple tax for all adults in his household, reflecting the government's desire to access labor. All of these taxation systems reified the household as a foundational unit of colonial domination. Taxation added to the financial challenges of the household head, who in turn likely drew on his household labor to help generate the cash or commodities required to pay the tax. In rural South Africa, for example, the burden was borne largely by women who were most vulnerable to the consequence of their male guardian's failure to pay tax: the loss of land rights.[33] Thus, the effort to make African societies legible at the level of the family encouraged administrators to turn a blind eye to internal family dynamics, including domestic violence. This process is what other scholars of Africa called the colonial project of domestication—that is, the process by which African households were connected to the political economy of colonialism.[34] Domestication was an economic process, but it also contributed to the consolidation of a moral authority and the reordering of household relations within the state and among members of the household itself.

Second, men's efforts during the colonial period to increase their control over the labor of their wives led to conflicts over the separate wealth and income that women controlled. In many parts of sub-Saharan Africa, property systems permitted wives to accumulate wealth that was separate from the general household wealth. In many cases, marriage brought male and female labor systems together for the benefit of the household, but wives retained some portion of their time after completing domestic and agricultural chores to devote to their own enterprises.[35] Income derived from these enterprises provided women with some autonomy within marriage and could be used for women's strategies to promote their own or their children's well-being. The financial demands of the colonial period, however, motivated household heads to exert increased control over women's wealth and to prevent women from using their labor independently from the household.[36] Such actions fall under the expanded definitions of domestic violence that scholars have recognized in recent years.

Finally, in much of Africa marriage was and is legitimated through bridewealth. Bridewealth — the third of these nested processes — was a strategic investment that built and maintained webs of kinship and organized and controlled labor. Bridewealth often involved the transfer over a number of years of goods (grain, livestock, and cash) and services (weaving, herding, and occasional farmwork) from the husband's kin to those of his bride. In return, the husband and his kin group received the rights to the bride's labor power (at least for that portion of the day customarily devoted to household chores and other activities which contributed to the well-being of the household, such as farming, weeding, and spinning,), her reproductive power, and her domestic services.[37]

Colonial administrators' failure to understand the complex flow of goods and obligations involved in bridewealth transfers was reflected in the legal systems they imposed. As the value of bridewealth increased in many places throughout the subcontinent during the colonial period, some husbands also understood the higher value of bridewealth to confer on them fuller control over their wives' labor and sexuality and enhanced patriarchal authority. At the same time, economic pressures often limited the ability of husbands to pay bridewealth and contributed, particularly in the postcolonial period, to a rise in long-term domestic relationships that did not attain the status of marriage. Domestic violence must be understood in relation to the complex ways in which local processes of change shaped household relationships.

In many ways, the analyses of domestic violence in this volume contribute to a greater understanding of a broader history of the family. Martina Salvante's chapter illustrates the creation of new forms of family life during the Italian colonization of Eritrea, while Emily Burrill, Richard Roberts, and Marie Rodet examine the reconfiguration of households in French Soudan (Mali) after the abolition of slavery there. Studying domestic violence forces us to examine the constant renegotiations of power relations within families.

DEFINING DOMESTIC VIOLENCE: HUMAN RIGHTS AND THE PROBLEM OF CULTURE

Efforts to combat domestic violence within Africa have been plagued by accusations that it is a Western concept without relevance to African cultures.

There is a certain truth to this charge. The emergence of an international feminist movement, with the resulting campaigns against domestic violence, has shaped much of the work done to combat domestic violence in Africa. However, this work also has local roots. One of the contributions of this volume is to demonstrate the complicated past of the cultural categories that people have used to make sense of domestic violence in Africa.

In the West, the identification of domestic violence as a problem has its origins in the child protection movement in industrializing countries during the middle of the nineteenth century, itself a result of the novel identification of childhood as a distinctive phase of human life.[38] Protection of children from cruelty became, in turn, a means of opening up the household to public scrutiny. This scrutiny also revealed other forms of family violence, including wife battering.

In the United States in the twentieth century, the problem of domestic violence became a medical one. The "battered child syndrome" was first used in the public health literature in the early 1960s.[39] By 1976, every state in the United States mandated reporting of evidence relating to the battered child syndrome. In the 1970s, the "battered wife syndrome" became a central element of the women's movement and shifted the problem of domestic violence out of the hands of the medical and social services and into the judicial sphere, as courts recognized a history of violent abuse as a defense in cases where women killed their abusive husbands.[40] Along with the medicalization of domestic violence came new legislation. By the early 1990s, major industrial countries had enacted new legislation criminalizing violence against women.[41]

These developments in the industrialized world intersected with the internationalizing human rights movement, giving rise to an international women's rights movement that played an important role in the mobilization of international actors and states to enact legislation protecting women against discrimination and against violence as basic human rights.[42] The concept of human rights emerged primarily out of Western political theories of the rights of the individual to autonomy and freedom. The concept gained legal status in the international legal system that emerged after World War II. The United Nations Charter (1945) and the Universal Declaration of Human Rights (1948) codified a normative system of rights that adhere to people precisely because they are human.[43] From the beginning, the conception of human rights articulated in this international system included gender equality. Campaigns by gender activists have made this commitment explicit, resulting in the 1979 Convention on the Elimination of All Forms of Discrimination Against Women (CEDAW); the Convention on the Rights of the Child followed in 1989.[44] Both conventions explicitly identify violence against women or children as a violation of their rights.

The strategies of the international women's movement have influenced struggles against domestic violence in Africa. However, human rights discourse has not been seamlessly translated into national or local legal arenas. Scholars have identified this as a problem of scale, in which different discourses and practices prevail at different levels.[45] As Sally Engle Merry recently argued, international discourses do not neatly fit into vernacular discourses about justice, dignity, and emancipation. Merry has emphasized the role of the "translator" in bridging this gap. She writes that "translators refashion global rights agendas for local contexts and reframe local grievances in terms of global human rights principles and activities."[46] Indeed, domestic violence programs that merge human rights discourse with local idioms have emerged in numerous African societies. However, states can resist global human rights discourses and regimes by arguing that such ideas are opposed to local culture and values.[47] Benedetta Faedi (in this volume) details the recourse to such cultural arguments in the exceptions that numerous African countries have to their ratification of CEDAW where its provisions conflict with local understandings of religious or customary law. As Faedi describes, states bowed to significant pressure to ratify international human rights conventions but sought ways to avoid implementing them. In place of what may be termed blunt international instruments of human rights, Faedi calls instead for empowering regionally based human rights commissions and courts as a way of resolving the tensions with what states invoke as "local culture" to delay implementation.

Few students of culture today would invoke Edward B. Tyler's classic late nineteenth-century definition of culture as "that complex whole which includes knowledge, belief, art, morals, law, custom, and any other capabilities and habits acquired by man as a member of society."[48] Tyler's description of culture as a bounded entity, shared by all members of the community, supported European understandings of Africa as a patchwork of distinct "tribal societies." Most scholars today would agree that culture is better understood as a composite of practices that are contested, changing, connected to relationships of power, and shaped by historical influences. Within popular discourse, however, culture remains a powerful concept that carries a sense of deep tradition and national essence.[49] In Africa, such references to culture often involve claims about the continuity of cultural structures from the precolonial to the postcolonial eras.

The chapters in this volume contribute to the analysis of the place of culture within both historical and current debates about women's rights and legal protections from violence and discrimination. Unfortunately, none of our contributors deals directly with precolonial Africa. We hope that this volume inspires future research in that vein. However, the work included here highlights the major reconfigurations in family ideology that took place across Africa during the colonial period. Chapters by Burrill and Roberts, Rodet,

Elizabeth Thornberry, and Salvante make clear that ideas about the duties and obligations of different family members changed over time. At stake in these debates was the status of the household head and his rights over his dependents. Far from being stable, during the colonial period these rights were constantly challenged in the face of pressures from women, junior dependents, and from colonial officials whose views of African families also changed, as chapters by Stacey Hynd and Elke Stockreiter describe. These findings do not exclude the possibility of continuities in cultural understandings of the family between the precolonial and postcolonial periods.[50] However, we should be suspicious of appeals to an unchanging culture, in Africa as elsewhere.

In her chapter in this volume, Saida Hodžić analyzes the very different trajectories of efforts to ban female genital cutting and domestic violence in Ghana, both of which emerged out of the international women's movement. Although it might seem likely that efforts to ban FGC would bump up against cultural justifications for the continuation of the practice, Hodžić describes the relatively frictionless process of banning the practice. In contrast, efforts to promote national legislation to prohibit domestic violence failed miserably. Hodžić explores the complex ways in which international human rights discourse was marshaled in Ghana and the place of government–civil society interactions during these two campaigns. Culture was invoked differently in each effort, which lends support to the contention that culture is a malleable element in the debates around women's rights and domestic violence.

Despite being a signatory to all the major international human rights conventions, Senegal is still a site of domestic violence, and reforms instituted by the state actually perpetuate the conditions of such violence. Scott London in this volume explores the ways in which women with complaints of domestic violence are required to attend mandatory reconciliation sessions. London describes how women's complaints go unheeded by male mediators who tend to defer to husbands' explanations of domestic "troubles" and thus reassert the power of patriarchy.

But culture is not invoked randomly in the debates about domestic violence in Africa. Codou Bop, a Senegalese activist, argues in her chapter that culture is repeatedly invoked as the prop for patriarchy and thus lies at the heart of the persistence of domestic violence. The only solution is to change the culture. Bop's conclusion raises questions about the possibility of translating alternative visions of power and authority into local idioms. But how is this to be accomplished?

In a bold argument about efforts to eliminate female genital cutting, Gerry Mackie has proposed mobilizing local pressure groups to change the conventions surrounding marriage so that FGC would no longer be seen as a precondition for proper marriage in sub-Saharan Africa.[51] Mackie makes clear that the success of such a campaign cannot rest on the actions of individuals or individual families but must be based on communities acting together to change cultural practices. Several African-based NGOs (nongovernmental organizations), such as Engender Health in South Africa and Raising Voices in Uganda, work with men and have pursued a similar strategy in their efforts to combat domestic violence. By using men's associations—especially age-grade associations—efforts are under way to harness cultural institutions to change cultural practices by creating new collective standards that disapprove of domestic violence.[52]

REGULATING DOMESTIC VIOLENCE: LEGAL SYSTEMS AND MORAL ECONOMIES

The tension between competing conceptions of domestic violence is not, however, present only in human rights discourse and its collision with notions of culture. It is a fundamental feature of the legal arena. All societies have some form of legal pluralism in which multiple systems of normative beliefs and legal practices coexist. In precolonial Africa, various forms of indigenous law existed side by side with shari'a (Islamic law) and, during the era of the slave trade, with forms of European and canon law.[53] Colonialism, however, generated what John Griffiths has termed juristic legal pluralism, which gave formal structure to the interactions between different legal systems.[54] The classic example of colonial legal pluralism was the dual legal system that recognized and separated preexisting "native" law from the received law of the metropole.[55] Colonial legal pluralism can be understood as an encounter between dynamic, local processes of change in indigenous societies that predated colonial conquest and continued after conquest, and dynamic and changing forms of colonialism.[56]

Colonial systems implemented dual legal systems for reasons of both practicality and international law. The protectorate, which granted indigenous authorities sovereignty over internal affairs while placing them under the guardianship of an imperial power, was the predominant international legal instrument of late nineteenth-century imperial expansion. This structure also allowed imperial powers to delegate much of the work of governance to indigenous rulers. The protectorate sliced off those characteristics of sovereignty that involved capital crimes and other crimes considered to be threats to public order and singled them out for criminal prosecution, usually in courts run by the European colonial officials. Disputes relating to families and personal status were relegated to a residual category of customary or family law, often controlled by existing native authorities. Thornberry (in this volume) examines the impact of this dual classification on sexual assault cases in South Africa, which often fell into the cracks between these two systems.

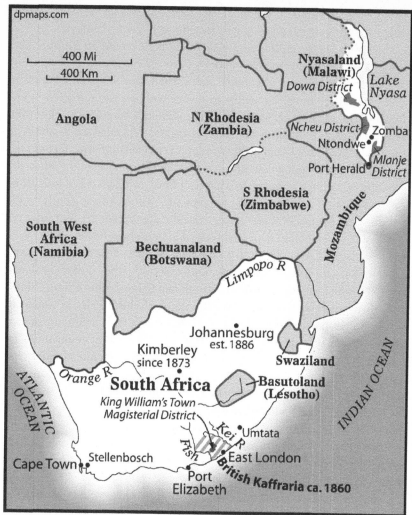

MAP 3. Southern and Central Africa

In order to exert some control over the African courts it supervised, the superior imperial power sought to make legible indigenous law. This process has been referred to as the invention of tradition, and it often took the form of collaboration between indigenous authorities (often merely male elders who were thought to be custodians of local knowledge) and colonial officials to generate handbooks of customary law. Indigenous law became customary law through this process and these handbooks served as guides to colonial magistrates in adjudicating cases and appeals brought to their courts.[57] The production of customary law gave significant power to native informants to reshape gender relations and forms of authority. Male household heads used these opportunities to consolidate their power. Colonial magistrates also shaped customary law according to their perceptions of African societies and African families.[58]

There were, however, limits on what could be invented. In Muslim communities, where the protectorate model recognized the regime of shari'a, and qadis became employees of colonial states when they served as assessors or judges on native courts, the ability to invent tradition was restricted by the circulation of written legal texts.[59] Even in nonliterate communities, however, the precarious hegemony of the colonial regime depended on its ability to manipulate the symbols and institutions of precolonial authority; it could not stray too far from popular consensus on the contents of custom.[60] Rather, the invention of tradition gave rise to what Sara Berry calls "an era of intensified contestations over custom, power, and property" within African courts.[61] One of the central focuses of these debates was the appropriate level of subservience that wives and other dependents owed to household heads.

The delegated sovereignty of the protectorate also generated policy and legal problems for colonial administrations, especially when custom or shari'a came in conflict with metropolitan and colonial rights. In this volume, Stockreiter discusses such a conflict, over the status of child brides in Zanzibar. Although British colonial legal policy granted shari'a wide autonomy in civil disputes in Zanzibar, a crisis was provoked when an activist colonial official decided that the child marriages condoned by shari'a resembled child rape cases in England and were therefore "repugnant" to civilization. Colonial officials were often deeply ambivalent about customary practices and occasionally intervened based on the repugnancy clauses found in most imperial legal codes. Thus, the British outlawed corporal punishments sanctioned by shari'a, and the French sought to mandate women's consent in marriage.[62] These actions contributed to the ongoing debates and struggles over the nature of custom that played out in colonial courts.

Using court cases, Rodet and Salvante (in this volume) describe how the French and Italian colonial states intervened in the domestic sphere if they felt that certain practices were undermining family stability or racial hierarchy. Rodet discusses how colonial policy changed as significant numbers of divorces were granted to women who complained of domestic violence. Worried about the lack of family stability, the colonial administration began to criminalize battered wives who left abusive husbands, sentencing them to prison terms. Salvante discusses how Italian Fascist ideas of racial purity led the colonial state in Italian East Africa to intervene aggressively in long-term domestic relationships between Italian settlers and African women. The police did not concern themselves with short-term sexual encounters across the racial divide but descended aggressively into the homes of Italian settlers if they suspected that stable, affective relationships existed.

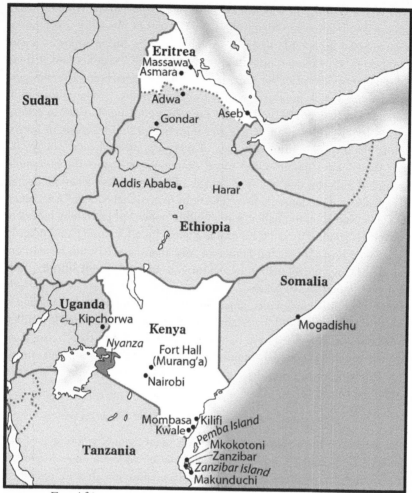

MAP 4. East Africa

However, neither the colonial state nor its male interlocutors managed to fully control the claims about domestic violence that were made in court. Several chapters in this volume demonstrate that women's agency in bringing cases of domestic violence to the courts challenged the practices of patriarchy. Stacey Hynd's chapter explores the challenges the colonial legal system faced when confronted with a wife who killed her violent husband. Rodet uses cases of domestic violence to examine women's efforts to end abusive relationships. Battered women may have escaped from abusive households in these individual cases, but they did not fundamentally challenge the bases of patriarchy and the logic of domestic violence. Burrill and Roberts propose in this volume that marriage and household formation should be seen as a form of "moral economy" in which men and women enter into a complex set of interlocking relationships that were shaped in part by prevailing assumptions regarding the acceptable limits of exploitation.[63] As Susan Amussen writes about domestic violence in early modern England, "No one denied there was an appropriate place for discipline within the household. The difficulty was ensuring that its use stayed within acceptable limits."[64] When those limits were exceeded, aggrieved individuals brought complaints forward to various forums for dispute resolution, whether informal kinship meetings or formal courts, often invoking this very idea of inappropriate violence. The WHO 2005 study lends support to the "moral economy" concept of the household because it indicates that high percentages of women accept a certain degree of violence in their domestic lives. The term "patriarchal bargain" was coined by Deniz Kandiyoti to challenge monolithic notions of patriarchy prevalent in Western feminist thought. Kandiyoti argued, from localized case studies in the Middle East, Africa, and Southeast Asia, that many Muslim women engaged in a bargain with patriarchy as a survival strategy.[65] Emily Burrill's study of domestic murders in Sikasso, Mali, demonstrates that wives were actively complicit in the maintenance of patriarchy—including domestic violence—as long as it remained within certain limits.[66] The limits recognized by women in Sikasso and elsewhere were not necessarily the same as those recognized by men, much less colonial administrators; but all of these groups did engage each other in an ongoing debate over the appropriate exercise of violence within the family.

AFRICAN VOICES IN THE COURTROOM

The authors in this volume rely heavily on court records as a source of evidence. Using court records to uncover domestic violence raises important epistemological questions. In her chapter, Hynd asks how students of domestic violence can use court records in the colonial past when the very concept of domestic violence was not yet invented and neither courts nor litigants used the term. However, many of the chapters in this volume—including Hynd's own—demonstrate the crucial importance of conceptions of family to both the practice and adjudication of certain forms of violence. In a variety of times and places, moral economies of violence permitted men to use violence against their wives, parents against their children, or household heads against their many dependents.

In seeking to reconstruct these moral economies, court records provide an invaluable resource. They reveal the importance of ideologies of family to kinds of violence that do not fit easily into definitions of domestic violence derived from international experience. Katherine Luongo peels away the layers of a witchcraft case to discover that sexual violence lay at its source. Luongo argues that Africans often understood and explained domestic violence through frameworks such as witchcraft. In her chapter, Thornberry describes the importance of ideas about family to the distinction between customary and criminal law in colonial South Africa. The testimony in these cases allows her to reconstruct understandings of sexual violence held by women and their families, which contradicted the understandings of colonial officials.

Court cases provide, as Koni Benson and Joyce Chadya have recently argued in their study of rape in colonial Bulawayo, a "rare opportunity to hear women speaking about their lived experiences."[67] Sally Engle Merry's study of law and colonialism in Hawai'i notes that court records provide an opportunity "to glimpse the tensions and conflicts of everyday life, to hear the stories of ordinary people who were not otherwise producing archival texts, and to understand the complex role of legal institutions" in the colonization of the islands.[68] Used carefully, court records can even provide some hints at the prevalence of domestic violence. The 1989 UN report stated that police reports "present only the tip of the iceberg" of the prevalence of domestic violence, and suggested that the level of domestic violence might be better estimated using records of divorce cases, especially in industrialized countries where violence in the family is often presented as ground for divorce.[69]

Court records also reveal the role played by legal processes in disrupting or reinforcing patterns of domestic violence. Susan Hirsch has applied linguistic and discourse analysis to Swahili women's disputes brought before the qadi's courts in Mombassa. Hirsch uses both records from the court and her own observations of disputes. By bringing disputes before the qadi's court, Swahili women both negotiated marital disputes and refashioned gender in the process. In narrating their troubles before the qadi, women confronted and reimagined Swahili gender norms that demand silence and subordination. Qadi's courts thus became "sites of resistance" not only because women challenged gendered norms but also because the judgments tended to favor women.[70] In Senegal, however, Scott London demonstrates in his chapter in this volume that, far from being empowered by their complaints of domestic violence, women found that court-mandated mediation sessions turned their complaints into criticisms regarding their lack of obedience to their husbands.

Using court records to write about domestic violence is, however, not straightforward. Records of domestic violence are often scattered among the various court systems. Such cases may have appeared before criminal courts in trials for rape, murder, or assault caused by violence in the domestic sphere (see chapters by Coe, Hynd, Luongo, and Thornberry) as well as before courts charged with dealing with civil disputes, such as divorce or child custody, where domestic violence in some form was invoked by the disputants (see chapters by Burrill and Roberts, London, Rodet, and Stockreiter).

Even when relevant cases are located, court records have limitations. They are not necessarily representative of the society that produced them; courts in communities with high levels of domestic violence might hear few cases about it, precisely because domestic violence is not considered a crime worthy of prosecution. The grievances we hear have been altered by the process of transforming the dispute into a legal wrong, by court procedures, by translating the testimony from local languages into colonial ones, and by the act of committing the claims to writing.[71] Students working with court records must also be mindful of the fact that the law changes. Procedures change; appeals exert backward pressure on legal practices; new legal categories and concepts are introduced.

Nor were these changes always intentional; there were always unintended consequences to the impositions of new legal regimes.[72] The French created exactly such conditions when they realized that the 1903 colonial legal system that provided opportunities to African women to seek divorce from their husbands actually created what they called "family instability." Here was a case where the French drew on recent metropolitan legal changes that permitted women to sue for divorce and imposed their sense of rights into a colonial situation.[73] Rodet in this volume discusses how the colonial administration of French Soudan sought to control the new rights given to wives (to seek divorce and to give consent in marriage) by punishing them for abandoning their conjugal homes. It is this mutual reconfiguring of legal and cultural definitions that makes the colonial period so important for understanding the history of domestic violence in Africa, as well as the challenges faced by those who are grappling with the problem today.

⇌

Amina Mama, a Nigerian feminist scholar, argues that activists and scholars concerned with domestic violence in Africa must look to the colonial period to understand the meaning and quality of African domestic violence in the present. She argues that colonial states sought to separate women and men into distinct, Eurocentric gender categories whereby women were relegated to so-called private spaces and restricted from movement and migration, while men were encouraged to work outside the home and engage with state tools in public (albeit highly monitored) ways.[74] Such processes of separation created a new domestic space for intimate violence. The chapters that follow support Mama's characterization of the colonial period and flesh out the nature of colonial contributions to the perpetuation of domestic violence. Despite occasional gestures toward liberal reform, the legal structures of colonial Africa tended to condone domestic violence, particularly violence perpetrated by husbands against their wives but also violence against children and older women. The state prioritized stability over the protection of vulnerable groups and relegated questions involving the family to the arena of custom.

Because of the colonial and postcolonial state's role in defining domestic space, Mama argues that the state cannot be the mechanism for change. Rather, grassroots, non-state-based solutions to violence in postcolonial African contexts have the most potential for combating household-based gender violence. However, Mama also notes a handful of promising state-funded projects especially in Uganda and Tanzania. In these cases, vocal elected officials, particularly female elected officials, and successful media and informational programming backed by state funding, provide hopeful models of state participation in anti–domestic violence reform.[75] These successes are linked to the fact that they emerged from localized knowledge production (a version of Merry's vernacularization), but they are also supported by international movements and organizations. The chapters in the third section of this volume, which focus on the contemporary period, analyze the successes and limitations of current approaches to domestic violence in several African countries. They demonstrate the lingering effects of the debates initiated during the colonial era.

It is the importance of these lasting repercussions that makes the conversation among historians, anthropologists, activists, and legal scholars over domestic violence in Africa initiated in this volume necessary. Interdisciplinary dialogue helps us understand the changing patterns of domestic violence over time, fleshing out the models of social scientists and explaining how changes in family structure and in broadly shared understandings of people's duties and obligations within the family have shaped patterns of violence within the family. The contributors to this volume remind us that because acts of domestic violence are ultimately about power and linked to larger sociocultural values, scholars should look more closely at the links between violence in the household, social and economic strife, and challenges to local political authorities and disputes over state power.[76] All of the contributors to this volume provide models for this interconnected research agenda through the use of legal records, court testimony, and debates about legislation, and thus provide inroads to new understandings of African domesticity, the family, and law during the colonial and postcolonial periods.

The history of domestic violence also provides a window onto the ways in which Africans interpreted the major social changes of the nineteenth and twentieth centuries. Members of households who violently subjugated other household members did so within the intimate space of family relationships, but these acts were part of larger sociohistorical connections. Court records and legal documents reveal that quite often, domestic violence took place under conditions of increasing shortages of material, political, and social resources associated with the shifting terrain of colonial rule and globalization. By contrast, victims of domestic violence sought out courts because they provided new avenues for confronting these shifting patterns of power consolidation. The history of domestic violence reveals the intimate, embodied experiences of power. Those chapters that examine the contemporary situation are also keenly aware of the challenges facing those who wish to implement greater protections for women within households.

The contributions to this volume reveal that, while the prevalence of domestic violence has changed over time, the problem of domestic violence has changed even more. It has been redefined as a problem for states, a problem for communities, a problem for families, and a problem for human rights activists. All of these definitions remain contested, and efforts to end domestic violence are, in no small part, efforts to control the definition of the problem. Regardless of how we define the problem, violence within the domestic sphere continues to take its toll on women, children, men, and society as a whole.

NOTES

This introduction grows out of an engagement with our contributors, colleagues, the anonymous readers of our manuscript, and the editors of the New Histories of Africa series at Ohio University Press. In particular, we want to thank Babacar Fall, Sarah Roberts, and Helen Stacy.

1. Linda Gordon, *Heroes of Their Own Lives: The Politics and History of Family Violence, Boston 1880–1960* (New York: Viking, 1988), 27–28.

2. By contrast, the term "family violence" is preferred by social science researchers who do not see gender as playing a significant role in domestic violence. See for example D. H. Currie, "Violent Men or Violent Women: Whose Definition Counts?" in *Issues in Intimate Violence*, ed. R. K. Bergen (Thousand Oaks, CA: Sage, 1998).

3. The best overviews of these theories appear in Sana Loue, *Intimate Partner Violence: Societal, Medical, Legal, and Individual Responses* (New York: Kluwer Academic/Plenum, 2001), 21–36; United Nations, *Violence against Women in the Family* (New York: Center for Social Development and Humanitarian Affairs, 1989), 25–33.

4. See especially Michael P. Johnson and Kathleen Ferraro, "Research on Domestic Violence in the 1990s: Making Distinctions," *Journal of Marriage and the Family* 62, no. 4 (2000): 948–63; Rosemary Ofeibea Ofei-Aboagye, "Altering the Strands of the Fabric: A Preliminary Look at Domestic Violence in Ghana," *Signs* 19, no. 4 (1994): 924–38.

5. See Albert Bandura, *Aggression: A Social Learning Analysis* (Englewood Cliffs, NJ: Prentice Hall, 1973). For a fascinating study about the cultural reproduction of learned behavior, see Paul Willis, *Learning to Labor: How Working Class Kids Get Working Class Jobs* (New York: Columbia University Press, 1981). A variant of the social learning theory is the "recipe for living," used by Catherine

Campbell in her study of Zulu masculinity and violence, "Learning to Kill? Masculinity, the Family, and Violence in Natal," *Journal of Southern African Studies* 18, no. 3 (1992): 614–28.

6. See Christopher Browning, "Collective Efficacy: Extending Social Disorganization Theory to Partner Violence," *Journal of Marriage and the Family* 64 (November 2002): 833–50. As Browning notes, social disorganization theory assumes that social norms disapprove of domestic violence but do not prevent it, failing to account for situations in which social norms in fact condone violence.

7. See Demie Kurtz, "Social Science Perspectives on Wife Abuse: Current Debates and Future Directions" *Gender and Society* 3, no. 4 (1989): 489–505.

8. L. L. Dahlburg and E. G. Krug, "Violence: A Global Health Problem," in *World Report on Violence and Health*, ed. E. G. Krug et al. (Geneva: World Health Organization, 2002).

9. These included the *Annaliste* (from the journal *Annales d'histoire économique et sociale*) approaches to the past and cliometrics in the form of demographic studies using large samples.

10. See, for example, Pamela Scully, *Liberating the Family? Gender and British Slave Emancipation in the Rural Western Cape, South Africa, 1823–1853* (Portsmouth, NH: Heinemann, 1997); Charles von Onselen, *The Seed Is Mine: The Life of Kas Maine, A South African Sharecropper, 1894–1985* (New York: Hill and Wang, 1996).

11. Jan Vansina, "Ambaca Society and the Slave Trade, c. 1760–1845," *The Journal of African History* (hereafter *JAH*) 46, no. 1 (2005); John Thornton, *The Kongolese Saint Anthony: Dona Beatriz Kimpa Vita and the Antonian Movement, 1684–1706* (New York: Cambridge University Press, 1998).

12. Donald Crummey, "Family and Property amongst the Amhara Nobility," *JAH* 24, no. 2 (1983): 207–20. The most famous tarikh for social history is 'Abd al-Ṛamān ibn 'Abd Allāh Sa'dī, *Tarikh es-Soudan*, translated by O. Houdas and Edmond Benoist (Paris: Adrien-Maisonneuve, 1964). Individual Muslim families, especially those belonging to notable lineages, have family chronicles. See also Timothy Cleaveland, *Becoming Walata: A History of Saharan Social Formation and Transformation* (Portsmouth, NH: Heinemann, 2002).

13. See the results of the School of Oriental and African Studies Conference on the History of the Family in Africa, particularly Shula Marks and Richard Rathbone, "The History of the Family in Africa: Introduction," *JAH* 24, no. 2 (1983): 145–61; Wyatt MacGaffey, "Lineage Structure, Marriage and the Family amongst the Central Bantu," *JAH* 24, no. 2 (1983): 173–87; and Megan Vaughan, "Which Family? Problems in the Reconstruction of the History of the Family as an Economic and Cultural Unit," *JAH* 24, no. 2 (1983): 275–83. For a sample of contemporary studies, see Yaw Oheneba-Sakyi and Bafour K. Takyi, eds., *African Families at the Turn of the 21st Century* (Westport, CT: Praeger, 2006), and for East African cases studies, see Thomas S. Weisner, Candice Bradley, and Philip L. Kilbride, eds., *African Families and the Crisis of Social Change* (Westport, CT: Bergin and Garvey, 1997).

14. Among this vast literature, see Lawrence Stone, *The Family, Sex and Marriage in England, 1500–1800* (London: Weidenfeld and Nicolson, 1977); Edward Shorter, *The Making of the Modern Family* (New York: Basic Books, 1976); David Levine, *Family Formation in an Age of Nascent Capitalism* (New York: Academic Press, 1977); Hans Medick, "The Proto-industrial Family Economy: The Structural Function of the Household and Family during the Transition from Peasant Society to Industrial Capitalism," *Social History* 1, no. 3 (1976): 291–315; J.-L. Flandrin, *Families in Former Times: Kinship, Household, and Sexuality*, translated by R. Southern (Cambridge: Cambridge University Press, 1979); and the classic study by P. Ariès, *Centuries of Childhood: A Social History of Family Life*, translated by R. Baldick (New York: Knopf, 1962).

15. Naomi Todamor, *Family and Friends in Eighteenth-Century England: Household, Kinship, and Patronage* (Cambridge: Cambridge University Press, 2001), 272; see also 9–15.

16. Jane Guyer, "Household and Community in African Studies," *African Studies Review* 24, no. 2–3 (1981): 199.

17. Jack Goody, "The Evolution of the Family," in *Household and Family in Past Time*, ed. Peter Laslett and Richard Wall (Cambridge: Cambridge University Press, 1972), 103–24.

18. Tamara Hareven, "The History of the Family and the Complexity of Social Change," *American Historical Review* 96, no. 1 (1991): 96, 111.

19. Charles Tilly, "Retrieving European Lives," and David W. Cohen, "Doing Social History from Pim's Doorway," in *Reliving the Past: The Worlds of Social History*, ed. Olivier Zunz (Chapel Hill: University of North Carolina Press, 1985), 11–52, 191–235, respectively.

20. Already in 1983, Marks and Rathbone drew attention to some of these themes, "The History of the Family in Africa: Introduction," 150.

21. See especially Claire Robertson and Martin Klein, eds., *Women and Slavery in Africa* (Madison: University of Wisconsin Press, 1983); Ester Boserup, *Woman's Role in Economic Development* (Aldershot: Gower, 1986).

22. Slavery was abolished in South Africa in 1834 as part of the British abolition of slavery in its crown colonies. Elsewhere in Africa, Britain pursued a more gradual policy. Suzanne Miers and Richard Roberts, eds., *The End of Slavery in Africa* (Madison: University of Wisconsin Press, 1988).

23. Richard Roberts and Martin Klein, "The Banamba Slave Exodus of 1905 and the Decline of Slavery in the Western Sudan," *JAH* 21, no. 3 (1980): 375–94; see also Miers and Roberts, eds., *End of Slavery*.

24. Martin Klein, *Slavery and Colonial Rule in French West Africa* (Cambridge: Cambridge University Press, 1998).

25. Megan Vaughan, *The Story of an African Famine: Gender and Famine in Twentieth-Century Malawi* (Cambridge: Cambridge University Press, 1987).

26. See, for example, Valentine Moghadam, *The "Feminization of Poverty" and Women's Human Rights* (Paris: UNESCO, 2005), and Randall Packard, *White Plague, Black Labor: Tuberculosis and the Political Economy of Health and Disease in South Africa* (Pietermaritzburg: University of Natal Press, 1989).

27. Jan Vansina, "Mwasi's Trials," *Daedalus* 111 (Spring 1982): 49–70; A. L. Epstein, *Politics in an Urban African Community* (Manchester: Manchester University Press, 1958).

28. Novels capture this tension especially well. See, among others, Chinua Achebe, *No Longer at Ease* (London: Heinemann, 1963), and Ayi Kwei Armah, *The Beautyful Ones Are Not Yet Born* (London: Heinemann, 1988). See also Shula Marks and Richard Rathbone, eds., *Industrialization and Social Change in South Africa: African Class, Culture, and Consciousness, 1870–1930* (London: Longman Group, 1982).

29. David W. Cohen and E. S. Atieno Odhiambo, *Burying SM: The Politics of Knowledge and the Sociology of Power in Africa* (Portsmouth, NH: Heinemann, 1992); James Ferguson, *Expectations of Modernity: Myths and Meanings of Urban Life on the Zambian Copperbelt* (Berkeley: University of California Press, 1999); Martin Chanock, "Paradigms, Policies, and Property: A Review of the Customary Law of Land Tenure," in *Law in Colonial Africa*, ed. Kristin Mann and Richard Roberts (Portsmouth, NH: Heinemann, 1991), 61–84.

30. *World Health Organization Multi-country Study on Women's Health and Domestic Violence against Women: Initial Results on Relevance, Health Outcomes and Women's Responses* (2005), available online: http://www.who.int/gender/violence/who_multicountry_study/en/ table 4.1, p. 28. Ethiopia had only a rural site, where 71 percent of the women ever experienced violence, and Namibia had only an urban site, where 36 percent of the women ever experienced violence. The higher incidence of rural violence appeared also in Bangladesh, Brazil, Peru, and Thailand.

31. See David W. Sabean, "The History of the Family in Africa and Europe: Some Comparative Perspectives," *JAH* 24, no. 2 (1983): 167–68; and James Scott, *Seeing Like a State: How Certain Schemes to Improve the Human Condition Have Failed* (New Haven, CT: Yale University Press, 1998).

32. Nancy Rose Hunt, *A Colonial Lexicon: Of Birth Ritual, Medicalization, and Mobility in the Congo* (Durham, NC: Duke University Press, 1999), 56.

33. Sean Redding, *Sorcery and Sovereignty: Taxation, Power, and Rebellion in South Africa, 1880–1963* (Athens: Ohio University Press, 2006).

34. Karen Tranberg Hansen, Introduction to *African Encounters with Domesticity*, ed. Karen Tranberg Hansen (New Brunswick, NJ: Rutgers University Press, 1992), 1–33.

35. Claire Robertson, *Sharing the Same Bowl: A Socioeconomic History of Women and Class in Accra, Ghana* (Bloomington: Indiana University Press, 1984); Jean Allman and Victoria Tashjian, *"I Will Not Eat Stone": A Women's History of Colonial Asante* (Portsmouth, NH: Heinemann, 2000); Richard Roberts, "Women's Work and Women's Property: Household Social Relations in the Maraka Textile Industry of the Nineteenth Century," *Comparative Studies in Society and History* 26, no. 2 (1984): 229–50.

36. See, for example, Susan M. Martin, *Palm Oil and Protest: An Economic History of the Ngwa Region, South-eastern Nigeria, 1800–1980* (Cambridge: Cambridge University Press, 1988).

37. There is a significant body of work on bridewealth in Africa. Major works that influence this study are John Comaroff, ed, *The Meaning of Marriage Payments* (New York: Academic Press, 1980); Camilla Toulmin, *Cattle, Women, and Wells: Managing Household Survival in the Sahel* (Oxford: Clarendon Press, 1992); and Brett Shadle, *"Girl Cases": Marriage and Colonialism in Gusiiland, Kenya, 1890–1970* (Portsmouth, NH: Heinemann, 2006).

38. See, for example, Ariès, *Centuries of Childhood;* Gareth Stedman Jones, *Outcast London* (New York: Pantheon Books, 1971); and Eric Hopkins, *Childhood Transformed: Working-Class Children in Nineteenth-Century England* (New York: St. Martin's Press, 1994).

39. In 1946, pediatric radiologists first identified the distinctive pattern of broken bones and healed fractures in children that led them to link these health issues to their caregivers. Charles Kempe, F. Silverman, B. Steele, and W. Droegemueller, "The Battered Child Syndrome," *American Journal of Medical Science* 181, no. 1 (1962): 17–24.

40. Richard Gelles, "Family Violence," *Annual Review of Sociology* 11 (1985): 347–48; Richard Gelles, "Demythologizing Child Abuse," *Family Coordinator* 25, no. 2 (1976): 135–42; Leonore Walker, *The Battered Woman Syndrome* (New York: Springer, 1984); Canadian Supreme Court ruling, *R. v. Lavalee,* 1991; Marilyn Kasias, Nicholas Spanos, Cheryl Terrance, and Suzanne Peebles, "Battered Women Who Kill: Jury Simulation and Legal Defenses," *Law and Human Behavior* 17, no. 3 (1993): 289–312; Regine A. Shuller and Neil Vidmar, "Battered Woman Syndrome Evidence in the Courtroom: A Review of the Literature," *Law and Human Behavior* 16, no. 3 (1992): 273–91.

41. See, for example, Nancy Meyer-Emerick, *The Violence against Women Act of 1994: An Analysis of Intent and Perception* (Westport, CT: Praeger, 2001).

42. See Elisabeth Friedman, "Women's Human Rights: The Emergence of a Movement," in *Women's Rights, Human Rights: International Feminist Perspectives,* ed. Julie Peters and Andrea Wolper (New York: Routledge, 1995), 18–35; Estelle Freedman, *No Turning Back: The History of Feminism and the Future of Women* (New York: Ballantine Books, 2002), 335–47.

43. There is a prehistory to human rights on the international scene, starting with the effort to abolish the slave trade, the Haitian revolution that borrowed foundational concepts from the French Revolution, and the effort to abolish slavery. See also the framing of international human rights even for colonial populations in articles 22–24 in the Covenant of the League of Nations (1919). See Lynn Hunt, *Inventing Human Rights* (New York: Norton, 2007).

44. Both conventions were preceded by UN declarations: the Declaration on the Elimination of Discrimination against Women in 1967 and the Declaration on the Rights of the Child in 1959. Unlike the conventions, the declarations were not ratified by individual countries and therefore had only persuasive power.

45. See, for example, Sally Engle Merry, "Conditions of Vulnerability," and Balakrishnan Rajagopal, "Encountering Ambivalence," in *The Practice of Human Rights: Tracking Law between the Global and the Local,* ed. Mark Goodale and Sally Engle Merry (Cambridge: Cambridge University Press, 2007).

46. Sally Engle Merry, "Transnational Human Rights and Local Activism: Mapping the Middle," *American Anthropologist* 108, no. 1 (2006): 39.

47. Sally Engle Merry, *Human Rights and Gender Violence: Translating International Law into Local Justice* (Chicago: University of Chicago Press, 2006), chap. 1. See also Sari Wastell, "Being Swazi, Being Human: Custom, Constitutionalism and Human Rights in an African Policy," in Goodale and Merry, *Practice of Human Rights*.

48. Edward B. Tyler, *Primitive Culture: Researches into the Development of Mythology, Philosophy, Religion, Art, and Custom* (Gloucester, MA: Smith, 1871), 2 vols., 1:1, quoted in Milton Singer, "Culture: The Concept of Culture," *International Encyclopedia of the Social Sciences*, ed. David Sills (New York: Macmillan and Free Press, 1968), 3:527.

49. Merry, *Human Rights and Gender Violence*, 12–16.

50. See the discussion of customary law, below, for more on this issue.

51. Gerry Mackie, "Female Genital Cutting: The Beginning of the End," in *Female "Circumcision" in Africa: Culture, Controversy, and Change*, ed. Bettina Shell-Duncan and Ylva Herlund (Boulder, CO: Lynne Rienner, 2000), 253–81.

52. We are reminded of the successful campaigns against foot-binding in late nineteenth-century China. Like female genital cutting in some areas sub-Saharan Africa, foot-binding was in parts of China a requirement for respectable marriage. No individual could give up the practice without risking her marriage prospects. Foot-binding began to end after hundreds of years when "pledge societies" emerged in the last part of the nineteenth century that made collective and public pledges to renounce the practice. Pledge societies spread together with public education programs that explained that the rest of the world did not practice foot-binding and that there were significant health and economic advantages to ending the practice. By 1911, when China enacted a legal prohibition against foot-binding, the practice was already discredited by these communal pledges. See Dorothy Ko, *Cinderella's Sisters: A Revisionist History of Footbinding* (Berkeley: University of California Press, 2005).

53. June Starr and Jane Collier have suggested that customary law was a colonial invention that needs to be analytically separate from what they term indigenous law, which was practiced before colonial conquest. June Starr and Jane Collier, eds., *History and Power in the Study of Law: New Directions in Legal Anthropology* (Ithaca, NY: Cornell University Press, 1989), 8–9. See also Omoniyi Adewoye, *The Judicial System in Southern Nigeria, 1854–1954* (London: Longman, 1977), and Martin Chanock, *The Making of South African Legal Culture, 1902–1936: Fear, Favour, and Prejudice* (Cambridge: Cambridge University Press, 2001).

54. John Griffiths, "What Is Legal Pluralism," *Journal of Legal Pluralism* 24, no. 1 (1986): 2–9. The concept of imposed law, applied in *The Imposition of Law*, ed. Sandra Burman and Barbara E. Harrell-Bond (New York: Academic Press, 1979), was designed to highlight the political context of legal pluralism in late nineteenth-century colonialism and in the twentieth-century global legal environment.

55. This is the concept that Mahmoud Mamdani applies in *Citizen and Subject: Contemporary Africa and the Legacy of Late Colonialism* (Princeton, NJ: Princeton University Press, 1996), 21–23, 108–28 ff.

56. Richard Roberts, *Litigants and Households: African Disputes and Colonial Courts in the French Soudan, 1895–1912* (Portsmouth, NH: Heinemann, 2005); Lauren Benton, *Law and Colonial Cultures: Legal Regimes and World History, 1400–1900* (New York: Cambridge University Press, 2002), 128, 137. See also Sally Engle Merry, "Legal Pluralism," *Law and Society Review* 22, no. 5 (1988): 879, and Sally Engle Merry, *Colonizing Hawai'i: The Cultural Power of Law* (Princeton, NJ: Princeton University Press, 2000).

57. See, for example, Isaac Schapera, *A Handbook of Tswana Law and Custom* (London: Oxford University Press, 1938). For context, see Terence Ranger, "The Invention of Tradition in Colonial Africa," in *The Invention of Tradition*, ed. Eric Hobsbawm and Terence Ranger (Cambridge: Cambridge University Press, 1983), 211–62; Martin Chanock, *Law, Custom, and Social Order: The Colonial Experience in Malawi and Zambia* (Cambridge: Cambridge University Press, 1985); Sally Falk Moore, "Treating Law as Knowledge: Telling Colonial Officers What to Say to Africans about Running 'Their Own' Native Courts," *Law and Society Review* 26, no. 1 (1992): 11–46; and Jean-Hervé Jézéquel, "'Collecting Customary Law': Educated Africans, Ethnographic Writings, and Colonial Justice in French West Africa," in *Intermediaries, Interpreters, and Clerks: Africans in the Making of Modern Africa*, ed. Benjamin N. Lawrance, Emily L. Osborn, and Richard L. Roberts (Madison: University of Wisconsin Press, 2006), 139–57.

58. Chanock, *Law, Custom, and Social Order*; Roberts, *Litigants and Households*.

59. See Shamil Jeppie, Ebrahim Moosa, and Richard Roberts, eds., *Muslim Family Law in Sub-Saharan Africa: Colonial Legacies and Postcolonial Challenges* (Amsterdam: Amsterdam University Press, 2009).

60. Thomas Spear, "Neo-Traditionalism and the Limits of Invention in British Colonal Africa," *JAH* 44, no. 1 (2003): 3–27.

61. Sara Berry, *No Condition Is Permanent: The Social Dynamics of Agrarian Change in Sub-Saharan Africa* (Madison: University of Wisconsin Press, 1993), 8.

62. In French West Africa and French Equatorial Africa this was enforced through the 1939 Mandel Decree. See Jeanne Maddox Toungara, "Changing the Meaning of Marriage: Women and Family Law in Côte d'Ivoire," in *African Feminism: The Politics of Survival in Sub-Saharan Africa*, ed. Gwendolyn Mikell (Philadelphia: University of Pennsylvania Press, 1997), 53–76; Abd-el Kadr Boye et al., "Marriage Law and Practice in the Sahel," *Studies in Family Planning* 22, no. 6 (1991): 343–49. On the outlawing of corporal punishment in British colonial Africa, see Lord Frederick Lugard, *The Dual Mandate in British Tropical Africa* (Edinburgh and London: W. Blackwood and Sons, 1922); Steven Pierce, "Punishment and the Political Body: Flogging and Colonialism in Northern Nigeria," in *Discipline and the Other Body: Correction, Corporeality, Colonialism*, ed. Steven Pierce and Anupama Rao (Durham, NC: Duke University Press, 2007), 186–214.

63. See, for example, E. P. Thompson, "The Moral Economy of the English Crowd in the Eighteenth Century," *Past and Present* 50 (February 1971): 76–136, and James Scott, *The Moral Economy of the Peasantry* (New Haven, CT: Yale University Press, 1976).

64. Susan Dwyer Amussen, "Punishment, Discipline, and Power: The Social Meanings of Violence in Early Modern England," *Journal of British Studies* 34, no. 1 (1995): 18.

65. Deniz Kandiyoti, "Bargaining with Patriarchy," *Gender and Society* 2, no. 3 (1988): 274–90.

66. Emily Burrill, "Disputing Wife Abuse: Tribunal Narratives of the Corporal Punishment of Wives in Colonial Sikasso, 1930s," *Cahiers d'Études Africaines* 47, no. 3–4 (2007): 603–22.

67. Koni Benson and Joyce M. Chadya, "*Ukubhinya*: Gender and Sexual Violence in Bulawayo, Colonial Zimbabwe, 1946–1956," *Journal of Southern African Studies* 31, no. 3 (2005): 587.

68. Merry, *Colonizing Hawai'i*, 9.

69. UN, *Violence against Women in the Family*, 17–19.

70. Susan F. Hirsch, *Pronouncing and Persevering: Gender and the Discourses of Disputing in an African Islamic Court* (Chicago: University of Chicago Press, 1998), 3–4, 136.

71. James Clifford, "Identity in Mashpee," in *The Predicament of Culture: Twentieth-Century Ethnography, Literature, and Art* (Cambridge: Harvard University, 1988), 277–346; William L. F. Felstiner, Richard L. Abel, and Austin Sarat, "The Emergence and Transformation of Disputes: Naming, Blaming, Claiming . . . ," *Law and Society Review* 15, no. 3–4 (1980): 631–54; Roberts, *Litigants and Households*; Kristin Mann, *Slavery and the Birth of an African City: Lagos, 1760–1900* (Bloomington: Indiana University Press, 2007).

72. See the classic study by Gregory Massell, "Law as an Instrument of Revolutionary Change in a Traditional Milieu: The Case of Soviet Central Asia," *Law and Society Review* 2, no. 2 (1968): 179–228.

73. See Roberts, *Litigants and Households*, chap. 4.

74. Amina Mama, "Sheroes and Villains: Conceptualizing Colonial and Contemporary Violence against Women in Africa," in *Feminist Genealogies, Colonial Legacies, Democratic Futures*, ed. M. Jacqui Alexander and Chandra Mohanty (London: Routledge, 1998), 46–62.

75. Ibid., 60.

76. See also Lynn Thomas, *Politics of the Womb: Women, Reproduction, and the State in Kenya* (Berkeley: University of California Press, 2003), and Dorothy Hodgson and Sheryl McCurdy, eds., *"Wicked" Women and the Reconfiguration of Gender in Africa* (Portsmouth, NH: Heinemann, 2002) for their discussions of the connections between gender relations at home and larger sociopolitical dynamics.

PART I

Domestic Violence,

Relationships of Servitude,

and the Family

THE FIRST PART of this book highlights early encounters between colonial law and shifting forms of power and authority in the twentieth century. In the early years of colonial state formation and the implementation of new legal systems, hierarchical relationships based on age and gender were particularly pronounced locations of household and kin-based violence. The chapters in this part demonstrate the ways in which legal structures sought to harden local practice into categories of acceptability and unacceptability, but they also emphasize the importance of extralegal moral economies and social mores in regulating domestic violence in the early years of colonial rule. As Martina Salvante's work in colonial Eritrea demonstrates, colonial governments were unable to exert full control even over European colonists. Attempts to remake African "customs" and to regulate African domesticity were even more difficult for the colonial state. Similarly, Marie Rodet argues that the criminalization of the actions of women who left their husbands was a genuinely "invented tradition," which ultimately did little to deter women from leaving their husbands during times of marital strife and abuse.

African societies tolerated certain kinds of domestic violence and condemned others. The limits placed on domestic violence varied over time and space, although they tended to reinforce existing power relations. Asymmetries of violence existed between husbands and wives, parents and children. The vulnerabilities of the pawned girls described in Cati Coe's chapter are typical: young, female, and with few economic resources, they were subject to high levels of violence. At the same time, the limits placed on domestic violence gave vulnerable groups a degree of protection against outright abuse, thereby giving them a stake in the maintenance of the moral economy itself. As Emily Burrill and Richard Roberts demonstrate for colonial Mali, such normative limitations on domestic violence placed both social and economic pressure on husbands to limit the severity of violence directed toward their wives.

Thus, this first part of the volume situates the shifting meaning and composition of African households and conjugal relationships within the larger sociopolitical transformations of the colonial period. These changes are thrown into relief through the incidents of domestic violence that emerge in the historical record.

1 ⤳ Domestic Violence, Colonial Courts, and the End of Slavery in French Soudan, 1905–12

EMILY BURRILL AND RICHARD ROBERTS

BETWEEN 1905 AND 1912, upward of one million slaves throughout French West Africa left their masters. Some headed back to their homelands; others moved to the expanding commercial centers scattered throughout the region along the lines of rail being built, along the major rivers, or simply away from their former masters.[1] Not all slaves left their masters; many slaves remained near their masters, if no longer with them. But in all cases, the end of slavery set in motion sets of social, cultural, and economic changes that transformed the worlds in which Africans lived. The degree and meanings of these changes remain hotly debated.[2]

In this chapter, we examine how immediate post-emancipation social transformations in French Soudan affected households and how these adaptations contributed to domestic violence in the regions of Banamba, Gumbu, Kita, and Sikasso.[3] These four regions are distinct: Banamba and Gumbu were centers of slave production; Sikasso was an area ravaged by wars of conquest and slave-raiding in the near past; and Kita was a growing population center based on French colonial enterprise and protection of freed and runaway slaves. As a result of these variations, the linked transformations of colonial conquest, the end of slavery, and the operation of the new courts in early twentieth-century French Soudan affected these regions differently. These linked transformations were certainly momentous, but they were also contested and uneven. Not only was there localized resistance to French rule, but slavery persisted and justice in the new courts was inconsistent. These transformations nonetheless challenged relationships of authority at many levels and threatened the obligations and expectations that bound people together in hierarchical relationships. At the same time, some people—slaves and free alike—chose to take risks in an effort to form their own family units and new social networks, thereby breaking away from relationships bounded by slavery.[4]

Although both of us have explored these interconnected historical changes elsewhere,[5] we have yet to consider the ways in which they affected or reflected incidents of domestic violence in African households. Most certainly, the decline of slavery and the early colonial period throughout Africa were periods of significant violence and social change, as Africans struggled over labor, dependents, and access to economic and political resources. Households and families were not immune to these societal ruptures and conflicts; in many instances, the contested nature of the relationships of slavery and bondage manifested itself within the courts as household conflicts and violence. Our argument is that slavery influenced relationships within African households—including those between free members of the household—and that the end of slavery contributed to efforts to redefine those relationships. Sometimes these efforts were smooth and frictionless; at other times, the end of slavery increased tensions within households, resulting in acts of domestic violence.

This chapter addresses the connections between the end of slavery, domestic violence, and the moral economy of marriage in French Soudan during early colonial rule. The patterns of violence and domestic desertion that took place in Banamba, Gumbu, Kita, and Sikasso were part of larger patterns of slave migration and the resultant redistribution of labor and power within households.[6] Such shifts in gendered labor obligations upset balances in the moral economy of marriages and frequently resulted in domestic desertion and violence within the household.

DOMESTIC VIOLENCE AND THE
MORAL ECONOMY OF MARRIAGE IN FRENCH SOUDAN

E. P. Thompson first introduced the idea of a moral economy in 1971, but James Scott's later intervention would lend the expression more currency in African studies.[7] Whereas Thompson used moral economy as a tool for explaining the motivations and actions of a working-class crowd in eighteenth-century England, Scott turned to moral economy as a conceptual framework for understanding peasant uprisings in Southeast Asia, particularly in the face of subsistence crises. There was nothing "moral" about the moral economy. It describes a system of exploitation in which individuals accepted exploitation in expectation of protection and subsistence. Moreover, the limits on exploitation were generally understood and accepted. Most scholars of African history who use moral economy apply the concept in similar ways: as an organizing principle for understanding the actions of male peasants and agrarian workers in struggles over land and labor in colonial contexts. Moral economy is potentially limited in its possibilities for analysis because it suggests a closed, unchanging, and potentially static system of rational choice. These critiques are to be taken seriously; however, despite these limitations, moral economy is useful as a way of understanding the meanings of protest, resistance, and seemingly disorderly struggle in contexts of unequal power distribution.

For these reasons, we turn to moral economy, but with an eye toward factors that have been left out of the discussion—namely, gender and the household. Rather than see moral economy as a governing network of obligations, entitlement, and provisions between workers and patrons, or proletariat and patricians, at the societal level, we extend the moral economy to the gendered and generational hierarchy of the household. This smaller and more intimate unit of analysis allows us to understand the ways in which systems of exchange and materiality are embedded in other social and cultural mores and values, especially those that govern marriage and the family. Here, then, the breaking point is not the food riot or the mass protest; it is the incident or pattern of domestic violence. As such, domestic violence signals the breach in the system of obligations and reciprocity governing a set of relations. It is not simply an act of hitting, withholding food, forcing extra work, or leaving the home that causes the breach; it is when these acts exceed the limits of acceptability and threaten the mutuality of interdependence and obligation. We are interested, then, in what potentially caused the breach, and we suggest that the end of slavery contributed to breaches in the moral economy of marriages. The evidence we use comes largely from the newly created colonial courts, which provided new resources to women and former slaves to resist changes in the moral economies that governed marriages. We believe that similar analyses could be applied to the precolonial period, but we do not have sufficient evidence for that period.

Various factors contributed to domestic violence among married men and women. The prevailing culture of patriarchy helped define the place of husbands and wives in a hierarchical but mutually dependent moral economy of marriage. Patriarchy contributed to male control over women, junior men, children, and the household's various dependents. Although the moral economy of marriage was deeply structured by gendered asymmetries in power, it was also shaped by a widely shared sense of entitlements and limits on exploitation. Men and women had discrete gendered tasks and responsibilities that defined the household. Husbands were required to provide for their wives' and children's subsistence, protection, and propriety. Wives were required to perform domestic and sexual labor, work in the household's fields for part of the day, and care for the children.

Of the varieties of intimate, kin-based violence (violence among married partners, child abuse, and elder abuse), we are concerned here only with violence among married or quasi-conjugal partners in domestic contexts.[8] Marriage in French Soudan at the beginning of the twentieth century was a complex affair that linked individuals with wide kinship groups and embedded the new married couple in a set of interlocking institutions. In French West Africa, a woman was always a daughter, a wife, a widow, and/or a mother or co-wife. Marriage in most of the region's Malinke, patrilineal, virilocal societies involved the transfer of rights to a woman's labor and reproductive power from her father's kin to that of her husband. Brides were rarely consulted on their wishes, and bridewealth solidified the transfer. Women almost always lived within domestic units headed by men.[9]

In her ethnographic study of the sahel, Camilla Toulmin describes Bambara marriage as "a particularly long term investment. While the woman's labour and services provide some immediate returns for the heavy wedding costs, many of the benefits will accrue over the following 30 years or more." Toulmin further notes that because the consequences of marriage are likely to be with the family for decades, care in making marriage choices is not left to the potential spouses. Spouses often come from groups already bound by existing marriage ties. "In this way, the household head hopes to ensure that marriages endure and are free of conflict."[10] Such was the practice in Banamba, Gumbu, and Kita.

In the Sikasso region, some marriages were forged among Malinke patrilineal groups in the manner described above. The Senufo who predominated in the Sikasso region practiced matrilineal forms of marriage. Normative accounts of Sikasso's past, in the form of ethnographies and oral accounts, depict turn-of-the-century marriage in Sikasso as a regulating force in Senufo society. Senufo men could gain wives in a number of ways that reinforced various units of membership: the virilocal household, the matrilineal descent group, age-grades, secret societies, and the village. The myriad paths to marriage complemented and contributed to these units of belonging, and maintained a political balance that privileged the authority of the matrilineal patriarchs of a community as well as the chief. Among Senufo farming families of the Sikasso region, labor obligations were deeply embedded in large social and cultural obligations, primarily those tied to matrilineal connections and marriage intentions.[11]

Marriage was thus a complex enterprise, and the challenges to it were many. The household head may have hoped that the marriage he entered his daughter or niece into would endure and be free of conflict, but the realities were often quite different. What we see in the courts are cases where the limits on exploitation have been exceeded, and where husbands and wives appealed to these limits in seeking the dissolution of their marriages.[12] The view of marriage from the courts clearly exacerbates the conflictual and contractual nature of the relationships in and surrounding marriage. But the use of court cases provides precious detail on actual marriages and allows us to identify evidence of domestic violence.

THE END OF SLAVERY
AND THE EARLY COURTS IN FRENCH SOUDAN

Any individual household was deeply enmeshed within networks of kinship and the wider world of early twentieth-century French West Africa in which violence was a ubiquitous feature. The state-building activities of medieval Soudanese empires had led to persistent warfare, exacerbated by the transatlantic and trans-Saharan slave trades that drew deeply from this region. The second half of the nineteenth century witnessed an increase in the scale of violence in the region associated with the Umarian jihad, subsequent widespread resistance to the Umarians, and the warfare associated with Samori and Tieba in the southern savanna region, centered on Sikasso and the neighboring district of Bouguni. French conquest fostered new violence, and it was not until 1898 that the French emerged militarily hegemonic, though small-scale resistance and raiding persisted.[13] Domestic relations within households were certainly affected by the political and economic contexts. Thus, when slaves began to leave their masters in 1905 and in ever-widening circles up to 1912, households were stressed yet again.

The end of slavery meant different things in Gumbu, Banamba, Kita, and Sikasso.[14] In Banamba and Gumbu, slavery was a significant part of the social and economic order. Households in Kita and Sikasso had slaves, but the proportion of slaves in the overall population was smaller. Kita was centrally located along the Bafing River close to the Bambuk goldfields and along a major commercial route from Kankan to the west. Slaves had served various roles in Kita, but the region did not develop into a major agricultural zone until the arrival of the French and especially the railway. Kita's population swelled from 1885 to 1905 when it served as the railhead. Kita became the site of one of the *villages de liberté,* which housed slaves freed by the French during their conquest and which provided a coercible pool of labor for railway construction and porterage.[15] In Banamba, slaves began to leave their masters in 1905.[16] Shortly thereafter in 1908, slaves began to leave Gumbu as well. Many of these slaves who left Banamba and Gumbu were part of slave-based agricultural systems and originally came from other parts of the Soudanese interior, such as Wasulu and Sikasso.[17] Merchants from the Saharan frontier and the northern savanna sold salt, cattle, and cloth on the Sikasso market, which was a significant entrepôt for the southern savanna, and purchased kola nuts that came from the region as well as slaves procured from the Wasulu countryside and villages of the Sikasso region for resale in the regional markets of Segu.

This trade was temporarily halted during the French invasion and conquest of the precolonial state of Kenedugu, which was centered on Sikasso. Market activity and trade caravans resumed relatively quickly after conquest.[18]

French policy on slavery was ambivalent. The French wanted to disrupt African societies and regional economies as little as possible, but they nonetheless introduced legislation that eroded the underpinnings of slavery and the slave trade. The Banamba slave exodus in 1905 forced the French to act, and in December 1905, the French decreed that new enslavement was illegal. This decree built on the 1903 legal code that prohibited the use of individuals' status, including the status of slaves, in the newly created native courts, thus ending state support for masters' control over their slaves. The Banamba slave exodus tested French policies and inaugurated a wide exodus throughout French West Africa. Beginning in 1905 large numbers of people began returning to Sikasso, Bouguni, and neighboring Wasulu, regions where they had been born and enslaved, in order to reintegrate into their households and communities. This shift came in waves. In May 1906, the colonial administrator noted that between 11 May and 1 June, 197 people passed through Sikasso on their way home from Banamba. Another group of approximately one hundred slaves entered Sikasso during these weeks of May and settled in the various villages or cantons of Sikasso.[19] The pattern of freed slaves returning to Sikasso or passing through the colonial cercle went on for years after 1905.

Returning slaves had a significant impact on the community of Sikasso. Although new labor was almost always wanted, the return of former slaves whose families had long since dispersed and who were without clear lines of kinship and patronage created new tensions. Former slaves returning to Sikasso after 1905 created new burdens on local resources and access to food, shelter, and work. They also posed political challenges, since they were not clearly integrated into patronage and kinship networks. In 1906, Georges Deherme, a colonial administrator charged with examining the condition of the colony, wrote that "the freed slave is a dissolvent, a fomenter of trouble in the village when he returns."[20] The return home of former slaves also coincided with the establishment of a colonial court system for African subjects in French Soudan. Thus, at the same time that administrators and local African magistrates struggled to define customary practice in the realm of marriage, they were faced with a growing population of people with shifting slave and free status.

In each region, wives and junior members of households took on the burden of agricultural labor in the wake of slave departures. As a result, some wives, citing mistreatment and abuse, chose to leave their households. In instances when slaves chose to remain near their former masters, the processes of postslavery integration were not always seamless or free of conflict. In some cases, slaves brought cases against their former masters to the newly created native courts, arguing that their former masters continued to exploit them or that they refused to renegotiate the terms of their dependency. Former slave women who appeared before the courts to test the bonds of their relationships in early postemancipation society often cited violence, abuse, and neglect in their relationships with former masters.[21]

Women and men brought their conflicts before the colonial courts in attempts to gain control over their lives during a period of rapid change in which colonial conquest led to the dissolution of local polities and forms of authority, the withdrawal of explicit state support of slavery, and the expansion of commerce. At the heart of these struggles was the desire to reduce social vulnerabilities and enhance stability through familial and social networks. These struggles did not necessarily challenge the gendered nature of power in the household, however. Social stability remained grounded in authority and protection: authority over junior members of a household, such as wives and slaves, and protection within patriarchal systems of belonging. The struggles we see within households in the aftermath of slavery most often surrounded efforts to reinscribe household relations within the broad parameters of a moral economy. Women, men, and former slaves were in court implicitly invoking the concept of moral economy as a way of demonstrating that enhanced forms of exploitation violated those norms and constituted forms of domestic violence.

In a study of family instability in Gumbu and Banamba published in 2007, Richard Roberts has assessed the impact of the end of slavery on African households.[22] The departure of the slaves meant that masters had to rely on themselves and their households for most of their agricultural labor needs. Using court data, Roberts saw a pattern of divorce and marriage cases that had a marked seasonality. Divorce disputes in Banamba and Gumbu reflected the pressures of the agricultural cycle throughout the year. In both Banamba and Gumbu, preparation of the fields and the crucial first weeding (April, May, June) and harvest (November, December, January) were the labor bottlenecks. Not surprisingly, these were also the months with the highest proportion of divorce disputes.[23] Since divorces (Banamba, n = 131; Gumbu, n = 138) were usually introduced by wives, their actions during these months indicate that they were reacting to increased pressures on their households, their lives, and the moral economy of marriage.

In contrast to divorce cases, marriage disputes to force a spouse to return to the conjugal home were brought exclusively by husbands petitioning the courts. Both the Banamba (n = 44) and Gumbu (n = 30) data on marriage disputes show seasonal patterns. In Banamba 45 percent of all the marriage disputes occurred during the two months of May and June—only one-sixth (17 percent) of the year, thus two and one-half times an averaged monthly rate. May and June were the peak weeding months, and this was the time that male household heads needed their wives' labor. In Gumbu, the critical labor bottlenecks occurred in March and April when the fields needed to be prepared and in July and August during peak weeding times. Husbands were in court to force their wives to return home to work the fields. It is not surprising that wives complained of mistreatment at the hands of their husbands.

COURTS AND COURT RECORDS

Well before the arrival of European colonialism, Africans brought their disputes to a variety of legal forums, including indigenous and Muslim courts.[24] These persisted into the colonial period, but the establishment of colonial tribunals shifted the landscape of dispute resolution and influenced decisions Africans made about where to bring their grievances. Regularizing dispute resolution among its subjects and controlling the authority of its own colonial officials were two primary objectives of the newly created government general of French West Africa in 1895. A new colonial legal code was promulgated on 10 November 1903, which essentially created two separate systems of courts and legal procedures, one for French citizens and those who had rights to French citizenship, and one for Africans who did not hold French citizenship.[25] The latter was the native court system, and its jurisdiction was extended to "subjects," whose disputes were heard by native judges applying "custom."[26]

The 1903 decree established three tiers of courts for African subjects that more or less resembled the three-tier court in the metropole. The first level courts were the *tribunaux de village*, which were designed as the forum for reconciling disputes at the village level.[27] Supervision of these tribunals fell to the French district officer, but few colonial officials had the time or the inclination to visit the village tribunals. Most litigants bypassed these courts because they were either not interested in having the village chief adjudicate or because they did not wish to be reconciled.[28]

Native courts of the second tier were the *tribunaux de province*. These courts heard civil disputes and misdemeanor offenses. The chief judge was the *chef de province*, the French appointed native ruler of the region, or another highly regarded notable, who was assisted by two other notables from the region. During the early stages of the court's operation, the French district administrator participated or closely supervised the court's proceedings. The 1903 decree also required that registers of the court's activities be kept, a task that fell largely to French administrative staff, since African literacy in French was fairly rare at the time.[29] Criminal cases were heard at the district tribunal level. In this chapter, we have used only the civil and commercial registers of the provincial tribunals, which are for our purposes the entry-level court for civil disputes.

Native courts on the third level were the *tribunaux de cercle*, which were charged with hearing all the appeals from the lower courts and with jurisdiction over criminal matters. In her chapter in this volume, Marie Rodet uses both civil and criminal registers to trace domestic violence accusations and the response of the colonial administration. At the *tribunal de cercle*, the district administrator presided, assisted by two African notables. The first of the new native courts began hearing disputes in 1905, and most districts had functioning courts by 1907. Colonial officials were surprised by the number and nature of the disputes brought before them, and they did not understand how the new legal system had empowered women, younger brothers, and sons to challenge the authority of male elders. Nor did they fully understand how the new colonial legal system channeled long-standing grievances in new directions, so that they would be "heard" by the new courts.[30] What went on in the courtroom was shaped by local legal practices, by litigants' strategies, and by the disposition of power accorded class, status, gender, and race.[31]

In what follows, we examine divorce and marriage cases from Gumbu, Banamba, Kita, and Sikasso in an effort to understand how these cases shed light on instances of domestic violence and the connections between domestic violence and the sociohistorical context in which such acts took place. A fine-grained analysis of the court records in these districts reveals patterns that were regional in nature.

DOMESTIC VIOLENCE AND THE END OF SLAVERY

The end of slavery initiated a huge population movement in a relatively short period. Picking up and leaving often meant leaving family behind. But former slaves were not the only group on the move during this period. Faced with the prospect of increased labor on the household farm, sons of former masters probably followed some of the same routes that former slaves had taken to areas in Senegal, Guinea, and Côte d'Ivoire that offered new employment opportunities in mining, construction, and temporary agricultural work. Sons left because there were new opportunities outside the household economy and because, with the departure of the slaves, sons had little to anticipate in terms of inheritable property and much to fear from increased labor obligations. In their study of the Soninke of Nioro District to the west of Gumbu, Eric Pollet and Grace Winter argue that the liberation of the slaves weakened the hierarchical principles of both the family and society.[32] Husbands also left their families, sometimes to seek work or to trade. Not all returned. We code these cases as abandonment. Abandonment ruptured the moral economy of marriage, for the husband failed to maintain the minimum necessary to sustain his wife and children. It was clearly a form of domestic violence.

Not all abandonment cases stemmed from slave households, nor can all absconding husbands be linked directly to the end of slavery, although contemporary French observers of the slaves' exodus pointed first to the "destructions of the family, abandonment of children, raping of children" as a consequence of the end of slavery.[33] The end of slavery contributed to household stresses that may have manifested themselves in domestic violence. There is no question, however, that domestic violence was a feature of African households in French Soudan at the beginning of the twentieth century.

Most plaintiffs seeking divorce in French Soudan in the early twentieth century were women. Of the range of causes for divorce, plaintiffs most often cited abandonment, mistreatment, failure to complete bridewealth payments, illness of one spouse, misbehavior, or incompatibility. Within divorce cases where women cited abandonment, mistreatment, or misbehavior, they produced evidence through testimony or proof of physical violence or the threat of such violence, coercive control, neglect, psychological or verbal abuse, and perceived ruptures to the limits on exploitation.[34] We interpret such cases and the testimony and proof behind them as instances of domestic violence.

Abandonment and Mistreatment

Abandonment and mistreatment overlap in effect, but the two are generally separable in the testimonies presented in court. Abandonment refers to the departure of one spouse (most often the husband) for some considerable period of time, anywhere from several months to a dozen years or more. Abandonment most often meant leaving the spouse and children without support. Mistreatment is a more capacious category. Within it fall classic characteristics of domestic violence such as physical violence, verbal abuse, and neglect. Neglect to live up to the moral economy of marriage and thus failure to provide for the subsistence of the wife and the children were common complaints. Although abandonment also involved neglect, the difference between abandonment and neglect was that the spouse was present in the household in instances of neglect.

Neglect cases resembled abandonment cases in that the plaintiffs complained of not being fed, clothed, or maintained by their spouses. Many cases of neglect simply state that the wife "requests divorce because the husband does not provide for her."[35] A woman justified leaving her husband's household because he "provided her with nothing." Her brother was in court and corroborated her complaints. The court granted a divorce, but ordered that the wife return the bridewealth.[36] Makandian K. was in court seeking a divorce from her husband on the ground that he was a "drunkard who does not work and does not provide for her or their children." The husband contested the divorce, but the court overruled his objections, granted the divorce, and gave temporary custody of the children to the mother until such time as the husband would claim them. At that point, he would have to compensate her for the care given.[37] Memoutou D. was also in court claiming that "her husband is a drunk who mistreats her, hits her continuously, and leaves her and her children in misery." The court granted a divorce but ordered that the children remain with their father.[38]

In Gumbu and Banamba, abandonment and mistreatment cases seem to be relatively evenly distributed over the months without demonstrating any marked seasonality. Abandonment was most prevalent in February, July, and September whereas mistreatment was most marked in April and August. Weeding was women's work, and thus taken together, mistreatment cases in July, August, and September, during the height of the intense agricultural season, constituted 33 percent of all the mistreatment cases.

In many ways the complaints that plaintiffs brought under the category of mistreatment more fully conform to the established definitions of domestic violence: physical violence, psychological and verbal abuse, and neglect.[39] Mistreatment disputes in Gumbu coincided directly with the departure of the slaves. Given the acute labor demands facing household heads with the end of slavery, household heads would most likely have turned to their households to make up for the labor needed after their slaves had left. As a result, we anticipate that women would have brought mistreatment cases as household heads used or forced their wives to work in the fields. Reflecting patterns of adjustments to the departures of slaves from nearby Banamba and Bamako, former slave-owning heads of households turned increasingly to their own wives and children to make up the shortfall in agricultural labor. Many wives of slave-owning household heads throughout the region probably felt like the woman quoted in a 1907 report from Bamako: "[M]y husband gives me nothing; my husband forces me to work. My husband does nothing himself and I, I work continuously."[40]

Often, mistreatment appears in the legal and political record in the form of control over the terms of a wife's mobility. In April 1907 in Sikasso, Tiébélé T. was charged with murdering his wife, who did not want to go to a neighboring village alone to engage in petty trade. Exasperated and enraged, he beat her to death.[41] In a 1912 Sikasso marriage case between Mame T. and his wife, Safi T., Safi complained that she wanted to leave her husband because he did not allow her to see her friends and that he circumscribed her mobility and prevented her from visiting her natal village.[42] The court ultimately ruled in Mame T.'s favor, requiring that Safi obey her husband. These cases had very different outcomes and very different premises—in the first case the deceased wife was resisting her husband's attempts to force her to travel alone, whereas in the second case the wife complained that her husband would not let her travel without him. However, both cases involved husbands' attempts to control the movement of their wives in ways that were ultimately about controlling behavior, a form of domestic violence.

Bridewealth disputes also provide some evidence of domestic violence and the moral economy of marriage. As we argued above, bridewealth was a form of contract that transferred rights to his wife's labor, her reproductive power, and rights of sexual access to her husband and his kinship group. While on the face of it cases involving bridewealth disputes may not be immediately concerned with domestic violence or abuse, the divorce cases brought by women who cited lack of bridewealth or the continuation of slave-based relationships reveal a form of exploitation and mistreatment that women found unsavory enough to bring before the colonial tribunal. There were attempts by magistrates, chiefs, and colonial administrators to pin down bridewealth practice, currency and property exchange. Where women were concerned, however, they often blurred the boundaries of marriage and slave-related contracts.[43]

Wives also left their husbands, and husbands were in court to force their wives to return. We code these cases as marriage disputes, and males constituted fully 95 percent of the plaintiffs in these cases.[44] Runaway wives certainly ruptured the moral economy of the household since marriage brought together gender-specific tasks necessary for subsistence. A wife's actions differed from a husband's abandonment because husbands were obligated by the moral economy of marriage to provide subsistence for their wives and children. Because of the bridewealth transfers, wives were obligated to work for their husbands and to contribute to overall household subsistence. In cases where bridewealth was fully transferred, the courts most often ruled in favor of husbands and ordered the runaway wives to return to the "conjugal unit." The courts rarely ruled in favor of divorce as they did when husbands abandoned their wives.

Physical and Verbal Abuse

It would be hard to imagine divorce requests on the basis of physical violence caused by a single incident. Husbands were permitted to discipline their wives, and claims for physical violence therefore had to exceed the customary limits on discipline. It is also hard to imagine that physical violence occurred without precursor events, such as verbal abuse. The court records do not give us a good sense of the history of verbal abuse, but Tonama C. was in court in Segu on 23 September 1906 claiming that he wanted the court to force his wife, Na C., to return to his home. Na C. refused and told the court that she left because Tonama insulted her.[45] The Segu provincial tribunal also agreed to a divorce when Nianson D. accused her husband of "insulting her and her parents."[46] Verbal and physical abuse often went hand in hand. In Kita, the court granted a divorce to a wife who complained that her husband "mistreats her and humiliates her in front of other wives."[47] In 1909, Kassiba B. was in court seeking a divorce from his wife. He claimed that his wife insulted him and "disobeyed him." Filifui K. responded in court that her husband beat her without justification "whenever he is drunk."[48]

The court was probably willing to accept a certain amount of beating as part of maintaining discipline in the household, but when beating exceeded a certain threshold, the court ruled in favor of the victim. In Timbuktu, the court dismissed a request for divorce from a wife who accused her husband of being "brutal" but warned him that if the abuse continued, it would grant the wife a divorce.[49] In 1905 Namasso D. was in court demanding that his wife return to him. She responded that she had left the conjugal home because her husband "was violent toward her and makes her work more than a man." Invoking what seems to be a sense of the moral economy of marriage, the court ordered the wife to return to her husband's home but ordered the husband to treat her better.[50] On a trip to Fouta Jallon from Kita in 1908, both of Lamine K.'s two wives accused him of abusing them. Lamine K. responded that he only hit his wives with justification, probably invoking the widely accepted right husbands had to discipline their wives.[51] Domestic discipline could easily get out of hand. Sama S. was in court claiming that her husband mistreated her. Her husband did not deny the charge but claimed that he beat her and "will continue to do so as long as she continues in shameful conduct." The court agreed to a divorce but demanded the return of bridewealth, which indicated that the wife was not considered blameless.[52]

On 29 August 1910, Samba Diallo S. came before the tribunal and accused her husband of "beating her ceaselessly." Her husband justified his actions by claiming that his child had died because of his wife's negligence and that she also had a lover. The court disregarded the husband's explanations and granted a divorce.[53] In Kita, a wife sued for divorce because her husband "brutalizes" her. Her husband argued that his wife "refuses to work" and that he was merely disciplining her. The court granted a divorce but required the return of the bridewealth.[54] Beating a wife who was ill clearly violated the moral economy of marriage. On 11 September 1911, Dianta M. was in court asking for a divorce on the ground that "her husband beat her while she was sick and could not work." The wife's claim was supported by witnesses, and her husband, Bo K., confessed to this in court. The court not only granted a divorce but also ruled that the wife need not return the bridewealth. Bo K.'s actions had clearly exceeded the limits on domestic violence and thus warranted drastic action.[55] Physical violence may have been grounds for divorce, but the degree of violence often shaped the court's judgment. For example, on 30 October 1911, Soro S. was in court requesting a divorce from her husband, who beat her with a stick. The court granted a divorce but ordered the wife to reimburse the bridewealth.[56] Malado A., wife of Oumare D., was in court in Jenne seeking a divorce. She stated that she detested her husband, who, together with his brothers, "beat her continuously." Oumare D. argued in court that his wife's claims were without merit. Witnesses, however, supported Malado A.'s claim. The court ruled in favor of Malado A.'s request for a divorce and ordered Oumare D. to pay his wife 40,000 cowries in compensation and to complete the bridewealth payments, which she was entitled to keep.[57]

In Sikasso, physical abuse was commonly cited as a woman's reason for appealing to the tribunal for divorce. Husbands often justified beating their wives in terms of the need to control their misbehavior. On 15 May 1908, Maoule S. brought her husband, Moussa C., to the Sikasso tribunal to request a divorce. Maoule S. claimed that her husband physically abused her. Her husband did not refute her claims of physical abuse but told the court that he beat her because she wanted to leave their household. The court found in favor of Maoule S.[58] Similarly, on 4 August 1911, Namoro S. brought her husband, Mamadi K., to the Sikasso tribunal and asked for divorce on grounds of physical abuse. Mamadi K. stated before the court that he beat his wife because she had a lover. The court found in favor of Namoro S.[59] As these cases suggest, the court did not always side with husbands and thus rejected their explanations for violence.

The bar for proof in cases of physical violence was high, and women who accused their husbands of physical abuse needed to have witnesses. Bourte C. was in court in Jenne on 27 August 1910 seeking a divorce from her husband, Souleymane D., for "mistreatment." Bourte C. had witnesses support her claim, and the court granted her a divorce.[60] In Segu, Dieneba M. was in court to seek a divorce from her husband because of his "brutality." She brought witnesses, and the court approved her request.[61] Consequences for false accusations could be severe. Aissata D. was in court on 4 December 1908 seeking a divorce from her husband for "serious" beatings. She did not have witnesses, and the court dismissed her case. Aissata D. appealed the judgment and was in court again on 28 December 1908, and this time brought a witness. However, the witness swore in court that he did not hear or see anything. The appeals court not only threw out the case, but fined Aissata D. a hefty twenty-five francs for frivolous appeal.[62] The Jenne court ruled against a wife who sought a divorce against her blind husband, arguing that his infirmity was not sufficient cause for divorce. Tiena C. appealed the judgment and was back in court 27 April 1910. Here she argued that her blind husband was also very "mean" to her, hoping that this added level of accusations would sway the court. Witnesses for the defense did not support Tiena C.'s claim, and the court not only dismissed the case, but fined the plaintiff a whopping one hundred francs for frivolous appeal. Failure to pay the fine would result in forty days' imprisonment.[63]

In a world where violence was ubiquitous, women also used physical violence. In Kita, both Faguimba K. and Yegue S. accused each other in court of violence against each other.[64] In Bouguni, the provincial tribunal listened to Dougoune K. seek a divorce from his wife for incompatibility, which the court rejected. However, he was back in court on 13 July 1911, complaining that his wife abused his son. Dougoune K. must have brought witnesses, who testified to his character and to his wife's actions, because the court now granted a divorce. Fatouma T. must have acted out in court, since the court sentenced her to one month in prison for "disrespect to the court."[65] Samake S. justified his beating his wife on the grounds that she had tried to kill him. Bamakan K. responded that her husband beat her without cause and threw her out of the home. The court sided with the wife and ruled that since the husband had sent her away, it granted a divorce and permitted the wife to keep the bridewealth.[66] Husbands were occasionally victims of domestic violence perpetrated by other family members. Amadou T. claimed in court, in response to his wife's request for a divorce on the basis of his "abandonment," that he only left because his wife's children from a previous marriage "threatened him."[67]

Polygynous marriages could provide a sense of community and shared domestic labor for the wives. But just as easily, these marriages could become sites of conflict. On 13 August 1907, Niakalemba C. was in court in Kita seeking a divorce from her husband because her husband's other wife "mistreats her." The tribunal tried to reconcile the disputants but agreed to a divorce when it was clear that these efforts were not going to prevail.[68] Cisse D. sought a divorce from her husband because he "mistreated her, did not give her food as he does to his other wives." The court granted the request.[69]

The courts evaluated cases of domestic violence according to a complex matrix that used the moral economy of marriage as a framework. A certain level of exploitation and physical disciplining was accepted. In this framework, however, the degree of violence was one factor among several. The court assessed whether responsibility for the violence was shared by both partners or caused by one primarily. Only when domestic violence exceeded the limits of the moral economy of marriage did the courts grant divorce and release the woman from returning the bridewealth.

꙳

We have suggested in this chapter that there was a moral economy of marriage that provided men and women with a framework for understanding what to expect from marriage. It also provided the African judges sitting on the newly created native courts with a framework for assessing the causes of domestic violence that came before them and how to rule in these cases. A certain degree of exploitation was an accepted part of marriage in the late precolonial and early colonial eras of West Africa. Exceeding those limits, however, ruptured the marriage, and many of these cases made their way to court.

The end of slavery contributed to household stresses, and these were often expressed as domestic violence. The end of slavery was a time of social upheaval, during which forms of social and political authority were tested and reconfigured by people in subservient or vulnerable situations. Often, when women or junior members of households tested household authority and the moral economies that defined them, the results were extreme; men responded with violence and abuse. Very little of the research on African marriage and gender has specifically examined domestic violence as a historical element of marriage and society. Scholarship on the history of marriage disputes, divorce, and other family-related civil conflicts sheds light on issues related to power and control in marriage, often examining how the management of marriage on the part of new states and local authorities changed during the colonial period.[70]

There is no question, however, that domestic violence was a feature of African households in French Soudan at the beginning of the twentieth century. We have argued that court cases provide a body of evidence to assess accusations of domestic violence at a time of accelerated social change. The end of slavery contributed to stresses on households already coping with the transition to colonialism. Explanations of why these forms of violence against women occurred bring to the fore contested societal notions of a woman's place in her household and society, and the prevailing sense of propriety surrounding a woman's behavior, particularly toward men. Work on domestic violence and gender violence reminds us that acts of domestic violence are ultimately political in nature and linked to larger sociocultural values. We should therefore look more closely at the links between violence directed toward women in their conjugal relationships and families, social and economic strife, and challenges to established political authorities.

NOTES

1. Martin Klein, *Slavery and Colonial Rule in French West Africa* (New York: Cambridge University Press, 1998), 197.

2. Most recently see Gregory Mann, *Native Sons: West African Veterans and France in the Twentieth Century* (Durham, NC: Duke University Press, 2006). See also Igor Kopytoff, "The Cultural Context of African Abolition," in *The End of Slavery in Africa*, ed. Suzanne Miers and Richard Roberts (Madison: University of Wisconsin Press, 1988), 485–503.

3. We use the name *French Soudan* throughout the chapter to refer to the colony, though it was known as Haut-Sénégal-Niger between 1904 and 1920. The territory became Soudan Français or French Soudan once again in 1920 and thus remained until independence in 1960.

4. See Sean Hanretta, *"Suffering for Our Father": Sufism and Social Change in French West Africa* (New York: Cambridge University Press, 2009), which explores

how former slaves and women gravitated to this new community because it offered opportunities to redefine gender and status.

5. Richard Roberts, *Litigants and Households: African Disputes and Colonial Courts in the French Soudan, 1895–1912* (Portsmouth, NH: Heinemann, 2005); Emily Susan Burrill, "Meanings of Marriage in a Market Town: Gender, Conjugality, and Law in Colonial Sikasso (French Soudan), 1895–1960" (PhD diss., Stanford University, 2007).

6. Marie Rodet, "Continuum of Gendered Violence," this volume.

7. Whereas Thompson used the concept of moral economy as a tool for explaining the motivations and actions of a "labouring class" crowd in eighteenth-century England, Scott turned to moral economy as a conceptual framework for understanding peasant uprisings in Southeast Asia, particularly in the face of food shortages. E. P. Thompson, "The Moral Economy of the English Crowd in the Eighteenth Century," *Past and Present* 50 (February 1971): 76–136; James Scott, *The Moral Economy of the Peasant: Rebellion and Subsistence in Southeast Asia* (New Haven, CT: Yale University Press, 1976). For the foundational works on moral economy in African history, see John Lonsdale, "The Moral Economy of Mau Mau: Wealth, Poverty and Civic Virtue in Kikuyu Political Thought," in *Unhappy Valley: Conflict in Kenya and Africa,* book 2: *Violence and Ethnicity,* by Bruce Berman and John Lonsdale (Athens: Ohio University Press, 1992), 315–468; Thomas Spear, *Mountain Farmers: Moral Economies of Land and Agricultural Development in Arusha and Meru* (Berkeley: University of California Press, 1997).

8. Patrick Tolman, Deborah Gorman-Smith, and David Henry, "Family Violence," *Annual Review of Psychology* 57 (2006): 560–61. The cases we use deal almost exclusively with marriage issues, especially those surrounding the rupture of a marriage. We have only isolated records of unmarried partners seeking the court's intervention in domestic violence, supporting our argument that the disputes are about the moral economy of marriage, not violence per se.

9. Martin Klein and Richard Roberts, "Gender and Emancipation in the French Soudan," in *Gender and Emancipation in Comparative Perspective,* ed. Diane Paton and Pam Scully (Durham, NC: Duke University Press, 2005), 162–80; Marcia Wright, *Strategies of Slaves and Women: Life-Stories from East/Central Africa* (New York: Lilian Barber Press, 1993).

10. Camilla Toulmin, *Cattle, Women, and Wells: Managing Household Survival in the Sahel* (Oxford: Clarendon Press, 1992), 4–5, chap. 13.

11. This is also reflected in ethnographic writings on the Minyanka of Koutiala. See Enquête sur l'organisation de la famille les fiancailles et le mariage, cercle de Koutiala, 1910, 1 D 198, Archives Nationalesat du Mali at Koulouba (hereafter ANM-K), Fonds Anciens (hereafter FA).

12. Two important exceptions need to be recognized: plaintiffs could cite the serious illness of one of the partners as cause for divorce, which would rupture the moral economy principles of marriage, and invoke incompatibility. The tribunals would sometimes grant divorce on the basis of mutual incompatibility, especially during the early years of their operation. Women seeking divorce found it much harder to do so after 1911.

13. 7 See Richard Roberts, *Warriors, Merchants and Slaves: The State and the Economy in the Middle Niger Valley, 1700–1914* (Stanford, CA: Stanford University Press, 1987); Andrew Hubbell, "A View of the Slave Trade from the Margin: Souroudougou in the Late Nineteenth-Century Slave Trade of the Niger Bend," *Journal of African History* 42, no. 1 (2001): 25–47; Martin Klein, "The Slave Trade and Decentralized Societies," *Journal of African History* 42, no. 1 (2001): 49–65.

14. We also use court data from neighboring cercles, such as Segu, Jenne, Mopi, and Timbuktu to augment the quality of the case materials presented.

15. Nicholas S. Hopkins, *Popular Government in an African Town: Kita, Mali* (Chicago: University of Chicago Press, 1972), 37–38; Diango Cissé, *Structures des Malinké de Kita: Contribution à une anthropologie sociale et politique du Mali* (Bamako: Éditions Populaires, 1970); Klein, *Slavery and Colonial Rule in French West Africa*; Denise Bouche, *Les villages de liberté en Afrique noire française, 1887–1910* (The Hague: Mouton, 1968).

16. Richard Roberts and Martin Klein, "The Banamba Slave Exodus of 1905 and the Decline of Slavery in the Western Sudan," *Journal of African History* 21, no. 3 (1980): 375–94.

17. Klein, *Slavery and Colonial Rule in French West Africa*; Roberts, *Litigants and Households*, 103; Claude Meillassoux, "État et conditions des esclaves à Gumbu (Mali) au XIXe siècle," in *L'esclavage en Afrique précoloniale*, ed. Claude Meillassoux (Paris: Maspero, 1975).

18. Rapport commercial, Sikasso, 1907, 1 Q 84, ANM-K, FA. Rapport administratif, Bougouni, 1907, 2 D 173, ANM, FA.

19. Rapport Politique, Sikasso, May. See, for example, *Lagui D. v. Foutoura D.*, 24 September 1912, Tribunal of Sikasso, 1906, 1 E 73, ANM-K, FA. See also Roberts and Klein, "The Banamba Slave Exodus of 1905"; and Brian J. Peterson, "Slave Emancipation, Trans-Local Social Processes, and the Spread of Islam in French Colonial Buguni (Southern Mali), 1893–1914," *Journal of African History* 45, no. 3 (2004): 421–44."

20. Georges Deherme, *L'Afrique occidentale française: Action politique, action économique, action sociale* (Paris: Bloud, 1906), 366.

21. See, for example, *Lagui D. v. Foutoura D.*, 24 September 1912, Tribunal of Sikasso.

22. Richard Roberts, "Women, Household Instability, and the End of Slavery in Banamba and Gumbu, French Soudan, 1905–12," in *Women and Slavery*, vol. 1: *Africa, the Indian Ocean World, and the Medieval North Atlantic*, ed. Gwyn Campbell, Suzanne Miers, and Joseph Miller (Athens: Ohio University Press, 2007), 281–305.

23. Procedure in the native courts was such that complainants could file a dispute and have a hearing on that disputes with a few days. Thus there was a close correlation between the kind of grievance expressed and when a dispute was heard.

24. In *History and Power in the Study of Law: New Directions in Legal Anthropology* (Ithaca, NY: Cornell University Press, 1989), June Starr and Jane Collier remind us that there were indigenous courts that preceded the colonial creation

of "customary" courts and persisted alongside these colonial inventions. See also Lauren Benton, *Law and Colonial Cultures: Legal Regimes in World History, 1400–1900* (New York: Cambridge University Press, 2002). We have not located records of qadi's decisions that were not part of the colonial legal system. Research in the Timbuktu manuscript collections indicates that there are a number of *fatwas*, which could provide insight on Muslim legal decision making. See Shamil Jeppie and Souleyman Bachir Diagne, eds, *The Meanings of Timbuktu* (Cape Town: HSRC Press, 2008).

25. Significant legal ambiguities surrounded the *originaires* (those Africans originally resident when the French established municipal government) of the four communes of Senegal, who, although mostly Muslims, were given the rights of French citizenship without actually becoming French citizens. For a preliminary discussion, see Dominique Sarr and Richard Roberts, "The Jurisdiction of Muslim Tribunals in Colonial Senegal, 1857–1922," in *Law in Colonial Africa*, ed. Kristin Mann and Richard Roberts (Portsmouth, NH: Heinemann, 1991), 131–45; J. W. Johnson, *The Emergence of Black Politics in Senegal: The Struggle for Power in the Four Communes* (Stanford, CA: Stanford University Press, 1971); Benton, *Law and Colonial Cultures*.

26. For more detail, see Roberts, *Litigants and Households*, chaps. 1, 3.

27. According to the 1903 decree, the village tribunal was not obliged to keep written records, and we have not seen any archival traces of the deliberations of these tribunals. We have seen only a tiny handful of cases in which one of the litigants appealed the judgment of the village tribunal to the provincial tribunal. Most litigants at the provincial tribunal probably bypassed the lower court altogether.

28. See, for example, Rapport sur le fonctionnement des tribunaux indigènes, 3d Quarter 1906, Bouguni, 2 M 59, ANM-K, FA; Rapport de M. l'Administrateur de cercle du Bamako sur le fonctionnement des tribunaux indigènes, 1st Quarter 1909, Bamako, 2 M 54, ANM-K, FA.

29. The requirement to keep records reflects efforts to regularize the colonial practices and to control for excesses. In the case of the courts, registers were required because of the professional magistrates of the procureur général's office in Dakar were charged with overseeing the functioning of the courts and the dispensation of punishments.

30. See David W. Cohen, "A Case for the Busoga," in *Law in Colonial Africa*, ed. Kristin Mann and Richard Roberts (Portsmouth, NH: Heinemann, 1991), 239–54; Richard Roberts, "Representation, Structure and Agency: Divorce in the French Soudan during the Early Twentieth Century," *Journal of African History* 40, no. 3 (1999): 389–410; Judith Byfield, "Women, Marriage, Divorce and the Emerging Colonial State in Abeokuta (Nigeria) 1892–1904," in *"Wicked" Women and the Reconfiguration of Gender in Colonial Africa*, ed. Dorothy L. Hodgson and Sheryl A. McCurdy (Portsmouth, NH: Heinemann, 2001), 27–46.

31. Where we have written records of the courts' transactions, the testimony of the litigants, witnesses, and judges (or magistrates) was shaped by traditions of literacy and the economies of administration. No matter how advanced, no

recorded testimony can capture the often telling silences and gestures of those giving testimony. See James Clifford's discussion of the 1976 Masphee Indian land claims case, James Clifford, *The Predicament of Culture: Twentieth-Century Ethnography, Literature, and Art* (Cambridge, MA: Harvard University Press, 1988).

32. Eric Pollet and Grace Winter, *La société Soninke* (Dyahunu, Mali) (Brussels: Université libre de Bruxelles, 1972), 371, 394.

33. Thoron de Laur, Rapport sur la tournée de recensement, 5 May 1909, Gumbu, 1 E 38, ANM-K, FA

34. This is our application of the definition of domestic violence, as informed by the 1989 UN Report and the WHO 2005 reports on domestic violence discussed in the introduction to this volume. UN, Center for Social Development and Humanitarian Affairs, *Violence against Women in the Family* (New York: Center for Social Development and Humanitarian Affairs, 1989); *World Health Organization Multicountry Study on Women's Health and Domestic Violence against Women: Initial Results on Relevance, Health Outcomes and Women's Responses* (2005), available online: http://www.who.int/gender/violence/who_multicountry_study/en/.

35. *M. D. v. Mala D.*, 16 May 1907, Tribunal de Province, Jenne. Due to privacy concerns raised by the regulation issued by the Republic of Mali in 2002 restricting the use of any records held by the National Archives of Mali that may "implicate the private lives of citizens," we use only the first name and the initial of the last name to identify disputants in court cases. For more information on court cases and privacy, see Richard Roberts, *Litigants and Household*, xi–xii.

36. *Buladougou M. v. Wange Koly K.*, 26 October 1908, Tribunal de Province, Kita.

37. *Makandian K.v. Mamadou D.*, 5 April 1909, Tribunal de Province, Kita.

38. *Memoutou D.v. Makandou K.*, 14 August 1905, Tribunal de Province, Kita.

39. WHO 2005 study.

40. Rapport politique, Bamako, May 1907, 1 E 19, ANM-K FA.

41. Rapport Politique, Sikasso, April 1907, 1 E 28, ANM-K FA.

42. *Mame T. v. Safi T.*, 5 January 1912, État des jugements rendus en matière civile et commerciale par le tribunal de province de Sikasso pendant le premier trimestre de l'année 1912, 1 E 28, ANM-K FA.

43. Jane Guyer writes on the haziness of such transfers in rights in people, particularly where women are involved. See Jane Guyer, "Lineal Identities and Lateral Networks: The Logic of Polyandrous Motherhood," in *Nuptiality in Sub-Saharan Africa: Contemporary Anthropological and Demographic Perspectives*, ed. Caroline Bledsoe and Gilles Pison (Oxford: Clarendon Press, 1994).

44. For more information see Roberts, *Litigants and Households*, chap. 5.

45. *Tonama C. v. Na C.*, 23 September 1906, Tribunal de Province, Segu. See also *N'Pe T. v. Ba T.*, 23 October 1905, Tribunal de Province, Segu.

46. *Nansa D. v. Kouiba T.*, 23 October 1905, Tribunal de Province, Segu.

47. *Awa S. v. Monhoro S.*, 1 February 1907, Tribunal de Province, Kita. This case also indicated that gender-specific uses of money may have been implicated in the dispute. The wife in this case claimed that she had received money from

the [Catholic] "mission" and that she bought cloth with it. Her husband claimed that she stole the money from him.

48. *Filifui K. v. Kassiba B.*, 27 September 1909, Tribunal de Province, Kita.

49. *Santa C. v. Alaman K.*, 7 August 1909, Tribunal de Province, Timbuktu.

50. *Namasso D. v. Fatimata S.*, 25 September 1905, Tribunal de Province, Kita.

51. *Mama D. and Dialiconi D. v. Lamine K.*, 17 February 1908, Tribunal de Province, Kita.

52. *Sama S. v. Bala C.*, 28 May 1912, Tribunal de Province, Kita.

53. *Samba Diallo S. v. Madhy K.*, 29 August 1910, Tribunal de Province, Kita.

54. *Yoro D. v. Mamadi K.*, 3 May 1909, Tribunal de Province, Kita.

55. *Dianta M. v. Bo K.*, 11 September 1911, Tribunal de Province, Kita.

56. *Soro S. v. Dougoufama D.*, 30 October 1911, Tribunal de Province, Kita.

57. *Malado A. v. Oumare D.*, 20 January 1908, Tribunal de Province, Jenne.

58. *Maoule S. v. Moussa C.*, 15 May 1908, Tribunal de Province, Sikasso.

59. *Namoro S. v. Mamadi K.*, 4 August 1911, Tribunal de Province, Sikasso.

60. *Bourte C. v. Souleymane D.*, 27 August 1910, Tribunal de province, Jenne.

61. *Dieneba M. v. Baba D.*, 20 January 1908, Tribunal de Province, Segu.

62. *Aissata D. v. Hama K.*, 4 December 1908, Tribunal de Province, Jenne; *Aissata D. v. Hama K.*, 28 December 1908, Tribunal de Cercle, Jenne.

63. *Tiena C. v. Fakoro B.*, 3 March 1910, Tribunal de Province, Jenne; *Tiene C.*, 27 April 1910, Tribunal de Cercle, Jenne.

64. *Faguimba K. v. Yegue S.*, 3 June 1907, Tribunal de Province, Kita

65. *Dougoue K. v. Fatouma T.*, 13 July 1911, Tribunal de Province, Bouguni.

66. *Bamakan K. v. Samake S.*, 7 September 1908, Kita.

67. *Amadu T. v. Tara T.*, 6 August 1909, Jenne.

68. *Niakalemba C. v. Sengoubou K.*, 13 August 1908, Kita.

69. *Cisse D. v. Yamadou K.*, 18 January 1909, Tribunal de Province, Kita.

70. See Byfield, "Women, Marriage, Divorce and the Emerging Colonial State"; Sean Hawkins, "'The Woman in Question': Marriage and Identity in the Colonial Courts of Northern Ghana, 1907–1954," in *Women in African Colonial Histories*, ed. Jean Allman, Susan Geiger, and Nakanyike Musisi (Bloomington: Indiana University Press, 2002), 116–43; Victoria Tashjian and Jean Allman, "Marrying and Marriage on a Shifting Terrain: Reconfigurations of Power and Authority in Early Colonial Asante," in Allman, Geiger, and Musisi, *Women in African Colonial Histories*, 237–25; Roberts, *Litigants and Households*.

2 ⇜ Domestic Violence and Child Circulation in the Southeastern Gold Coast, 1905–28

CATI COE

IN JULY 1918, Delphina Ocquaye brought a woman, Afua Fearon, to the highest colonial court of the Eastern Province of the Gold Coast for repayment of debt.[1] The situation, like many court cases, was more complex than initially met the eye. The reason that Delphina was demanding Afua repay the debt now was because a girl or young woman,[2] Nah Adaye, had run away from her house after Delphina threw soup at her. How were the debt and the movement of this girl connected?

According to the story told by participants, eight to ten years before the case came to court, Nah Adaye's mother was ill. At that time, Nah Adaye's mother was living with her sister Afua, a bead seller, in the town of Nsawam in the Eastern Province. Nsawam was a hub of cocoa trading and commercial activity that grew rapidly after a railway linking coastal Accra and inland Kumasi, two important cities of the Gold Coast, reached the town in 1910. Nah Adaye's mother asked Afua to place her daughter as a servant with someone else. Afua turned to her landlady, Delphina Ocquaye. We do not know much about Delphina, but her European first name suggests that she had been baptized or gone to mission schools.[3] She gave her occupation as "trader" in the court documents, an occupation common to women and appropriate to the commercial town of Nsawam. A teacher in Nsawam had placed his wife with Delphina as an apprentice to be a seamstress, paying Delphina for the training. Delphina's ownership of a building in a rapidly expanding town attests to her prosperity, and she attracted people to her household as a result.

In response to Afua's request, Delphina agreed to take on the girl Nah Adaye, and gave Afua eight pounds in exchange, which Afua passed along to Nah Adaye's mother. Unfortunately, the mother then died, and after some years of service,[4] Nah Adaye ran away to Afua, who by then was living in Pakro, another commercial town farther up the railway line.[5] Delphina had come to get Nah Adaye once, but to no avail. Two months prior to the court case, Afua testified that Delphina's husband "came to Pakro and the child was given to him without my knowledge." In her work as a bead seller, Afua probably did a fair amount of traveling, and she may have been absent during the husband's visit, or she may have gone to live elsewhere, leaving Nah Adaye behind in Pakro, for her current residence was noted as being in Accra. Nah Adaye apparently ran away from him as well, because Delphina brought Afua to court.

Afua launched two counterclaims against Delphina's claim of debt. Afua testified that Nah Adaye complained that Delphina's husband had sexual "connection" with her when he had taken her away from Afua's residence in Pakro.[6] Afua furthermore argued that Nah Adaye should have received wages for her time of service to Delphina's household at a rate of seven pounds sixteen shillings per month. Delphina then countered these charges of wage employment by saying that Nah Adaye had been sent to live with her to receive good discipline and training, what is known as fostering in the anthropological literature. Delphina testified: "She [her mother or Afua; it is unclear] wanted to place the girl because she was so proud she needed checking by someone." She had fed her and clothed her as is "customary." Under these conditions, she suggested, paying Nah Adaye was inappropriate. As the court questioned Afua, Afua admitted, "The child was bought or pawned the same way as when a native buys a wife. The person paying the pawn money has absolute control." Pawning (also called pledging) referred to a practice in which, when a person received a loan from another, the debtor transferred a person into the hands of the creditor as security for the loan, to stay with and work for the creditor until the loan or the loan and interest were repaid.

One of the tasks of a court is to determine which kind of wrong is applicable to a particular case.[7] As we see in this case, participants made many different claims because they were uncertain which wrong would carry weight in the court's decision making. The court decided that although Afua's counterclaim for wages was excessive, they accepted her underlying rationale and decided that Delphina should have paid for Nah Adaye's services. At the same time, they decided that Delphina's loan should be repaid. As a result, they assessed Delphina and Afua eight pounds apiece, in effect canceling their obligations to one another in an attempt to resolve the conflict. In its ruling, the court ignored the accusation of rape and the implied relationships of pawning or fostering; what the court overlooked will be the focus of this chapter.

As others in this volume argue, domestic violence as a concept differentiates between the kinds of violence, harm, and exploitation that occur in the domestic sphere and those that occur in society more generally, yet households and the wider society in which they operate are deeply linked. First, the domestic household in the Gold Coast—unlike the Western ideal of the nuclear family—often contained members of different families, including slaves, pawns, fostered children, and tenants. However, it is important to note that all households, even Western nuclear families, are made up of strangers, who can be made into family over time, whether through communal practices of eating and sleeping together, reciprocities of exchange, and/or kinship ideologies around the transfer of fluids, such as blood.[8] Second, households are constituted socially. In the colonial Gold Coast, children were incorporated into and dispersed from households based on that household's relative well-being or poverty. Nah Adaye's presence in Delphina's domestic household was the result of the relative prosperity of Delphina, a landlord and businesswoman who was able to give out loans, in contrast to the crisis facing Nah Adaye's mother, who was sick with an illness that probably resulted in her death. More prosperous or stable households tended to attract children, whether through extending credit or through their enhanced ability to provide children with training and opportunities for future livelihood. Under conditions of migration and trade, membership of households was fluid with adults and children often moving in and out of the household temporarily or permanently. The demographic composition of a domestic household—who lived with whom—was therefore shaped by the affective and economic relations between men and women, adults and children, and patrons and clients.

Viewing households in this way highlights that the domestic unit is not a single unit governed by a man, as anthropologists have long pointed out about both families and households,[9] but rather that people in households and families have different interests, access to resources, roles, and perceptions. A focus on domestic violence reveals the fractures between conjugal partners and between parents and children, between those we might otherwise idealize as "a family." Domestic violence as a lived practice is part of the repertoire of negotiations and reciprocities between unequals in a household. Two acts of violence are mentioned in this case by Afua: Delphina's throwing soup and her husband's sexual intercourse with Nah Adaye, actions that were probably part of a long string of interactions, conflicts, and negotiations between these parties. Yet contemporary thinking about domestic violence may not account for how participants in that situation interpret and evaluate these actions as wrongs. The forms of violence are socially learned, with patterns in who tends to enact different kinds of actions. Because both violence itself and its meaning are social, and because of the way that the domestic sphere is interlinked with other households and larger social inequalities, an analysis of violence within the domestic space makes visible changing social relations both within and beyond the domestic household. Gold Coast households, with their circulation of children involved in different kinds of reciprocal exchanges, make this insight particularly clear.

For this discussion, I focus on court cases involving children and adolescents living apart from their parents in Akuapem, an area that included the town of Nsawam. Located about thirty miles from Accra and the coast, towns and villages in Akuapem were multiethnic: although Akan and Guan peoples predominated, Krobo, Ga, and Ewe people lived among them. From the 1890s to the 1930s, Akuapem was taken over by "cocoa fever": companies of Akuapem farmers moved from their towns on the ridge to forest areas in the west to plant cocoa farms, getting initial capital from their earnings as migrant craftsmen and clerks, from trade, and from oil palm and rubber.[10] Men and women also traveled further afield—such as to the north, the inland city of Kumasi, or the coastal city of Sekondi—to participate in the growing commercial sector. Commercial towns like Nsawam and Pakro, towns founded by cocoa farmers from the Akuapem town of Aburi in the early 1890s, were growing rapidly during this time period. Colonial rule was present sporadically through the district commissioner's periodic visits to settle numerous chieftaincy disputes, the building of roads and railways, and the presence of police officers at Akuse and later Nsawam.[11]

The data on children and adolescents living in other people's households are sketchy and slim, buried in cases of debt, witchcraft, land, pawning, and sexual abuse. Court records are an interesting if limited source because they reveal relationships that were troublesome and conflictual at a particular historical moment, illuminating social fractures.[12] Situations that came to court were those of conflict, in which people had differing interests and conceptions of what was wrong. Courts were part of a process of contestation, some of which is visible to us and some of which is not. What is missing from court records are conflicts that never made it to court due to practical matters such as the cost or difficulty of traveling and getting witnesses to the court, or because of other forms of mediation within the community or social norms about who could be party to a conflict in court.[13] Another limitation with court records is that court cases tend to sever relationships; people who are more interested in altering or negotiating the terms of that relationship are likely to seek informal means of mediation.[14] As the case of *Delphina Ocquaye v. Afua Fearon* illustrates, people came to court only when other kinds of interventions had been attempted and failed; so often cases were quite complicated, having festered over time. I supplement the court records with oral histories conducted by Polly Hill among Akuapem cocoa farmers and Basel Mission sources, the main church in the area, which contain letters and reports from the European missionaries and articles by African Christians and ministers in a monthly Twi-language periodical, *Kristofo Sɛnkekafo*, published by the Basel Mission 1883–88, 1893–95, and 1905–17.

I combed the civil and criminal records of colonial courts at the High Commandment Court in Accra from 1869 to 1902 and its replacement, the Supreme Court in Accra, from 1902 to 1909. A criminal court opened in the Eastern Province at Nsawam in 1896, and I looked at its records along with those from the Supreme Court for the Eastern Province from 1909 to 1928. It is evident from the Gold Coast archival records that those who lived closest to the colonial courts were most likely to use them, particularly in the nineteenth century, and that in the twentieth century, as the courts became more accessible because of the increased ease of transportation, people were pursuing the same cases simultaneously or serially in different courts, hoping for a favorable verdict in at least one. Akuapem people found the distance to Accra a hindrance, and they appeared infrequently in those courts.[15]

As was the case elsewhere in Africa, there were multiple court systems operating simultaneously, and so not only did colonial courts operate, drawing on English common law, but so do did chiefly courts, or native tribunals, using "customary" law. In the Gold Coast, "chiefly courts remained very much in competition with a highly developed British-style Supreme Court."[16] While the British government formally recognized chiefly judicial power in the 1883 Native Jurisdiction Ordinance, native tribunals were not given the scope to deal with serious crimes, which were in the hands of colonial district commissioners, but only with civil matters. In 1910, an amendment to this ordinance made it possible to appeal the decisions made in the chiefly courts to the colony's administrative courts and required chiefs to keep written records or report to the district commissioner on the tribunal's monthly activities. These actions set in motion a process in which chiefly tribunals and colonial courts each adopted practices of the other, as illustrated by Delphina's reference to "custom" in a colonial court using English common law. While chiefly tribunals were meant to be cheaper than colonial courts because lawyers were excluded, lawyers found their way into them, and the fines and fees associated with them often made them more expensive than their British counterparts.[17] Court fees and fines were critical to "the impoverishment and reduction in status and class" of ordinary citizens to the benefit of those who sat on the chief's council.[18]

Beginning in 1905, there are extensive court records from four different chiefly tribunals, run by chiefs, in the major towns of Akuapem, although the court records are not necessarily continuous. These tribunals existed previously, but the extensive records after 1905 demonstrate that they came under colonial oversight during this time. I had access to the records for chiefly tribunals in four different towns in Akuapem: Abiriw (1913–1920), Aburi (1914–20, 1923–25), Adukrom (1911–1933), and Akropong (1905–1925). Many of the records provided detailed accounts of the court proceedings, including the testimony of plaintiffs, defendants, and witnesses, although the verbal exchange was usually in either the Twi or Guan language and the written account was usually in English, so that it could be accessed by colonial officials. Most of the cases that the chiefly tribunals heard concerned, in order of frequency, debt, ownership and possession of land, marriage, child custody, and witchcraft.[19] My focus is on the first three decades of the twentieth century in Akuapem in the Eastern Province, but I draw on court cases from the late nineteenth century and from other areas of the southeastern Gold Coast when necessary to place my data in context.

Basing my account on the limited evidence from court documents, supplemented by missionary sources, I explore Nah Adaye's move to Delphina's household and how that may have affected the way that she was treated.

NAH ADAYE AS A PAWN? A WAGE SERVANT?

A CHILD SENT FOR TRAINING?

CHILDREN'S CIRCULATION BETWEEN HOUSEHOLDS

In the early twentieth century in Akuapem, children circulated among households in different ways, but in general, their circulation resulted from transactions and exchanges between adults, of whom at least one was a child's relative.[20] A child's residence in any household implied both that the household head would provide basic sustenance, such as food and clothing, to the child and that the child would reciprocally contribute labor to the household, whether that involved household duties, commercial labor, and/or agricultural work. The different kinds of exchanges that prompted a child's circulation to another household had implications for the terms by which that child might leave that household. Although previous generations of mainly non-Akuapem children had circulated to households in Akuapem through slavery, by the early twentieth century, active slave trading in Akuapem had ceased.[21] Two of the most significant forms of child circulation in the early twentieth century in Akuapem were pawning and kin fostering.[22] In both situations, the child's ties to his or her birth parents and lineage were not severed, and the child might visit back and forth.

As related briefly above, pawning involved one person's receiving a loan in exchange for placing a person (a pawn) in the creditor's household, a person who could be redeemed when the sum or the sum and interest was repaid. Until the loan's repayment, the pawn had to live with the creditor and work for him (or, in fewer cases, her). Scholars of pawning have documented that kin groups acted as corporate bodies that had rights in and responsibilities to family members, which they could transfer to another lineage in return for goods or money through slavery and pawning.[23] Within this context, the concept of individual freedom does not make sense, since all people belonged in some way to a lineage for whom they worked during their lifetimes, although people within the lineage would have differential access to lineage resources.[24] There was not a sense of moral wrong associated with pawning, which was used in a situation of crisis, when there were no other avenues for help.[25] In colonial Akuapem, the most common relationships of pawning were family heads who pawned junior members of the family to secure family debts, older brothers who pawned younger brothers, and parents who pawned their children. They pawned them to people they knew or friends of friends, in the same town or towns nearby. These relationships provided some security for all involved: the creditor could rest assured that the debtor would want to release a close relation from bondage, and the debtor could supervise how his or her relative was being treated while living with the creditor.

The spread of the commercial economy in the southeastern Gold Coast meant that people required capital for new commercial ventures or to buy land for cocoa, and pawning of slave descendants and junior relatives was a way to raise that capital.[26] "Pawning is common," said one witness in a court case in Berekuso, Akuapem, in 1907.[27] Although it was a common practice, the colonial government considered it to be illegal and a form of slavery that had been outlawed with the Emancipation Ordinance of 1874. However, not much was done to prosecute slavery and pawning after the Emancipation Ordinance, except in cases of outright cruelty or when a slave or pawn transaction had recently taken place, because colonial officials were concerned about overly disrupting the existing social order.[28]

As a result, although it was commonly practiced, it had to be kept somewhat hidden from colonial officials. As with slavery, one of the strategies by which this was accomplished was through using younger pawns. Young people in the Gold Coast were often used as pawns, as they were elsewhere in West Africa.[29] Generally, however, they were over the age of eight, because they were valuable for the work they would provide to the creditor.

Awareness of pawning and its possibility of prosecution in Akuapem was heightened by the government's arrest of two debtors and a creditor in 1911 for pawning two children; the violators were punished with several months' imprisonment.[30] Pawning became better hidden in Akuapem after this successful prosecution, with fewer numbers of pawns exchanged at a time for a loan and with participants expressing concerns about the legality of pawning in court cases, although one can continue to find pawning cases well into the 1920s. The arrests also prompted the Basel Mission to reaffirm its guidelines that pawns held by Christians be paid a monthly wage.[31]

The reason why child pawns—rather than adult pawns—could be hidden from the law was because they could be presented to colonial officials as children who were being fostered. Colonial officials were aware of this: in 1890, the colonial government issued a circular ordering all district commissioners that as they enforced the abolition laws they should pay particular attention to "apprenticed children."[32] Fosterage is a common practice in West Africa, and in Akuapem in the early twentieth century, it seemed to be most often practiced between women, in which women gave their children to other women, whether kin or not, to raise and take care of for a variety of reasons. In some cases, the mother felt that the foster mother could better train her child's character or give her particular occupational skills, as Delphina alluded. In many cases, the foster parent was living in a commercial town and may have attracted dependents because of his or her relative wealth or access to commercial opportunities in which children could be employed. In some cases of crisis fostering, babies and toddlers were fostered by female relatives after their mothers had died.[33] Beginning in the late 1910s and particularly in the 1920s, some boys were sent to live with men in Accra to go to school.[34] Children also seemed to go on short-term stays to help relatives with their cocoa fields.[35]

Like pawning, fosterage indexed networks of relationships and patronage between adults, although often kin fostered children. Parents of a fostered child might also receive small loans or gifts from the fostering parent. Pawning and fosterage looked similar from the outside—a girl goes to live with a woman not her mother and works for her as she would work for her mother— and court cases from earlier periods and not in Akuapem reflect the ways that participants attempted to negotiate the ambiguities between slavery, pawning, and fosterage. Although there was some negotiability around these roles because they all entailed the everyday routines of coresidence and domestic service as well as the possible exchange of money, participants agreed on the conceptual distinction between them, implying different rights to the girl. In three court cases in the 1870s in the Accra court, in which the custody of a girl was at stake, the woman with whom the girl was living presented the situation as one of pawning, whereas the girl herself or her closer relatives presented the situation as one of child fosterage.[36] Pawning implied that a creditor had more control over a child's labor and residence than a foster parent would.

However, in Nah Adaye's case, in Nsawam in 1918, the argument goes the other way than in Accra in the 1870s, with Delphina claiming that Nah Adaye is a fostered child and Afua claiming she is a wage servant. The actions of both Delphina and Afua suggest that they understood Nah Adaye to be a pawn: Delphina gave Afua, as the representative of Nah Adaye's mother, a loan when she brought Nah Adaye to live with her and sought to have the loan repaid when Nah Adaye, the security for the loan, left her household. The loan Delphina provided of eight pounds was close to the average loan for a pawn at the time.[37] Yet because pawning was a crime for which both debtor and creditor could be charged, both Delphina and Afua did not talk about the arrangement as one of pawning.

If Nah Adaye was a debt pawn—rather than a fostered child or a wage servant—did that make her more vulnerable to violence—whether rape by other household members (such as Delphina Ocquaye's husband), beatings, or other forms of harm, such as the throwing of soup or the denial of food? I do not have any proof of circulating children suffering from more violence from other household members or other members of the community than children staying with their birth parents, which would require far more cases in the archival records for anything to be statistically significant. In contemporary Ghana, people commonly believe that children living with nonrelatives—assumed to be house help—are more likely to be beaten, mistreated, and denied educational opportunities than either children who belong to one's family or the child of one's own womb. It is important to note, however, that all children, whether fostered, pawned, or living with their parents, were social and economic dependents in their households, subject to a gerontocratic ideology that valued elders. Many children circulated to other households over the course of their childhoods, whether temporarily or more permanently, and thus the situation was not unusual. Furthermore, Delphina's statement about "checking" Nah Adaye suggests that a contemporary ideology about raising children to be hard-working, respectful, resourceful, and resilient was also common in the early twentieth century. For such child-raising goals, a harsh regime of punishment and hard work—not to the extent of permanently damaging a child—could be particularly valued.[38] In contemporary Akuapem, foster parents, like Delphina, are seen as particularly good at training children precisely for their stranger value: the child is apt to be more shy and more likely to obey such a person than the child's own mother. Training considered oppressive by children as they were growing up is often, although not always, appreciated by those now adults for how it has helped them be resilient in the face of many kinds of hardship.[39]

Children of course had agency under these conditions. The primary way for children to deal with mistreatment was to run away, an informal and non-legal mechanism that occurs over and over again in the court cases on pawning and which fostered children and household help use today.[40] However, children had differential access to this form of action. Slave children had the least recourse in this regard because they were generally brought from far away; if brought at a very young age, they might not even know how to find their own families. Pawns usually lived near their family, but if they ran away, their relatives might be displeased because they would have to repay the debt; they might bring them back to the creditor or might try to raise the money to repay the loan in other ways. Nah Adaye was in a particularly vulnerable situation in this regard, because her mother had died, although Afua was behaving appropriately like her mother's relation in taking responsibility for her. In all situations, whether as a debt pawn or a child living with someone for training, children's ability to protect themselves from mistreatment depended on the support that they received from other people to take them in, generally with a similar arrangement of living with and laboring for that person.

However, there is some evidence that female pawns in general were more vulnerable to unwanted sexual intercourse.

SEXUAL RELATIONS WITH PAWNS

The label of domestic violence signals a wrong that may not necessarily be viewed that way by participants in the situation. The participants in Nah Adaye's court case were negotiating their relationships through concepts of what they thought was morally appropriate and what was not in this situation. Afua implied that Delphina's husband was wrong to have sexual relations with Nah Adaye and by extension, that his action reduced the force of Delphina's claim to the debt.

Colonial anthropologist R. S. Rattray, in describing pawning among the Asante from his fieldwork in the 1910s and 1920s, states that a creditor had the full right to have sexual intercourse with a female pawn.[41] Rattray's assertions are based on very limited data—namely, conversations with a few elderly men in Asante—and were biased to further their interests.[42] These statements may also have been stated more strongly to Rattray than used in practice, given colonial administrators' desire to codify "a loose fluid body of social rules" into customary law.[43] Similar claims about creditors' sexual access to pawns were made in the court cases I saw, although they were scattered and always contested.[44] Furthermore, there is some evidence that female pawns were more valued by creditors than male pawns as a result.[45] Thus, we might expect that Nah Adaye's pawn status made her more vulnerable to rape by her creditor (if a man) or members of her creditor's family.

In her claim, Afua implied that sexual relationships with pawns were problematic, showing that this social norm—if it was one—was contested. Others in other court cases in the second decade of the twentieth century in Akuapem made similar claims, arguing that sexual intercourse with a pawn was a breach of agreement with the creditor. For instance, in the backstory to one case heard in 1914,[46] eleven years prior, in 1903, a man had borrowed eighteen pounds from another man, Kwajo Budu, to travel to the town of Kumasi, leaving his two daughters behind with him. Upon his return ten years later, the father had married one of his daughters, Afua Otubea, to a Christian chief of an Akuapem cocoa-growing village.[47] The question before the court was whether the father or Budu had the right to determine whom the daughters married and to accept their marriage payments. The father claimed that he did because he had repaid the debt owed to Budu, telling him: "The debt was eighteen pounds." The debt was "all pd [paid]" with money sent from Kumasi, "but my children remained with you." When Budu retorted that all the debts had not been repaid, the father responded, "You had s. c. [sexual connection] with Fosua [Ofosua, the second daughter] so I refused to pay the eight pounds she owed," a debt that must have been acquired by Fosua during the time that her father was away. The father thus claimed that the sexual relationship erased the debt associated with Fosua. Despite the father's argument about sexual relations with a pawn canceling the debt, the court took it as a straightforward custody case—in which the rights of fathers to control whom their daughters married trumped those of creditors.

Other cases suggest that creditors' rights to sexual relationships with pawns were contested. In 1908, in one case, a pawn initially said no to her creditor's request for sex, but then agreed when the creditor agreed to "dash" or forgive her debt as compensation.[48] Another interesting case occurred in 1909, when a man Teteh Kwadjo had "connection" with his brother's pawn. His brother, the creditor, responded by sending the girl back to "the father debtor," and Teteh said he would repay the debt, although further complications ensued that resulted in his not doing so.[49] Both cases suggest that sexual relations with the pawn eliminated the debt.

One of the reasons that sexual relations with pawns perhaps became more problematic in the early twentieth century was because the balance between creditors and debtors was shifting in favor of debtors and pawns. Rather than serving as the security for high-interest loans as in the late nineteenth century,[50] by the second decade of the twentieth century, a pawn tended to serve in lieu of interest on the loan.[51] Pawns also began to be treated with increased care by both debtor relatives and creditors in the twentieth century. Some pawns were asked by debtors if they would be willing to be pawned.[52] Some wanted to be pledged, knowing that it would result in greater family wealth that would benefit them later.[53] Increasingly, in the second decade of the twentieth century, male pawns were given land by creditors on which to work, which they sometimes claimed as their own later.[54] Or male pawns claimed that they deserved a portion of the land that had been bought with the loan for which they served.[55] Pawns tended to run away after a short period of time, some after as little as a month, but sometimes after a year,[56] and because of the illegality of the practice, creditors had a difficult time forcing the debtor to repay the debt when this happened. In response, creditors were changing the kinds of agreements they were making, refusing pawns as a less rewarding and more risky security and asking for land instead.

A second reason had to do with the rapid increase in marriage payments. Basel missionaries noted in 1875 that gifts were given to mark a marriage in Akuapem,[57] but by the early part of the twentieth century, cash payments were increasingly promised at the time of marriage, and marriage payments increased rapidly in the early twentieth century, to the point where they were sometimes higher than the amount of a loan for which a pawn served as security.[58]

One result of this development was that from about 1908 onward marriage came to look more like pawning in Akuapem. Jean Allman and Victoria Tashjian and Beverly Grier have described a similar process in Asante during the 1930s and 1940s.[59] Conflicts over whether a particular sexual relationship was one of pawning or marriage increased in the first two decades of the twentieth century in Akuapem chiefly tribunals. These cases constituted a set of characteristic "trouble cases" or "a body of disputes that clustered around specific fault lines of social and economic change."[60] In the early twentieth century, women seeking loans slept with their creditors so that they would pay their debts[61] or were raped when they sought a loan.[62] Men generally claimed that the money they gave women was a marriage payment. During a time when men were losing access to the labor of slaves and pawns at the same time as new cocoa farms required inputs of labor, they turned to wives and children as sources of labor. With higher marriage payments, husbands' rights over their wives and their children increased, including rights to control their labor and residence, as if the wives and children were pawns. However, women challenged these rights and left marriages by finding another man to repay the previous marriage payment. Furthermore, in court cases, they generally claimed the money exchanged was just a loan. Being a pawn at this point in time, therefore, implied that the woman had more control over her own labor and sexual relationships than she did as a wife. One man, wanting to remarry his ex-wife, paid off all her debts associated with her new marriage. When she came to live with him reluctantly, however, she would not sleep with him because she told him, as he reported to the court, "she wasn't my wife but she was with me as a pawn," whereupon he sent her back to her mother and asked for repayment of the loan.[63] In Asante, marriage also meant that men controlled the labor and residence of their wives, such that the women had to accompany the men to their cocoa fields far from where the women could earn other income.[64]

As marriage and pawning became confused with each other in the early twentieth century, pawns were increasingly female and adult, rather than children. Akuapem data, based on a small number of cases from the court records, corroborates data from Asante.[65]

TABLE 1 Pawning in Akuapem: male and female, 1890–1929

Decade	Total number of pawns	Total number of pawns whose gender can be determined	Female	Male
1890–99	11	11	2 (18%)	9 (82%)
1900–1909	49	38	11 (29%)	27 (71%)
1910–19	55	55	27 (50%)	27 (50%)
1920–29	27	27	19 (70%)	8 (30%)

Sources: See note 66.

TABLE 2 Pawning in Akuapem court cases: children and adults, 1890–1929

Decade	Total number of pawns	Total number of pawns whose child or adult status can be determined	Children	Adults
1890–99	11	8	8 (100%)	0
1900–1909	49	43	20 (46%)	23 (53%)
1910–19	55	37	13 (35%)	24 (65%)
1920–29	27	20	4 (20%)	16 (80%)

Sources: See note 66.

In Akuapem, although cases of pawning continued to appear in court records into the 1920s, pawning gradually transformed in three ways. One was toward wage employment, as advocated by the Basel Mission church and encouraged by the colonial government, as we see in its decision in Nah Adaye's case. A second was in using land, rather than people, to secure a loan.[67] Last, pawning became absorbed into marriage. Because of these developments, the incidence of children as pawns declined, as young men pawned themselves into wage employment and young women entered into marriages with creditor-husbands.

Children, however, continued to circulate into other households, although less and less as debt pawns. Perhaps their mothers could not balance child care and work, or perhaps a parent died, and so they were placed with grandmothers and aunts; perhaps they were sent to another household for discipline and training; perhaps their parents could not pay for their education, and so they would be sent to live with a relative who could; and perhaps as adolescents they went to help a woman with her housework and child care, hoping to receive at the end of their service the wherewithal to enter an apprenticeship that would ensure their future livelihood. Despite the prevalence of practices that tend to distribute child care to those households with the financial or social resources best able to sustain children, Akuapem people are engaged in an ongoing conversation about whether children will be treated well in nonparental households.

THINKING ABOUT "DOMESTIC VIOLENCE" IN AFRICA

Domestic violence as a concept implies that the kind of violence that occurs in the domestic sphere is different from that which occurs in other contexts. The domestic sphere conflates household and family: the nuclear family lives together. Furthermore, the term is meant to undo our notion of the happy nuclear family with a shared project, as a political move, because such violence has been downplayed by the law and societies. This move to expose the dark side of family life is perhaps less necessary in Africa, where it is more acknowledged, whether in contemporary versions of evangelical Christianity where family members may expose one to the devil or witchcraft, or through slavery and pawning where one's relatives sell or loan one to another household.[68]

The cases from Akuapem in the early twentieth century help clarify several characteristics of domestic violence in Africa. Certainly, one lesson is that we should not conflate household and kin. Many children circulated to nonfamilial households in the colonial Gold Coast, as they do in contemporary Africa. Furthermore, if kinship is a process of belonging accomplished over time, then people living together can be on a continuum of being kin or part of the family.

Second, we need to pay attention to the internal differentiation of the household unit, and how members may have different access to resources, interests, and repertoires for negotiation, whether throwing soup or running away. The roles and repertoires attached to such positions shift in response to the contestations between such people, such that the meaning of these actions—particularly whether or not they are considered wrong—changes over time.

Finally, whether we think of the domestic as households or families, we need to see households as deeply connected to the society in which they are placed. People's positions within households and their resources in negotiating relationships with other household members are bound up in relations between households—such as Nah Adaye's coming to Delphina's household in exchange for a loan to her mother. Nah Adaye's presence signals the well-being of Delphina's household—in terms of both wealth and health—relative to that of her mother's: her debt pawnage is due to the difficulties her previous household faced. Thus, Delphina and her husband's harm to Nah Adaye are bound up not only in their positions as unrelated adults in a household where Nah Adaye is a dependent but also in Delphina's creditor role in relation to Nah Adaye's mother and the differences in overall well-being between Delphina's household and that of Nah Adaye's relations. Thus the term "domestic violence" should not obscure the ways that people's positions and roles within their families or households are enabled by their relationships, roles, and positions within a larger society simultaneously, including the privileges and constraints given to them by virtue of their gender or social class position.

NOTES

I am grateful to Deborah Augsburger, Heather Levi, Ann Peters, Rachel Reynolds, Diane Sicotte, and the editors for their thoughtful comments and suggestions for revising this paper. Rutgers University, through the Childhood Studies Center and the Research Council, provided the funding that enabled me to do this research.

1. *Delphina Ocquaye v. Afua Fearon*, 26 July 1918, Civil Record Book, Supreme Court for Nsawam, 2 May 1918–30 October 1920, SCT 38/4/1, Ghana National Archives (hereafter GNA).

2. It is unclear how old Nah Adaye was at the time of the trial, but I suspect that she was an adolescent or older, given that she initially went to live with Delphina eight years prior.

3. In 1911, 14 percent of the women in Nsawam were estimated to be able to read and write, as were 45 percent of the men (*Kristofo Sɛnkekafo* 8, no. 6 [1913]: 70, D II y.4001, Basler Mission Archive [hereafter BMA]).

4. The length of time which Nah Adaye served was under dispute: Nah Adaye said about two years, and Afua said three years.

5. Pakro was growing rapidly during this period. When the railway station opened there in 1911, the recorded population of Pakro was only 521, but by 1921 it had doubled in population to 1,145 (Pakro File, Box 2, Folder 1, The Polly Hill Papers, Northwestern University Library).

6. *Connection* was the formal courtroom term used in England in the same time period (Shani D'Cruze, *Crimes of Outrage: Sex, Violence, and Victorian Working Women* [DeKalb: Northern Illinois University Press, 1998], 99).

7. Lloyd A. Fallers, *Law without Precedent: Legal Ideas in Action in the Courts of Colonial Basoga* (Chicago: University of Chicago Press, 1969).

8. Janet Carsten, *The Heat of the Hearth: The Process of Kinship in a Malay Fishing Community* (Oxford: Clarendon Press, 1997).

9. Diane L. Wolf, *Factory Daughters: Gender, Household Dynamics, and Industrialization in Java* (Berkeley: University of California Press, 1992); Margery Wolf, *Women and the Family in Rural Taiwan* (Stanford, CA: Stanford University Press, 1972); and Ann Whitehead, "Men and Women, Kinship and Property: Some General Issues," in *Women and Property, Women as Property*, ed. Renée Hirschon (London: Croom Helm, 1984), 176–92.

10. Polly Hill, "The Migration of Cocoa Farmers, 1890–1914," in *Akwapim Handbook*, ed. David Brokensha (Accra-Tema: Ghana Publishing Corporation, 1972), 69–74, and Polly Hill, *The Migrant Cocoa-farmers of Southern Ghana: A Study in Rural Capitalism* (Cambridge: Cambridge University Press, 1963).

11. Akwapim Native Affairs, 1902–15, ADM 11/1/1101, GNA, Accra.

12. Fallers, *Law without Precedent*; Richard Roberts, *Litigants and Households: African Disputes and Colonial Courts in the French Soudan, 1895–1912* (Portsmouth, NH: Heinemann, 2005).

13. Anne M. O. Griffiths, *In the Shadow of Marriage: Gender and Justice in an African Community* (Chicago: University of Chicago Press, 1997).

14. Igor Kopytoff, "The Cultural Context of African Abolition," in *The End of Slavery in Africa*, ed. Suzanne Miers and Richard Roberts (Madison: University of Wisconsin Press, 1988), 485–503. Drawing on contemporary court cases in Koforidua, Ghana, Michael Lowy similarly finds that litigants with less long-standing relationships were more likely to use the court only, rather than in combination with other dispute-settling agencies, such as household adjudication or supernatural authorities (Michael J. Lowy, "A Good Name Is Worth More Than Money: Strategies of Court Use in Urban Ghana," in *The Disputing Process: Law in Ten Societies*, ed. Laura Nader and Harry F. Todd Jr. [New York: Columbia University Press, 1978], 181–208).

15. However, Akuapem people were turning to the colonial courts in the 1850s ("Mante," in Notebook, Sch. 3.10, 130–32, D-20, BMA).

16. Roger Gocking, "Colonial Rule and the 'Legal Factor' in Ghana and Lesotho," *Africa* 67, no. 1 (1997): 63.

17. Roger Gocking, "British Justice and the Native Tribunals of the Southern Gold Coast Colony," *Journal of African History* 34, no. 1 (1993): 93–113.

18. Beverly Grier, "Pawns, Porters, and Petty Traders: Women in the Transition to Cash Crop Agriculture in Colonial Ghana," *Signs* 17, no. 2 (1992): 307.

19. See also Gocking, "Colonial Rule."

20. Suzanne Lallemand, *La circulation des enfants en société traditionelle: Prêt, don, échange* (Paris : Editions L'Harmattan, 1993).

21. Nathaniel Clerk, a pastor and teacher for the Basel Mission, felt in 1894 that many Akuapem Christians received pawns, but he doubted that they bought slaves ("*Wogye nwowa yen asafo horo yi pi mu; nkoa de, minnim se wɔtɔ bi ana.*" N. Clerk, "Ia. *Sakasaka a ɛwɔ asafo nom' a ɛto pi hintidua ne sɛnea wonyi no hɔ,*" *Christian Messenger* 1, no. 9–10 [May and July 1894]: 75). The last trade in slaves that was prosecuted in the Eastern Province occurred in 1903 (*Queen v. Dedy*, 29 March 1903, Criminal Record Book, 1896–1904, ADM 29/4/1, GNA). The first "slave-calling" case in which someone brought another person to court for calling his mother a slave appeared in Akuapem in 1905, indicating that the domestic slave trade had been an experience of the past generation, but not the present one (*Afriyie v. Ayi Kofi*, 13 November 1905, Civil Record Book, Akwapim, 23 June 1905–1 February 1906, ECRG 16/1/1, Eastern Regional Archives [hereafter ERA]); in the 1920s, these claims were being made about grandmothers (*Osae Kwadwo v. Kwaku Amaka*, 22 April 1924, Civil Record Book of the Native Tribunal of Adontenhene of Akuapem, Aburi, 15 October 1923–10 January 1925, ECRG 16/1/24, ERA). Taking the court cases and the comments by missionaries and Christians in the Basel Mission together, it would seem that the buying of slaves in Akuapem declined during the 1890s to the point of becoming virtually nonexistent in the early twentieth century, although the descendants of those slaves remained in Akuapem households and families.

22. E. N. Goody, *Parenthood and Social Reproduction: Fostering and Occupational Roles in West Africa* (Cambridge: Cambridge University Press, 1982).

23. Suzanne Miers and Igor Kopytoff, "African 'Slavery' as an Institution of Marginality," in *Slavery in Africa: Historical and Anthropological Perspectives*, ed. Suzanne Miers and Igor Kopytoff (Madison: University of Wisconsin Press, 1977), 10. See also the discussion by Toyin Falola and Paul E. Lovejoy, "Pawnship in Historical Perspective," in *Pawnship, Slavery, and Colonialism in Africa*, ed. Paul E. Lovejoy and Toyin Falola (Trenton, NJ: Africa World Press, 2003), 1–26.

24. Whitehead, "Men and Women, Kinship and Property."

25. Martin Klein and Richard Roberts make a similar case that pawning was used in times of crisis, such as during the depression in the 1930s in French West Africa: Martin Klein and Richard Roberts, "The Resurgence of Pawning in French West Africa during the Depression of the 1930s," in Lovejoy and Falola, *Pawnship, Slavery, and Colonialism in Africa*, 409–26.

26. See Polly Hill, "The Acquisition of Land by Larteh Cocoa Farmers," Cocoa Research Series No. 14, Economics Research Division, University College of Ghana, November 1958, Box 6, Folder 4, The Polly Hill Papers, Northwestern University Library for Akuapem; and for Asante, see Gareth Austin, *Labour, Land, and Capital in Ghana: From Slavery to Free Labour in Asante, 1807–1956* (Rochester, NY: University of Rochester Press, 2004).

27. *Rex v. Osaku*, 15 January 1907, Supreme Court, Accra, Criminal Record Book, 6 April 1905–20 July 1907, GNA, SCT 2/5/16.

28. Peter Haenger, *Slaves and Slave Holders on the Gold Coast: Towards an Understanding of Social Bondage in West Africa* (Basel: P. Schlettwein, 2000). Between 1877 and 1884, slavery or pawning cases represented between 5 and 11 percent of all cases in the Supreme Court of the Gold Coast and the Criminal Record Book of the High Court, both in Accra.

29. Don Ohadike, "The Decline of Slavery among the Igbo People," in *The End of Slavery in Africa*, ed. Suzanne Miers and Richard Roberts (Madison: University of Wisconsin Press, 1988), 437–61. See also Falola and Lovejoy, "Pawnship." Children had been pawns previously in Akuapem [*Brehooase of Obosomase v. Quay of same place*, 13 January 1875, Court of Civil Commandant, Ussher Fort, Accra, 31 July 1874–18 June 1875. GNA, SCT 2/4/11, in which children are captured for debt to work on palm oil plantations], but court records suggest that children became more popular as pawns in the 1890s. Whereas for previous decades (admittedly with a very small number of cases), children had constituted 33 percent of the pawns where adult or child status could be determined, during the 1890s, all eight Akuapem pawns whose status was given seem to have been children.

30. *Rex v. Oben Cudjoe and others*, 24 April 1911, Criminal Record Book, High Court, Accra 5 November 1909–25 July 1911, SCT 2/5/19, GNA.

31. *Kristofo Sɛnkekafo* 6, no. 1 (31 January 1911), 11, and *Kristofo Sɛnkekafo* 6, no. 8 (31 August 1911), 93–94, D II y.4001, BMA.

32. K. Opare-Akurang, "The Administration of the Abolition Laws, African Responses, and Post-Proclamation Slavery in the Gold Coast, 1874–1940," *Slavery and Abolition* 19, no. 2 (1998): 149–66.

33. *Yao Ofori v. Akrong*, 31 July 1914, Civil Record Book, Native Tribunal, Adukrom, 9 March 1912–23 November 1914, ECRG 16/1/12, ERA; *F. N. Adum v. Kwabena Ntow*, 8 April 1915, Civil Record Book, Native Tribunal of Akropong, 7 April 1914–27 November 1915, ECRG 16/1/18, ERA.

34. Charles Amponsa for *Ya Odi v. Adu Kumi*, 29 April 1919, Civil Record Book, Native Tribunal at Abiriw, 19 February 1913–31, May 1920, ECRG 16/1/15, ERA.

35. See *Kwafo Kwasi v. Kwaku Yirenchi*, 17 February 1909, Civil Record Book, Native Tribunal of Akropong, 9 January 1909–9 August 1909, ECRG 16/1/4, ERA, in which a man takes his sister's daughter to farm; and *Kwasi Jareboah v. Kofi Amoah*, 27 September 1915, Civil Record Book, Native Tribunal of Akropong, 7 April 1914–27 November 1915, ECRG 16/1/18, ERA, in which a girl went to stay with her cousin and her husband to help them dry the cocoa on their farm.

36. *Tawiah v. Johanna*, 2 August 1871, Civil Commandants Court, Accra, 17 May 1870–1 November 1872, SCT 2/4/8, GNA; and *Quamin Yaw v. Mansah*, 22 July 1873, and *Adooquaye Lydia of Accra v. Lum Yoccor of Accra*, 11 February 1873, both in SCT 2/4/10, GNA.

37. Between 1910 and 1919, the average loan for a female pawn in Akuapem was seven and a half pounds (n = 19), with a range of three to sixteen pounds; the average loan for a child was eight pounds (n = 8), with a range of three to thirteen pounds.

38. Caroline Bledsoe, "'No Success without Struggle': Social Mobility and Hardship for Foster Children in Sierra Leone," *Man* 25, no. 1 (1990): 70–88.

39. Cati Coe, "How Transnational Migration Has Affected the Distribution of Childcare in Ghana," Manuscript for the Multinational Working Group on Children and Youth, CODESRIA, December 2008.

40. On the strategies of legal inferiors, see Caroline H. Bledsoe, *Women and Men in Kpelle Society* (Stanford, CA: Stanford University Press, 1980), 187.

41. R. S. Rattray, *Ashanti Law and Constitution* (New York: Negro Universities Press, 1969).

42. Sara Berry, "Unsettled Accounts: Stool Debts, Chieftaincy Disputes, and the Question of Asante Constitutionalism," *Journal of African History* 39, no. 1 (1998): 39–62.

43. Martin Chanock, *Law, Custom, and Social Order: The Colonial Experience in Malawi and Zambia* (New York: Cambridge University Press, 1985), 53.

44. *Edward Repino Pinto of Ningo v. Appiadjaye of Ningo now at Accra*, 14 February1872, SCT 2/4/10, GNA.

45. One creditor refused a male pawn but accepted a female one, with whom he then had "connection" (*Kwasi Manu v. Kwaku Nsia*, 4 May 1922, Civil Record Book, Native Tribunal of the Nifahene, Akwapim, 25 February 1921–4 May 1923, ECRG 16/1/22, ERA).

46. *George Paul Kumi v. Kwajo Budu*, 15 October 1914, Civil Record Book, Native Tribunal of Akropong, 7 April 1914–27 November 1915, ECRG 16/1/18, ERA.

47. Hill, *Migrant Cocoa-farmers of Southern Ghana*, 220.

48. *Akrong Kwaben v. Addi Affua*, 5 February 1908, ECRG 16/1/2, ERA.

49. *John Kumi v. Teteh Kwadjo*, 17 February 1909, Civil Record Book, Omanhene's Court, Akropong-Akwapim, 9 January 1909–9 August 1909, ECRG 16/1/4, ERA.

50. In the 1870s, debtors generally paid high interest (up to 50 percent) on loans even when guaranteed by a pawn (Paul Jenkins, "Asante, Mohr, and Werner on Slave Emancipation Commission, 26 Jun 1875," in *Abstracts from the Correspondence of the Basel Mission Archives, 1852–1898* [Manuscript in Thesis Room, Balme Library, University of Ghana, Legon, 1970]). But Austin points out that the interest rate may have been lower when guaranteed by a pawn (Austin, *Labour, Land, and Capital in Ghana*).

51. A statement from one court case illustrates this trend: in 1914, Kwasi Ahamfro, a farmer from the ridge town of Dawu, Akuapem, said that he got a loan of ten pounds "and gave my son Aboagyi [Aboagye] to plaintiff to stay with him to forfeit the interest and if the boy failed to stay I will pay interest to plaintiff" (*Eller Kwadjoe Konor v. Kwasi Ahamfro*, 24 June 1914, Civil Record Book, Native Tribunal, Adukrom, 9 March 1912–23 November 1914, ECRG 16/1/12, ERA).

52. For instance, in the Okorase chiefly tribunal, in 1918, a man brought his two step-siblings to the chief's court and "put the matter before them that I was going to pledge [pawn] them for a loan in payment of the debt due by their late brother, for if the land he sold them they have finished; plaintiff and other refused to be in servitude." Upon their refusal, he put the land into pledge (*Ofosu v. Linguist Kwadjo*, 19 November 1918 in *The Native Tribunal of Okorase-Akwapim, Selected*

Land Cases, 1918–1919, ed. Polly Hill [Legon: Institute of African Studies, University of Ghana, 1964]).

53. E. O. Walker of Larteh remembered not wanting to go to school so he could be pledged to help his parents buy land (Notes on the Manuscript Book by James Lawrence Tete, taken 7/10/58, Box 4, Folder 7, The Polly Hill Papers, Northwestern University Library).

54. For example, see *Kwasi Panyin v. Kwasi Sakyi*, 28 October 1924, Civil Record Book, Akwapim, Superior Court of Omanhene of Akwapim, Akropong, 23 May 1919–23 March 1925, ECRG 16/1/21, ERA; and *Kwasi Mensa v. Otete Kwasi, both of Larteh*, 21 August 1908, Civil Record Book, Omanhene's Court, Akwapim, 17 October 1907–29 December 1908, ECRG 16/1/2, ERA.

55. *Kwaku Nipanka of Akropong v. Kwame Awuku of Akropong*, 6 April 1910, Civil Record Book, Omanhene's Court, Akwapim, 8 January 1910–17 September 1910, ECRG 16/1/5, ERA. See also *Kwasi Apema v. Kwaku Adade*, 6 October 1928, Adukrom Tribunal, Civil Record Book, 14 April 1928–24 October 1931, ECRG 16/1/27, ERA.

56. *Adawura of Amanprobi v. Kwaku Donkor of Akropong*, 25 June 1910, ECRG 16/1/5, ERA.

57. Jenkins, "Asante, Mohr and Werner on the Slave Emancipation Commission, dd 26 June 1875," in *Abstracts from the Correspondence of the Basel Mission Archives, 1852–1898*.

58. The average loan for which a pawn served increased slightly from nine pounds in 1900–1909 to eleven pounds in 1910–29.

59. Grier, "Pawns, Porters, and Petty Traders," and Jean Allman and Victoria Tashjian, *"I Will Not Eat Stone": A Women's History of Colonial Asante* (Portsmouth, NH: Heinemann, 2000).

60. Roberts, *Litigants and Households*, 2, drawing on Fallers, *Law without Precedent*, 83.

61. *Kwabina Kumi v. Akosua Akrofibea*, n.d. (between 9 January and 23 February 1909), ECRG 16/1/3, ERA; *Akrong Kwaben v. Addi Affua*, 5 February 1908, ECRG 16/1/2, ERA.

62. *Kwasi Defo v. Akosua Ayim*, 30 April 1915, ECRG 16/1/18, ERA; *Salome Adjoa Assi v. Odonkoi*, 9 September 1914, ECRG 16/1/19, ERA.

63. *Kwasi Wusu v. Amah Dakoa and Yah Asamaniwa*, 8 April 1908, ECRG 16/1/3, ERA.

64. In one case, after a man redeemed a woman from debt, he complained that she did not come to live with him. She countered that while she agreed to marry him, she said she would be willing to go to Kumasi, a large town, but not Akyeremateng, a cocoa-growing village in Akuapem, with him (*Kwame Bah v. Kwaw Aboagye, Meansah, Afua Wusua*, 10 March 1909, Civil Record Book, Adukrom, Akwapim, 13 October 1906–25 January 1909, ECRG 16/1/3, ERA).

65. Austin, *Labour, Land, and Capital in Ghana*.

66. The data for tables 2.1 and 2.2 come from my analysis of the following sources: ADM 29/4/1, SCT 2/4/5, SCT 2/4/6, SCT 2/4/53, SCT 2/4/54, SCT 2/5/11,

SCT 2/5/13, SCT 2/5/15, SCT 2/5/16, SCT 2/5/17, SCT 2/5/18, SCT 2/5/19, SCT 2/5/20, SCT 38/4/1, SCT 38/4/2, SCT 38/5/1, SCT 38/5/2 (all in GNA); and ECRG 16/1/1, ECRG 16/1/2, ECRG 16/1/3, ECRG 16/1/4, ECRG 16/1/5, ECRG 16/1/8, ECRG 16/1/11, ECRG 16/1/12, ECRG 16/1/13, ECRG 16/1/14, ECRG 16/1/15, ECRG 16/1/16, ECRG 16/1/17, ECRG 16/1/18, ECRG 16/1/19, ECRG 16/1/20, ECRG 16/1/21, ECRG 16/1/22, ECRG 16/1/23, ECRG 16/1/24, ECRG 16/1/26, ECRG 16/1/27, ECRG 16/2/1 (all in ERA).

67. In March 1912, in Berekuso, a man asked Kofi Adoo for a loan of thirteen pounds in exchange for a "young girl." A witness testified, "Kofi Adoo told him that this was illegal and that he couldn't do that. And that if he could give him a farm as surety or if someone would be surety for him, he would give him the amount" (COP v. Ofosu, 1 March 1912, Criminal Record Book, Supreme Court, in Nsawam, 1909–1912, SCT 38/5/2, GNA). Austin, *Labour, Land, and Capital in Ghana,* notes that land was pawned once it became valuable through cocoa farming.

68. Birgit Meyer, *Translating the Devil: Religion and Modernity among the Ewe in Ghana* (London: Edinburgh University Press for the International African Institute, 1997).

3 ↫ Continuum of Gendered Violence

The Colonial Invention of Female Desertion as a Customary Criminal Offense, French Soudan, 1900–1949

MARIE RODET

IN SEPTEMBER 1909, Filifin K. from Fodébougou came to the court of Kita to ask for divorce and request the reimbursement of bridewealth. He claimed that his wife, Kaniba B., intended to leave him following an argument during which he beat her because she insulted and disobeyed him.[1] Kaniba claimed that Filifin constantly attacked her when he was drunk and that she did not wish to live with him any longer. The court pronounced the divorce but found the wife liable for repayment of the bridewealth to her husband.

This court case is revealing on two levels. First, the husband considered himself to be the one suffering a loss: not only did his wife disobey and insult him (and therefore she deserved to be punished), but she wished to leave him. This was why he was in court to request a divorce and the reimbursement of the bridewealth. Second, his condemnation of his wife's "loose behavior" was backed by the court of Kita, which found her at fault in the divorce and ordered her to reimburse the bridewealth. The colonial administrator, who retranscribed the case for the legal records, supported the husband and concluded that the court's sentence was reasonable. "[S]he [could not] refuse to live with her husband just because of a simple quarrel which [was] a very common fact in indigenous households." Unfortunately, the record does not tell us much about the exact circumstances of the wife's battery. However, in a previous judgment on the same day Filifin K. asked the court to authorize him and his mother to leave the region because his older brother called him a "bastard." We can suspect that his quarrel with his wife and her intent to ask for divorce were a direct consequence of his decision to leave the region. His wife probably refused to follow him.

Although the transcripts of the court cases found in the Malian archives for the first half of the twentieth century are often very brief and elusive on the precise context of the case, they remain a precious source of information about gender conflicts, as the majority of the cases heard in civil courts at this time concerned marriage disputes. An attentive study of the court cases heard in the region of Kayes[2] can furthermore help us question the degree of colonial interference into "indigenous family matters."

Following the implementation of a new colonial legal system and the establishment of colonial native courts in French West Africa (hereafter FWA) in 1903,[3] the idea of respect for African custom became the pivot of the French politics of domination. The 1903 legislation guaranteed that the colonial courts would enforce African customs for African subjects. The compulsory use of customary law for defining and judging civil law offenses was reinforced by the decree of 16 August 1912, which officially recognized the "personal status" of French subjects.[4] Colonial respect for local customs facilitated above all colonial control over native courts, by ensuring that the "traditional power" became the loyal ally of the administration. The colonial administration was in charge of formalizing and unifying the content of customary laws. This formalization was based on what the "traditional power," the jurisprudence of colonial courts, and the colonial administration viewed as "customary law." It also aimed at unifying and standardizing customs, the colonial administration being convinced that the different customs used in French Soudan were fundamentally similar.[5]

Moreover, the colonial obsession with the coercive control of the population and the "preservation of the traditional African family" ultimately entailed a certain "invention of tradition"[6] pertaining to family law. This invention was facilitated as many local chiefs and notables used this opportunity to manipulate customary law for their own benefit. This simultaneous colonial and local manipulation of customary family law was often to the detriment of women.

In this chapter I examine to what extent certain forms of colonial inventions of tradition contributed to the persistence of violence and to new forms of violence against women, from domestic and intimate violence to violence structured by the colonial state. Here, I define domestic violence as a continuum of behaviors enacted by a member of a family or household against another member of the family or household that is intended to result in physical and psychological harm such as degrading remarks, bodily injury, assault, sexual assault or homicide, or a threat of such physical and psychological violence.

This chapter focuses on domestic abuses between married partners and more specifically on husbands' physical abuse of their wives that resulted in wives asking for a divorce and/or deserting their husbands. Through the specific case of female desertion of the marital home, I aim to better understand the tenuous and often blurred limits between what was considered legitimate and illegitimate violence in a specific colonial setting. By enforcing the law, the colonial state in French Soudan claimed to monopolize legitimate force. However, by its attempts to regulate the behavior of colonial subjects and to develop penal and legal institutions, it also organized violence against its subjects. The colonial state created a context in which violence could be generated. But the logic of colonial state interests is not sufficient to account for violence. Between the level of the colonial state and that of the perpetrators of domestic violence, we can find local and regional power brokers who used the colonial context of violence to reappropriate parts of the monopoly of force they had lost during colonization. The examination of the nature of colonial state and local power is therefore important to an understanding of the complex interplay between explicit colonial repression and gendered violence of daily life. The distinctions between private and colonial forms of violence became increasingly troubled during the colonial era to the detriment of women.

The study of jurisprudence in the region of Kayes demonstrates that from the 1910s onward, wives accused of desertion were increasingly forced by the courts to return to their husbands, even in case of alleged domestic abuse. From 1914 onward, colonial courts went further in restricting the possibility that a woman could leave a marriage by imposing prison sentences in case of female desertion, as both the "traditional power" and the colonial administration had agreed to declare female desertion a "customary offense." Female desertions were a form of "misbehavior" that had to be controlled by the court. Effectively, the native courts under colonial rule became complicit in the practice of domestic violence because they increasingly refused to grant divorce to women who were beaten by their husbands. Furthermore, the native courts criminalized battered women who fled their husbands.

THE PENALIZATION OF FEMALE DESERTION: THE LOSS SUFFERED BY THE DESERTED HUSBAND VERSUS THE HUSBAND'S ILL-TREATMENT OF THE WIFE

The examination of the colonial compilation of customary laws in French West Africa at the end of the nineteenth century demonstrates that female desertion of the marital home was only rarely an issue in divorce cases.[7] A woman could leave her husband but had to reimburse the bridewealth, as divorce was then recognized as her fault. There were few officially accepted causes that granted women the right to ask that the divorce be declared her husband's fault and thus avoid the obligation to reimburse the bridewealth fully or partially. The causes recognized in this version of customary law included serious domestic violence, sterility, serious illness, nonpayment of the bridewealth, and abandonment. If a woman wanted to leave her husband, she would first flee to her family in order to signal her desire to divorce and to assure the family's protection and approval for divorce. In November 1908, Diali Mady S.

declared to the court of Kita that he was married to the daughter of Danté D., but the latter took his daughter back and refused to let her return to him.[8] The father stated that Diali kept beating his daughter and that was why he took her back. The court pronounced the divorce and ordered Danté's daughter to reimburse the bridewealth.

Following the flight of the wife, the two families would begin negotiations in order to convince the woman to return to her husband. However, if the woman persisted in her refusal to continue living with her husband, and if the breach of the marriage was not recognized as the husband's fault, both families agreed that the bridewealth should be reimbursed. This marked the official end of the marriage. This was a common feature of the divorce cases brought to the courts of the region of Kayes in the first years of their existence.

Between 1907 and 1912, the number of women asking for divorce at the court of Kayes constantly increased. Figure 1 shows for the same period the percentage of divorce cases heard by the Kayes civil court in which the plaintiff is the wife. The frequency of divorce requests made by women is not surprising, since few women consented to their first marriages.[9] Marriage at the time was the result of long negotiations between two lineages. It was embedded in a complex system of preexisting lineage alliances that left little room for personal marriage choices by either men or women. It was likely to be a source of tension between future spouses, even though these kinship bonds through marriage ties over several generations were supposed to limit conflicts between spouses.

Beginning in 1911, the majority of those seeking divorce were men. The details of the cases, however, show that in most instances men brought their

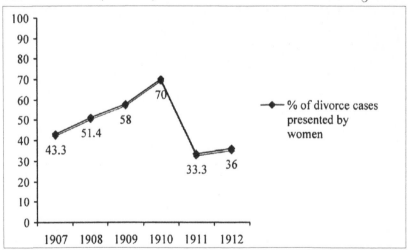

FIGURE 1 Percentage of divorce cases heard by the court of province in Kayes in which the plaintiffs are women (1907–12), N = 174. *Source:* Civil court records, Kayes, 1901–20, 2 M 123, ANM Koulouba, fonds anciens.

wives to the court because the latter, who wished to divorce, had already left the marital home. Female desertion of the marital home (cases in which wives left their husbands and asked for divorce) account for 23 percent of the civil cases heard by the court of Kayes between 1907 and 1912 (174 divorce cases for a total of 748 civil cases). Cases in which deserted husbands tried to force their wives to return to the marital home with the help of the native courts constitute more than 65 percent of the marriage cases (264 marriage cases heard by the civil court of Kayes between 1907 and 1912). In most cases, the two parties would come to the court only when they could not agree among themselves and with their kin to reconcile or to separate, or when there was disagreement over the status of the bridewealth.

By the time the case was heard in court many of the women were already in new relationships with other men. As a result, the abandoned husband's objective was often not to force the wife to return, but rather to force her or her family to reimburse the bridewealth or to obtain custody of their children. Women did not remain unmarried long once they had deserted and divorced their husbands. It was extremely difficult for women in patrilineal and virilocal societies such as those of the region of Kayes to remain unmarried, since unmarried women were without "protection."

Disputes also came to the courts when a woman's family could not or was not willing to reimburse the bridewealth. Courts took the opinions expressed by women's families into account when considering divorce cases. In November 1909, Soussaba M., married to Moussa B., declared to the court that she wanted to divorce, since she and her husband could not get along together.[10] We can assume here that the claim that they "could not get along together" was a euphemism for disputes involving domestic violence, since in other similar cases acts of domestic violence were always embedded in the details of the testimony. Since Soussaba's father stated that he did not have any reservations against his daughter staying with her husband, Soussaba's demand was rejected. When the family was not willing to reimburse the bridewealth, it was all the more inclined to force the daughter to go back to her husband by any possible means. In May 1911, the court of Kita charged Madigué C. with ill-treatment of his sister. He was sentenced to fifteen days' imprisonment because he beat her as a result of her inability to get along with her husband and wanted to desert the marital home.[11]

In the first years of their existence, the courts of the region of Kayes were inclined to grant divorce to deserting women who asked for it[12] and whose husbands agreed to it.[13] However, the courts still required women to prove serious ill-treatment or another officially recognized cause for divorce to get it pronounced as the husband's fault. In March 1911, Dialli D. came to the court of Kayes to declare that her brother-in-law, Koumadia S., whom she married following the death of her husband, kept beating her. He had recently beaten her so brutally that he injured her arm. She therefore asked for divorce and protection from the court. The court sentenced Koumadia to three months' imprisonment and the payment of a cow to Dialli as compensation for her injury. The transcript does not tell us whether the divorce was pronounced. Dialli's own statements to the court imply that a certain amount of domestic violence was socially legitimate and therefore tolerated by women themselves as long as it did not involve serious injuries. Only when violence exceeded some threshold did women desert their husbands and ask for divorce.

A battered wife's decision to leave her husband was facilitated if she met a man willing to marry her. In this case, the future husband would repay the bridewealth to the former husband, especially when her family was not willing to support her in her wish to get divorced. In April 1911, Fatoumata T. declared to the court of Kayes that she bore the ill-treatment of her husband Alassane D. as long as her daughter was young.[14] Six years earlier, she agreed to follow another man, a *tirailleur* (an African soldier in the French army), to Kayes. She now asked for her freedom and the custody of her daughter. Alassane agreed to accept the divorce. The court therefore pronounced the divorce but gave the custody of the child to the father.

The issue of child custody was an important pressure upon women not to desert, even when they were regularly subjected to violence by their husband. In the case of divorce, custody was almost always granted to the husband except when the children were too young to do without their mother's care. In some cases, women would retain custody of their daughters until they reached the age of marriage. At that moment custody would be passed on to the former husband so that he could collect the bridewealth for his daughter's future marriage.

When a wife asking for divorce declared to the court that she was brutalized by her husband, the judges determined the seriousness of the alleged mistreatment. Overall, judges were skeptical of women's claims of abuse. During the period 1905–20, judges in the region of Kayes tended to declare that there was a lack of evidence of serious ill-treatment and therefore no valid cause for divorce when the husband refused to divorce. Even when the husband agreed to a divorce, the courts usually pronounced the divorce on the grounds of the wife's abandonment of the marital home rather than the husband's mistreatment of his wife, therefore making the wife liable for the repayment of the bridewealth. In October 1908, Sounkarou D., ill-treated by her husband, came to the court of Kayes to ask for divorce.[15] The court judged that ill-treatment was not a sufficient motive for pronouncing the divorce. Sounkarou declared to the court that she did not want to reconsider her decision. Her husband finally accepted the divorce, which was pronounced as the fault of his wife, who had to reimburse the bridewealth. In July 1910, Moussa F. came to the court of Nioro to ask for the payment of the rest of the bridewealth that his brother-in-law still owed.[16] His sister had come to him because her husband beat her and because, she alleged, he had repudiated her. Her husband denied the repudiation, but affirmed she had asked to be divorced in exchange for the reimbursement of the bridewealth. The court decided that there were no grounds for pronouncing the divorce and ordered the wife to return to the marital home. In September 1911, Lamine D. complained to the court of Kayes that his wife had left him.[17] His wife asserted that she was ill-treated by her husband. As he refused to divorce her, the court ordered his wife to go back to her husband but also advised her to find witnesses and to bring them to the court in case her husband abused her again. In May 1920, Yaté T. declared to the court of Kayes that he had been married to Sediko S., the daughter of Assa Awa S. residing in Kayes, for four years.[18] The year before, he sent his pregnant wife to her parents so that she could deliver her baby there. A few days after the delivery, the child died. Since then, she had refused to return to the marital home. The husband sent kinsmen to her mother to request her return four times but Assa refused. Assa stated that during the pregnancy of her daughter, she and her husband had had an argument in the course of which he beat her with a stick. Following this quarrel, the daughter ran away to her mother where she delivered the baby who died several days later. The daughter confirmed her mother's statements and declared to the court that she did not want to return to her husband as he kept brutalizing her. But as she could not present any witnesses, she was ordered to return to the marital home.

Courts progressively increased control over women by implementing a specific jurisprudence forcing women to go back to their husbands when they deserted and making divorce gradually more difficult for them to obtain, even in cases of alleged ill-treatment. This change helps explain the shift visible in figure 1, which shows a sudden decrease in the percentage of divorce cases whose plaintiffs were women.[19]

This shift in the jurisprudence does not seem to be linked to changes in the legal staff, which remained largely the same for the first fifteen years of the existence of the court of Kayes.[20] The cause is more probably to be found in the general economical and social context of the 1910s. The progressive tightening of the jurisprudence in the 1910s occurred at a time when the region of Kayes was experiencing tremendous social and economic change, which set in motion an increasing mobility of the population, both socially and geographically. In the first twenty years of the twentieth century, the region of Kayes experienced two closely linked phenomena: a series of economic and ecological crises and the departure of former slaves. Between 1897 and 1915, the region of Kayes suffered fourteen years of bad harvests and food shortages, with the most severe crises in 1905–7 and 1913–15. The period 1913–14 was the worst.[21] The region again experienced serious food shortages in 1918–19. These crises stimulated the emigration of a substantial part of the area's population.[22] Slaves were part of this wave of emigration as their masters were not able to provide them with their daily sustenance, and the colonial administration promoted the end of slavery.[23] Some women (both slave and free) tried to take advantage of the weakening power of the head of the family in times of severe food crises in order to free themselves from their male guardians and husbands.[24] In 1923, the commandant of the Nioro noticed:

> It is incredible to see today the number of people—women in particular—who turn up in order to divorce—unfaithful or too old wives, little reliable or too old husbands. It was so striking that we meant well by encouraging natives of the cercle to delay registering their complaints during the cultivation, but to wait for after the harvest, which, looking promising, could encourage some of them to return to a better frame of mind.[25]

Not only did the end of slavery and the constant economic crises increase tensions within households, resulting in an expansion of economic violence against women,[26] but acts of domestic violence against women were soon backed by both the colonial and the local power: the idea of penalizing women for their "loose behavior" made its way into the jurisprudence of the colonial native courts. By pronouncing divorce as women's fault when they deserted, even in cases of ill-treatment, the courts of the region of Kayes had already determined that a deserted husband suffered a greater loss than a beaten wife. In the 1920s, the colonial administration and the courts began to consider women seeking divorce a threat to social stability.[27] The courts therefore increasingly penalized women who attempted to leave unwanted marriages.[28] In September 1925, Antoine S. came to the court of Kayes and declared that he had had an argument with his wife, Sountou D.[29] As she left for her mother's field, he caught up with her and beat her. Having heard what happened, Sountou's father came to take his daughter back and to ask for divorce. Sountou declared that her husband had beat her and stripped her clothes off, arguing that he had the right to do so since he had paid for the bridewealth and the clothes. The court recognized that such serious violence was a valid cause for divorce according to the Muslim Sarakolé custom. However, the court pronounced the divorce as the wife's fault and ordered her to reimburse the bridewealth. As husbands noticed that the decisions of the courts in cases of desertion of the marital home increasingly favored them, they turned more often to the courts in order to force their wives to return to the marital home, especially when the traditional negotiations between the two families failed. In October 1921, a Muslim man called Baba D. came to the court of Kayes to complain about his wife who had left the marital home six months previously. His wife, Néné S., answered the court that she refused to return because her husband did not support her adequately and kept hitting her mother.[30] However, she could not present any witnesses to confirm her assertions. Her husband, Baba D., who was a Muslim, transferred only seventy-five francs from an agreed bridewealth of two hundred francs. The court of Kayes declared: "According to the fetishist customary law as well as the Muslim law, Néné has to return to the marital home." The court's decision was important in two ways. First, it overturned previous jurisprudence that failure to complete bridewealth payments was a cause for divorce, and second, it effectively equated Muslim family law and local custom. It was becoming clear to husbands that they could no longer be threatened with divorce when resorting to violence against their wives and that the use of the courts was a very effective way to force their runaway wives to return to them.[31] With the approval of the colonial administration from 1914 onward, the courts sent women who refused to return to the marital home to prison.

FEMALE DESERTION OF THE MARITAL HOME:
VIOLENT COLONIAL INVENTION OF A CUSTOMARY OFFENSE

In November 1911, a desertion case was heard by the criminal court of Kayes. This case appears to represent a turning point in the jurisprudence: before this date, the colonial administration of justice always invalidated judgments regarding family matters pronounced by a criminal court instead of a civil court. Lamine D. declared to the court that his wife had deserted the marital home and refused to return. The court ordered Siora T. to return immediately. Although no fine was imposed, this case signaled the beginning of a period in which criminal courts began to hear an increasing number of marriage disputes.[32]

The court records from 1912 to 1945 and the prison register clearly reveal a shift in the jurisprudence of female desertion of the marital home. Before 1910, women were occasionally ordered to return to the marital home or to reimburse the bridewealth in the case of divorce. Sometimes women were ordered to prison but only as a result of the failure to reimburse bridewealth.[33] A different pattern seems to have emerged in the 1910s. After this date, a deserting woman victim of domestic violence could henceforth not be considered as having valid reasons for divorce as long as she was economically well maintained by her husband. Desertion became therefore a crime whose female perpetrators had to be punished when they refused to return to the marital home, since deserting women were thought to be a threat to social and economical stability. A striking example of this shift in the jurisprudence is the

Sodié S. case: in 1914, Sodié S., who categorically refused to return to the marital home, was sentenced by the court of Nioro to one month's imprisonment. Earlier in the year, a political report on Nioro specifically noted the significant number of women leaving their villages for employment in more prosperous regions because of food shortages.[34] This movement left the villages of the region deserted.[35] The harsh sentence in Sodié S.'s case may have represented an effort to deter women from leaving the region. Following this case, the commandant of the cercle asked the governor of the colony if the courts could apply Bambara customary law in such cases, which "considers as a customary criminal offense the fact that a woman refuses to return to the marital home."[36] The attorney general, whose opinion had also been solicited, approved the judgment since it was within the provisions of customary law. Both the "traditional power" and the colonial administration were in agreement that a deserting woman's refusal to return to the marital home was officially recognized as a "customary criminal offense." This shift of desertion to criminal law was facilitated because offenses were not defined by the decrees of 1903 and 1912, which left the substance of customary law to be determined by the courts themselves. But as the Sodié S. case reveals, the ultimate judge of local custom was the colonial power and not the native courts.

The intent of this policy was to deter women from deserting and seeking divorce from the court. It appears to have been effective, deterring even those women who were mistreated by their husbands. There are only a few cases of female desertion to be found in the legal records after 1912. The incomplete state of the legal archives for the period 1912–45 is one factor of the lack of visibility of these cases in the archives.[37] However, close examination of the prison registers of Kayes allows us to trace back some cases where women were sentenced to prison for desertion.

In December 1926, Diénéba K. from Kayes-Liberté was put in prison for six months because of desertion.[38] In July 1936, Fatouma D. from Kayes was sentenced to three months' imprisonment for refusing to return to the marital home. In July of the same year, Sira Sidibé was also sentenced to three months' imprisonment for refusing to return to the marital home.[39]

Since the colonial administration supported the new jurisprudential move, women faced greater hurdles in presenting domestic violence cases before the native courts.[40] As the case presented in the introduction of this chapter shows, victims of domestic violence were systematically suspected by the colonial administration, as in France at the same period, of exaggerating the ill-treatment or even lying about it in order to obtain a divorce.[41]

Some deserting women certainly tried to manipulate the issue of ill-treatment in order to gain divorce, but knowing that they risked prison sentences in case of desertion and that false declarations were also punished by the court, it seems unlikely that many took this risk. In October 1905, Diara D. asked the court of Kita to force his wife, Maniouma K., who had left him to go live with her relative N'Tiékouram, to return to him.[42] Maniouma K. complained of mistreatment by her husband and asked the court for a divorce. However, as the motives given by Maniouma were judged false by the court, she was ordered to return to her husband immediately. Her failure to do so led the court to impose a one-month imprisonment for desertion of the marital home. Maniouma appealed the sentence, but the appeals judge sentenced her to two months' imprisonment for false testimony. There was debate within the administration about the legality of sentencing deserting wives to prison. Although this 1905 case may have been an anomaly, by 1914 such sentences were recognized as completely regular. The colonial administration was increasingly concerned with the disappearance of the "traditional African family."

An important part of the colonial policy of population control at the time was the effort to maintain the "traditional" family organization on which the colonial power intended to base its domination. The colonial administration attempted to control and to prevent female desertion, which challenged both the colonial view of the African family and stability of the colonial order. At a time when the metropole was also threatened by war, reaffirming power over recently colonized populations such as the ones from French Soudan became increasingly important to the colonial administration. It therefore attempted in the 1920s and 1930s to fight against the "dispersal of the elements constituting the communities,"[43] which undermined the power of the traditional chiefs on which the colonial administration rested.[44]

This colonial concern with the "moral crisis" in the indigenous society became intensified with the economic crisis of the 1930s that coincided with a series of bad harvests after 1927,[45] leading to a large immigration of the populations into colonial cities such as Kayes or Bamako. The administration was especially worried by the increase in the number of the "non-desirable idle in the big centers"[46] and therefore implemented policies driving back urban dwellers to their rural homes. In Kayes, "purges" of the "floating population" were organized in 1941, forcing three hundred to four hundred persons, including women, to leave the city.[47]

Women who were determined to resist local and colonial coercive control of their mobility, and the penalties for desertion in particular, had to make sure that they could use alternative or informal structures of power to protect them against their husbands and the court. In 1922, Ousmane B., a tailor in Dakar, sent a petition to the administration in order to complain that the administrator of Kayes had not answered his letter.[48] In this first letter, he had asked the president of the court to summon Djibi N. from a village near Kayes, the husband of his sister, Hava B., in order to force him to explain the causes that led to Hava's desertion of the marital home. Hava had come to live with her brother following the ill-treatment she suffered from her husband. She complained about the lack of food and clothing and that she was often beaten. Having no response from the administration, and believing his sister's declarations since her husband had not come to demand her return, Ousmane went to the qadi, president of the Muslim court in Dakar, who declared Hava as henceforth legally divorced. Ousmane, however, asked the administration for confirmation of the divorce. The administrator of Kayes confirmed that he transmitted Ousmane's letter to the president of the court of Kayes, who then forwarded it to Djibi N., but the latter never answered. Late in the process the husband had come to Kayes to complain that his wife had left without grounds, that the divorce had never been pronounced, and that the bride-wealth had never been reimbursed.[49] Further investigation revealed that Hava had once before deserted her husband, but had been forced to return by the commandant of the cercle.

The second time she left her husband, Hava chose to go to Dakar, where she probably hoped that the distance would protect her. She may also have sought the protection of a relative who could help her navigate the mechanics of the colonial administration. Indeed, the case shows that Ousmane B. skillfully addressed his petition to the legal administration in Kayes, to the qadi of the Muslim court in Dakar, and finally to the colonial administration in Dakar. Unfortunately, the archival record does not give us the outcome of the case.

Another case illustrates the tactics women could use to avoid being penalized for desertion. In 1939, Mariam Diodo H. was accused by her husband, Mamadou S., a city councillor in Kayes, of desertion of the marital home.[50] He registered a complaint at the court of Kayes after Mariam H. took refuge with her family in Dakar. But before she left, she had also begun divorce proceedings, declaring that she was ill-treated by her husband. Since she refused to return to the marital home, a summons ordered her to come back to Kayes for a hearing. The Senegalese colonial administration decided to defend Mariam H. against the Soudanese proceedings and suspended the summons because of the lack of gravity of the offense.[51]

The administrator of Kayes rejected the opinion of his colleague in Dakar. In the correspondence, he emphasized that there were no witnesses to corroborate her claims of ill-treatment. Unlike his Senegalese counterpart, the administrator of Kayes considered it important to punish such insubordinate behavior by legal action in the criminal court, lest it encourage the dissolution of the African family and social unrest more generally.[52] This case reveals both the patriarchal alliance between the local powers and the colonial administration in French Soudan in order to control women with the threat of prison sentences, even in cases of alleged domestic violence, and the contradictory attitudes of the colonial administration during the Popular Front era. Under Vichy, however, the colonial administration hardened its attitude to women who deserted their husbands.[53]

The close link between the colonial administration and customary power in French Soudan is particularly visible when we examine the suppression of the native criminal law in French colonies in 1946.[54] Criminal law came under European law, which eliminated the crime of desertion of the marital home, which did not exist in French metropolitan law. In October 1947, the governor of French Soudan observed:

> As desertion of the marital home is no longer an offense, there is from now no means by which it can be penalized and if a woman, even without valid reason, refuses to return to her husband, sooner or later he is obliged to ask for divorce, the result being the diminishment of paternal and marital authority. For several months the number of claims for divorce — all made by wives — has significantly increased and nothing allows us today to slow this moral crisis. Many married men declare that it is citizenship, which has brought them unpleasant drawbacks. This declaration is confirmed even by the évolués.
>
> Because they fear the dissolution of their marital home, a lot of respectable people have asked members of the Parliament to attempt the impossible in order to accommodate certain laws so that the desertion of the marital home can be penalized independently from adultery.[55]

For a short period of time, the suppression of the criminal offense of desertion of the marital home and the introduction of citizenship for both sexes became an opportunity for women to reaffirm their civil rights in terms of divorce. However, responding to male complaints and administrative concerns about the weakening of family stability, on 19 November 1947 the French colonial administration promulgated a decree that reinstated criminal sanctions against wives deserting their marital homes but only if they were married under customary law: if the wife deserted the marital home without serious cause or without the grounds for divorce recognized by customary laws, she could be sentenced to prison for a period ranging from three months to two years.[56] Only the husband could henceforth end the sentence by agreeing to take his wife back. Thus, even in cases of serious physical abuse, which had been recognized as a valid cause for desertion under customary laws, it was very unlikely that a woman would win a divorce on these grounds unless she could find support from an alternative power structure, as happened in the two cases of desertion to Dakar. The use of prison against women who left their husbands, or at least the legal threat of prison, was recognized by the court and the colonial administration as legitimate legal violence to be used in order to counter the social threat of a possible "dissolution of the African family." In 1949, the administrator of the cercle of Kayes wrote in answer to a circular from the central administration in Bamako concerning women's work in prison that:

> It is indisputable that since criminal law came exclusively under the European jurisdiction, the number of incarcerated women has kept increasing. While the custom for cases of adultery and desertion from the marital home—crimes which concern more particularly women— often manages to settle them by resorting to familial pressures, the European justice, in this regard, penalizes them through the temporary privation of liberty.[57]

This official response shows the complex interplay between colonial state violence and domestic violence in the colonial history of French Soudan, both sustaining each other and resulting in a general atmosphere of violence.

ᘒ

Since control over the population in times of social and economic change was as central to the colonial administration as it was to local African authorities, it is not surprising that these two powers ultimately agreed to force women to return to the marital home, even in cases of proven ill-treatment, by threat of sending them to prison. Colonial organization of native justice imposed "a grid of Western legal institutions on African grievances"[58] and contributed to the "invasion of the colonial criminal law" into the jurisprudence of the native courts in French Soudan. The colonial authoritarian control over the subjects, especially through the systematic use of the code de l'indigénat, contributed to an increased use of prison by the agents of the administration.[59] This punitive strategy was quickly reappropriated by native courts as a common way to control the "misbehavior" of women, thereby confirming the power of husbands to use violence against their wives.

NOTES

1. Due to privacy concerns raised by the regulation issued by the Republic of Mali in 2002 restricting the use of any records held by the National Archives of Mali that may "implicate the private lives of citizens," I use only the first name and the initial of the last name to identify disputants in court cases. For

more information on court cases and privacy, see Richard Roberts, *Litigants and Households: African Disputes and Colonial Courts in the Fench Soudan, 1895–1912* (Portsmouth, NH: Heinemann, 2005), xi–xii.

2. In the French colonial archives, the Region of Kayes refers to the cercles (districts) of Bafoulabé, Kayes, Kita, Nioro, and Satadougou.

3. *Journal officiel de la République Française*, 24 November 1903, no. 319: 7094–97. The 1903 colonial legal system created three levels of native courts in each colony: the *tribunal de village*, the *tribunal de province*, and the *tribunal de cercle*. The *tribunal de village* was presided over by the village chief and had a reconciliation role, whereas the *tribunal de province*, which was also presided over by a local notable, had to deal with civil disputes and offenses that could not be settled by the village tribunal. Judgments rendered by the *tribunaux de province* could be appealed at the *tribunal de cercle*, whose president was the commandant of the cercle. The village courts were not always able to resolve conflicts, and the plaintiffs often preferred the colonial administration as referee; parties were therefore eager to address their personal disputes directly to the *tribunal de province* or the colonial administration. The Decree of 1912 did not change the nature of this three-level court system; only the names of the courts changed. The Decree of 1924 suppressed the village court.

4. See section 7 of the decree, *Journal officiel d'Afrique Occidentale Française* 5, no. 408 (October 1912): 623–30.

5. Instructions to the administrators of the Sénégambie-Niger regarding the application of the Decree of 10 November 1903, 2 M 459, Archives Nationales du Mali. Mali now has two archival depots: the one on Koulouba (hereafter referred to as ANM-K) contains the *fonds anciens* (hereafter referred to as FA) and part of the *fonds récents* (hereafter referred to as FR); the new depot at the Bibliothèque Nationale (hereafter referred to as ANM-B) contains the rest of the *fonds récents*. The reference to this document is thus 2 M 459, ANM-K, FA. This tendency to standardize is clearly to be seen in the way the court registers were written in the first twenty years of the colonial court system in French Soudan: Up to 1912, the law under which the litigants were judged was not specified in the court registers. Then, the Decree of 1912 only asked the courts to make the distinction between Muslim and non-Muslim/Fetishist status. Customary and Islamic law could not, however, always be disentangled easily: Islamic law had influenced customary law in some parts of the region of Kayes, especially in the North, for several centuries. Moreover, the recognition of different "personal statuses" within the same legal system regularly led to legal and political contention: the different litigants tried to play simultaneously on the different legal traditions to win their case, whereas the colonial power attempted to act on the jurisprudence and to affect the native judgments in order to pursue their own policy agenda toward the Muslim and non-Muslim powers. This designation was finally abandoned in the Decree of 1924, which asked the courts to specify precisely the law used for each case.

6. Eric J. Hobsbawm and Terence Ranger, "Introduction: Inventing Traditions," in *The Invention of Tradition*, ed. Eric J. Hobsbawm and Terence Ranger

(Cambridge: Cambridge University Press, 1993), 1–14. See also in the same volume Terence Ranger, "The Invention of Tradition in Colonial Africa," 211–62. Another insightful study on similar processes but in Malawi and Zambia is Martin Chanock, *Law, Custom, and Social Order: The Colonial Experience in Malawi and Zambia* (Portsmouth, NH: Heinemann, 1998).

7. Coutumier juridique, Soudan français, Barrat, 1897, 1 G 229, Archives Nationales du Sénégal (hereafter ANS), Fonds du Gouvernement général d'Afrique occidentale française (GGAOF), fonds anciens (FA).

8. État des jugements civils et commerciaux, tribunal de province de Kita, 4th quarter 1908, 2 M 124, ANM-K, FA.

9. See, for example, the classic West African woman's life history, Mary Smith, *Baba of Karo, a Woman of the Muslim Hausa* (New Haven, CT: Yale University Press, 1981).

10. État des jugements civils et commerciaux, tribunal de province de Kayes, 3d quarter 1909, 2 M 123, ANM-K, FA.

11. État des jugements correctionnels, tribunal de province de Kita, 2d quarter 1911, 2 M 124, ANM-K, FA.

12. Marie Rodet, "Disrupting Masculinist Discourse on African Migration: The Study of Neglected Forms of Female Migration," in *Crossing Places: New Research in African Studies*, ed. Charlotte Baker and Zoë Norridge (Newcastle, UK: Cambridge Scholars Publishing, 2007), 28–50.

13. Divorce would ordinarily be granted only if the husband agreed to it. If he did not, the woman was simply sent back to her husband for a lack of valid grounds for divorce.

14. État des jugements civils et commerciaux, tribunal de province de Kayes, 2d quarter 1911, 2 M 123, ANM-K, FA.

15. État des jugements civils et commerciaux, tribunal de province de Kayes, 4th quarter 1908, 2 M 123, ANM-K, FA.

16. État des jugements civils et commerciaux, tribunal de province de Nioro, 3d quarter 1910, 2 M 135, ANM-K, FA.

17. État des jugements civils et commerciaux, tribunal de province de Kayes, 2d quarter 1911, 2 M 123, ANM-K, FA.

18. État des jugements civils et commerciaux, tribunal de subdivision de Kayes, 2d quarter 1920, 2 M 123, ANM-K, FA.

19. From the late 1900s, women also began to be prosecuted when they left their husbands before the divorce was pronounced and the bridewealth reimbursed. In May 1909, the court of Kayes pronounced the divorce between Kantara D. and his wife Moussoufiman, but it also sentenced her to a fine of twenty francs because she left her husband before getting divorced. In December 1912, Guimba K. came to the court of Kayes to ask for the reimbursement of the bridewealth he paid since his wife Maryam D. wished to divorce. The court pronounced the divorce but ordered Maryam to stay with her husband until the complete reimbursement of the bridewealth. Maryam appealed against this judgment, but the second judgment confirmed the decision of December 1912, although Maryam declared that she did

not want to stay one minute longer with her husband, who, she claimed, insulted her parents. État des jugements civils et commerciaux, tribunal de province de Kayes, 2d quarter 1909 and 4th quarter 1912, 2 M 123, ANM-K, FA.

20. See 2 M 236, ANM-K, FA.

21. See the political reports for this period: 1 E 17, 1 E 44, 1 E 45, 1 E 48, 1 E 61, 1 E 69, ANM-K, FA.

22. Rapports politiques trimestriels. 1st, 2d, and 3d quarters 1922, Soudan fran-çais, 2 G 22/11, Centre Archives d'Outre-Mer (hereafter CAOM) GGAOF micro-film (hereafter mf), fonds moderns (hereafter FM).

23. Rapport politique annuel, 1912, H-S-N, 2 G 12/13, CAOM, GGAOF mf FA.

24. Marie Rodet, "Migrants in French Sudan: Gender Biases in the Historiog-raphy," in *Trans-Atlantic Migration: The Paradoxes of Exile*, ed. Toyin Falola and Niyi Afolabi (New York: Routledge, 2007), 165–82.

25. Rapport politique trimestriel, 3d quarter 1923, Cercle de Nioro, 1 E 36, ANM-K, fonds récent (hereafter FR).

26. Emily Burrill and Richard Roberts, "Domestic Violence, Colonial Courts, and the End of Slavery in French Soudan, 1905–12," this volume.

27. The court's decisions in divorce cases during the 1920s also demonstrated the gradual legal formalization of the concept of female desertion. In the records of the court of Kayes, the term "female desertion" as such does not appear before the end of 1910. Until this date, only the description of the case can help to identify a desertion of the marital home: "Maka asks for his wife who fled to her father's and wants her back or the bridewealth to be reimbursed." From 1910, the term "de-sertion of the marital home" specifically appears in statements like: "demand for divorce because of desertion." The statements in the records become even more precise from 1918–19 with formulations such as: "The customary law prescribes the return of X to the marital home." See in particular: 2 M 135 and 2 M 103, ANM-K, FA; 1 M 2283, 1 M 895, 1 M 908, and 1 M 88, ANM-B.

28. In Nioro, the restriction over women's mobility out of marriage went a step further in the 1920s by systematic fining of women who asked for divorce. In Decem-ber 1920, Bokary Kaba D. came to the court of Nioro following divorce from his wife Fatoumata D. pronounced by the same court in August 1920. He appealed against the first judgment because the court had not imposed a fine, despite the local inter-pretation of Islamic law that imposed such a fine when a woman asked for divorce without sufficient grounds. Because Fatoumata D. refused to stay with her husband under any conditions, the court decided that she had to pay an indemnity to him of one hundred francs (État des jugements civils et commerciaux [appel], tribunal de cercle de Nioro, December 1920, 2 M 135, ANM-K, FA). The Qur'an does not prescribe this fine. According to the 1899 compilation of customary laws by Barrat, this provision was only applied by the Djennenke. It seemed here that this local custom was later reappropriated by the Muslim populations of the region of Nioro and implemented by the local jurisprudence as a Muslim tradition.

29. État des jugements rendus, tribunal du 1er degré de Kayes en matière civile, September 1925, 1 M 895, ANM-B.

30. États des jugements civils et commerciaux, tribunal de subdivision de Kayes, October 1921, 1 M 88, ANM-B.

31. *Mamadou S. v. Awa D.*, tribunal de subdivision de Kayes, 21 December 1920, 2 M 123, ANM-K, FR.

32. Marital disputes had already been present in criminal courts in the form of adultery cases. For the period 1907–12, the majority of the desertion cases heard in criminal courts were presented as adultery cases. Female adultery had been considered a crime by the native courts from the time of their inception in 1903. As in France at the time, adultery was punishable by imprisonment. Desertion often led to finding a new lover, and thus desertion often involved adultery. Well into the 1940s, prison registers and the statistical reports on the functioning of the indigenous courts of the region of Kayes clearly differentiated between adultery and desertion by specifying whether a sentence was pronounced because of adultery, refusal to return to the marital home, or both.

33. Rebecca A. Shereikis, "Customized Courts: French Colonial Legal Institutions in Kayes, French Soudan, c. 1880–c. 1913" (PhD diss., Northwestern University, 2003), 213.

34. Rapport politique mensuel, February 1914, Cercle de Nioro, 1 E 61, ANM-K, FA. One of my oral informants confirmed that in times of severe food shortages in French Soudan, numerous women used to come on their own to the Bundu in order to get employed in less affected villages. Interview in Kidira with Siramdou Diakité, 3 November 2004.

35. Rapport politique mensuel, May 1914, Nioro, 1 E 61, ANM-K, FA.

36. Letter no. 77 G on the functioning of the indigenous justice in the colony of Haut-Sénégal-Niger (2d and 3d quarters 1914), 30 March 1915, public prosecutor to governor general of French West Africa (hereafter FWA), 2 M 1, ANM-K, FA.

37. During my research in 2008–9, I discovered unclassified legal records in cercle archives. These may provide more information for future research. A first examination of these documents tends to demonstrate that deserting women in Kayes started being increasingly sent to prison from 1924. The argument to be found in the court cases is that, according to the customary law, a deserting woman deserved to be beaten a predetermined number of times by a rope, but as this sanction was considered by the criminal court—which was henceforth presided over by the commandant of the cercle since the Decree of 1924—to be contrary to the French principles of humanity, it had to be transformed into prison sentences. The use of prison instead of rope beating was here introduced and justified by the colonial administration as both civilizing and corrective. It seemed also to have been legitimized by the colonial administration as the only discipline language women seemed to understand. Desertion was a form of female resistance, which had to be harshly punished. However, it did not always prevent women from deserting again, once released. If the husband refused to divorce, he could bring his case again to the criminal court, and his wife would be sentenced to prison once more.

38. Extrait du registre d'écrou, Kayes, July 1927, 1 M 2000, ANM-B.

39. Extrait du registre d'écrou, Kayes, October 1936, 1 M 2280, ANM-B.

40. Marie Rodet, "Genre, coutumes et droit colonial au Soudan français (1918–1939)," in "Les femmes, le droit et la justice," special issue, *Cahiers d'Études Africaines* 187–88, no. 3–4 (2007): 583–602.

41. The Savineau report, 33, 17 G 381, CAOM, GGAOF mf FM.

42. État des jugements civils et commerciaux, tribunal de province de Kita, 4th quarter 1905, 2 M 124, ANM-K, FA.

43. Rapport politique annuel, 1934, Soudan français, 2 G 34/6, CAOM, GGAOF mf FM.

44. Rapport politique annuel, 1930, Soudan français, Affpol 160, CAOM.

45. Rapports politiques trimestriels, 2d quarter 1927 and 2d quarter 1930, 1 E 36, ANM, FA: Agriculture Bafoulabé, 1933, Disette à méditer par les commandants de Bafoulabé, 1 R 2162, ANM-B.

46. Rapport annuel sur le fonctionnement de la justice indigène, Afrique occidentale française 1931, 59 B 32, CAOM, Commission Guernut (hereafter CG).

47. Letter, 26 September 1941, administrateur-adjoint Sutils to administrateur commandant cercle de Kayes, 1 E 57, ANM-K, FR.

48. Petition, 20 February 1922, Ousmane Bokoum to délégué of the government of Senegal in Dakar, 2 M 211, ANM-K, FR.

49. Letter, March 1922, délégué of the governor in Kayes to governor of French Soudan in Koulouba, 2 M 211, ANM-K, FA.

50. The H. case, 1939, 15 G 16, CAOM, GGAOF mf FM. For a more detailed account and analysis of this case, see Rodet, "Genre, coutumes et droit colonial au Soudan français."

51. Letter no. 117 AP/S, 12 July 1939, governor general of FWA to governor of French Soudan, 15 G 16, CAOM, GGAOF mf FM.

52. Letter no. 1839 APA3, 8 August 1939, governor of French Soudan to governor general of FWA, 15 G 16, CAOM, GGAOF mf FM.

53. For example, in April 1941, Fanta Dramé from Kayes was put in jail for one month for desertion of the marital home. In May 1941 the court of Bafoulabé condemned to six months' imprisonment Moussoumakan D. for adultery and desertion of the marital home. Extrait du registre d'écrou, Kayes, and Bafoulabé, April 1941, 1 M 693, ANM-B.

54. Decree of 30 April 1946 on the suppression of the indigenous penal justice in the territories coming under the ministry for overseas territories. René Pautrat, *La justice locale et la justice musulmane en A.O.F.* (Rufisque: Imprimerie du Haut Commissariat de la République en Afrique occidentale française, 1957), 115.

55. Rapport politique, 3d quarter 1947, Soudan français, 2 G 47/142, CAOM, GGAOF mf FM.

56. Pautrat, *La justice locale*, 169. See especially the revised article 337 of the criminal code, which had been introduced under Vichy in the early 1940s.

57. Letter no. 1084 on women's work in prison, 26 July 1949, administrator of the cercle of Kayes to the governor of French Soudan, nonclassified, Archives du Ministère de l'Administration territoriale et des collectivités locales.

58. Roberts, *Litigants and Households*, 81.

59. Ibrahima Thioub, "Sénégal: La prison à l'époque coloniale: Significations, évitement et évasions," in *Enfermement, prison et châtiments*, ed. Florence Bernault (Paris: Karthala, 1999), 288.

4 ⤚ Violated Domesticity in Italian East Africa, 1937–40

MARTINA SALVANTE

ON 5 OCTOBER 1938 the young Ethiopian Destà Agos asked for police intervention in her home against the Italian Giovanni Spano, who, she claimed, had hit her. According to police testimonies during the proceeding, the woman had already denounced the man in the previous days for mistreatment. Successive police interrogations yielded evidence that the two had been having a relationship for the previous four months in spite of the fact that racially mixed unions had been prohibited by the Italian Fascist government in 1937. On this ground Giovanni Spano was brought to court. On 19 November 1938 the criminal court accused Spano of the crime of *madamato*, a quasi-conjugal relationship between an Italian citizen and a native woman, banned by law. Magistrates found that

> The psychological element [of a relation characterized by *affectio maritalis*] is recurrent in this case, evidence of which is not only the cohabiting customs of the couple but also the violent possessive behavior of the man, who did not want his *"madama"* to talk to other men, especially white men. He prohibited her from leaning out of the window overlooking the road; he gave her a dress as a present; he expected her to go to the hospital to visit him; he escaped more than once from the hospital without permission to reach her; and he beat her, because she had been forced to "sell herself" in order to get the means of subsistence.[1]

Taking into account the "material element"—that Agos and Spano lived together—and the above-mentioned psychological, or spiritual, element,

94

the court explained that "there could hardly be imagined a more complete form of '*more uxorio*' cohabitation."[2] This statement indicates that, paradoxically, Spano's abuse of Agos provided evidence of his possessiveness, which was taken as proof of his affection toward the woman. The court was not interested in the alleged physical abuses but only that these acts incriminated the defendant, showing that he had committed an offense against "the prestige of the race of superior civilization" by carrying out a relationship with a native woman. At the core of Italian Fascist policing of its racial policy in East Africa was the belief that domestic violence paradoxically proved the existence of prohibited conjugal-like relationships. According to current views, as outlined in particular by the 2005 WHO study on domestic violence, behavior such as Spano's would be classified as "controlling behaviour" and therefore a form of domestic violence.[3]

My chapter therefore focuses on the role of colonial courts in defining the place of domestic violence in racially mixed unions. The courts' action took place under the rule of the Fascist dictatorship, which was seeking to formalize its racial policies in its new African empire and to outlaw racial diversity in the metropole.

DEFINITIONS AND INTERPRETATIONS

In another document by the World Health Organization, published in 2002, violence is classified as "an extremely diffused and complex phenomenon. Defining it is not an exact science but a matter of judgment. Notions of what is acceptable and unacceptable in terms of behaviour, and what constitutes harm, are culturally influenced, and constantly under review as values and social norms evolve."[4] To measure domestic violence at specific times in history is even more complex. At the end of the 1930s, domestic violence was a concept not yet fully developed in either social or legal worlds in Italy. Italian legislation at the time proscribed certain violent acts but evinced greater tolerance toward the behavior of the person invested with *auctoritas* in his dealings with "subordinates" (women, minors, and servants) living in the same household. Patently abusive behavior was sometimes punished, but it was more often condoned in the case of the paterfamilias, according to a traditionally patriarchal set of rules.[5] The situation was even more complicated in the colonial context, where the conventionally unequal relationship between men and women was compounded by differences in race and class. Studies of domestic violence should, therefore, take into account variations in family structures over time and the complexity of family configurations in different cultural and geographical contexts. In particular, families in colonial territories were often the result of interracial relationships and, thus, of intercultural interactions.

Reconstructing the history of domestic violence in Italian colonies is hindered by the lack of appropriate sources. Single episodes of domestic violence can be studied through the cases brought to colonial court; however, these represent only a tiny fraction of daily occurrences. The number of documented proceedings "does not quantify all the committed crimes, but only the cases brought to court; and consequently, it only serves to measure the functioning of the justice system and not the actual magnitude of the crime."[6] To add to the difficulties encountered by the historian in reconstructing daily life in the Italian colonies, much of the documentation produced by the Italian colonial administration has been lost.[7]

For this chapter, I have used a set of published verdicts, drawn from criminal courts in the Italian colonies in East Africa concerning the prosecution of Italian men accused of engaging in relationships with indigenous women, which, as mentioned, were banned by law in 1937. What makes these verdicts even more relevant is the peculiar interpretation of violence used by the courts. The element of domestic violence arose in most cases from witnesses' declarations and police denunciations, but it was never explicitly judged per se, for it was usually seen "only" as an element of the "bigger" crime of unlawful cohabitation. In fact, the verdicts I examined were not for the crime of violence that occurred in domestic spaces but for transgression of the ban on conjugal-type relationships between citizens and subjects. Violence appeared in some cases but was mainly interpreted as unequivocal evidence of Italian men's transgressive behavior. I analyze this interpretative knot by drawing on some general considerations of violence in a colonial context, where violence—in different forms (sexual, legal, ethnic, etc.)—played a central role in reproducing racial hierarchies and in shaping relationships.

The title of this chapter highlights the various forms of aggression perpetrated against domesticity, not just by Italian men upon indigenous women but also by the state, which through the police and the judiciary intruded upon the relationships of madamato. Hence, domesticity was a "space" violated on more than one front.

The events discussed are to be read within the framework of codified relations between men and women as well as within the racial hierarchies of the time. However, an important note of caution must be added. Although frequently present, violence was not an intrinsic element of all madamato relationships. In several cases affection, interest, and love were the driving forces of the relationships. However, my attention is focused on tracing cases of violence that occurred in domestic spaces and on recovering the categories by which they were understood and judged by the colonial legal system.

LEGISLATION REGULATING RACIALLY MIXED UNIONS

Historians of Italian colonialism in East Africa have identified continuities between the liberal and Fascist periods, but they acknowledge that native policy started to change in the 1920s. In parallel with the transformation of the dictatorship toward a totalitarian model in the metropole, the Fascist approach to colonial policy changed after the second half of the 1920s.[8] But it was later in the 1930s, when Fascist imperialism reached its apex—marked by the Ethiopian war (1935–36) and the proclamation of the Italian empire in East Africa in 1936—that a structured racist policy took shape.

Until the 1930s, the composition of the Italian population residing in the colonies was made up mainly of male members of the army and of the public administration. In Irma Taddia's words, the empire was "un mondo al maschile" (a male world).[9] There were few Italian women in the colonies until the Fascist regime decided to encourage the immigration of entire family groups and women, especially in the thirties.[10] The encouragement of family and female emigration to the colonies was designed to reduce the demographic disparity between the local population and settlers and to promote the myth of the "place in the sun" as a site of hopeful fulfillment for thousands of Italians in search of job opportunities. As Charles Burdett has put it, female settlers "openly reinforced the notion of colonialism as an essentially male activity in which women performed a secondary role—solving practical realities, providing moral support, creating the domestic space."[11]

As a consequence of the prevailing male presence among the settlers, the number of interracial relationships increased. From the outset of Italian colonialism in the Horn of Africa these relations between Italian men and indigenous women had been acknowledged under the label of *madamato* (or *madamismo*). In addition to madamato, there existed a form of more or less official prostitution by local women known as *sciarmutte*.[12] In actual fact, madamato was born from an "erroneous" interpretation by colonizers of a form of "contractual marriage" (*demoz*), widespread among Tigrinya and Amhara people.[13] This sort of local bridewealth, which involved the transfer of goods in exchange for the bride's labor and procreative power over a number of years, was often seen by colonial settlers as an evidence of the lack of morality and uninhibited sexual habits of locals. Italian colonizers "translated" the marriage system of *demoz* into the new interracial institution of madamato, which was actually more similar to a *more uxorio* cohabitation than a marriage and did not offer any legal recognition or right to the concubines. In addition, this relationship was complicated by the unbalanced distribution of powers within it, due to the different civil status (citizen/subject), to the often existing hierarchical relation of employer/servant, and, obviously, to the racial component. The male erotic imagination pictured African black women as sexually uninhibited and precocious (and therefore desirable), to the extent that in some cases the sexual abuse of minors was justified, as we will see later.

The authorities were especially suspicious of madamato because of its higher potential for the creation of mixed-race children.[14] Until the 1930s, however, the Italian colonial administration's ambiguous attitude toward mixed unions—alternately tolerated and morally condemned—allowed such unions to proliferate, resulting in high numbers of mixed-blood offspring, who were more often than not denied recognition by their Italian fathers.

In 1937 madamato unions were explicitly banned. The royal decree by law no. 880 of 19 April 1937 established that "an Italian citizen who . . . has a relation of conjugal type with a subject of Italian East Africa . . . is to be punished with imprisonment between one and five years."[15] This piece of legislation highlights how the Italian government bizarrely condemned relationships based on stability and affection, while at the same time preserving the rights of Italian men who sought mercenary relations with local women. The justification lay in the perceived threat that stable relationships posed to the "prestige" of the Italian race, as well as in the increased probability of the birth of mixed-race children.[16]

In 1938 the promulgation of the "Measures for the Defense of the Italian Race"[17] introduced new racial laws for the whole national territory, not only in the colonies. It ratified among other laws the prohibition of mixed marriages.[18] The 1939 law concerning "Penalties for the Defense of the Prestige of the Race in regard to Italian African Natives" clarified further the strict racial separation and the consequent punishment for every transgression.[19] The first article condemned as punishable "any act thought to diminish the moral character of Italians." Other articles listed the actual behaviors, which were considered damaging to the prestige of the "Aryan race." Article 10 defined conjugal-type relationships between settlers and natives as a crime, to be punished by imprisonment from one to five years.

Further on, article 11 of the 1939 *Sanzioni penali per la difesa del prestigio di razza* (Penalties for the Defense of the Prestige of the Race) prescribed that, in the case of the birth of a mixed-race child (a clear transgression to the 1937 law) an investigation was to be opened to trace the transgressor. Such an investigation was a clearly repressive and intimidating procedure, considering that the Italian civil code prohibited paternity searches.[20] As Gianluca Gabrielli has observed, "[T]he anonymity of the male, guaranteed by the codes, was overruled in that case for racial reasons. We can say that the gender hierarchy was here set aside to secure the racial hierarchy."[21] With this new law the traditional patriarchal line of transmission (of name, culture, and heredity) was denied and opposed for purely racial reasons. There was a conflict between the racial concerns of the state authorities and the tradition of the paterfamilias.

COURT CASES AND OTHER SOURCES

My chapter focuses on the court cases involving Italian citizens accused of having engaged in loving (as opposed to purely sexual) relationships with local women, in violation of new legislation, with the result of "damaging the colonizers' prestige." The documentary sources used here have been drawn from law journals that reported and commented on sentences considered particularly representative of the modes of application of legislated racial policies. Thanks to these published sources we can shift our investigation from legislation, which from 1937 onward gave rise to a de facto system of racial discrimination, to jurisprudence, that is, the concrete application of law. Although the analysis of the juridical discourse offers a fundamental insight into how colonial powers defined "legal domesticity and colonial morals," it does not permit us to fully determine "how people really lived in the colonies and what were the real experiences and emotions of the individuals involved."[22]

In its first year (1940), the journal *Razza e civiltà* published forty-one verdicts (some in their entirety, most, however, in the form of excerpts), reached by the courts of Italian East Africa. These forty-one verdicts included twelve trials in the courts of the first degree from Addis Ababa, Gondar, Harar, and Asmara and twenty-nine from the court of second degree—the Court of Appeal of Addis Ababa. They all related to the crime of madamato, which highlights the propagandistic centrality of this issue. *Razza e civiltà* was the official publication of the Executive Council for Demography and Race (best known as *Demorazza*), within the Ministry for Internal Affairs. Other periodicals that published and commented on the verdicts in relation to the crime of madamato include the *Rivista giuridica del medio ed estremo oriente e giustizia coloniale*, *Il diritto razzista*, and the *Rivista di diritto coloniale*.[23] These journals did not publish as many sentences (three to five a year on average), but they provided more in-depth commentaries. Since not all trials involving madamato were reported by these journals, it is difficult to establish the number of such cases. Other sources, including the actual court records, have not survived.

From the analysis of the published court verdicts it is possible to reconstruct, although partially, the type of relationships Italian men engaged in with local women, or at least how these relationships were viewed. The court verdicts that we have are only representative, and not exhaustive, of the real number of mixed unions. As reported by Italians who lived in the colonies, most found ways of eschewing police controls and ignored the legal ban.

> In Mogadishu there was no racism among us Italians. Only declared Fascists were rather arrogant and absolutely did not want to see any Italian man in the company of a black woman. . . . In reality, in everyday life, things happened differently. The majority of Italians, there in Mogadishu, did not have a wife, and had a so-called madama, a local woman, as servant but also as cohabitant. I had one for all the time I stayed there without having any troubles, because I passed her

for my servant, and nobody was able to check. I even had a son from a Somali woman.[24]

In the summaries of the events prefacing the sentences in the journals' reports, we find references to the daily lives of couples and, in some cases, to their behavior and their actual voices in court. We can also find information on the police and carabinieri's control forms for each case, and in the courts' judgments and opinions.

The comparison of verdicts shows diversity in the interpretation of the new racial norms, especially in relation to what constituted evidence proving that relationships were of an affective nature. The colonial judiciary, charged with defining the nature of the relationship, focused at first on *affectio maritalis*, a term taken from ancient Roman law.[25] Later, this was no longer considered a necessary element in the definition of a relationship of conjugal type, as madamato was more similar to concubinage than real marriage.[26]

Indeed, the search for evidence to prove the conjugal nature of a relationship was not at all clear-cut. Therefore, the publication of the verdicts on madamato in the law journals was useful for the jurisprudential debate around what actually constituted a conjugal union for the purposes of the regulation of racial matters. It is important to remember that these court cases were more important for their propagandistic and "educative" relevance than for their jurisprudential standing. The Fascist regime intended to "train" Italians through the use of penal threats to consider themselves racially superior and to avoid any sort of "dangerous" unions with the natives. This is why sanctions explicitly punished Italian citizens. Further debates ensued as to the degree to which indigenous women would be punished.[27]

DOMESTIC VIOLENCE AND STATE VIOLENCE

The verdicts we have refer to different types of violence perpetrated within the domestic sphere. We find, on the one hand, the violence to which white men subjected local women, often reported to the authorities by the women themselves. On the other hand, we find the violence carried out by colonial police in their search to uncover illicit relationships. Police were given carte blanche to forcefully enter private homes in order to ascertain whether citizens had more than occasional sexual intercourse with local women. Any evidence that the man shared his house with a local woman was thoroughly investigated in these police raids.[28]

The Italian Police Department in Africa (PAI from the Italian name), initially known as the Colonial Police Corps, was formed in June 1937 and shortly thereafter (from 14 December 1937) replaced the "normal" state police and the royal carabinieri in the colonies. Its staff reported to the Ministry of Italian

Africa and was trained at the School of Tivoli near Rome. The territory of AOI (Africa Orientale Italiana, Italian East Africa) was divided into six jurisdictions (including the municipality of Addis Ababa), each with its own police headquarters. The first PAI contingent left from Naples for Addis Ababa in December 1937.[29] In order to carry out its mission of control and supervision of the population, both indigenous and Italian, the PAI immediately created a network of informants and initiated mail censorship. The PAI's power was especially strong in urban areas, where the Italian presence and police control networks were greater. Means of repression included PAI's frequent raids on the homes of Italian men who had been reported to be in the company of local women. These police controls were intended to establish the nature of the relationship, whether a temporary sexual liaison—a work relationship legally remunerated—or an "affectionate" relationship. Gifts, jealousy, and cohabitation were all considered evidence of a sentimental relationship. The following case of an indigenous prostitute, working in a bar, discovered in the house and bed of her employer, an Italian citizen, is an example of the police practice of observing and shadowing couples considered possible transgressors of the 1937 law.

> External signs of affection and intimacy made one suspicious that a madamismo relationship was blossoming between the two, for a police marshal once saw the local woman caressing the national's face, which persuaded him to break into the house of the Italian, where he found the two lying together.[30]

Affection as represented, for example, by a caress, made the transgression more probable and justified the police raid to verify the supposed existence of a madamato relation. The fact that the police carried out strict control of the citizens' private lives, at least in urban areas, is proved by another verdict, which stated:

> The colonial police (which has established a special squad investigating madamismo), having been informed of the fact that Mr. Sodano had been having conjugal relations for many months with an indigenous woman, broke into his house during the night and discovered the Italian lying with the colored woman. . . . It is a reality that the madamismo squad found them lying together in the same bed.[31]

This passage suggests that a police squad had been formed specifically charged with investigations on madamato. The Statute of the Italian Africa Police, promulgated by Royal decree no. 1480 of 14 September 1939, assigned to it the control over prostitution and over licenses for prostitution, but never mentioned madamato.[32] Informants were feared, and some police reports reveal the practice adopted by some madamas to enter the house of their lovers through the window in order to avoid neighbors' unwanted attention. One such report says, "When interrogated, the woman . . . said that for four months she has been spending every night in her lover's house, that she received gifts, and that she regularly enters through the window, clearly to avoid the attention of the neighbours."[33]

State violence took the form of aggressive intrusion of colonial police into people's private lives with the objective of ensuring that the colonizer/colonized hierarchy was not being compromised. A white employer's relationship with the woman employed as a servant, waitress, or washerwoman fell within a "normal" relational scheme between the Italian and the indigenous populations. While it was permissible for an Italian employer to "vent" his physical needs on his servant, no feeling or affection was allowed between the two.

> To find grounds for the crime of madamato, it is not sufficient to have evidence of sexual intercourse; cohabitation—an unofficial but de facto marriage tinted by *honor matrimonii*—has to be proved. This excludes the case in which a woman is considered and treated as a servant by her employer, who occasionally engages in sex with her.[34]

Gabrielli has pointed out that "the law functioned as a means of repression and in particular as a means of intimidation to outlaw all behaviors not conforming to the master/subject scheme."[35] What is striking is how quickly the first trials took place following the implementation of the 1937 decree: the first trial was held in September of the same year, and many other trials followed.[36]

DOMESTIC VIOLENCE AND COLONIALISM

Court transcripts demonstrate that the violence perpetrated by some Italian men against local women was not condemned as an abuse of the human rights of the woman but was interpreted instead as evidence of the existence of a loving relationship between them.[37] That an Italian man expected exclusivity from his lover and acted to deny her the freedom to meet and engage in sexual relationships with other men was considered by the courts as a sign of a conjugal relationship. Similarly, caresses and violent behavior were both considered evidence of an exclusive relationship. In the judges' opinions, violent outbursts of possessiveness, beatings, and mistreatment were often seen as sufficient proof of an existing emotional tie between the accused and the woman. Such behavior would not have been plausible in a "normal" master-servant or client-prostitute relationship. The tribunal court of Gondar in 1938 ruled on a case brought against a man accused of the crime of madamato in the following manner:

> In order to prove a conjugal relationship, it is sufficient to have evidence of cohabitation, over a reasonably long period of time and with the presence of regular sexual activity. This is because cohabitation brings with it a spiritual and psychological element, embodied by a special tie or spiritual bond, which resembles, in a certain way, the *affectio maritalis* mentioned in the national legislation. A certain proof of the existence of this psychological dimension is when the man displays a violent possessive behavior.[38]

And another case in 1938 stated

> Between the man and the woman there was even (an element which does not occur in all cases) *affectio maritalis*, which the defendant denies, but it is sufficient to prove that he was possessive and beat the woman for this reason, while at the same time giving presents to her sister, significant evidence of how involved the man was in the relationship, which extended to the relatives of the woman.[39]

On the contrary, violence perpetrated by an Italian against a black woman for the purpose of obtaining sexual favors from her cleared the man of the crime of madamato, because "it is hard to understand the existence of a relation of conjugal type, in which the woman denies sexual intercourse, so that the man arrives to hit and also to beat her to get her favors, so much so that to avoid such misfortunes the woman went to the police."[40] Thus the meaning of the terms "violence" and Italian "racial prestige" were implemented opportunistically.[41] The legal interpretation of violence ended up depending on social, racial, and gender variables. On this subject Ann Laura Stoler and Frederick Cooper have well explained the partiality of colonial law in defining rights and duties.[42]

The possibility that the man's violent behavior may represent an abuse of the woman's human rights was not even taken into consideration. The fact that she was a subject and that indigenous sexual customs were believed to be deeply different from Italian mores (it was also believed that African women reached puberty earlier than European women) contributed to the application of unequal standards for judgment. Black African women shaped the sexual fantasies of Italian men, who often understood Africa as the place of sexual opportunities.[43] A clear example of this was the case of a Mr. Lanfranconi, who had been accused of raping a thirteen-year-old girl. He was first acquitted on the grounds that thirteen- year-old Abyssinian women were to be considered adults in sexual terms, in contravention of article 519 of the Italian penal code, which prescribed fourteen as the age below which statutory rape occurred.[44] In spite of the acquittal in the first instance, the case went to the Court of Appeal. The final conviction came not as the just punishment for an act of aggression against a woman, but based on the fact that

> Italians living in a colony have a greater duty to behave responsibly than do Italians living in the mainland: each of us represents in small our national character in front of the indigenous population; every undignified act represents in the eyes of the indigenous populations (primitives that they are . . .) a fault in the dominant race. . . . To say, as the courts did, that an Italian in Africa could enjoy thirteen-year-old girls only because they are of a different race is a juridical mistake, and it is at odds with the will of the State, which, in order to avoid the persistence of uncivilized and disgusting customs, has extended the implementation of our laws to the whole Empire.[45]

Based on a study of these verdicts, the anthropologist Barbara Sòrgoni states that "the Eritrean woman becomes a mere mute body upon which to discuss and decide, an object whose characteristics (age, physical and psychological maturity, consent, adherence to traditional norms) are studied with the objective of achieving a better organization of the juridical structure of the territory."[46] The woman's voice—to use a "classic" theme of subaltern studies—fundamentally remains silenced.[47] However, Giulia Barrera states that

> Even if the law on *madamato* was not intended to protect African women, women could manipulate it to secure protection against Italian men who behaved like masters. Often court decisions reflected that a man was convicted because of the incriminating testimony given by his *madama*. Unfortunately, it is difficult to tell whether the *madame* in these cases were intentionally incriminating their partners.[48]

Barrera's statement is surely interesting, because it supposes a discreet shrewdness on the part of indigenous women in manipulating prohibitions imposed by the Italian colonial power. We know that men accused by their madamas were never punished for violence against them, but the abuses were often used to prove the existence of conjugal relations. In case of a conviction, which resulted in her lover's imprisonment, the accusing woman at least had put an end to her sufferings. Without access to oral histories or testimonies, it is not possible to analyze women's intentions in these cases. But African urban women almost certainly knew about colonial restrictions on mixed-race unions and could use that knowledge to get the colonial state to help them escape these abusive relationships.

DEBATING MISTREATMENT IN THE HOUSEHOLD

The debate surrounding mistreatment in the family reveals that the law was interpreted differently in the colonies than in the metropole.[49] On the mainland, doctrinal discussions considered concubines as well as relatives potential victims of domestic violence. Although it had been customary for Italian settlers to live *more uxorio* with indigenous women, in the colonies concubines were never taken into account.

As mentioned above, madamismo "was a colonial adaptation of existing customs of concubinage, or contractual conjugal arrangements, which coexisted with formally sanctioned long-term marriages."[50] Italians considered it a temporary concubinage, which released men from any obligation or duty toward their partners and the possible children born from those relationships. However, according to indigenous customs, these de facto marriages implied a series of reciprocal obligations between the partners, the legitimacy of the children, and an arranged provision for wife and children, should the relationship be dissolved.

According to Gabriella Campassi, Italians used autochthonous practice to guarantee for themselves partners/servants who were not entitled to any rights.[51] These unions were usually sanctioned by traditional forms of negotiation, which should have guaranteed women a certain security in native patriarchal terms, but Italian men were not always prepared to recognize these rights. More complexly, in the opinion of Ruth Iyob, "The madama can also be seen . . . as a wage earner who developed a new position based on her proximity to those in power," but "if she failed to meet [her master's] demands, the alternative was to join the growing number of bordellos subsidized by the colonial government."[52] Such an attitude of neglect, shown by many male colonizers, proves that the colonial legal system frequently rested on the discretional concern of customary practices and rules of behavior and that institutional violence "which governed the ordering of the colonial world . . . tirelessly punctuated the destruction of the indigenous social fabric."[53] The promulgation of racist and segregationist laws from 1937 further complicated the social and legal bases of mixed-race unions. Even those Italian men who may have considered marrying their indigenous partners were prevented from doing so by the new legislation. Nonetheless, as the following testimony reveals, Italian settlers continued to establish conjugal unions with African women.

> It is true that there was a law prohibiting cohabitation with black women, in order to protect from diseases and for motivations of prestige,

however this law was rarely observed. We did everything secretly. Some children were born, from unions between African women and white men, but they were not legitimated. . . . I too had a black woman, and I had a normal life. I took her when she was thirteen years old, and I was over twenty. I kept her for two years: then I left her. It was better to have a woman at home than to go outside, because something bad could happen. I was happy. I found her a house in the center of Addis Ababa and she lived well. She was considered a servant, but I kept her also during the night, even if it was not allowed. There were always some excuses; it was difficult to verify; moreover she had a separate bedroom, and therefore I have never had troubles. Although, if I wanted to marry her, there was no way I could.[54]

As I have mentioned above, a sort of juridical "invisibility" was common to all concubines, because Italian legislation protected above all the legitimate family. In the late 1930s, legislators and jurists in the metropole initiated a doctrinal discussion of the possibility of considering the *more uxorio* cohabitant as the injured party in the crime of "mistreatment in the family." Although it was not possible to consider her as a relative or a family member, one commentator observed that

It should be recognized that, even if deprived of juridical character, the *more uxorio* cohabiting creates between the man and the woman a relationship that could be de facto entirely similar to that at the basis of the conjugal society. This relationship can easily give rise to subjugation, which is the basis of the concept of authority. This in turn is a necessary element, together with others, for the occurrence of the crime here taken into account.[55]

Despite this enlightened opinion, the jurisprudence did not appear to implement such an interpretation of the norm in that period of time. Without entering here into details that are beyond the scope of this study, the Fascist penal code of 1930 had redefined mistreatment as a crime against family care (title XI, art. 572). Prior to this act, domestic mistreatment had been considered a crime against personal integrity in the previous liberal code (book II, item VI, art. 390). Under the old code, the victim was forced to bring legal action against the perpetrator of the violence, and the punishment never exceeded thirty months' imprisonment; under the new code the crime was made indictable, and the sentence was extended to a maximum of five years. However, article 572 of the new code did not provide an unambiguous definition of domestic violence and only mentioned the repeated occurrence of mistreatment.

In the colonies the situation was complicated by the ethnic character of the women involved, which put them in a subordinate position to the Italian settlers. As a consequence, the domestic mistreatment they were subjected to could not be prosecuted as "mistreatment in the family," because, although concubines had legal rights, they were not typically considered as having the status of a family member. In addition, prosecution for mistreatment was left to the discretion of judges. Paradoxically, the only protection African women received from the colonial legal system came after 1937 when their complaints were used as evidence to prosecute Italian men for having entered into mixed-race conjugal relationships, thus releasing women from abusive relationships. Although the objective of prosecuting and imprisoning men who were violent in the home was reached in any case, the reasons that led to the conviction differed significantly. The imprisonment of violent male abusers was paradoxically the product of a legal system that promoted racism and segregation and punished transgressors.

⌒

The Fascist dictatorship approached domesticity through a new brand of laws and institutions, which were devoted to regulating behavior and purifying categories related to gender, race, and class. Some of the verdicts mentioned here clearly show "the strong ideological options of the political culture" of colonial judges at the end of the thirties; the verdicts expressed "a coherent adhesion to the new norms aimed at defining a strong racial bias."[56] A serious historical reconstruction of Italian colonization cannot ignore "the role of jurists in the coresponsibility of drafting, implementing, and interpreting legislation, including racist laws."[57] Such a study would have to examine the families, education, and prior experience of the judges and the civil servants posted to the colonies. This is exactly what Barbara Sòrgoni did in her work on the public official Alberto Pollera, who acted as judge in Eritrea and whose life represented conflicts between private and public experiences and roles.[58]

The Fascist era introduced new scrutiny into the domestic spheres both in the mainland and in the colonies. Fascist-era legislation also differentiated between the legal responsibilities of Italian men and African women and sought to educate them on their proper roles. According to the 1939 law, Italians caught in flagrante with African women faced prosecution for violating the "internal borders" of the Italian East Africa's colonial society, although madamas were not guilty of the same crime. It was Italians who were expected to behave in accordance with their "superior race" and avoid "impure mixed unions."

> The family was the crucial site in which future subjects and loyal
> citizens were to be made. Thus the domestic life of individuals was

increasingly subject to public scrutiny by a wide range of private and government organizations that charged themselves with the task of policing the moral borderlands of the European community and the psychological sensibilities of its marginal, as well as supposedly full-fledged, members.[59]

Let us not forget that policemen and judges were all men: these situations were therefore expressions of racial and gender inequalities. The culturally and legally subordinated position of women within every Italian couple was, in the case of mixed unions, further complicated by the different ethnic origin of the two partners and their belonging to the categories of colonizer and colonized. Thus, the central paradox of the Fascist prohibitions on mixed-race conjugal unions was that domestic violence through controlling behavior and other forms of abuse, which revealed the very normalcy of the union, was used to prosecute the male settler.

> In the study of empire more than that of nation, the analytic of gender is entwined with that of race as "an organizing principle and a powerful rhetorical theme" that infiltrated every layer of the colonial interface. The general instability of subject positions in the landscape of empire meant that the work of defining and maintaining otherness was continuous, as sexual difference was reordered in relation to shifting categories of race, class, or caste.[60]

Moreover, in the colonies these unions were not sanctioned by any juridical norm, but they imitated and reinterpreted indigenous customs. The fear of miscegenation pushed Fascist legislators to issue the royal decree by law no. 880 of 19 April 1937 and the slightly revised law no. 2590 of 30 December 1937 against quasi-conjugal relations. Fascist legislators and judges feared that these relationships would produce mixed-blood children, which helps to explain the zeal of colonial judges in interpreting and implementing this law.[61] An intensive campaign against mixed-race unions was launched by the authorities and was supported by well-known members of academia and the judiciary, who were influenced by an increasingly racially biased Italian scientific community. Furthermore, law no. 822 of 13 May 1940, "Norms Concerning Mixed-Blood Children," prohibited Italian men from recognizing their children born from African women. In his speech to the chamber, the minister for Italian Africa, Attilio Teruzzi,[62] confirmed the ideological nature of the law, intended to repress *métissage*.[63]

Private lives of both colonizers and colonized were deeply embedded in a larger context of violent relations provoked by the colonial experience. The

Fascist dictatorship increasingly imposed its boundaries and clear-cut definitions on the colonial society, although sometimes that trend produced the corrosion of common cultural practices (for example, gender hierarchy or patrilinearity). The strong relevance given by the regime to the centrality of the legitimate family within the Fascist state was neglected in the colonies in the name of presumed racial reasons. In actual fact, interracial unions were considered illegal family units, because "white opinion as well as judicial opinions upheld the notion that to be a black woman was indeed not to be a woman at all."[64] Such an attitude showed that Fascist praise was reserved not so much for the family but rather for a specific kind of family, whose characteristics were also determined on a strictly racial basis.

NOTES

I warmly thank my sister Raffaella Salvante for her help in translating this paper. Unless otherwise noted, all translations are mine or my sister's.

1. Tribunal of Gondar, 19 November 1938—President and drafter Maistro, Public Prosecutor Ruffini, defendant Spano, *Razza e civiltà* 1 (1940): 130.

2. Tribunal of Gondar, 19 November 1938, 130. The fact that the couple shared their living, eating, and sleeping habits and that the woman did the housework, in addition to having sexual intercourse, indicated that she was not just a prostitute, used occasionally by the man to satisfy his sexual needs.

3. See box 2.1 in World Health Organization, *WHO Multi-country Study on Women's Health and Domestic Violence against Women: Initial Results on Relevance, Health Outcomes and Women's Responses* (2005), http://www.who.int/gender/violence/who_multicountry_study/en/, 14.

4. WHO, *World Report on Violence and Health. Summary* (2002), http://www.who.int/violence_injury_prevention/violence/world_report/en/summary_en.pdf, 4.

5. For example, article no. 340 against *Abuso dei mezzi di correzione* [abuse of *ius corrigendi*] addressed crimes against the person in the Zanardelli penal code of 1889; however, transformed into art. no. 571 in the Rocco penal code (the Fascist code of 1930), it came to tackle crimes against familial care. Nevertheless, a moderate use of strength was considered a fundamental tool in education.

6. Mario Sbriccoli, "Fonti giudiziarie e fonti giuridiche. Riflessioni sulla fase attuale degli studi di storia del crimine e della giustizia criminale," *Studi storici* 29, no. 2 (1988): 494.

7. Federica Tamarozzi and Giovanni Focardi, "L'Italie et ses colonies: la destine des archives et des musées," in *Corse-Colonies. Colloque 19–20 septembre 2002*, ed. Musée de la Corse (Ajaccio: Musée de la Corse-Éditions Alain Piazzola, 2002), 241–61. But for some interesting discoveries in Eritrean archives, see Francesca Locatelli, "The Archives of the Municipality and the High Court of Asmara, Eritrea: Discovering the Eritrea 'Hidden from History,'" *History in Africa* 31 (2004): 469–78.

8. Cf. Luigi Goglia, "Sul razzismo coloniale italiano," *Materiali di lavoro* 10, no. 2–3 (1992): 203–4.

9. Irma Taddia, *La memoria dell'Impero: Autobiografie d'Africa Orientale* (Manduria: P. Lacaita, 1988), 41. See also Vittorio Castellano, "Considerazioni su alcuni fenomeni demografici della popolazione italiana dell'Eritrea dal 1882 al 1923," *Rivista italiana di demografia e statistica* 23, no. 3 (1948): 386–417; Castellano, "La popolazione italiana dell'Eritrea dal 1924 al 1940," *Rivista italiana di demografia e statistica* 2, no. 4 (1948): 530–40; Gabriele Ciampi, "La popolazione dell'Eritrea," *Bollettino della Società geografica italiana* ser. 11, vol. 12, no. 4 (1995): 487–524.

10. For information on women living in the colonies, see Cristina Lombardi-Diop, "Pioneering Female Modernity: Fascist Women in Colonial Africa," in *Italian Colonialism*, ed. Ruth Ben-Ghiat and Mia Fuller (New York: Palgrave Macmillan, 2005), 145–54; Barbara Sòrgoni, "Donne in colonia tra definizione giuridica e immaginario di genere," in *Oltremare. Diritto e istituzioni dal Colonialismo all'età postcoloniale*, ed. Aldo Mazzacane (Naples: Cuen, 2006), 235–65.

11. Charles Burdett, "Journeys to Italian East Africa 1936–1941: Narratives of Settlement," *Journal of Modern Italian Studies* 2, no. 2 (2000): 217.

12. "Sciarmutta was an Italianization of the Arabic term 'sharmāta' and stood for prostitute" (Giulia Barrera, *Dangerous Liaisons: Colonial Concubinage in Eritrea, 1890–1941*, PAS Working Paper No. 1 [Evanston, IL: Northwestern University, 1996], 1). Some male witnesses wrote about prostitution in the African colonies in their diaries and memoirs collected by Nicola Labanca, *Posti al sole. Diari e memorie di vita e di lavoro dalle colonie d'Africa* (Rovereto: Museo storico italiano della guerra, 2001), 253–56.

13. For an explanation on the difference between *demoz* and *madamato*, see Barbara Sòrgoni, *Parole e corpi: Antropologia, discorso giuridico e politiche sessuali interrazziali nella colonia Eritrea, 1890–1941* (Naples: Liguori, 1998), 127–38.

14. Among many, see the considerations of Ferdinando Martini (1841–1928), man of letters and politician, who became governor of Eritrea from 1897 to 1907. Cf. Ferdinando Martini, *Diario eritreo* (Florence: Vallecchi, 1943), 4:48–49.

15. During the drafting phase of the decree, the civil servant Alberto Pollera wrote a text to be sent to Minister Alessandro Lessona, to show his opposition to the planned racial segregation foreseen by the new law; see Luigi Goglia, "Una diversa politica razziale coloniale in un documento inedito di Alberto Pollera del 1937," *Storia contemporanea* 16, no. 5–6 (1985): 1071–92. Pollera, resident in the colony for a long time, had fathered six *métis* children born two different mothers. He not only recognized his children but also strove for Italian citizenship for them. About his role as ethnologist and private man, see Barbara Sòrgoni, *Etnografia e colonialismo. L'Eritrea e l'Etiopia di Alberto Pollera (1873–1939)* (Turin: Bollati Boringhieri, 2001).

16. See Giovanni Rosso, "Definizione dell'espressione 'relazione d'indole coniugale' del reato di madamismo," *Razza e civiltà* 1, No. 8 (1940): 680–83.

17. Royal decree by law no. 1728 of 17 November 1938, *Provvedimenti per la difesa della razza intaliana.*

18. Luciano Martone's considerations on the use "of the colony as a place of penal experimentation" are remarkable. He maintains that "the decisions of the judges of the Italian East Africa were helpful to an advanced verification of the Italian judiciary consensus in favour of the racial policy, which would shortly after be promulgated by the Fascist government through the anti-Jewish laws." Martone, "Magistrati italiani nella Colonia Eritrea. Immagini d'Africa e riflessioni giuridiche (1886–1941)," in *Amicitiae pignus: Studi in ricordo di Adriano Cavanna*, ed. Antonio Padoa Schioppa, Gigliola di Renzo Villata, and Gian Paolo Massetto (Milan: Giuffré, 2003), 2:1399.

19. Law no. 1004 of 29 June 1939, *Sanzioni penali per la difesa del prestigio di razza di fronte ai nativi dell'Africa italiana*. For the parliamentary debating sessions, see *Atti Parlamentari*, XXX Legislatura, 1 sessione della Camera dei fasci e delle corporazioni, Commissioni legislative, 20 April 1939, Commissione Africa Italiana, 3–4.

20. On the contrary, the search for paternity was accepted and foreseen by the indigenous law, as ethnologist Alberto Pollera has also remarked in his book on Ethiopian women. See Pollera, *La donna in Etiopia* (Rome: SAI, 1922), 78–79.

21. Gianluca Gabrielli, "La persecuzione delle 'unioni miste' (1937–1940) nei testi delle sentenze pubblicate e nel dibattito giuridico," *Studi piacentini* 20, no. 2 (1996): 127–28, n. 14.

22. Sòrgoni, "Donne in colonia," 254. For a detailed summary on the law system existing in Colonia Eritrea, see Irma Taddia, *L'Eritrea-colonia 1890–1952: Paesaggi, strutture, uomini del colonialismo* (Milan: Franco Angeli, 1986), 61–71.

23. The *Rivista giuridica del medio ed estremo oriente e giustizia coloniale* (1932–1940), based in Rome, was directed by professor and lawyer Vincenzo Taormina. *Il diritto razzista* (1939–1942) was established and directed by Stefano M. Cutelli and was published in Bologna. Finally, the Rome-based *Rivista di diritto coloniale* (1938–1942) was edited by professor and lawyer Saverio Ilardi.

24. Oral testimony by S. G., Mirandola, Modena—born 22 May 1911 and left for Africa in March 1935—collected by Taddia, *La memoria dell'Impero*, 90–91.

25. The Latin expression *affectio maritalis* indicated in the ancient Roman law reciprocal affection and support between wife and husband in a marriage. Being an essential requisite for a conjugal relation to exist, the relation ended when *affectio* was no longer present. See "Affectio maritalis," in *La nuova enciclopedia del diritto e dell'economia Garzanti* (Milan: Garzanti, 1987), 29.

26. See Rosso, "Definizione dell'espressione," 680–83.

27. See Giovanni Leone, "La non punibilità dell'indigena per il delitto di madamato," *Rivista italiana di diritto penale* 11 (1939): 85–89, and Rosso, "Il reato di madamismo nei confronti dell'indigena che abbia una relazione di indole coniugale con un cittadino italiano," *Razza e civiltà* 1 (1940): 131–39.

28. Minister of Colonies Alessandro Lessona wrote in 1937: "The coupling with inferior creatures has to be considered not only for the abnormality of the physiological event, nor only for the signal harmful consequences, but as a slipping towards a familiar promiscuity in which our best qualities as dominator stock

could drown. To dominate others it is necessary to learn dominating oneself. That is what Italians should remember and desire, from humble to high." Cited from Alessandro Lessona, *Memorie* (Florence: Sansoni, 1958), 352. Lessona was minister of the colonies from June 1936 to November 1937.

29. The royal decree by law no. 2374 of 4 December 1936 created the Colonial Police Corps, dependent on the Ministry of the Colonies, which was then called the Ministry for Italian Africa with the royal decree no. 431 of 8 April 1937. Consequently, the colonial police force, active also in Libya, was renamed Italian Africa Police, best known as PAI (law no. 748 of 15 May 1939).

30. Court of Appeal of Addis Ababa (11 July 1939—President Carnaroli, drafter Nigro; defendant De Gioia), *Razza e civiltà* 1, no. 8 (1940): 673.

31. Court of Appeal of Addis Ababa (24 January 1939—President Carnaroli; defendant Sodano.—*Madamismo*—Constitutive elements), *Rivista di diritto coloniale* 2, no. 2–3 (1939): 400–401.

32. Title VII. *On prostitution* (articles 191–210). See Archivio centrale dello Stato, Ministero dell'Africa Italiana, b. 2053, *Polizia: Corpo della Polizia coloniale P.A.I.*

33. Court of Appeal of Addis Ababa (26 September 1939—President Guerrazzi, drafter Nigro; defendant Romersa), *Razza e civiltà* 1, no. 5–6–7 (1940): 549. The text ended with the remark that "it suffices to prove the nature of the relationship between the two the fact that the woman entered every day through the window after having all day long worked in the same house and going out in the evening" (ibid.).

34. Court of Appeal of Addis Ababa (7 March 1939—President Russo, drafter Guerrazzi; defendant Russo), *Razza e civiltà* 1, no. 5–6–7 (1940): 676.

35. Gabrielli, "Un aspetto della politica razzista nell'impero: il 'problema dei meticci,'" *Passato e presente* 15, no. 41 (1997): 94n61.

36. Cf. Gabrielli, "La persecuzione," 83–140.

37. As Martone says, the colonial juridical experience had "always reduced the guarantees for indigenous accused and adopted a strictly inquiring method," but, after the establishment of the AOI, it "distinguished itself everywhere for a marked racial characterization" (Martone, *Giustizia coloniale: Modelli e prassi penale per i sudditi d'Africa dall'età giolittiana al fascismo* [Naples: Jovene, 2002], 312).

38. Penal Tribunal of Gondar (19 November 1938—President Maisto; defendant Spano), *Rivista di diritto coloniale* 2, no. 1 (1939): 97.

39. Court of Appeal of Addis Ababa, 13 December 1938 President Carnaroli; defendant Angello, *Il diritto cazzista* 2, no. 1 (1940): 37.

40. Court of Appeal of Addis Ababa (27 September 1939—President Guerrazzi, defendant Cerullo), *Razza e civiltà* 1, No. 5–6–7 (1940): 558. See also Sòrgoni, *Parole e corpi*, 237–38.

41. "The notion of prestige occupies a central place in all colonial discourse but may have held a special meaning for Italians, who viewed empire as an escape route from a subordinate international position" (Ben-Ghiat, *Fascist Modernities: Italy, 1922–1945*, [Berkeley: University of California Press, 2001], 130).

42. Cf. Ann Laura Stoler and Frederick Cooper, "Between Metropole and Colony. Rethinking a Research Agenda," in *Tensions of Empire: Colonial Cultures in a Bourgeois World*, ed. Ann Laura Stoler and Frederick Cooper (Berkeley: University of California Press, 1997), 6.

43. Cf. Araia Tseggai, "Eritrean Women and Italian Soldiers: Status of Eritrean Women under Italian Rule," *Journal of Eritrean Studies* 4, no. 1–4 (1989–90): 7–12, and Giulietta Stefani, *Colonia per maschi. Italiani in Africa Orientale: Una storia di genere* (Verona: Ombre Corte, 2007), 97–108. See also Dorothy Roberts, *Killing the Black Body: Race, Reproduction, and the Meaning of Liberty* (New York: Pantheon Books, 1997).

44. Tribunal of Addis Ababa (8 February 1938—President and drafter Buongiorno; defendant Lanfranconi et al. Rape—age of the victim—indigenous subject), *Rivista giuridica del medio ed estremo oriente e giustizia coloniale* 2 (1938): 253–58. Court of Appeal of Addis Ababa (20 May 1938—President Carnaroli; defendant Lanfranchi [sic] et al.), *Rivista del medio ed estremo oriente e giustizia coloniale* 2 (1938): 369–72. Cf. also Sòrgoni, *Parole e corpi*, 239–41.

45. Court of Appeal of Addis Ababa, 20 May 1938, 372. Frantz Fanon wrote evocative pages on the animalized representation of the colonized by the colonizer. See *The Wretched of the Earth* (New York: Grove, 2004), 7.

46. Sòrgoni, *Parole e corpi*, 238–39.

47. See Gayatri C. Spivak, "Can the Subaltern Speak?" in *Marxism and the Interpretation of Culture*, ed. Cary Nelson and Lawrence Grossberg (Urbana: University of Illinois Press, 1988), 271–313.

48. Barrera, *Dangerous Liaisons*, 57. See also Barrera, "Colonial Affairs: Italian Men, Eritrean Women, and the Construction of Racial Hierarchies in Colonial Eritrea" (PhD diss., Northwestern University, 2002). On the contradictory position of *madamas* within the colonial society, see Ruth Iyob, "Madamismo and Beyond: The Construction of Eritrean Women," in Ben-Ghiat and Fuller, *Italian Colonialism*, 233–44.

49. See Raffaello Gioffredi, "Maltrattamenti in famiglia o verso i fanciulli," in *Nuovo digesto italiano*, ed. Mariano D'Amelio (Turin: Utet, 1939), 8:37–41.

50. Iyob, "Madamismo and Beyond," 236.

51. Gabriella Campassi, "Il madamato in Africa Orientale. Relazioni tra italiani e indigene come forma di aggressione coloniale," *Miscellanea di storia delle esplorazioni* 12 (1987): 219–60.

52. Iyob, "Madamismo and Beyond," 237.

53. Fanon, *Wretched of the Earth*, 7–9.

54. Witness account by V. B., San Posidonio, Modena, born 18 March 1911 and left for Africa 5 April 1935. He was first a soldier and then a truck driver in Ethiopia. This oral story was collected, with others, by Taddia, *La memoria dell'Impero*, 98. Another witness, who left for Africa as a soldier, narrated: "In spite of the little money, we soldiers felt well, we were happy twenty-year-olds. We had our women, as everyone, the indigenous women, because the Italian women came later, when the war was over. Our women were young girls, they worked for us, they were twelve or thirteen years old, over there a thirty-year-old woman is already old"

(Taddia, *La memoria dell'Impero*, 118; oral testimony by L. C., Ferrara, born in January 1916, who left for Africa in September 1935).

55. Gaetano Sardiello, "Le condizioni della donna convivente more uxorio ed il reato di maltrattamenti," *Rivista penale* 653, no. 2 (1939): 228.

56. Martone, "Magistrati italiani," 1399. In this essay, Martone, in addition to outlining the guidelines of the jurisprudential practice in the colonies, drafts the biographies of the most influential magistrates operating in the colonies in the liberal era (Mariano D'Amelio, William Caffarell, Adelgiso Ravizza, etc.).

57. Giovanni Focardi, "Gli 'africani' di Palazzo Spada: tracce biografiche dei consiglieri di Stato," *Quaderni fiorentini per la storia del pensiero giuridico moderno* 33/34 (2004–2005): 1167. Focardi's essay concerns the Counsellors of State of the VI section (created in 1939) devoted to Italian Africa's matters.

58. Sòrgoni, *Etnografia e colonialismo.*

59. Ann Stoler, "Sexual Affronts and Racial Frontiers: European Identities and the Cultural Politics of Exclusion in Colonial Southeast Asia," *Comparative Studies in Society and History* 34, no. 3 (1992): 521.

60. Kathleen Canning, *Gender History in Practice: Historical Perspectives on Bodies, Class, and Citizenship* (Ithaca, NY: Cornell University Press, 2006), 37–38.

61. Stoler has written: "The tension between concubinage as a confirmation and compromise of racial hierarchy was realized in the progeny that it produced, 'mixed-bloods,' poor 'indos,' and abandoned 'métis' children who straddled the divisions of ruler and ruled threatened to blur the colonial divide" (Ann Stoler, "Making Empire Respectable: The Politics of Race and Sexual Morality in Twentieth-Century Colonial Cultures," *American Ethnologist* 16, no. 4 [1989]: 638).

62. Teruzzi succeeded Mussolini at the Ministry for Italian Africa (from November 1939 to July 1943).

63. Introduction of the bill to the Chamber by the Minister for Italian Africa, Attilio Teruzzi, 16 April 1940 (doc. 716); cited from *Le leggi* (Rome, 1940), 865–66.

64. Pamela Scully, *Race and Ethnicity in Women's and Gender History in Global Perspective*, Working Paper "Women's and Gender History in Global Perspective," American Historical Association and the Committee on Women Historians (Washington, DC, 2006), 20.

PART II

⸺

Narrating Domestic Violence

TESTIMONY AND NARRATIVES of violence feature prominently in the second part of this volume. The stories that emerge from these sources demonstrate that across the diversity of colonial experiences, European rule in Africa tended to increase the vulnerability of women and children to domestic violence. Even in places where the colonial administration made attempts to raise the status of women, the imperative of maintaining order quickly trumped concerns for women's welfare. Thus, Elke Stockreiter finds that in colonial Zanzibar, a lone official's crusade against child marriages was suppressed by an administration more concerned with political stability. In many places, colonial regimes systematically tried to procure the cooperation of male elders by reinforcing their power over women and younger men. Colonial officials also brought European models of patriarchal control to their administrative practices. In colonial Kenya and Malawi, Stacey Hynd finds that colonial officials regularly commuted sentences for men convicted of murdering their wives, and Elizabeth Thornberry's research in South Africa reveals the reluctance of British administrators to believe women's accusations of rape. In South Africa, dissatisfaction with colonial responses to sexual assault led Africans to maintain parallel judicial systems that avoided the colonial state entirely. Katherine Luongo shows the ways in which victims of epistemological and intimate violence, manifested in witchcraft, narrated their suffering within cases of physical violence that the Kenyan colonial state recognized as actionable.

5 ⇆ Sex, Violence, and Family in South Africa's Eastern Cape

ELIZABETH THORNBERRY

IN OCTOBER 1893, a Xhosa-speaking woman named Nondaba described to the resident magistrate of King William's Town the following experience:

> I was sleeping in our hut with my mother, Nosenti, Noponi, and Nosayiti, and I was awoke late in the night or towards the morning by someone having connection [intercourse] with me. I was lying on my side and the person was behind me. I could feel when I awoke that he had penetrated me. I jumped up and caught hold of him, and then I screamed out and my mother came and shut the door of the hut. The other women were aroused; we threw up the fire and found the person Christmas. We kept him there till the next morning when we handed him over to the police. I was examined next morning by a board of matrons. . . . I was a virgin up to that night.[1]

In the nineteenth-century Eastern Cape, Nondaba's experience was not unusual. In King William's Town district alone, thirty-eight cases with a similar pattern of facts—a woman complaining of sexual assault while sleeping, often in the presence of several witnesses—appeared before the magistrate between 1847 and 1902. In Xhosa, such assaults were labeled *ukuzuma*, and defined to a 1950s ethnographer as to "have sexual relations with a woman while asleep," with the further explanation that someone who commits ukuzuma "is despised . . . his punishment is that he should be thrashed when caught."[2] The colonial court system, however, was more lenient. Christmas, the man Nondaba accused of raping her, was found not guilty at his trial.

These cases do not fit contemporary definitions of "domestic violence," including that employed in this volume. The parties involved were not family members, or husband and wife. In most cases, they had no prior intimate relationship—while a few of the assailants claimed to be the lovers or "sweethearts" of the women they assaulted, most did not.[3] Nor were these cases recognized as domestic violence by the men and women of the nineteenth century who dealt with them. Although the term "domestic violence" had not come into common usage yet, British colonial administrators recognized categories such as "wife-beating," while African men and women understood certain kinds of violence within the family as operating according to different rules than extrafamilial violence.

However, the adjudication of ukuzuma cases reveals that ideas about the separation between public and domestic spheres influenced a much broader range of cases than those which are normally understood as domestic violence. I argue in this chapter that an analysis of ukuzuma cases—and, particularly, of the reluctance of the British administration to convict the men who committed these offenses—illuminates the broader history of domestic violence. These cases crossed the boundaries between customary and criminal law that the colonial administration was trying to create; they brought "domestic" issues of sexuality and family relationships into the sphere of the criminal court system. An analysis of their adjudication therefore reveals the British colonial system's commitment to maintaining a separation between these spheres, and the consequences of that commitment for their ability to comprehend and apply Xhosa custom in colonial courts.

Definitions of domestic violence in both the nineteenth century and the contemporary period center on an idea of the family as part of the "private" sphere, defined in opposition to such "public" institutions as the state, the workplace, and even religious institutions. Feminist critiques of domestic violence in recent Western history argue that this division between the private family and public institutions has insulated violence within the family from state intervention.[4] However, historians have described institutions of the family as operating in very different ways in many African contexts. Slavery in Africa has famously been understood as operating through the language of kinship, while other studies have emphasized the importance of ideas of relatedness to religious identity and trade networks.[5]

In Southern Africa, including Xhosaland, family ties were a fundamental idiom of political culture. Writing in 1934, the Xhosa intellectual J. H. Soga described the "tribe" as "an aggregation of clan units, as the latter is of family units, all descended from one progenitor."[6] In precolonial Xhosaland, precisely because of the centrality of concepts of relatedness to political and social life, the term family could cover a wide range of relationships. Relatives could be people of the same clan, with whom intermarriage was forbidden even if the exact genealogical connection was unknown. They could be members of the same patrilineal household; they might include a man's younger brothers and their descendents as well as his own wives, unmarried daughters, sons, and sons' wives and children. Within that household, however, uterine families— one mother and her children within a polygynous family—might feel particularly strong affective bonds, and form alliances in family disputes.[7] For women marriage entailed entry into a new lineage. Wives experienced their marital household very differently from their natal household, owing great deference to their parents-in-law and avoiding spaces (such as the cattle kraal) to which daughters of the family were allowed access. Well into maturity, a woman might turn to her natal family for support in disputes with her husband, or her husband's family.

Meanwhile, British colonial officials brought with them their own emergent idea of the private sphere of the family, in which the normative family involved a man and women united in monogamous marriage as well as their children. Inculcation of this model of family relations was one of the major concerns of British missionaries working in the area, from whose families many early colonial officials emerged.[8] African converts, numerous in nineteenth-century Xhosaland, integrated these different models of the family in a variety of ways, with some renouncing polygyny and embracing a version of British domesticity and others formulating new defenses of polygyny.

This proliferation of models of the family posed a problem for the British colonial administration. Colonial officials struggled to create a recognizable judicial structure with which to govern Xhosaland. The structure that emerged depended—as I argue below—on a separation between criminal law and civil law in which civil law became the repository for Xhosa custom. This separation, in turn, was determined in large part by an ideology that saw family relations as fundamentally outside the purview of state control.

The men in several ukuzuma cases explained their actions with reference to marriage. Of all the articulations of family in nineteenth-century Xhosaland, marriage was one of the most recognizable to British eyes. Colonial courts systematically recognized the claims of women's assailants to some kind of domestic status, defining these cases as lovers' quarrels that ought to be left to African families to resolve according to African "custom." These cases reveal the creation of legal categories that marked off violence within the family as different from other, more public, forms of violence. The ambiguous nature of these cases entangled British officials, African women and their families, and the African men accused of assault in an ongoing argument over what kinds of violence were worthy of state attention.

This issue is an important one for African history. As discussed elsewhere in this volume, contemporary legal and political discourses on domestic violence often emphasize the foreignness of the category to African conceptions of family relationships. This claim implies, in turn, that contemporary African states need not intervene in situations of family violence. It is certainly true that in the Eastern Cape in the nineteenth century no one talked about domestic violence as such. However, the separation of violence within the family from other kinds of violence was more a product of colonial interventions than precolonial African legal norms—and while some Africans welcomed this innovation, others argued vigorously against it.

VIOLENT ACTS

Domestic violence in its more obvious forms did appear in the colonial court system on a regular basis. Incidents of domestic violence—including that directed by men at wives, but also violence between siblings, against children, or against aging parents (usually women)—were prosecuted in criminal courts. In 1884, Nhlane was fined forty shillings for "beating and otherwise ill-treating his wife."[9] Assault cases constituted a substantial part of magistrates' caseloads. Prosecutions for crimes such as imputing witchcraft, arson, and even theft also contain evidence of domestic violence. The most detailed evidence can be found in cases of murder. When Booy Swart was convicted of murdering his wife in 1861, the investigation revealed a lengthy history of abuse.[10]

As in colonial Mali and Zanzibar, domestic violence also came to judicial notice during divorce proceedings (see chapters by Rodet, Stockreiter, Burrill and Roberts in this volume). Divorces in customary marriages were handled according to British interpretations of customary law. The interpretation of customary law that prevailed in British Kaffraria, the administrative district that included King William's Town, recognized domestic violence as a legitimate reason for divorce. John Maclean's *Compendium of Kafir Laws and Customs* informed its readers that "if a woman absolutely refuses to live with her husband, on account of ill-usage . . . the only remedy he has is to demand that the dowry be refunded to him; but the law will not support him even in this, if she has borne him a family of children."[11] Sigidi, a wealthy older man, similarly explained to a government commission on Xhosa law that "if the husband is entirely in the wrong, and his conduct forces her to leave him . . . then the cattle need not be returned to the husband, or only in part, where there are children."[12] If the woman was childless, bridewealth might have to be returned, but women could use evidence of abuse as leverage against their own parents. Such evidence could persuade magistrates to order the marriage dissolved and the bridewealth refunded despite the reluctance of the wife's family.

As a result, the archives are relatively rich in evidence about the prosecution of domestic violence in the colonial Eastern Cape.[13] A brief survey of cases from King William's Town reveals a colonial administration relatively unconcerned about violence directed by men against their wives and other dependents. Allegations of abuse raised in divorce cases almost never resulted in a criminal investigation; they did not always even result in divorce. Magistrates dealt with most criminal cases of domestic violence using their summary jurisdiction, typically giving sentences of a month's imprisonment or less.[14] There is substantial room for future research on this subject. This chapter, however, focuses on cases that involved violence on the margins of family structure—incidents of ukuzuma, in which women were sexually assaulted within their homes. These cases forced British officials and African families into debates over the appropriate roles of family and state in regulating violence. They illustrate the effects of the colonial courts' tendency to separate customary law and criminal law—and to define the difference in a way that excluded certain violent acts from criminal prosecution precisely because they were seen as too domestic.

Nondaba's case, quoted at the beginning of this chapter, was far from unique. It was one of thirty-eight ukuzuma cases that found their way into the colonial court system between 1866 and 1902—almost a third of the total number of cases of rape and attempted rape.[15] In 1888, Martha Sdimile told the court that she was "sleeping in the same hut [as] my sister Lydia, my grandmother Mabula, my brothers Samuel, Elijah, Mark, and Isaac, and Gijana, the prisoner," when she awoke to find Gijana having sex with her. Unsurprisingly, when she woke up and screamed, Gijana was quickly apprehended.[16]

Very few of these thirty-eight cases resulted in convictions. Only ten (26 percent) even went to trial. The rest were dismissed by the solicitor general or remitted to the resident magistrate on lesser charges. African women routinely faced skepticism about their lack of consent in cases of sexual assault. Testifying before the Cape Colony's 1883 Commission on Native Law and Custom, Frank Streatfield, a resident magistrate in the Transkei, told the Commission on Native Law and Custom that "I . . . give lashes . . . for rape, or what is called rape by natives, always. No case of bona fide rape has ever come before me."[17] Streatfield's skepticism of women's claims of rape was typical, although his choice to accommodate them in the court system nonetheless was not. Nor was such skepticism limited to Britain's colonies. In early nineteenth-century Britain, Anna Clark has estimated that only 17 percent of rape complaints resulted in a guilty verdict at trial.[18] In King William's Town, only two of six sexual assault cases involving Europeans as both complainants and accused resulted in guilty verdicts. However, in the Eastern Cape, women assaulted at night and in domestic space faced greater skepticism than those assaulted on the road or in another public space. A full 57 percent of the sexual assault cases with African protagonists that fell into the latter categories went to trial—a rate twice as high as for ukuzuma cases. The stories of women like Nondaba simply did not fit with magistrate's ideas of what criminal sexual assault looked like.

The Roman-Dutch common law governing the Cape Colony defined rape as "unlawful sexual intercourse with a woman without her consent," and incidents of rape were to be prosecuted in criminal courts that had jurisdiction over both African and European inhabitants of the region.[19] However, the colonial judicial system was not the only forum for adjudicating cases of sexual assault. Cases might be settled, and cattle or other goods paid by the man's family to the woman's, through informal negotiations or an appeal to authority figures outside the colonial legal system. Although the officially appointed headmen were legally forbidden to settle cases, many did so anyway. Even within the colonial judicial system, there were alternatives to criminal charges for women and their families. Magistrates did a brisk business settling cases in which a man was charged with seduction or adultery—categories that would cover most of the sexual assault cases considered here. The presence of alternative methods for adjudicating sexual assault cases forces us to ask how they were assigned to different legal categories. I argue in this chapter that magistrates regarded these criminal rape cases as, in fact, violations of civil or customary law.[20]

CRIME, TORT, CUSTOM:
DEFINING JURISDICTIONS IN BRITISH KAFFRARIA

King William's Town lies in the western part of South Africa's contemporary Eastern Cape Province, an area known in English during the nineteenth century as Kaffraria and then British Kaffraria, and in the twentieth century as the Ciskei.[21] For the Xhosa-speaking inhabitants, it was kwaXhosa or kwaRharhabe, named after two esteemed chiefs of earlier generations. Home to a number of different Xhosa polities, the area was a contested frontier between the Cape Colony and independent chiefdoms for the first half of the nineteenth century, and was gradually incorporated into the colony during the second half of the period.

The complex judicial landscape of the nineteenth-century Eastern Cape arose from a fundamental indecision on the part of colonial administrators. On the one hand, their presence in the area was justified largely through the language of "civilization," and the benefits of British civilization included access to British justice. On the other hand, the Eastern Cape frontier remained a politically unstable place. The easiest way to keep the peace was often to interfere as little as possible in the internal affairs of African communities, and to rely instead on chiefs and other preexisting structures of authority. In short, officials in the Eastern Cape were torn between what were later labeled direct and indirect rule. In the legal arena, they had to choose between applying British laws in British courts or continuing to enforce some version of "native law and custom." This was not a struggle in any way unique to the

Eastern Cape, or even to British colonialism. However, the conquest of the Eastern Cape forced the issue at a time when British colonial policy was in flux, and theories of indirect rule were still being formulated. The result was a particularly complex legal landscape.

The Cape Colony annexed British Kaffraria in 1866 at the culmination of a long period of political turmoil. Before colonial conquest began in the early part of the century, the area had been inhabited primarily by various Xhosa-speaking polities. Disputes were resolved either directly between families or in courts of male elders presided over by chiefs, who articulated the decision of the court.[22] Death sentences and corporal punishment seem to have been rare, limited to cases of witchcraft and offenses against the chief; more common were fines imposed on offenders, which might be distributed to the family of the victim of a crime, or kept by the chief himself.[23] Chiefly authority was articulated through genealogy, but depended in large part on political prowess. Commoners disgruntled with a chief's decision might appeal to a more powerful chief or even choose to switch allegiance entirely.

After an abortive attempt at annexation to the Cape Colony in 1835, British Kaffraria was proclaimed a British colony in 1848 at the end of a major war.[24] Civil commissioners were instructed to "rule the British Kafrarians through the medium of their chiefs."[25] In practice, the area remained under martial law until 1853. In 1855, chiefs were given government salaries in return for giving up personal control over fines paid in their courts. Magistrates were also posted with chiefs "to assist . . . in their deliberations and sentences." In the long term, the colonial government hoped that "European laws will, by imperceptible degrees, replace their barbarous customs."[26] In 1860, an ordinance extended the laws of the Cape Colony to British Kaffraria; in 1866 it was formally annexed to the Cape.[27] From 1860 onward, then, British Kaffraria was officially governed by the Roman-Dutch common law of the Cape.[28]

Immediately, however, practical problems in implementing Roman-Dutch law became apparent. The most pressing issue was the law of inheritance. Most of the area's residents were unwilling to marry in civil or religious ceremonies, which would limit husbands to one wife. From the perspective of colonial law, then, almost all Xhosa children were illegitimate and would not inherit. To remedy this situation, the 1864 Native Succession Ordinance recognized marriages according to "Native custom" and provided that the estates of Africans who had been married in this way would also be divided according to customary rules.[29]

The 1864 act thus gave legal status to African custom within the Eastern Cape's legal system.[30] Although this legal status was technically confined to marriage and inheritance, in practice magistrates in British Kaffraria applied it much more broadly. Magistrates in the Cape Colony presided over courts with summary jurisdiction in minor criminal and civil cases.[31] Faced with African litigants who claimed rights and obligations in the language of custom, magistrates found it necessary to give some recognition to customary law—at least in civil cases. In King William's Town district there were by the 1880s three special magistrates who tried "native cases, cases of ukulobola [bridewealth], and civil cases between the natives" according to their understanding of Xhosa custom.[32] As one of them later explained, "I have since my appointment deemed it part of my duty to adjudicate upon all Native Civil Cases brought to the Special Magistrates Court for hearing. They have always been dealt with as informal cases . . . and decided according to native law and custom."[33] According to James Rose Innes, the Undersecretary for Native Affairs and former resident magistrate in King William's Town, "special magistrates . . . exercised jurisdiction, and to my mind improperly because illegally."[34] I refer to the patchwork of courts that in some way recognized customary law in civil cases as the informal court system, following the language used by magistrates themselves.[35]

This recognition of custom in civil cases was tolerated by the administrators who were painfully aware of their own failure to monopolize judicial authority in the area. As the colony continued to extend its reach east beyond the Kei River, the chief magistrate of the newly acquired territories warned that "if natives do not consider the laws framed for their government just and suitable to their condition, there is the fear that they will take their cases to the Chiefs and Headmen, which will be a very serious retrograde move."[36] Indeed, despite the best efforts of the colonial government, many Africans continued to do just that. The archives of the colonial courts are peppered with cases that had previously been decided by a chief or headman. Kama, a powerful chief in the King William's Town area, spent much of the 1860s negotiating with colonial authorities to allow him some authority to settle civil cases.[37] A modus vivendi was eventually reached: whereas in 1862 the magistrate tried to suspend a headman for deciding an adultery case, by the 1880s his successor was hearing bridewealth cases appealed from the court of Kama's son without objection.[38] However, the state was less willing to tolerate the usurpation of its authority in criminal cases: a headman who heard a case of rape in 1893 was forced to apologize to the court, saying, "I know I am not allowed to try cases. The man was brought to me a prisoner, and yet I tried the case and let him off."[39]

The informal solution that was reached in British Kaffraria was formalized when the Cape Colony annexed the first part of the Transkei in 1877. Courts were authorized to apply "native law" in civil suits between two Africans, while criminal code was a modified version of Roman-Dutch law.[40] Not all civil law, then, was customary law. In the Transkei, disputes where at least one party was European were adjudicated according to Roman-Dutch law. This clause protected the property interests of white traders who did business in the Transkei, as well as European employers. In practice, it meant that the bulk of customary law cases dealt either with family law (marriage and divorce, adultery and seduction, and inheritance) or land disputes. In British Kaffraria, the division was even more blatant. Because the customary law system came into being as an ad hoc measure, it covered only litigation that magistrates decided could not be properly handled by European civil law—again, primarily family law cases and small property disputes.

By contrast, although there was a category for civil Roman-Dutch law, there was no category for customary criminal law. Disputes could be adjudicated according to customary or criminal law, but not a combination of the two. Magistrates had to decide whether complaints made to them in the language of custom properly belonged in civil court, in which case customary law could apply, or criminal court, in which case Roman-Dutch law was applicable. However, the division between criminal and civil law was derived from the British common law, not from Xhosa or other African legal traditions. Applying it to customary law fundamentally altered the content of custom. Since the publication of Martin Chanock's *Law, Custom and Social Order*, scholars of African legal history have acknowledged the changes necessary to create a relatively stable customary law out of the living tradition of customary practice, although debate continues over the relative contribution of British and African ideas to the end result.[41] This debate has mostly taken place over the sets of issues that typically came to be included in customary law: the law of marriage, inheritance, and property. The influence of the process on shaping criminal law has received comparatively little attention. However, the actions taken by magistrates in dealing with these rape cases illustrate how the bifurcation of criminal and civil law and the consequent definition of all customary law as civil could excise certain kinds of violent acts from the purview of criminal law.

The equation of customary and civil law in colonial governance had its roots in British understandings of their own legal system. Chanock himself notes the prevalence in Northern Rhodesia and Nyasaland (present-day Zambia and Malawi) of the idea that, in the words of one administrator, "in Early Law all Crimes are Torts"—as opposed to English law, which recognized the "clear distinction between the *civil* wrong which is compensated by damages to the individual, and the *criminal* wrong which is compensated by fine or forced labor extracted by the community."[42] From their earliest attempts to describe Xhosa legal traditions, British administrators in Xhosaland called on the categories of "civil" and "criminal" law. The 1858 publication of John Maclean's *Compendium* was the first major attempt to collect and disseminate information about Xhosa "law and custom" in order to aid local administrators.[43] One of volume's contributors explained that:

> For convenience, Kafir Laws may perhaps be divided into Criminal and Civil, as with us; but then the cases classed under these two heads will be a very different classification from ours.
>
> Criminal Cases will comprise such only as are prosecuted by the chiefs themselves, and the fines for which are claimed by them as their inalienable right; and which fines are denominated 'izizi.' . . .
>
> All other cases will come under the head of Civil Cases. These are prosecuted by the plaintiffs, and the fines, or compensation, are always awarded to, and claimed of right by them.[44]

The division of wrongs into civil and criminal categories was emerging in the nineteenth century as a fundamental category of English common law. In his *Commentaries on the Laws of England*, William Blackstone described the division as one between private and public wrongs.[45] A few decades later Jeremy Bentham reformulated the difference, defining criminal laws as those which the state had singled out for punishment, a framework that shaped theories of the law through the nineteenth century.[46] The distinction was increasingly recognized in practice as well. Peter King has found that, in Essex, the proportion of assault cases in which nominal fines were imposed (usually in conjunction with an out-of-court compensation settlement) fell from 83 percent of guilty verdicts in 1748–52 to 22 percent in 1819–21, while the percentage ending in imprisonment rose from 7 percent to 60 percent over the same time period.[47]

The use of categories imported from European legal philosophy created difficulties for administrators in describing African legal practice. William Brownlee, a former chief magistrate of the Transkei, who was raised in King William's Town, acknowledged in 1925 that "the distinction between civil and criminal cases as drawn by the natives was not quite the same as drawn by us."[48] Despite this discrepancy, Brownlee explained that "since our rule has displaced that of the native chief, no chief or headman is permitted to decide any criminal case, these are all dealt with by our courts. In any civil case or dispute, chiefs and headmen are allowed to arbitrate." The distinction between civil and criminal law was also the dividing line between chiefly and magisterial authority, between "native custom" and British law. In order for the system to work, British administrators had to define these spheres as mutually exclusive.

SEXUAL ASSAULT, MARRIAGE, AND THE FAMILY

Shoehorning Xhosa customary law into British legal categories worked best when the acts in question could be easily identified in those categories. Killing, in other words, could be easily labeled as murder, or perhaps culpable homicide. Disputes about bridewealth could be subsumed under divorce law. To be sure, the process of identification stripped these disputes of their thick meanings and transformed them into technically defined wrongs—such transformations are characteristic of all legal systems.[49] Some disputes, however, proved much harder to categorize. Witchcraft, for example, had no place in Roman-Dutch criminal law, but Africans seemed to recognize it as criminal, sometimes executing suspected witches. The colonial administration responded by creating new statutory crimes for both the practice of witchcraft and false accusations of witchcraft.

Sexual assault presented another major difficulty for British officials seeking to divide disputes into customary and criminal wrongs. Rape cases confounded administrators who wanted to use demands for compensation (rather than penal punishment or fines that would accrue to the state) as a criterion to distinguish between civil and criminal acts. Many rape victims—in both ukuzuma and other rape cases—demanded compensation. As one woman told the court, "I should not have brought a case against him, but he now denies the whole matter and refuses to pay my husband damages."[50] Such statements were common, if counterproductive. Explaining, as another woman did, that if her assailant "had given the cattle both my husband and myself would have been satisfied. This would have been according to Kafir Custom" did not convince the solicitor general to prosecute her case. Many British officials shared the view that the status of a wrong in Xhosa "law and custom" could be deduced from the punishment exacted from an offender—and that offenses for which compensation was paid to families were not criminal at all. Rather, they fell properly under the rubric of "civil" law and, by extension, African "custom." In Xhosaland, this conception of criminal law meant that the willingness of magistrates to prosecute sexual assault depended on victims' families' willingness to remove themselves and their claims for compensation from the legal arena.

Families who demanded payment of damages for the rape of a daughter or wife were accused of "condon[ing] the crime by offering to take cattle as payment."[51] In order to persuade magistrates to take them seriously, they had to strenuously deny "agreeing that [the accused] should pay for having had connection with my daughter."[52] Testimony that a woman's husband had demanded payment of a "fine" after her assault was enough to convince the solicitor general that there was "no evidence of a rape being committed upon the prosecutrix."[53] In the eyes of British colonial officials, the desire for compensation was incompatible with recognition of the crime of rape. Their fixation on evidence of compensation, moreover, located this categorization in African rather than British legal categories. Magistrates did not argue that Africans were responding inappropriately to acts of rape. Instead, they interpreted demands for compensation as evidence that rape had not occurred. If any offense had been committed, it was a customary (civil) rather than a criminal one. Indeed, cases that involved forcible sex were tried in the informal customary court system. In one such case, Songo sued Nongqala for "having assaulted his [Songo's] wife and had [sic] forcible connection with her." Songo received "two head of cattle or 10 pounds."[54] Unlike criminal fines, the money was paid to Songo himself and not to the government. In hearing rape charges as civil cases (a clear distinction in the record-keeping systems, if not always in practice), magistrates made space in the law for families who wished to seek restitution in cases of sexual assault—but they did so by defining them out of the criminal court system.

Ukuzuma cases were troubling for other reasons as well. British officials simply did not accept that women in these cases had not consented. In 1875, for example, Botshani was fined five pounds in civil court after Nante brought a charge of rape against him. The magistrate's verdict recorded that it was "proved that Botshani entered the hut of Nante and lodged there during the night. If anything occurred it must have been partly allowed by the woman. I very much doubt if Rape can take place when there are two grown up girls in the same hut."[55] This case was actually heard in the informal civil court system, probably because Nante's family had demanded compensation. Although recorded as a civil charge of rape, this case had been effectively downgraded to one of adultery; five pounds was a typical fine for cases of adultery and seduction. The solicitor general remarked in one case prosecuted in criminal court that the victim's "story as to the rape is an extremely improbable one" and described another as "a very peculiar case."[56] British administrators expected rape victims' bodies to bear the signs of violent struggle, and repeatedly questioned why the victims in ukuzuma cases had not struggled more. While Xhosa men and women took for granted that men might succeed in sneaking in to have sex with an unconsenting woman while she was asleep—and that they deserved to be punished for it—British administrators found the whole idea implausible.

In order to understand such cases, British officials examined the statements of both victims and assailants for explanations other than violent sexual assault. Although most men accused in these sexual assault cases declined to make any statement, a few explained their actions either directly to the court or to others who reported their explanations. Their statements returned again and again to the theme of marriage. In doing so, they located their acts in a particular kind of kin relation, positioning themselves as potential sons-in-law to women's fathers. Kupiso, whose confession resulted in one of the four guilty verdicts, told the court, "I wanted to steal Nontozonke and make her my wife. . . . I woke her up for the purpose of asking her to be my wife." When she refused and began to call for her father, Kupiso "threw her down and ravished her."[57] Nomngqwala also alluded to the connection between marriage and sex when she told the court that her attacker "had every day called me his wife, but I thought he was only joking."[58] The testimony in another case also linked the assault to marriage; Katazwa's erstwhile sweetheart raped her after her father warned him to stay away and arranged her marriage to another, much older, man.[59] Mary's assailant claimed (and she denied) that "I proposed to Mary and she accepted me," seeking to explain his presence in her family's home as a part of courtship behavior.[60] Xam Nkokhla, accused of the rape of a fourteen-year-old girl, reportedly approached her first and "said I want to make you my wife."[61] All of these men framed their assaults in terms of marriage rather than sex.

Women and their families also equated marriage and sex. Jesse Swaartland, assaulted in her own hut at night, testified that she woke up and "asked [her assailant] if I was his wife."[62] Nor was such rhetoric limited to sexual assaults within the home. Nosamunti, assaulted on a footpath, used the same language, also telling the court that she "asked [her assailant] if I was his wife."[63] This man later defended his actions by saying that he "did not know she was a married woman—I thought she was a girl."

These statements should not be taken to indicate approval of the sexual assault of unmarried girls; after all, the men in all of these cases ended up in court. Rather, they suggest that Xhosa men and women perceived a fundamental link between sex and marriage. They objected to sexual assault in part because it was sex outside of marriage—a wrong in and of itself. Litigation over adultery and the seduction of unmarried women formed a substantial portion of the caseload in the civil court system.[64] Indeed, after bridewealth cases, seduction and adultery cases were the most important reasons that magistrates were forced to recognize customary law in their attempts to satisfy Africans' demands for a properly functioning justice system. While seduction and adultery were both torts in Roman-Dutch common law, they had largely fallen into disuse, and the standards of evidence were difficult to meet. Most obviously, suing for adultery under the common law required proof of civil or Christian marriage. Veldtman, a prominent headman living in the Transkei, responded when asked about the defects of colonial law with the complaint that "there is no law providing for the seduction of girls in the colony, and it is equally so with married women. . . . There is no law punishing adultery. A man's wife may return to her friends, and in the colony he cannot get his dowry back."[65] Older African men, at least, were heavily invested in asserting their control over female sexuality through litigation over seduction and adultery.[66]

Marriage itself, however, was a circumstance in which at least some residents of the Eastern Cape sanctioned coercion, and even violence. Ngqaba, a Xhosa man, told the 1883 Commission on Native Law and Custom that a woman "is not consulted" before her marriage:

She is called to the kraal where the men are assembled, and they say to her, "you must smear yourself with red clay to-day, we are going to send you to so-and-so," meaning her intended husband. She then gets herself ready and the bridal party leaves accordingly. Even if the girl says she does not wish to go with the man mentioned, she will be compelled to do so. If she goes to the chief, she would be ordered to obey her parents.[67]

Ngqaba was a relatively wealthy man, with an interest in convincing the colonial government of his rights over his children. He acknowledged under questioning that "sometimes, when she is very obstinate, they send the man's cattle back again" to dissolve the marriage. William Shaw Kama, a well-known chief and Methodist preacher, testified that whereas "according to the old custom, if a girl refused to go where her father wished her, she was beaten," things had changed: "When a girl refuses a marriage because she doesn't like the man who wished to marry her, her will now-a-days carries the point."[68] The necessity of women's consent for marriage was hotly debated in nineteenth-century Xhosaland.

British officials took from such statements the idea—only partially correct, as the caveats of African men themselves reveal—that forced marriages were part of Xhosa custom. They also understood adultery and seduction as wrongs against a girl's family rather than against herself—and in this case, they agreed with the bulk of Xhosa public opinion. In seeking to understand ukuzuma cases, then, they turned to the concepts of seduction, adultery, and even marriage. All of these legal categories fell under customary civil law rather than Roman-Dutch criminal law.

The categorization of ukuzuma rape cases was, theoretically, based on an understanding of Xhosa customary law. However, Xhosa women and their families did not share the need to delineate precisely between civil and criminal offenses. They objected to ukuzuma because it was sex outside marriage, *and* because it was nonconsensual. While Xhosa fathers, in particular, might support coercion in the context of marriage, they were nonetheless indignant about coerced sex outside of marriage. The testimony of Bobani, a sixty-seven-year-old man interviewed in the 1950s, is worth quoting at length:

A person who *zuma* (have sexual relations with women who are asleep) is always having a difficult time because women are always talking about him. . . . All the people of the location are always talking about his ukuzuma (creeping practices). An *izuma* [person who commits ukuzuma] has no *isimilo* [good character] because he is a cruel man. . . . Women dislike an izuma very much. They dislike to have sexual relations with a person who has nothing to do with them (not in love with them). It is like *ukuba* (stealing). . . .

An izuma is like a thief as you would hear people saying to him, since you leave so late in the night you want to take away other people's goats. . . .

Among the Xhosa, the *izimilo* [character traits] that are regarded as *utterly bad* are *ubusela* (thieving) and ukuzuma (creeping). An izuma is hated by everybody. People insult others by *ubuzuma* (being an izuma).[69]

In his explanation—the substance of which is confirmed in other interviews done at the same time—Bobani differentiates ukuzuma from rape committed during the day or by force, but he also distinguishes it sharply from consensual seduction or adultery, such as might occur between a woman and someone who is in love with her. Moreover, he emphasizes the objection of women themselves, rather than their fathers or husbands, to ukuzuma.

In the nineteenth-century cases as well, it is clear that women and their families did not perceive ukuzuma as equivalent to seduction or adultery. They insisted that "I never consented to his having connection with me," or that "I screamed and he got on top of me. . . . I resisted all I could, but he was too strong for me."[70] Many of them desired compensation, and in this the assailants may have been lucky; if not for the British presence, they might have found themselves the recipients of immediate and violent retaliation, which Bobani described as the traditional punishment for ukuzuma: "An izuma . . . is simply caught by the woman victim and then the other women are aroused by her shouts. They all take pieces of wood and attack him. Men also come and hit the izuma."[71] In any case, the women who brought criminal cases after ukuzuma assaults saw no contradiction between their desire for compensation and their assertion that they had been assaulted against their will. They and their families objected to ukuzuma both because it happened outside of marriage and because it was nonconsensual. However, the British colonial legal system could only recognize one or the other wrong. In interpreting ukuzuma sex as a civil offense, best dealt with through customary law, they forced women to choose between defining the wrong done to them as rape, in which case the British courts were likely to reject their claims entirely, and receiving compensation for the wrong done to them.

～

The outcomes of the ukuzuma cases discussed in this chapter were the result of two distinct processes. Men who committed these assaults framed them in terms of marriage, either because they actually aspired to marry the women involved or because they wished to avoid punishment by mimicking consensual sexual relationships. Magistrates were extremely unlikely to find assailants guilty of rape. They believed that sex had occurred but that it was consensual. Any hint that a family sought compensation confirmed this view, as did references to marriage.

Over the long term, the view prevailed that some kinds of sexual assault—particularly those in which assailants aspired to marriage—were appropriately understood not as criminal but rather as customary civil offenses. The British colonial legal system defined certain kinds of assaults as outside the purview of the criminal justice system because of their association with the family. The opposition of customary and criminal law, and the association of the realm of the family with the former, made it almost impossible to prosecute one of the most common types of sexual assault in a criminal court.

Although ukuzuma cases would not meet common descriptions of domestic violence, their outcome was determined by their association with familial categories: seduction, adultery, and marriage. This bifurcation of the legal system into criminal and customary law, combined with an understanding of customary law as the law appropriate for the domestic sphere, set the stage for claims about the customary status of certain kinds of coerced sex, claims that continue to have consequences in contemporary South Africa. By taking men's claims of wanting to marry women as evidence for women's consent to sex, courts naturalized violence within a broad range of "family" relationships.

NOTES

1. Preliminary Evidence in the Case of Christmas, 10/2/93, SGG 1/1/124, Western Cape Provincial Archives and Records Service, Cape Town (hereafter CA). Dates given in court cases refer to the date of file creation or reception, as noted in the SGG series, for ease of reference.

2. MS 16891, Archives of the Institute for Social and Economic Research, Cory Library, Grahamstown (hereafter ISER). Although I have not found the word "ukuzuma" used in nineteenth-century documents—probably because the relevant material is almost all in English—I apply it to the material because the definitions given by this informant and others fit nearly perfectly the set of practices that appear in the nineteenth-century sources. The word is distinguished from *ukudwengula*, which implies rape by violent force.

3. "Sweetheart" was the standard nineteenth-century translation of the Xhosa word *imetsha*, from the verb *ukumetsha*. See a discussion of ukumetsha relationships later in this chapter.

4. For a synthesis of such critiques, see Kristin Kelly, *Domestic Violence and the Politics of Privacy* (Ithaca, NY: Cornell University Press, 2003).

5. Igor Kopytoff and Suzanne Miers, "African 'Slavery' as an Institution of Marginality," in *Slavery in Africa: Historical and Anthropological Perspectives*, ed. Igor

Kopytoff and Suzanne Miers (Madison: University of Wisconsin Press, 1977), 3–81; Timothy Cleaveland, *Becoming Walata: A History of Saharan Social Formation and Transformation* (Portsmouth, NH: Heinemann, 2002).

6. J. H. Soga, *The Ama-Xosa: Life and Customs* (Lovedale, South Africa: Lovedale Press, 1932).

7. The term is borrowed from Margery Wolf, *Women and the Family in Rural Taiwan* (Palo Alto, CA: Stanford University Press, 1972).

8. See Natasha Erlank, "Missionary Views on Sexuality in Xhosaland in the Nineteenth Century," *Le Fait Missionaire* 11 (September 2001): 9–43.

9. 17 January 1884, 1/MDT 1/2/1, CA.

10. Amatole Museum, Record Book of the Supreme Court of British Kaffraria, 25 September 1861.

11. "Mr Brownlee's Notes," in *Compendium of Native Laws and Customs*, ed. John Maclean (Grahamstown, South Africa: J. Slater, 1906), 72.

12. *Report of the Commission on Native Law and Custom, Cape of Good Hope* (Cape Town: Government Printers, 1883), Minutes of Evidence, testimony of Make, Sigidi, Ngcweleshie, Sipiki, et al., 468. Unless otherwise specified, all citations of the commission report refer to the Minutes of Evidence.

13. Although this chapter deals with King William's Town district, this statement applies broadly in the Eastern Cape.

14. See 1/KWT 1/1/1/1–324, CA, for criminal cases. Divorce cases appear most commonly in the informal court system described later in this chapter. The divorce cases are scattered throughout the following series: MDS, 1/MDT, 1/KHK, 1/TAM.

15. See SGG 2/1/1/1–2/1/1/5, CA. These records mention 164 cases of rape and attempted rape, of which 121 had complete records. Of these, 99 involved Africans as both assailants and victims; the 38 cases thus constitute more than a third of the cases of sexual assault between Africans.

16. SGG 1/1/321, CA: Preliminary Examination in the Case of Gijana, 11 January 1888.

17. *Report of the Commission on Native Law and Custom*, Frank Streatfield, 275.

18. Anna Clark, *Women's Silence, Men's Violence: Sexual Assault in England, 1770–1845* (New York: Pandora, 1987), 71. Clark's data suggest that roughly 17 percent of complaints might result in both a trial and a guilty verdict. Clark's data are from the early part of the century and are thus not directly comparable, but they do provide the best published case for comparison.

19. F. G. Gardiner and C. W. H. Lansdowne, *South African Criminal Law and Procedure* (Cape Town: Juta, 1919), 431.

20. The term *civil law* is used throughout this chapter to refer to the body of law defined in opposition to criminal law, and not to refer to a codified system of law defined in opposition to the common law. This usage is congruent with nineteenth-century British practice.

21. A note on terminology: although the word *kaffir*, or *kafir*, became in the twentieth century an extremely denigrating racial insult, it was used in the

nineteenth century as a synonym for *Xhosa*, including by those Xhosa who spoke English. I have tried not to use the word gratuitously in quoted material, but there is no avoiding its presence in the official name for this region for much of the nineteenth century.

22. See John Maclean, ed., *Compendium of Kafir Laws and Customs* (1856; Cape Town, 1906), esp. "Rev H. H. Dugmore's Papers," 35–45.

23. J. D. Warner, "Mr. Warner's Notes," in *Compendium of Kafir Laws and Customs*. Warner equated cases in which the chief kept the fines as criminal cases, and all others as civil cases, but this differentiation is suspect.

24. For a discussion of the impact of this first attempt at annexation on later administrative structures, see Alan Lester, "Settlers, the State, and Colonial Power: The Colonization of Queen Adelaide Province, 1834–37," *Journal of African History* 39, no. 2 (1998): 241–43.

25. Smith to Mackinnon, undated enclosure in Smith to Grey, 4 January 1848, Papers Relative to the State of the Kaffir Tribes, 204, 1847–48, British Parliamentary Papers (hereafter BPP).

26. Despatch from Governor Sir George Grey to the Right Hon. Sir William Molesworthy (No. 46, High Commissioner), 18 December 1855, Further Papers Relative to the State of the Kaffir Tribes, 6 June 1856, No. 9, BPP.

27. Ordinance 1 of 1860, Crown Colony of British Kaffraria.

28. The Cape Colony was governed by a version of Roman-Dutch law with strong English influences, the result of successive Dutch and British colonial regimes. For a concise history of the sources of Cape law, see Reinhard Zimmerman and Daniel Visser, eds., *Southern Cross: Civil Law and Common Law in South Africa* (Oxford: Clarendon Press, 1996).

29. British Kaffraria No. 10 of 1864, same as Cape Colony No. 18 of 1864. Note that the Cape was not the only part of the empire grappling with this problem at the time. In 1865, the Indian Succession Act made similar provisions for British India.

30. The idea of "custom" already had a precise meaning in British law, where popularly accepted rights and responsibilities (usually in the relationship between landholders and surrounding farming communities) carried legal force. (See E. P. Thompson, *Customs in Common: Studies in Traditional Popular Culture* [New York: New Press, 1993]. For a nineteenth-century British perspective on the role of custom in law, see J. H. Balfour Browne, *The Law of Usages and Customs: A Practical Law Tract* [London: Stephen & Haynes, 1875]). Within South Africa, too, the legal concept of custom had played an important role in reconciling the Roman-Dutch and English legal systems. In fact, the failure of Africanists to take into account the history of the idea of custom in British legal thought represents a major failure in our current explanations of the development of customary law in British Africa. However, remedying this gap is beyond the scope of this chapter.

31. Resident Magistrates' Courts Act, No. 20 of 1856, Cape Colony. The act gave magistrates jurisdiction in civil cases where the damages claimed were less than twenty pounds, and in criminal cases where the sentence imposed was less than two years, although the limits of this jurisdiction evolved slightly over the years.

32. *Report and Proceedimgs with Appendices of the Commission on Native Laws and Customs* (Cape Town: W. A. Richards and Sons, 1883), testimony of W. B. Chalmers), 261. *Ukulobola* (to pay bridewealth/*ikazi*) refers to the gift (usually of cattle) made by a husband to his bride's family. If marriages failed, for whatever reason, men commonly brought court cases to demand the return of their bridewealth.

33. Robert J. Dick to Civil Commissioner, King William's Town. Tamacha, 15 January 1890, 1/TAM, CA.

34. *Report of the Commission on Native Laws and Customs*, James Rose Innes, 499.

35. Thus, in Middledrift, the formal court of the resident magistrate, which handled both civil and criminal cases according to Roman-Dutch law, coexisted with an informal court, which handled mostly cases involving bridewealth, seduction, and adultery. Compare 1/KWT H2/2/1, CA, with 1/MDT 3/1/1, CA. When the area received its own magistrate in 1894, he too appears to have operated a parallel court system. Compare 1/MDT 3/1/1/1–12, CA, with 1/MDT 2/2/1/2, CA. For reference to "informal" cases see *Hlakaya v. Kausela*, 23 April 1885, 1/KWT H2/1/2, CA.

36. Letter from H. G. Elliot, Chief Magistrate, Tembuland, *Report of the Commission on Native Laws and Customs*, Appendix I, 396.

37. See Statement by Kama, 22 September 1862, and Statement by Kama, 13 November 1865, BK 88, CA. As the second statement in particular reveals, the hierarchy of judicial authority was closely aligned to the hierarchy of political authority. When a headman complained that Kama did not have the authority to hear appeals from cases that the headman had settled, he did so as part of an assertion that Kama was not, in fact, a chief.

38. See letter from A. Bissett, 18 March 1865, BK 88, CA; 16 August 1886, *Zake v. Cweka*, 1/KWT H2/1/3, CA.

39. Preliminary Examination in the Case of Dyassop, 24/3/93, SGG 1/1/425, CA.

40. Transkei Annexation Act (Act 13 of 1877); Proclamations 110 and 112 of 1879.

41. Martin Chanock, *Law, Custom, and Social Order: The Colonial Experience in Malawi and Zambia* (Cambridge: Cambridge University Press, 1985).

42. P. J. Macdonnel, quoted ibid., 75.

43. Maclean, *Compendium of Kafir Laws*.

44. J. D. Warner, "Mr. Warner's Notes," ibid., 55.

45. William Blackstone, *Commentary on the Laws of England*, 4 vols. (Oxford: Clarendon Press, 1765–69). This characterization of Blackstone's writing is drawn from David Lieberman, "Mapping Criminal Law: Blackstone and the Categories of English Jurisprudence," in *Law, Crime and English Society, 1660–1800*, ed. Norma Landau (Cambridge: Cambridge University Press, 2002), 139–64.

46. Lindsay Farmer, "Reconstructing the English Codification Debate," *Law and History Review* 18, no. 2 (2000): 417–22. See also John Beattie, *Crime and the Courts in England, 1660–1800* (Princeton, NJ: Princeton University Press, 1986), 457; Norma Landau, "Indictment for Fun and Profit: A Prosecutor's Reward at

Eighteenth-Century Quarter Sessions," *Law and History Review* 17, no. 3 (1999): 507–36.

47. Peter King, "Punishing Assault: The Transformation of Attitudes in the English Courts," *Journal of Interdisciplinary History* 27, no. 1 (1996): 49.

48. William Brownlee, "The Transkeian Territories: Notes on Native Law and Customs. Part I," *Journal of the Royal African Society* 24, no. 95 (1925): 111.

49. See William Felstiner, Richard Abel, and Austin Sarat, "The Emergence and Transformation of Disputes: Naming, Blaming, Claiming . . . ," *Law and Society Review* 15, no. 3 (1980–81): 631–54.

50. Preliminary Evidence in the Case of Bantshu, 12 May 1876, SGG 1/1/118, CA.

51. Preliminary Examination in the Case of Jordan, 2 May1880, SGG 1/1/181, CA.

52. Preliminary Examination in the Case of Dickaway, 2 June 1894, SGG 1/1/448, CA.

53. Preliminary Evidence in the Case of Bantshu, 12 May 1876, SGG 1/1/118, CA.

54. *Songo v. Nongqala*, 8 May 1884, 1/KWT H/2/2/1, CA.

55. *Nante v. Botshani*, 7 June 1875, MDS 2, CA.

56. Preliminary Examination in the Case of Nywebeni, 26 June 1874, SGG 1/1/97, CA; Preliminary Examination in the Case of Kwahluka, 2 October 1868, SGG 1/1/28, CA.

57. Preliminary Examination in the Case of Kupiso, 7 March 1870, SGG 1/1/62, CA.

58. Preliminary Examination in the Case of Gqeke, 25 January 1/77, SGG 1/1/135, CA.

59. Preliminary Examination in the Case of Jordan, 10 August 1880, SGG 1/1/181, CA.

60. Preliminary Examination in the Case of Bota Soduwa, 4 May 1893, SGG 1/1/442, CA.

61. Preliminary Examination in the Case of Xam Nkokhla, 6 January 1897, SGG 1/1/535, CA.

62. Preliminary Examination in the Case of Kolis Lukazi, 4 May 1897, SGG 1/1/535, CA.

63. Preliminary Examination in the Case of Dyassop, 24 March 1893, SGG 1/1/425, CA.

64. Not all sex outside of marriage was subject to litigation; widows and divorced women were permitted greater sexual freedom.

65. Testimony of Veldtman, *Report of the Commission on Native Law and Custom*, 476.

66. For an analysis of the meaning of seduction and adultery litigation to women and younger men, see Pule Phoofolo, "Female Extramarital Relationships and Their Regulation in Early Colonial Thembuland, South Africa, 1875–95," *Journal of Family History* 30, no. 1 (2005): 3–47.

67. Testimony of Ngqaba, *Report of the Commission on Native Law and Custom*, 94.

68. Testimony of William Shaw Kama, *Report of the Commission on Native Law and Custom*, 240.

69. MS 16891, ISER. Translations or explanations in parentheses are original to the transcription; those in brackets are my own.

70. Preliminary Examination in the Case of Jacob Gawshe, 26 September 1876, SGG 1/1/124, CA; Preliminary Examination in the Case of Somnazi, 3 January 1895, SGG 1/1/493, CA.

71. MS 16891, ISER.

6 ↫ Child Marriage and Domestic Violence

Islamic and Colonial Discourses on Gender Relations and Female Status in Zanzibar, 1900–1950s

ELKE E. STOCKREITER

ISLAMIC COURT RECORDS and archival sources reveal rare evidence about the approaches of Muslim judges, known as qadis on the Swahili coast, and British colonial officers to incidents of domestic violence and child marriage in Zanzibar from 1900 until the 1950s. Even though the Penal Decree of 1934 made it an offense to cause a woman below the age of thirteen to be married and raped, thus explicitly linking child marriage to child wives' exposure to rape and domestic violence, colonial officials failed to provide redress to child wives and women suffering from domestic violence. Colonial officers' failure to address these sensitive issues derived from their ambivalent attitude toward Islamic law. On the one hand, colonial representatives avoided interference with Islamic family law, which they recognized as the blueprint of Zanzibar's social order.[1] On the other hand, due to a colonial bias against Islamic law, reforms restricted qadis' jurisdiction to civil cases and obliged qadis to enforce common law-based rules of evidence and procedure. As qadis continuously applied Islamic rules of evidence and colonial rules of procedure, wives' success in establishing claims of domestic violence in the qadi's courts was limited. Qadis refused to dissolve marital ties on the ground of the husband's cruelty if the wife failed to provide witnesses who proved her claim. The social and economic importance of marriage, which was the only accepted form of a partnership, further accounted for qadis' reluctance to pronounce a divorce.

In the late 1940s, economic instability due to a decline in the export of cloves followed Zanzibar's prosperous economic period during World War II and contributed to the frequent occurrence of child marriage in rural areas, which then came to the attention of colonial officers. While Islamic law allows the contraction of child marriage, it prohibits its consummation until the wife is physically mature. Ensuing debates on child marriage reveal that qadis sought to reconcile Islamic legal regulations with colonial sensibilities and local practice, while colonial interference in private matters of the sultan's subjects was largely constrained by acknowledging Zanzibar's patriarchal social structure and fear of Muslim opposition. In this chapter I argue that in interplay with local constructions of gender norms, British colonial officers' interpretation of Islamic law pertaining to child marriage and women's status provided little redress for Zanzibari girls and women trying to escape domestic violence. As the civil cases referring to domestic violence I studied are scattered over the first half of the twentieth century, I provide an exemplary account of qadis' approach toward this issue rather than a chronological account.

HISTORICAL AND LEGAL BACKGROUND

The island of Zanzibar and the island of Pemba became part of the Omani Sultanate in the early nineteenth century. The Omani Bu Saidi sultans pioneered the institutionalization of Zanzibar's Islamic legal system, which was first established in town and later expanded into rural areas. Since the Omani dynasty adhered to the Ibadi creed, the sultans appointed Ibadi qadis in addition to qadis administering Shafi'i law to the predominantly Sunni population. There are four schools of law in Sunni Islam: Hanafi, Hanbali, Maliki and Shafi'i. Along the East African coast, the Shafi'i school has spread since the introduction of Islam in the eighth century.[2]

The British approach toward Islamic law in Zanzibar circumscribed qadis' application of shari'a during the colonial period. When Zanzibar became a British Protectorate in 1890, the British agreed to preserve at least formally the islands' political structure as a sultanate and Islamic law as its legal basis. In accordance with the policy of "indirect rule," Islamic law remained the fundamental law throughout the colonial period. However, driven by a strong bias against its application, the colonial government interfered considerably in the Islamic legal sphere, reducing the scope of jurisdiction of the qadi's courts and ousting Islamic legal rules by enacting orders in council and colonial decrees. From the early nineteenth century onward, British and other European powers sought to remove European subjects from the sultan's jurisdiction and bring them under British jurisdiction. From as early as 1822 various treaties that sanctioned the interference of foreign powers with the sultan's jurisdiction laid the basis for this aim.[3]

Because British officials conceived of Islamic law as irrational, draconian in some respects while too lenient in others,[4] criminal jurisdiction was taken away from the qadis from 1908 onward.[5] The supposed irrationality of Islamic law was informed by the lack of written records and alleged procedural deficiencies. *Hadd* punishment in criminal cases, which, depending on the

offense, prescribes amputation of limbs, lashing, or stoning, prompted accusations of brutality.[6] To the relief of the British resident, Major F. B. Pearce, "the
mutilation of criminals by cutting off their hands for theft, which was only too
frequent an occurrence in the Eastern code of justice, administered under
autocratic auspices"[7] was not applied in Zanzibar. Yet a strong colonial bias
against shari'a remained. The British acknowledgment of Zanzibar as an Arab
sultanate and perception of a patriarchal social structure also shaped their
understanding of women's status on the island.

COLONIAL DISCOURSES ON THE STATUS OF WOMEN
AND QADIS' APPROACH TO DOMESTIC VIOLENCE

In Zanzibar visible manifestations of gender relations both informed and dis-
torted colonial officers' understanding of women's status. Obvious features
were the ideologies of purdah and patriarchy,[8] subject to continuous debates
by colonial representatives, who almost exclusively referred to women by
their "purdah habit."[9] When the sultan's role as arbitrator was discussed in
1930, Chief Justice G. H. Pickering argued that his exercise of judicial powers "would be to some extent a protection to Arab ladies, whose dread of the
publicity of an open Court, certainly places them under a disability when
their interests conflict with male members of their family."[10] Similarly, the
Marriage and Divorce (Mahommedan) Registration Decree, No. 8, 1935, acknowledged the practice of women observing purdah and therefore provided
that these women would not have to appear before the registrar but may give
their signature in the presence of only the husband or guardian.[11]

British perceptions of women's status in Zanzibari society, built on obvious
symbols of male dominance, such as purdah and veiling, were exacerbated by
understanding Islamic laws as discriminating against women. These perceptions
focused on the unequal distribution of rights and duties between the spouses,
such as polygyny, the husband's unilateral right of divorce by repudiation, and
the guardianship of women in marriage. According to Shafi'i and Ibadi laws,
women need a male guardian to contract a marriage. Under Shafi'i law, virgins can be given into marriage by their father and paternal grandfather
without their consent, although the girl or woman should be consulted.[12]
Ibadis hold that only minor virgins can be married off against their will, and
they can petition for the dissolution of their marriage upon attainment of
majority.[13] Although under Islamic law the dower is the property of the wife,
by Zanzibari custom, her elders received the dower from the husband and
decided whether to hand over the entire amount to her. Such complementary
rather than egalitarian constructions of the relationship between husband and
wife created potential conflict but also offered bargaining opportunities for the
wife. Legally, the husband is the sole provider and has to maintain the wife as

long as she is obedient to him. The husband's failure to provide maintenance is a ground for divorce under Shafi'i and Ibadi laws.

The wife's obedience to the husband is based on the Qur'an 4:34, which may be interpreted as allowing the husband to chastise the wife, if necessary by beating, thus justifying domestic violence. Some classical jurists argued that the beating could range from being merely symbolic, such as with a small stick that the Prophet used to clean his teeth, to forceful corporal punishment.[14] Hemedi, a Shafi'i qadi in Tanga, Tanganyika, who retired in 1934, argued that the husband could respond to a disobedient wife by leaving her bed. If she persisted in her disobedience, "he may strike her, but not so as to cause her actual harm, only gently. If she still does not listen, he should bring her before the Kadhi."[15] El-Busaidy, who served as provincial administrator, magistrate, and on the bench in the court of appeal in Tanganyika,[16] held that Islam permitted the husband to beat his wife, though not with strokes that might hurt her, but only in a way to admonish and frighten her. Also, the husband should take care not to hurt the wife on "certain limbs as well as in the face."[17] He added that it was contrary to Islamic law to beat the wife for an unlawful reason and to hurt her badly.[18] This indicates that Swahili jurists cautioned husbands about using force against recalcitrant wives, yet as they did not strictly forbid husbands to strike their wives, they also provided justification for corporal punishment of wives.

It is a striking indication of female agency that incidents of domestic violence found entry into civil cases adjudicated by qadis. From 1900 to the 1950s, not more than fifteen scholars served as qadis, which indicates that the resolution of disputes in the qadi's courts was left to a few individuals, chosen and appointed by the colonial government.[19] In the period after 1908, when qadis tried only civil cases, incidents of domestic violence appear to have been settled in the first instance by *shehas*, village or town elders, and *mudirs*, in charge of a district, or *mudiria*. If parties wanted to file an accusation, they had to address the magistrate's court. Under Shafi'i and Ibadi laws, the wife may petition the court for a dissolution of her marriage on the ground of defects of the husband (such as impotence, incurable or infectious disease) and his willful nonprovision of maintenance. Ibadi rules also recognize cruelty as grounds for such a petition. Wives referred to incidents of cruelty to back up claims for maintenance, dower, and/or the dissolution of their marriage, as well as to justify why they had left the matrimonial home if their husband sued for restitution of conjugal rights. Although cruelty does not constitute a ground for divorce per se under Shafi'i law, Shafi'i qadis may order a temporary judicial separation in case of domestic violence. How qadis approached allegations of the husband's cruelty toward the wife are important indications of qadis' support of women's rights within the framework of Islamic law.[20]

Although interpretations of Islamic law provide different options for Ibadi and Shafi'i qadis in case of the wife's ill-treatment by her husband, the realization of Shafi'i and Ibadi qadis' power to enable women to escape domestic violence was strikingly similar. Unfortunately, qadi's court records rarely provide the context for incidents of domestic violence, most probably because they were not the focus of the claim, nor do these records reveal the range of the social networks of the litigants. When Ameir[21] sued his wife Chausiku for restitution of conjugal rights in 1909, Chausiku, most likely a former slave, countered that she had left him because of ill-treatment. In response to the wife's assertion that she left her husband because of a beating, the Ibadi qadi Sheikh (Sh.) Ali b. Muhammad al-Mundhiri[22] asked her to bring witnesses. Although Chausiku said there were witnesses, they did not appear in court.[23] In another restitution of conjugal rights case of that year, Sh. Ali did not seem to consider the wife's counterclaim that her husband had beaten her, previously resulting in a mediation and reconciliation between the spouses. As the wife insisted on a divorce, Sh. Ali proposed that the couple should agree on its terms. They agreed that the wife would financially compensate her husband for the divorce.[24]

The Ibadi qadi Sh. Said b. Nasir al-Ghaythi took a more sympathetic approach toward a wife's claim as it was substantiated by evidence. In 1941, Khamisi b. Mwinyisheha was sued by his wife Mwanaidi bt. Fundi Kombo for maintenance and suitable accommodation or divorce. Khamisi was known for his bad behavior, "even by the neighbors whose houses are distant from him."[25] Although the husband's cruelty was not mentioned in the plaint, Sh. Said b. Nasir found that the wife should not return to her husband "until she agrees with her heart to his company."[26] Among the witnesses whom the wife brought were her mother, described by the qadi as a virtuous, trustworthy person, and Ibadi qadi Sh. Said b. Rashid al-Ghaythi. Based on the husband's established violent behavior and his failure to provide maintenance as well as suitable accommodation, the qadi ruled for a judicial separation until the husband complied with this order. The qadi, however, did not dissolve the marriage, possibly because cruelty was not mentioned as grounds for divorce in the plaint.[27]

Wives' claims of cruelty were shaped by the strict rules of procedure laid down by colonial reforms as well as the necessity of obtaining proof under Islamic law. Colonial rules of procedure obliged qadis to refer domestic violence cases to magistrates, while Islamic laws of evidence, which qadis continued to apply even though the Evidence Decree of 1917 excluded Islamic rules of evidence from the courts,[28] demanded testimonies from two upright male Muslim witnesses, or one male and two female witnesses, to establish claims of cruelty. In 1943, the Ibadi qadi Sh. Said b. Rashid al-Ghaythi responded to a wife's claim of judicial separation on the ground of ill-treatment (beating and sexual intercourse during her menstruation)[29] by pointing out that this claim could not be heard unless an accusation was filed. Aware of the colonial boundaries of his jurisdiction, the qadi referred the wife to the magistrate's court where criminal cases were tried.[30] Yet Sh. Said b. Rashid accepted the claim of Sheikha bt. Umar b. Muhammad al-Barwani that her husband forced her to forgo her dower, furniture, and household items because two male witnesses confirmed this claim. The husband had previously been fined by the magistrate for beating.[31] When Khadija bt. Seif b. Hamid al-Ba Kathir filed for judicial divorce on the ground of cruelty, the same qadi dissolved her marriage because two male witnesses confirmed the wife's mistreatment by her husband and his father. The court records reveal that the couple sought previous mediation after a fight that had left the wife with a mark on her hand. The mediator, possibly a mudir or sheha, ordered her to return to the husband.[32] In a case of 1956, the Ibadi qadi Sh. Muhammad b. Salim Ruwwahi ruled that the wife's ground for divorce, her husband's cruelty, was not proven since she failed to provide witnesses. Therefore, the qadi regarded her moving out of the matrimonial home as disobedience.[33] Although Ibadi qadis could dissolve a marriage on the ground of cruelty, they seem to have strictly adhered to the establishment of evidence by two male witnesses for such claims. Neighbors and relatives appear to have been those most likely in a position to testify against husbands' cruelty toward wives.[34] Given the difficulties of providing witnesses for acts of domestic violence due to the intimate nature of these acts and arguably the reluctance of neighbors and relatives to take side, the rules of evidence worked to the disadvantage of women.[35]

Shafi'i qadis also required substantial evidence for allegations of cruelty. In 1913 Sh. Tahir b. Abibakr al-Amawi[36] did not record Fatma bt. Abdallah al-Yarubi's allegation that her husband had intercourse with her during her menstruation. Fatma reasoned that "Sh Tahir did not record it perhaps because it is such a disgraceful thing."[37] On appeal, she referred to this incident as a ground for divorce. The unlawful incident was not cast as rape but rather in Islamic terms, as an impermissible act, since menstruation temporarily puts women into a state of impurity. In this appeal case, the two qadis and the British judge[38] considered the witness who corroborated Fatma's account, her *ayah*, or nurse, as hostile toward the husband. They held that there was no substantial proof to establish the allegation of unlawful intercourse. Fatma further mentioned that her husband had threatened her. Yet again, she failed to substantiate her claim to the satisfaction of the court.[39] In several other cases in which wives claimed to have been suffering from the husband's violent behavior, their allegations were not considered by Shafi'i qadis because they failed to produce evidence for their claims.[40]

However, if a wife could prove ill-treatment, Shafi'i qadis might order her to live near a trustworthy person. Shafi'i qadi Sh. Tahir applied this rule in a case of 1932, in which relatives confirmed the wife's maltreatment,[41] and in another case of 1927, in which neighbors gave testimony that the husband had beaten his wife. In the latter case, Sh. Tahir took it as a sign of the husband's guilt that he remained silent. Yet Sh. Tahir made the wife swear an oath that she left her husband in fear and not in disobedience. Having established the husband's cruelty, the wife was entitled to maintenance, even though she did not stay with the husband.[42]

Under Islamic law, a husband may make divorce contingent on a certain condition, such as drinking alcohol or beating his wife. Such a divorce is known as a suspended divorce. The divorce is effected when this condition has occurred. In 1905 Shafi'i qadi Sh. Burhan b. Abd al-Aziz al-Amawi[43] pronounced a divorce that the husband had suspended upon beating his wife. The beating was confirmed by witnesses, whose relationship to the wife, however, was not indicated.[44] When Mwamini bt. Baruti sued her husband Zuberi b. Hamedi for divorce in 1919, which he had suspended on receiving financial compensation from her, she argued that he had annoyed and beaten her. Sh. Burhan did not pursue these implications of cruelty, most likely because the case focused on the divorce bargain and Mwamini's claim that she had handed over money to Zuberi so he would divorce her.[45]

In these examples of civil suits, revolving around the unequal rights and duties between the spouses, wives backed up claims for divorce or countered the husband's allegation of disobedience by referring to his cruelty. Both Shafi'i and Ibadi qadis did not readily pursue allegations of domestic violence, as they felt obliged to adhere to their scope of jurisdiction and rules of evidence. Wives faced considerable difficulties in providing witnesses; without such proof, however, qadis considered wives who left their violent husband disobedient. In practice, qadis' emphasis on procedure prioritized the maintenance of marriage as a social institution over women's rights to leave a violent husband, while rhetorically confirming this right.

CHILD MARRIAGE, LEGAL NORMS, AND SOCIAL PRACTICE

Debates on child marriage in Zanzibar reveal the power constellation among the actors and the interplay of customary norms, colonial law, and shari'a during a period of socioeconomic changes. The frequent occurrence of child marriages in the late 1940s coincided with a period of economic difficulties in the years after World War II, when Zanzibar's main export product, cloves, yielded poor harvests. The negative ramifications on the population were compounded by droughts threatening crops and food production.[46] At the same time, the institution of marriage underwent a publicly debated crisis, which turned around exorbitant demands of dower by elders and the balance of power between husband and kin. These debates centered on the material implications of marriage, as some men reproached elders for requesting inflated amounts of dower and additional markers of status, such as jewelry, a wedding dress, or a cook.[47] In rural areas, dire financial straits caused some elders to send minor daughters to their husbands and keep the dower for themselves, even though Shafi'i and Ibadi laws state that a child wife should stay with her family until she becomes mature. Elders' violation of this provision exposed child wives to cruelty and premature consummation of the marriage according to shari'a as well as colonial law if the wife was below the age of thirteen. Even though child marriages violated colonial penal law, most colonial officers tolerated this practice. Acknowledging the public consensus on the acceptability of child marriage, British colonial officials were reluctant to intervene. Public opinion, the government's acceptance of a patriarchal social structure, and misconceptions about Islamic legal doctrines shaped the lives of Zanzibari minor girls, whose inferior sociolegal status made them especially vulnerable.

Informed by an understanding of restricted female agency, colonial interference in the application of Islamic law in Zanzibar appears to have had the direct intention neither of improving women's lot nor of curtailing their rights. Exploring the complexity of marital practices and colonial rule in Gusiiland, Kenya, Brett Shadle describes colonial reluctance in intervening in forced marriage and bridewealth disputes.[48] The approach of individual officers toward women was characterized by an underlying ambiguity and contradiction, as Elizabeth Schmidt has suggested for colonial Zimbabwe.[49] If women benefited from colonial enactments pertaining to marriage, it was rather a by-product of the government's primary goal of maintaining social order. As in other Muslim countries, compulsory registration of marriages increased colonial control over Zanzibari subjects while theoretically making child marriages more difficult.[50]

In the Palestinian context, Annelies Moors argues that the state revised forms of marriage contracts (for instance, by allowing stipulations) to achieve changes in legal gender relations without changing the law. How women made use of this provision seemed to depend on their social background.[51] In Zambia in the 1930s, the colonial administration debated the compulsory registration of marriage to reestablish elders,' women's, and men's belief in marriage.[52] While legislative intentions in requiring the registration of marriage may have varied, there do not seem to be any indications that the colonial government in Zanzibar had any larger goals than keeping track of marital ties. The compulsory registration of marriage was part of colonial legal reforms, tailored to establish and maintain a bureaucratic framework and to bring the native population closer to modernity.

In Zanzibar, marriage contracts seem to have been concluded mostly, if not exclusively, orally.[53] After the Marriage and Divorce (Mahommedan) Registration Decree of 1922 made the registration of marriages compulsory, marriage registers provided evidence of between whom and under which conditions marriages were contracted.[54] These registers recorded the bride's minority or majority under Islamic law, the amount of dower, and the names of the guardian and the witnesses. They served as evidence in future disputes, providing security for the wife and enabling her to back up claims in court.[55] Although the government form lacked a column for stipulations, usually registrars and qadis registered requests by the wife not to move to the countryside or to stay in her own house, which suggests that they supported women's concerns.[56] A different picture, however, emerges regarding the registration of minor wives. Even though marriage officers attested to the frequent occurrence of the consummation of child marriages in rural areas,[57] samples from the registers in Zanzibar Town show very few minor brides, which suggests that registrars failed to verify the wife's age. Since registrars rarely entered minor brides, the registration of marriage did not prove to be a safeguard for minor girls.

The consummation of child marriages, in which the wife is below the age of puberty, illustrates on the one hand the divergence of customary practices and Shafi'i as well as Ibadi laws, and on the other how the latter were reconciled with colonial decrees through the mediation of qadis and colonial officers. Possibly seeking to appease the Muslim population, colonial officers interpreted shari'a as legitimizing child marriages, whereas qadis interpreted it in support of the Penal Decree of 1934. Section 133 (2) of this decree made it an offense for a man to have intercourse with his wife below both puberty and the age of thirteen, unless it was reasonable that he may have thought that she was older. Under this decree, it was also a criminal act to take away or detain a woman, or cause her to be married and raped.[58] These stipulations might have led to the punishment of a father or grandfather who, following Shafi'i law, exercised his right to marry off his virgin daughter or granddaughter without her consent.[59]

Work by Kristin Mann and Richard Roberts elsewhere in Africa, as well as by Allan Christelow in Algeria, has outlined how European officers' condemnation of child marriage during the early colonial period slowly evolved into a preoccupation with women's lack of morality during the later years of colonial rule.[60] In Zanzibar, at least one European official, the senior welfare officer Ian Edward Ferguson Moultrie, embarked on a mission to save child wives in the late colonial period. I have not found evidence that would yield insight into the colonial government's approach toward this issue in the early colonial period. As for qadis, a case filed in Zanzibar Town in 1902 attests to the astonishment of the Ibadi qadi about the young age of a wife whom her husband sued for disobedience. Given that the wife obviously was a minor, given into marriage by her father, the qadi sent her to stay with her parents until her majority.[61] As evident in this case, qadis distinguished between contracting and consummating a child marriage. Under Shafi'i and Ibadi laws, a marriage can be consummated only if the wife is "physically ready."[62] However, since by consensus among Muslim scholars puberty starts at the age of nine,[63] this rule still allowed the consummation of child marriages by Western, twentieth-century standards. Lacking additional evidence, we can at least assume that qadis followed Islamic legal regulations and prohibited sexual intercourse with child wives below the age of nine.

After World War II, Zanzibaris faced general economic difficulties, including scarcity of goods and rising costs of living while wages largely remained steady. These problems, compounded by poor work conditions predominantly affecting migrant workers from the mainland, led to a general strike in 1948. Eventually not only dock workers but African women and men in domestic service and casual laborers participated in this strike, which brought the economy in Zanzibar Town to a halt during August and September 1948. This general strike not only paralyzed the island's urban center but also caused severe food shortages in rural areas.[64] These food shortages may have caused parents to send their children to work in domestic service in town, as described by the acting British resident in 1949.[65] It is difficult to establish the precise impact of these general economic crises after World War II on households whose elders allowed the consummation of child marriages by sending minor daughters to stay with their husband. Difficult material circumstances seem to have forced elders to cede to the husband's request to have the wife stay at his place, as the husband had to provide maintenance for the wife once the marriage was consummated. It is likely that material deprivation played a decisive factor in the practice of child marriages in rural areas, such as Makunduchi, where 70 percent of the peasants mortgaged their coconut trees to eke out a living between clove harvests in the 1940s.[66]

In November 1949, the mudir of Mkokotoni addressed the senior commissioner about marriages of girls, aged ten to twelve years, to elderly men. Their fathers had married them off for a dower and a customary present. The mudir suggested that measures should be introduced to stop girls getting married below the age of fifteen.[67] However, he failed to receive support from other mudirs. When the district commissioner raised this issue with villagers in Makunduchi, they argued that early marriage dissuaded girls from "going astray."[68] They further justified the practice by saying that if the girls were married to boys of their age, they would engage in "promiscuity." Partly convinced, and mainly concerned about the consequences of any attempt at interference, the district commissioner postponed any action until a future change in public opinion: "and not till then do we have the right to make laws about so private a matter."[69]

In 1956, "so private a matter" again came to the notice of colonial officers. On 30 May 1956, Zena bt. Rafiki, about nine years old, arrived at Ng'ambo police station in Zanzibar Town after being assaulted by her husband. The husband, Vuai b. Mkomo, was charged by the police officer because the senior welfare officer Ian Moultrie insisted that a sexual assault had occurred.[70] About three years earlier, Zena's father had brought her from Pemba to Zanzibar to be raised by her aunt, Binti Farahani. Vuai b. Mkomo, the husband of Binti Farahani in whose house Zena lived, married Zena without the consent of her father before Binti Farahani died. After Binti Farahani's death, her paternal sisters and their mother wanted to raise Zena, but Vuai refused and took her to the countryside.[71] Although the senior resident magistrate made a serious effort to entice Vuai to divorce Zena, Vuai refused until he was promised that the prosecution would be dropped. The senior welfare officer Moultrie was skeptical of parents' innocence in cases of child marriage such as Zena's. Since a previous case of child marriage had also not resulted in any consequences for the husband, Moultrie was worried about the precedent being set and launched inquiries.[72]

Moultrie gathered another piece of evidence when he heard about the arrangement of a secret adoption of a baby, whose mother was twelve years old, in Makunduchi. He found out that the girl was only one among several child mothers in the area and was disturbed that some of his colleagues were party to the "concealment of felony."[73] Despite Moultrie's concern about this issue, the senior commissioner was reluctant to press for change, for fear of hurting Muslim feelings and possibly causing unrest.[74] Obsessed with this issue, Moultrie felt ignored because no action was taken and the cover-up of such offenses by colonial officers confirmed as government policy. His insistent letters began to annoy the senior commissioner, who scribbled "So what?" in the margin of Moultrie's letter.[75]

Despite the promises made to Vuai b. Mkomo, Zena's case was tried before the resident magistrate's court in 1957. The man who had contracted her marriage on 11 February 1955 was Ameir Tajo, a well-known sheikh and member of the Legislative and the Executive Councils who would become chief qadi under the revolutionary government. Sh. Tajo registered that Zena's father authorized the marriage. The assistant judge, E. J. E. Law, described Zena as "a simple young village girl, [who] took the extreme step of leaving her husband and putting herself under the protection of the police. She would not have taken such a step unless sthg. [something] very serious had happened."[76] Assistant Judge Law clearly contrasted modern British values with Muslim tradition, referring to the Prophet's marriage with Aisha, but maintaining that circumstances had changed. He expressed distaste for the practice of child marriage and pointed to the alleged inadaptability of shari'a. However, despite Law's harsh words and his finding that Vuai b. Mkomo was guilty of defiling Zena, the penalty was mild. Law argued that the girl had suffered no harm, nearly attained puberty and was Vuai's wife. He declared Vuai a sick man, unfit for imprisonment. Law acknowledged the severity of the case and the harm done to Zena but set a different example with his sentence: one day of imprisonment and a fine of one hundred shillings.[77] The maximum sentence for this crime was imprisonment for life.

Correspondence between colonial officers reveals that this ambiguous stance on child marriages was not unique. The acting attorney general N. P. Carrick-Allan expressed an opinion that echoed Law's rhetoric even as he disputed the outcome. Carrick-Allan acknowledged the difficulties in obtaining evidence and the general feeling among Zanzibaris against prosecution in such cases. Nevertheless, it appeared to him that the punishment contradicted modern ideas of decency and the protection of children. In his opinion, the sentence should have shown the government's disapproval of such practices, and he considered protesting to the chief justice.[78]

Once Moultrie had embarked on his mission to save child wives from their misery, he worked continuously on this issue. On 27 May 1957, Moultrie replied to the chief secretary's and the senior commissioner's memorandum on institutions and practices similar to slavery by saying that a practice similar to slavery indeed existed in Zanzibar. "[A] woman, without the right to refuse, is given in marriage on payment of a consideration in money or in kind to her parents."[79] Thus referring to the father's (and grandfather's) right to give his virgin daughter into marriage against her wish, Moultrie explained that in rural areas, the father did not give the dower to his daughter, who did not sue her father for it. Moultrie assumed that

> 6. [t]he sanctions which compel a woman to accept a condition similar to slavery would appear to be the obligation on grounds of conscience in accordance with her religion and the economic compulsion of the need of maintenance either by her husband or parents.

> 7. If my understanding of Muslim shari'a is correct it is difficult to see what can be done without giving offence to Muslims to prevent the occurrence of adult women being married without their consent. I gather that such marriages are rare and may be expected to become progressively more rare with any decrease in the economic disabilities of Muslim women.[80]

What Moultrie could not accept and pursued until exhaustion, to the annoyance of his superiors, was the practice of forced marriages of minor girls. He thereby ignored instructions from magistrates and the probation officer not to pursue criminal proceedings, which indicates once more the anxiety of some government representatives about provoking Muslim opposition as well as the acknowledgment of "patriarchal Arab rule."[81]

Moultrie considered that introducing a minimum age of marriage, like that in Egypt, would solve the problem.[82] He proposed a plan of action that envisaged Ramadan broadcasts by qadi Sh. Abdallah Salih Farsy, explanatory meetings by qadi Sh. Umar b. Ahmad b. Sumayt and Sh. Abdallah with marriage officers and policemen, shehas and prominent members of society in rural areas, as well as the launch of a program to educate the public about Islamic regulations of marriage.[83] Sh. Umar and Sh. Abdallah should talk to male schoolteachers who would then instruct boys of their roles as husbands and fathers in higher classes of boys' schools. For girls, however, it was agreed that sexual matters should not be discussed with "immature [sic] children."[84] Only girls who had attained the age of puberty would be instructed in their roles as mothers and aunts.[85] It appears that colonial officers shared with male Muslims the perception that women needed to be protected. Thus men decided that women only needed information on how to duly fulfill their prescribed social roles as mothers and kin.

In their memorandum issued after a meeting with the senior education officer on 1 April 1957, the Shafi'i qadis Sh. Umar and Sh. Abdallah mentioned as first point the local inapplicability of the Hanafi doctrine, under which an adult woman can give herself into marriage and a minor can dissolve a forced marriage upon attainment of majority, if someone other than the father or paternal grandfather was the guardian.[86] The dissolution of forced marriages, however, was possible under Ibadi law, whose adherents had largely converted to the Shafi'i school by the late 1950s. The two Shafi'i qadis made clear in their memorandum that the Penal Decree did not contradict shari'a. They argued that under shari'a, nine years was the absolute minimum age of a wife, and since it was forbidden for a husband to have intercourse with a wife below the age of puberty, the Penal Decree, which postulated the age of thirteen, being above and not below the minimum age under shari'a, conformed with shari'a. They further reminded marriage registrars of their duty and made clear that an adult wife could not refuse intercourse unless on one of the grounds acceptable under shari'a.[87]

While finding a compromise between shari'a and the Penal Decree, the qadis did not deviate from what they believed to be substantial requirements of a Shafi'i marriage, such as the wife's physical maturity for its consummation, two witnesses, and the wife's consent unless she was a virgin. This suggests that qadis sought to reconcile contradictory attitudes of colonial officers and fellow Muslims pertaining to child marriage. The qadis condemned the consummation of such marriages, though not their conclusion. Given the dire financial straits of parents, some (elderly) men took advantage of this situation and consummated the marriage with minor girls who, according to Islamic legal rules, were not physically ready for intercourse.

The outcome of Moultrie's efforts was a booklet. Supported by the qadis, whom he held as influential, and the chief justice, he thus aimed to convince Muslims that shari'a conformed with the criminal law in force.[88]

> In a campaign against the custom of child marriage it appeared that the instruction given to the public by Kadhis and other Muslim teachers had beneficial effects, and that the only further measure needed was legislation to ensure that all Muslim marriage solemnisations should be conducted by or in the presence of a Register [sic] of Marriages who had been fully instructed by a Kadhi, and that in the case of marriage to child brides the parties should be made fully aware of the provisions of the Protectorate's penal laws for the protection of child wives. To that end the Senior Welfare Officer submitted draft amendments to the Marriage and Divorce (Mohammedan) Registration Decree 1935 which were under consideration at the end of the year [1960].[89]

Although the Annual Report of 1960 draws a largely optimistic picture of Moultrie's mission, further historical inquiries are needed to reveal whether women actually benefited from this campaign and whether the consummation of child marriage was prevented by educating the Muslim population about Islamic law.

ᗐ

This chapter has shown that the legal framework created during the colonial period, with qadis' strict application of the rules of procedure and evidence being compounded by the presence of the colonial supervisor, was the biggest obstacle women faced in escaping domestic violence. Women's agency in court is manifest in their attempts to refer to husbands' acts of violence as a legal strategy in order to support or counter claims. Although Ibadi qadis could dissolve a marriage on the ground of cruelty, they insisted on establishing evidence and tried to achieve a reconciliation before granting a divorce. Their reluctance to help wives escape permanently from domestic violence raises further questions about the institution of marriage in Zanzibari society. Marriage was the only socially accepted form of partnership and was an expense for the husband, who had to provide the dower and maintain the wife. I suggest that the social importance of marriage and husbands' perception of marriage as a material investment accounts for qadis' approach to domestic violence—their unwillingness to easily dissolve socially and materially important marital ties.

The debates on child marriage, whose consummation was recognized as a cause of domestic violence and was an offense under the Penal Decree of 1934, demonstrate how British perceptions of women's sociolegal status shaped their restrictive, individual agency, characterized by ambiguity and a patriarchal view of local social structures. Qadis sought to accommodate the Penal Decree with Islamic law, yet clearly differentiated between the contraction of child marriages and their consummation. They thereby adopted a solution that sought to protect minor girls and suited social practice. Since the cases of child marriage seem to have arisen mostly in rural areas, minor girls in town may have been less likely to be forced into marriage, or at least these marriages were not consummated. Although a legal tool for preventing child marriages existed from 1922 onward, registrars' inaccuracy in registering the age of wives—or their joining hands with male elders in marrying off minor girls—and the custom of not registering marriages account for the failure of this decree to act as a safeguard for minor girls. Due to unequal power relations and ambiguous approaches by colonial officers and qadis to wives who wanted to dissolve their marriage because of ill-treatment, women rarely benefited from the possibility of dissolving a marriage on the ground of cruelty.

NOTES

My thanks go to Anne Bang, Jim Brennan, Emily Burrill, Richard Roberts, Liz Thornberry, Lynn Welchman, and the reviewers for their thoughtful comments on previous versions. This chapter draws on parts of my dissertation, "Tying and Untying the Knot: *Kadhi*'s Courts and the Negotiation of Social Status in Zanzibar Town, 1900–1963" (PhD diss., School of Oriental and African Studies, University of London, 2008).

1. See Annelies Moors, "Debating Islamic Family Law: Legal Texts and Social Practices," in *Social History of Women and Gender in the Modern Middle East*, ed. Margaret L. Meriwether and Judith E. Tucker (Boulder, CO: Westview Press, 1999), 150, on colonial powers' limited interest in interfering with Islamic family law, which, unlike property laws, they perceived as a "highly sensitive issue."

2. See Randall L. Pouwels, "The East African Coast, c. 780 to 1900 C.E.," in *The History of Islam in Africa*, ed. Nehemia Levtzion and Randall L. Pouwels (Athens: Ohio University Press, 2000), 252, and 22–24, for a summary of Islamization along the Swahili coast in its early stages. The Ibadis are a branch of a less well known group called Khawarij in Arabic.

3. J. H. Vaughan, *The Dual Jurisdiction in Zanzibar* (Zanzibar: Government Printer, 1935), 11–12.

4. Although on the one hand Western countries increasingly perceived mutilating penalties as inappropriate, on the other the leniency of Islamic criminal law

was a concern to British officers. See Rudolph Peters, *Crime and Punishment in Islamic Law: Theory and Practice from the Sixteenth to the Twenty-first Century* (Cambridge: Cambridge University Press, 2005), 103–6.

5. I have explored this further in chapter 1 of my dissertation, "Tying and Untying the Knot."

6. Although it is beyond the scope of this chapter, I would like to point out that it is questionable to what extent these sentences were historically applied in Muslim societies.

7. Major F. B. Pearce, *Zanzibar: The Island Metropolis of Eastern Africa* (London: T. Fisher Unwin, 1920), 268.

8. McClintock offers an intriguing argument about the reinvention of patriarchy through the colonial bureaucracy at the time when the father figure vanished in the metropole. See Anne McClintock, *Imperial Leather: Race, Gender and Sexuality in the Colonial Contest* (New York: Routledge, 1994), 240. See also Julia Clancy-Smith, "Islam, Gender, and Identities in the Making of French Algeria, 1830–1962," in *Domesticating the Empire: Race, Gender, and Family Life in French and Dutch Colonialism*, ed. Julia Clancy-Smith and Frances Gouda (Charlottesville: University Press of Virginia, 1998), 154–74, and Haim Gerber, "Social and Economic Position of Women in an Ottoman City, Bursa, 1600–1700," *International Journal of Middle East Studies* 12, no. 3 (1980): 231, on the alleged Muslim women's suffering that exists in popular belief.

9. Annual Report of the Social Welfare Section of the Provincial Administration 1950, CO 822/677, National Archives Kew (hereafter NAK).

10. Memorandum by Chief Justice G. H. Pickering, 24 November 1930, CO 618/49/1, NAK.

11. Decree to Provide for the Registration of Mahommedan Marriages and Divorces, No. 8, 1935, CO 618/65/7, NAK.

12. L. W. C. van den Berg, *Minhadj at-talibin. Le guide des zélés croyants. Manuel de jurisprudence musulmane selon le rite de Chafi'i*. Arabic text, published on behalf of the government, translated and annoted by L. W. C. van den Berg, vol. 2 (Batavia: Imprimerie du Gouvernement, 1883), 322.

13. J. N. D. Anderson, *Islamic Law in Africa*, new impression with preface (London: Frank Cass, 1970), 71.

14. On different interpretations of Qur'an 4:34, see Barbara Stowasser, "Gender Issues and Contemporary Quran Interpretation," in *Islam, Gender, and Social Change*, ed. Yvonne Yazbeck Haddad and John L. Esposito (Oxford: Oxford University Press, 1998), 30–44.

15. Ali bin Hemedi, *Nikahi: A Handbook of the Law of Marriage in Islam*, translated into English by J. W. T. Allen (n.p., 1934), 9. Kadhi is the East African Swahili spelling of qadi and is here retained in direct quotes.

16. James R. Brennan, "Nation, Race, and Urbanization in Dar es-Salaam, Tanzania, 1916–1976" (PhD diss., Northwestern University, 2002), 114n116.

17. Hamed bin Saleh al-Busaidy, *Ndoa na talaka* (Nairobi, Kenya: East African Literature Bureau, 1962), 31.

18. Ibid., 32.

19. How qadis operated within the colonial legal framework is discussed in Anne K. Bang, *Sufis and Scholars of the Sea: Family Networks in East Africa, 1860–1925* (London: RoutledgeCurzon, 2003), 153–72.

20. See Allan Christelow, *Muslim Law Courts and the French Colonial State in Algeria* (Princeton, NJ: Princeton University Press, 1985), 90.

21. I have changed the names of the litigants but kept the original format, which is the genealogical chain. If a person was mentioned with her or his father's and grandfather's name as well as a clan name, this suggests that her or his status was higher than the one of someone listed with her or his personal name only.

22. Bang, *Sufis and Scholars*, 154–55, provides a short biography of qadi Sh. Ali.

23. HC9/98, Zanzibar National Archives (hereafter ZNA). The court records (HC8, HC9, HC10, HC28/29) are in Arabic and the translations are mine unless indicated otherwise.

24. HC9/89, ZNA.

25. HC10/761, ZNA.

26. HC10/761, ZNA.

27. HC10/761, ZNA.

28. Anderson, *Islamic Law*, 60.

29. Women are ritually impure during their menses, which makes intercourse unlawful (Qur'an 2:222).

30. HC10/1141, ZNA.

31. HC10/1403, ZNA.

32. HC10/1276, ZNA.

33. HC10/3302 (original in English), ZNA.

34. See also HC9/131, ZNA, where neighbors testified to the husband's ill-treatment. Husband and wife achieved a reconciliation.

35. On the difficulties of proving incidents of domestic violence under Islamic laws of evidence, see Anderson, *Islamic Law*, 25.

36. For a discussion of Sh. Tahir as a scholar and servant of the colonial government, see Anne K. Bang, "Another Scholar for All Seasons? Tahir b. Abi Bakr al-Amawi (1877–1938), *qadi* of Zanzibar, c. 1900–1933," in *The Global Worlds of the Swahili: Interfaces of Islam, Identity and Space in Nineteenth- and Twentieth-Century East Africa*, ed. Roman Loimeier and Rüdiger Seesemann (Berlin: Lit Verlag, 2006), 273–88.

37. HC8/86 (original in English), ZNA.

38. At the time, two qadis, a Shafi'i and an Ibadi, and a judge formed a quorum in appeal cases from qadi's courts.

39. HC8/86 (original in English and Arabic), ZNA. On this case, see also Laura Fair, *Pastimes and Politics: Culture, Community, and Identity in Post-Abolition Urban Zanzibar, 1890–1945* (Athens: Ohio University Press, 2001), 203–4.

40. See HC9/65, ZNA, where the wife said the witnesses would not testify to incidents of domestic violence and that her husband had been punished by the magistrate for beating her. In HC9/112 and HC9/129, ZNA, wives failed to prove the beating and the threat of beating by their husbands, respectively.

41. HC10/42, ZNA.

42. HC10/15, ZNA.

43. Sh. Burhan was the son of a well-respected scholar, Sh. Abd al-Aziz b. Abd al-Ghani al-Amawi. The family was originally from Brava, Somalia. See Bang, *Sufis and Scholars*, 155.

44. HC9/116, ZNA.

45. HC9/62, ZNA.

46. Samuel G. Ayany, *A History of Zanzibar: A Study in Constitutional Development, 1934–1964* (Nairobi: East African Literature Bureau, 1970), 21–22; Norman R. Bennett, *A History of the Arab State of Zanzibar* (London: Methuen, 1978), 241–42.

47. These debates can be traced in the newspaper *al-Falaq*, issues 29 June; 13, 20, 27 July; and 14 September 1946.

48. Brett L. Shadle, *"Girl Cases": Marriage and Colonialism in Gusiiland, Kenya, 1890–1970* (Portsmouth, NH: Heinemann, 2006), 195–97.

49. Elizabeth Schmidt, "Negotiated Spaces and Contested Terrain: Men, Women and the Law in Colonial Zimbabwe, 1890–1939," *Journal of Southern African Studies* 16, no. 4 (1990): 627.

50. For Egypt, see Ron Shaham, *Family and the Courts in Modern Egypt: A Study Based on Decisions by the Sharia Courts, 1900–1955* (Leiden: E. J. Brill, 1997), chap. 3.

51. Moors, "Debating Islamic Family Law," 161.

52. Martin Chanock, *Law, Custom, and Social Order: The Colonial Experience in Malawi and Zambia* (Cambridge: Cambridge University Press, 1985), 207–12.

53. Interview with Sh. Habib Ali Kombo, 24 March 2004.

54. Vaughan, *Dual Jurisdiction*, 44–45.

55. On the interaction between society and the registration of marriage in earlier twentieth-century Egypt, see Ron Shaham, "Custom, Islamic Law, and Statutory Legislation: Marriage Registration and Minimum Age at Marriage in the Egyptian Sharia Courts," *Islamic Law and Society* 2, no. 3 (1995): 258–81.

56. Sample of Marriage Registers, 1940 and 1945, *Mambo Msiige*, Zanzibar Town.

57. Senior commissioner I. E. Moultrie to chief secretary and senior commissioner, 27 May 1957, AB71/7, ZNA.

58. Anderson, *Islamic Law*, 62.

59. Ibid., 62n5. In the Aden Protectorate, the Child Marriage Restraint Ordinance of 1939 penalized men who contracted child marriages as well as those who assisted in contracting them. In Nigeria a provision similar to the one in Zanzibar was in force, albeit the Criminal Code Ordinance did not make the premature consummation of child marriage an offense per se (Anderson, *Islamic Law*, 35 and 177 respectively).

60. See Kristin Mann and Richard Roberts, eds., *Law in Colonial Africa* (Portsmouth, NH: Heinemann, 1991), 41; Christelow, *Muslim Law Courts*, 124–28. Mbilinyi accounts for the attention that the issue of forced marriage received in London in the 1930s after an incident of a young woman in Tanganyika. See Marjorie Mbilinyi, "Women's Resistance in 'Customary' Marriage: Tanzania's

Runaway Wives," in *Forced Labour and Migration: Patterns of Movement within Africa*, ed. Abebe Zegeye and Shubi Ishemo (London: Hans Zell, 1989), 239–47.

61. Entry #842, no. 360, 22 Dhu l-Hijja [1319]/1 April 1902, HC28/29, ZNA.

62. In a Hanafi context, see Mahmoud Yazbak, "Minor Marriages and *khiyar bulugh* in Ottoman Palestine: A Note on Women's Strategies in a Patriarchal Society," *Islamic Law and Society* 9, no. 3 (2002): 391–92.

63. The Prophet's marriage to Aisha when she was six or seven years old serves as the paradigm for the age of marriage for girls. However, according to hadiths (accounts of what the Prophet said and did), the marriage was not consummated until she was nine. Hence the age of nine has by consensus been taken as the minimum age of marriage for a girl.

64. Anthony Clayton, *The Zanzibar Revolution and Its Aftermath* (London: Hurst, 1981), 23–35.

65. Acting British resident to the secretary of state for the colonies, 16 March 1949, AB71/7, ZNA.

66. Abdul Sheriff, "The Peasantry under Imperialism, 1873–1963," in *Zanzibar under Colonial Rule*, ed. Abdul Sheriff and Ed Ferguson (London: James Currey, 1991), 126. In the 1890s, similar circumstances of material deprivation seem to have prevailed on the Kenyan coast, where colonial officers refrained from interfering with parents who sold their children, or forced them into child marriage due to famine (Shadle, *"Girl Cases,"* 44–45).

67. Mudir of Mkokotoni to senior commissioner, 29 November 1949, AK5/25, ZNA. It is not indicated why he proposed the age of fifteen.

68. In 1906 in Aden, a qadi justified a marriage of a minor girl, given into marriage by a guardian who was unacceptable according to shari'a, with the argument that it would cause hardship if she were not married. See Scott Reese, "Bureaucrats and Notables: Re-imagining Social and Religious Authority in Colonial Aden," paper presented at the workshop on Shifting the Meaning: Time, Space, Connectivity and Its Challenges in the Western Indian Ocean, Berlin, 21–23 May 2007.

69. District commissioner to senior commissioner, 16 December 1949, AK5/25, ZNA.

70. Officer in charge, Ng'ambo Police Station, to woman welfare officer, 30 May 1956, and senior welfare officer to senior commissioner, 8 June 1956, AK5/25, ZNA, respectively.

71. Welfare officer, Pemba, to senior welfare officer, Zanzibar, 11 June 1956, and evidence of Zena bt. Rafiki in Juvenile Court, 14 June 1956, AK5/25, ZNA.

72. Senior welfare officer to superintendent of police, 15 June 1956, AK5/25, ZNA.

73. Senior welfare officer to senior commissioner, 28 June 1956, AK5/25, ZNA.

74. Acting senior commissioner to commissioner of police, 11 June 1956, AK5/25, ZNA.

75. Senior welfare officer to senior commissioner, 10 August 1956, AK5/25, ZNA.

76. No. 3/1957 from criminal case no. 1554/1956 of the resident magistrate's court, in His Highness the Sultan's Court, Zanzibar Court, AK5/25, ZNA.

77. No. 3/1957 from criminal case no. 1554/1956 of the resident magistrate's court, in His Highness the Sultan's Court, Zanzibar Court, AK5/25, ZNA.

78. Attorney general to British resident, 16 April 1957, AK5/25, ZNA.

79. AB71/7, ZNA. Also Harold Ingrams, secretary to the director of education in Zanzibar during the 1920s, described the guardianship of women as slavery. See W. H. Ingrams, *Zanzibar: Its History and Its People* (London: H. F. & G. Witherby, 1931), 204–5. There are also striking similarities to the French Soudan, where colonial administrators equated the social condition of women as close to slavery. See Richard Roberts, *Litigants and Households: African Disputes and Colonial Courts in the French Soudan, 1895–1912* (Portsmouth, NH: Heinemann, 2005), 133. In 1910, the administrator of Koutiala described marriages as disguised sales, lamenting that young girls were taken from their mothers and given into marriage by a male relative in exchange for a bridewealth. The reply this administrator received echoed the one of Moultrie: "Do not meddle in native custom except with the utmost circumspection" (Roberts, *Litigants and Households*, 135). For the same reasons that concerned Moultrie, the French feminist Hubertine Auclert spoke of Arab marriage as "child rape." See Julia Clancy-Smith, "La femme arabe: Women and Sexuality in France's North African Empire," in *Women, the Family, and Divorce Laws in Islamic History*, ed. Amina El Azhary Sonbol (Syracuse, NY: Syracuse University Press, 1996), 61.

80. Senior welfare officer I. E. Moultrie to chief secretary and senior commissioner, 27 May 1957, AB71/7, ZNA.

81. Senior welfare officer I. E. Moultrie to chief secretary and senior commissioner, 27 May 1957, AB71/7, ZNA.

82. In Egypt, women's movements pressed for raising the age of marriage, an effort that resulted in a first failed attempt in 1914. However, a few years later the consummation of a marriage with a child below the age of twelve became prosecuted as rape. The method adopted was to prevent the registration of marriages in which woman and man were below the age of sixteen and eighteen respectively. Yet it was neither an offense not to register a marriage nor did a marriage become invalid because it was not registered (Shaham, *Family and the Courts*, 53–54, 56).

83. Senior welfare officer I. E. Moultrie to chief secretary and senior commissioner, 27 May, 1957, AB71/7, ZNA.

84. Record of the Agreed Conclusions of a Meeting Held in the Office of the Senior Education Officer, 1 April 1957, AB71/1, ZNA.

85. The same attitude can be gleaned from an earlier correspondence. When the opening of a school for African and Arab girls was discussed in 1926, the aim was to make girls "better house-wives and more intelligent mothers" (G. B. Johnson, 9 November 1926, CO 618/40/13, NAK).

86. Muslim Sharia and Doctrine in Regard to Marriage as Explained to the Senior Welfare Officer by Sh. Abdallah Salih Farsy and sayyid Umar, AB71/7, ZNA.

87. Sh. Abdallah and Sh. Umar quoted menstruation, childbirth, the wife's illness, insanity or infectious disease of the husband as well as "if the male organ is too big" as grounds which exempted wives from sexual submission (Muslim

Sharia and Doctrine in Regard to Marriage as Explained to the Senior Welfare Officer by Sh. Abdallah Salih Farsy and Sayyid Umar, AB71/7, ZNA).

88. Senior welfare officer to senior commissioner, 20 January 1958, AK5/25, ZNA.

89. *Annual Report of the Provincial Administration, 1960* (Zanzibar: Government Printer, 1960), 5.

7 ⮑ Fatal Families

Narratives of Spousal Killing and Domestic Violence in Murder Trials in Kenya and Nyasaland, c. 1930–56

STACEY HYND

> I admit I killed my husband. He used to beat me up and he had beaten me the day that I killed him. I wanted to revenge myself and be rid of him, I waited until he had gone to sleep and when he was fast asleep I hanged him with a rope and thus killed him.

Tabule, wife of Kipruto arap Soi, a Lumbwa woman from Kenya, pleaded guilty in 1947 to killing her husband by strangling him with a rope in his sleep. They had been married for eight years, had three children, and Tabule was pregnant with her fourth child. However, as the district officer (DO) of Kericho reported, she had suffered "severe persecution from her husband. He had repeatedly beaten her, and was known to be like a wild animal when drunk." Tabule's experience of domestic abuse roused the colonial state's sympathy, and her death sentence was commuted to five months' imprisonment.[1]

Domestic violence was one of the most commonly attributed reasons for murder in colonial courts in both Kenya and Nyasaland from 1920 to 1956, both in cases such as Tabule's when someone resorted to lethal violence to escape abuse and in cases where abuse escalated into murder. As Katherine Luongo shows in "Domestic Dramas and Occult Acts," colonial legal settings had few tropes available for talking about domestic violence: witchcraft was one, but murder was another arena in which acts of domestic abuse were brought to light.[2] In colonial Africa, murder trials were an arena where notions of "violence" and socially acceptable behavior clashed and were contested, where private lives became the subject of public discourses. This chapter analyzes domestic violence in Kenya and Nyasaland though the medium of High Court and Supreme Court murder trials, focusing both on the colonial judge's

159

perceptions of the accused as perpetrators of domestic violence, and on the accused person's representations of his or her own "criminality." The attitudes of native assessors and local communities toward the domestic violence reported are also revealed. Trial transcripts, judgments, and commutation reports here highlight the discourses surrounding domestic violence and how crimes resulting from such violence were sentenced by colonial courts, showing how this varied over time, location, and circumstance.

CAPITAL PUNISHMENT IN COLONIAL COURTS — DEATH, MERCY, AND CULTURAL DEFENSES

In Nyasaland and Kenya, as throughout British colonial Africa, the legal system was based on English common law, which provided a mandatory death sentence for a murder conviction on a capital charge.[3] This did not necessarily mean that convicted persons were executed, however: in Nyasaland, from 857 capital trials between 1908 and 1946, only 181 resulted in execution, and only 459 cases from 1,108 in Kenya between 1908 and 1956 (exclusive of Mau Mau trials) saw the extreme penalty enforced.[4] Colonial judges were not "hanging judges," and governors were themselves often opposed to capital punishment. The courts that tried cases of domestic violence and murder were not monolithic blocks but sites of contestation where values and beliefs were expressed and shaped.[5] Capital punishment is different from other legal penalties in that it contains an expressly political element: the Governor's Prerogative of Mercy. After sentencing and appeal, capital cases went to the governor-in-council for final disposition, and it was this process of mercy that spared many condemned African murderers. While some mercy decisions were based solely on legal principles and the facts of a case, it is clear that many sentences were commuted because of "cultural defenses." These portrayed Africans as "impulsive savages" prone to violence, who deserved mercy because they could not be expected to conform to "civilized" standards of behavior because of their "primitive mentalities" and low states of culture and society. Such narratives brought mercy at the price of reinforcing discriminatory hegemonic social relations.[6] These "cultural defenses" and their mediation of colonial understandings of African societies informed the sentencing of domestic murders in Kenya and Nyasaland and indicated the emergence of what can be seen as a specifically colonial form of justice.

The view granted of domestic violence through the investigation of capital trials is intermittent and exceptional, due to the very nature of the evidence, with a limited number of cases available, and those being of variable quality. These were not the everyday, routine examples of domestic violence, but those where the violence escalated to a lethal degree and was reported by either the victim's family, local authorities, or the perpetrator themselves, bringing the colonial gaze and judicial power down upon the suspected killer. The investigation of domestic violence in murder cases here is based on an analysis of 1,108 capital cases in Kenya between 1908 and 1956, and 897 cases in Nyasaland between 1903 and 1947, of which a qualitative assessment has determined that 145 of the Kenyan murder convictions between 1939 and 1955 resulted from domestic violence, and some 147 of the Nyasaland convictions between 1920 and 1947: these are the only years from which qualitative evidence remains from murder trials in these territories.[7] As officials noted, "beer and women" were the main causes of violent crime in colonial Africa during this period, both of which had a significant impact on domestic murders.[8] As many of the capital trial records for these archives contain no details of the circumstances of the crime or of the victim's relationship to their killer, it is likely that the actual number of murder cases involving some form of domestic violence is far higher. As the disposition of cases is so closely linked to the widely varied circumstances of the crimes, it is also difficult to determine even localized changes in attitudes toward domestic violence among African communities and individual judges, particularly over a relatively short time period. Although there are numerous good social histories of African communities in Kenya and Nyasaland, few deal explicitly with domestic abuse in any systematic way.[9] As such, we cannot accurately determine how the murders discussed here relate to wider patterns of domestic violence. The general trends elucidated here may be as much a result of changing attitudes to murder and capital punishment as they are of changing incidences or perceptions of domestic violence. The hypotheses that follow are based on subjective qualitative assessments of the material more than empirical analysis. Rather than attempting to explain the structures of domestic violence, this chapter analyzes its lethal manifestation in Nyasaland and Kenya as a form of culturally embedded violence, using the lens of trial narratives to elucidate what colonial officers and African communities thought of such crimes, and to highlight the tensions within—and between—these sectors of colonial society.

Significantly, it is notable that the frequency of domestic violence in capital convictions was much lower in Africa than in Britain at the time, where 65 percent of murder convictions were a result of domestic violence against spouses, lovers, children, or parents, suggesting that violence was less "privatized" in Africa, and levels of interpersonal violence were higher than in Britain.[10] It is generally regarded around the world that domestic murders are viewed by states as less threatening to public order, and are consequently less likely to be punished by a death sentence and result in execution.[11] The death penalty is interpreted therefore as a dramatic symbol of the lesser dignity attached to the security and peace of the domestic sphere as compared with the realms of commerce and social intercourse between nonintimates.[12] However, an analysis of the Nyasaland and Kenyan cases would seem to contradict this assumption: the incidence of convictions for domestic violence was lower but its punishment more severe. Between 1940 and 1956 in Kenya 48 percent of capital convictions for domestic murders resulted in execution, compared to an overall figure of 30 percent.[13] In Nyasaland, 43 percent of domestic murderers were executed, against 40 percent of all convicted murderers overall. More significantly, 70 percent of wife murderers—the main category of domestic murders—in Nyasaland were executed, and 60 percent in Kenya. Due to the incomplete nature of the capital trial archives, these figures are contestable, but they do strongly suggest that domestic murders were a recognized category of capital crime that the colonial state punished severely. In England at this time there is evidence of decreasing acceptance of wife-beating in criminal judgments, an attitude that seems to have carried over into the colonial sphere.[14] The functioning of capital punishment in colonial Africa was primarily didactic and deterrent, with the crimes perceived as most threatening to the social order receiving the greatest punishment. Such treatment of domestic murders suggests that not only was the legal system geared to the maintenance of colonial law and order but that it was also employed to manage violence within African communities.

Domestic murder is taken here to connote the infliction of lethal physical violence following an apparent pattern of abuse, physical or otherwise, inflicted upon a member of a household and/or close kinship relationship. What makes such cases *domestic* violence is not simply that the abuse occurs within the private sphere of household relations but that it results from systemic tensions within this sphere. As such, the killing of a father by his son at a beer drink after a long-standing quarrel about the son's bridewealth and marriage can be counted as domestic violence, as can the drowning of a co-wife's child by a second wife. Similarly, violence cannot simply be understood in instrumental terms; many of the acts of lethal violence discussed below contained—or reacted against—verbal, psychological, or cultural acts of aggression and transgression. The rules of violence that mark out its boundaries are often broken, but these disruptions are themselves within the rules, as it is through such transgressions that frontiers are established, fortified, and moved.[15] As such, the exceptional violence of a domestic murder reshaped the debates and narratives about domestic violence, and re-created the boundaries between legitimate and unacceptable use of force within the domestic sphere.

In the early colonial period in Nyasaland, the colonial government took a strong stand against spousal murders. In 1910, Ngahotoka was executed for beating his wife Nabeta to death with a stick after she had refused to sleep with him for two months. Judge Griffin wrote of the case: "This according to European ideas would not form an adequate motive for murder, but such a refusal on a wife's part is considered a serious matter by a Native as it is supposed to indicate that the wife has committed adultery." Governor Sharpe, however, sent Ngahotoka to the gallows, alongside many other men who killed their wives.[16] This attitude was not constant, however. By the 1920s, this firm stance against domestic violence had lessened, most probably in the light of increasing gender tensions and colonial support for African patriarchs. Additionally, there was a growing belief that capital punishment was not an effective deterrent in crimes of passion. Nonetheless, officials disliked sanctioning openly misogynistic opinions from assessors and local communities; when Principal Headman Machaka commented on the case of Chengwani, convicted in 1935 for murdering her husband: "She had no right when her husband was down and the knife out of his hand to hit him with the axe. If after her nagging, the husband had hit her with the axe it would have been all right, but not for her to hit him," Chief Justice Reed retorted this sounded like "a man-made law administered by men," and recommended her to mercy.[17]

The situation regarding spousal murder in Kenya also changed over time. For Ukutafi Shifushi, convicted of murdering his wife after a *tembe* (palm wine) party in Nyanza in 1940, Judge Thacker wrote, "The cause of the assault seems to have been some trivial dispute over his wife's cooking or the food in the house. I have no recommendation to make."[18] By the 1930s governors-in-council were taking a strong line against men convicted of murdering their wives without grave provocation.[19] In the 1940s this strict application of justice was extended to men who killed their current or former mistresses, or a woman whom they had attempted to abduct.[20] Mercy then became applied only in cases where it was determined that the woman had been of "bad character" or was judged to have provoked the man, particularly through committing adultery.[21] Tolerance of male violence was decreasing, particularly when related to drunkenness or wife-beating, but there was still a persistent belief that female delinquency was a potent threat to masculine self-control and that women who did not conform to gendered norms were less deserving of a court's sympathy, as Scott London demonstrates has occurred in Senegal's family tribunals.[22]

The way in which these cases were brought to court also affects records of domestic murder: although a disproportionate number of the cases from Kenya involve Kalenjin peoples, it does not follow that there were necessarily higher rates of domestic violence among the Kalenjin. It can be suggested rather that this predominance might be due to a high level of cooperation with colonial authorities by local chiefs in reporting such murders, or perhaps because there was a strong taboo against the killing of women in Kalenjin societies.[23] It is likely that a vast majority of domestic murders never made it to a conviction in the higher courts, being either prosecuted in native courts or district courts on lesser charges, being dismissed for lack of evidence, or never being reported to the colonial authorities. Such limits of knowledge and issues of credibility are particularly salient in domestic murders, where private crimes were crafted into public knowledge. Colonial courts had to weigh competing testimonies and notions of truth, and genealogies of violence shifted as colonial peoples exploited colonial misunderstandings about the nature of violence.[24] Overall, it should be noted that the differences in sentencing between Kenya and Nyasaland are less noteworthy than the varying treatment of diverse types of domestic violence.

"SHE LAUGHED AT ME AND THEN SAID 'YOU ARE TOO OLD'": PUNISHING A DISOBEDIENT WIFE

Domestic violence is both a cause and consequence of gender inequality and must be understood within its cultural milieu, forming part of a continually negotiated set of actions and reactions for which social legitimacy was contested. Overall, few domestic murders were regarded as premeditated, and most were viewed as stemming from "impulsive" outbursts of violence and quarrels.[25] Commonly cited reasons for quarrels among spouses included the refusal or failure of the wife to cook meals, not providing hospitality, answering back to her husband, and threatening to leave him for another man. It was the failure to fulfill these gendered, and generational, obligations that frequently led to lethal violence. By the 1940s quarrels over money became a significant source of domestic dispute, particularly in households where access to the money was controlled by the patriarch.[26] In the case of Bendulo Kachimango, who killed his wife during a quarrel over her "spoiling his money" by spending £2, native opinion was reported as being "generally not bitter or inclined to regard the crime as anything more than domestic trouble advanced to the pitch of assault resulting from brooding anger consequent on the loss of a sum of money." The district officer of Ncheu reported that "The subservience of the wife to the husband in native custom makes the offence of spoiling money more serious than it can ever be in European eyes."[27] That many domestic murders appear to have occurred in communities experiencing severe socioeconomic pressure—in the form of land hunger, widespread hunger, increased poverty, and increased social differentiation—suggests that such conditions contributed to levels of domestic violence.[28]

Additionally, many of the men convicted of spousal murder appear to have lashed out violently in response to insults from their wives.[29] John Seremani, an elderly Mang'anja Village Headman in Mlanje district, Nyasaland, was convicted in 1922 of murdering his young wife Asnett, a former slave. In a confession written for a mercy petition, he wrote:

> I said [to Asnett], 'I told you to make a gruel, have you made it?' She said, 'I have not done it and I won't do it.' She laughed at me then

and said, 'You are too old and have a rough beard.' I got angry and asked her if she wanted a younger man and she said, 'Yes and I shall go and see the young men if I want too' . . . I got very angry so in my anger . . . I pushed her down onto the floor and beat her with this piece of wood. . . . I did not mean to kill my wife when I hit her with this piece of wood but I was half drunk and so angry with what she said to me. [30]

The most common motivation ascribed by colonial courts to spousal murders, and one frequently admitted by accused men, was quarreling over sexual access to the wife and her agency in controlling her own sexuality. Desertion by a wife in favor of another lover could provoke extreme acts of violence by repudiated husbands; such acts of violence were interpreted as vengeful and punished harshly by the colonial state. In Kenya, one Gusii man petitioned that "I killed my wife as she had gone to live with another man named Chebuny."[31] Another man, a Makonde, asserted, "It is the custom of my tribe to kill your wife if she goes away with another man."[32] Both of these men were, however, executed by the Kenyan state. Many spousal murders appear to have been actuated through jealousy, particularly where one spouse felt their partner's affections transferred to another person.[33] Bride-price and divorce were other notable motivations for the anger and violence that erupted when a wife was caught after leaving her husband.[34]

Infidelity, either actual or suspected, was frequently cited by men to justify, or at least explain, their murders of their wives or mistresses.[35] Whilst catching a wife *in flagrante delicto*—in the act of adultery—was always held as sufficient provocation to reduce murder to manslaughter, many men acted on mere suspicion of their wife's infidelity or killed their wife or her lover too long after the adulterous act for the offense to qualify as the "grave and sudden provocation" that manslaughter convictions required.[36] Particularly in Nyasaland, many of the men convicted of murdering their spouses were migrant laborers, who spent months laboring in the mines of South Africa or Rhodesia, only to return home and find their wife had taken up with another man in their absence. One such man was Bwezani who murdered his pregnant wife because he suspected adultery. Acting Judge Belcher wrote, "In England this man would be hanged, but allowance should be made for a native in the circumstances."[37] Another man, Mbalati, had his death sentence for the murder of his wife commuted to life imprisonment, partly because it was revealed that he had previously charged his wife with adultery in the native courts on four occasions, and his wife was "shown in evidence to be of a bad character." Judge Belcher reported: "The case is one typical of a great many, where the habits of the wife have driven the husband to rage and despair and dissatisfied with the legal redress open to him, he kills her, making no serious attempt to deny his crime or to run away."[38] In Kenya, Jalou elders in 1952 discussed James Robert Omolo's murder of his wife—who was suspected of committing adultery—and reported that "The killing of a wife for whom dowry has been paid is regarded locally as a folly rather than a crime, being a destruction of personal property. In this case it is felt that the woman brought her own death about by driving her husband to distraction with her behavior."[39]

The refusal of sex by a wife was another significant cause of quarrels that directly motivated a physical assault and murder by the husband.[40] The perception of many colonial officials of such killings was that "for a native to be deprived of sexual intercourse with his wife for so long a period cannot fail to produce in him some abnormal condition."[41] Judge Lockhart-Smith noted of a young girl Alefa, who had been murdered by her new husband Mjepa in 1947 after refusing him sex, that she "naturally had not yet assimilated the code of submission to her husband which would have obtained in the case of a mature and more experienced wife."[42] A woman's refusal to fulfill her marital duties by having intercourse with her husband was considered serious provocation, and little consideration was given to marital rape in the assessment of mercy for men who killed their wives. Recent studies confirm that strong links between sexual access and wife-beating still persist in Kenya, and marital rape remains a contentious arena of legal and civil debate.[43]

Domestic sexual assault resulting in murder could highlight tensions between African and European opinions about gender violence. In one notable Nyasaland case, an elderly man Viaji from Kuleti village was convicted of killing a young woman Msayu, whom he had inherited in a leviratic marriage from his deceased brother. The court found that after a quarrel about her refusing to have sex with Viaji, he beat her unconscious and then proceeded to rape her with a knife, causing her to die of shock and hemorrhage. The three African assessors all found Viaji guilty only of manslaughter, as Msayu's refusal of sex was grave provocation. Judge Morgan told the court that "They have taken a lenient view of your offence and shown you mercy. I would not like it to be said that a European judge is less merciful than his native advisers, so I shall accept their advice . . . [but] award a severe sentence."[44]

LETHAL VIOLENCE OR CUSTOMARY CHASTISEMENT: "ACCEPTABLE" LEVELS OF VIOLENCE IN WIFE-BEATING

As other chapters have demonstrated, one of the difficulties in assessing domestic violence historically in Africa is that, aside from the usual problematics and paucity of sources, the term *domestic violence* is itself ahistorical. Certainly, it was never employed by the colonial courts, whose capital case trial narratives speak instead of "wife-beating," "chastisement" and "domestic quarrels." Our contemporary term emphasizes *violence*, thus connoting the perceived illegitimacy of the physical force employed.[45] Much of the violence employed within domestic spheres in colonial Africa though was perceived as legitimate, not just by the perpetrator, but by the local community and even by the victims themselves. The colonial state, if it did not openly condone such violence, accepted its existence and supported the social hierarchies and networks of power that generated much of the violence.[46]

Courts and governments in Nyasaland and Kenya did periodically try to take a symbolic stance against severe cases of wife-beating. The Chewa man Bester was found guilty of kicking his wife, Elina, to death in Dowa, Nyasaland, in 1935, despite the fact that Judge Belcher found there was "no intention to kill, merely the usual native view that a husband is entitled to knock his wife about for petty faults to any extent short of death or maiming. It is desirable to disabuse the native mind of this idea."[47] A man who claimed that "I only mean to beat her with a stick, but by mistake I took an axe and struck her with it" was lucky to escape the gallows with a life sentence.[48] However, colonial officials were aware that in many cases, violence by husbands against their wives was regarded as legitimate, or at least not opposed by the community, as long as it did not result in permanent or obvious physical damage that required external intervention and medical treatment, or transgressed other social customs and taboos. In Kenya, an assessor, Ladislans Mogoba, commenting in 1951 on the case of Kerubo wife of Ayienda, who claimed she had burnt her husband and co-wife's hut after he beat her and stripped her naked, stated, "I find her statement may be true, because usually men flog their wives."[49] Wife-beating appears to be accepted as normative among the majority of opinions in both Kenya and Nyasaland throughout this period.[50] As such, courts took levels of violence perpetrated by an aggrieved husband into account when assessing murder, differentiating between "grievous harm" and "customary chastisement." Omodin son of Simame was convicted of killing his wife, Okuda, in Nyanza Province, Kenya, in 1946 in what Judge Horne called "an excess of what an African deems chastisement of a rebellious wife."[51] If it could be proved that a man had intended only to chastise his wife, and did not beat her sufficiently to prove intention of causing grievous harm or death, then he could be convicted only of manslaughter. In the case of Mkwapatila, in Dowa in 1928, Judge Hanagin wrote that:

> Had the stick been used by Mr. Sandow [European assessor] in a like manner upon a civilized female, I would have no hesitation in recommending a verdict of murder; but if a jury were satisfied that the accused was only administering a beating such as he frequently gave to his wife without serious result, the correct finding should be manslaughter.[52]

Judges were supported in such leniency toward domestic violence by the African assessors who advised their judgments. Assessors would state that although it was wrong "under the Government today" for a man to kill his wife, men should still be allowed to discipline their wives. In the 1910 Nyasaland case of *R. v. Majawa*, where the accused claimed he had cut his wife's throat due to her constant nagging, hiding his things, and allegedly throwing their child onto the fire during a quarrel, Native Assessor Syasya recorded that:

> Before the white men came here the women were afraid to behave ill to their husbands, they would have been punished at first and her witnesses to marriage would be made to pay, and they would most certainly have been killed had they committed adultery. . . . Majawa has killed his wife and if he is killed it is as the law is now, but we chiefs do not think that he deserves to be put to death. Many women are giving trouble because they no longer fear their husbands. If Majawa is killed it will have a bad effect on all our women who are often troublesome now.[53]

In the end, Majawa was given a life sentence, to be reconsidered after five years. African assessors, usually headmen or elders, looked to reinforce their own authority by repeatedly asserting that if a couple were having marital difficulties, they should report the matter to their native authority, or their *ankhose* (marriage guardians) in the parts of Nyasaland where this system operated, rather than resort to unsanctioned violence.[54]

FATAL FEMALES: DOMESTIC MURDERS BY WOMEN

Trial narratives of female perpetrators of domestic murder differ from those of male perpetrators in their two main competing discourses. Colonial courts frequently depicted such women as lacking the emotional and mental development to be fully responsible for their actions and consequently not liable for the death penalty. In Kenya and Nyasaland, only two women were executed in this period, and those were for premeditated, nondomestic murders. What challenged this benevolent, if chauvinistic, patriarchal discourse were the actions and responses of the women themselves, who transgressed supposed gender stereotypes and social hierarchies in their use of lethal violence against husbands, children, relatives, and co-wives. Violent African female offenders asserted themselves, not as weak or mentally unstable women, but rather as rational actors who chose to kill those close to them, usually being driven to do so through their own suffering of domestic violence.[55] Kabon, wife of Kirop, a Kamasia woman who killed her husband in his sleep in 1946, openly stated in Kabarnet's Magistrate's Court that:

I admit that I killed my husband, but I had good reason for doing so. He had ill treated me every year since we were married. He gave me no chance to leave him and take another husband. . . . I decided that I would kill my husband and if Government wanted to hang me they could do so.[56]

Many of the women who were convicted of murdering their husbands were reacting against long-term patterns of domestic violence, and violent beatings in particular. A Kikuyu woman, Nyakihinyo, wife of Wiathenyi, killed her abusive husband in his sleep in 1949. The district commissioner (DC) of Fort Hall wrote of the case:

All the evidence shows that the murderer, as wife of the deceased, had led a miserable existence as a result of her husband's cruelty, drunkenness and neglect. Public opinion in the community . . . is in sympathy with the prisoner and appreciates the hardships by which she was beset. . . . Her act appears to have been one of despair, committed in order to remove him whom she considered the source of all her troubles.

That Nyakihinyo was a mother of several children whom she struggled to care for and was losing her secure position as favored wife to a younger woman were also cited as contributing factors in her actions. Nyakihinyo asserted that the native tribunal had known about the abuse she endured for the past thirteen years. In her statement she told of how her husband, Waithanji, had arrived home drunk one evening and beaten her:

He said, you should be happy, you have a house I have built you and five children. We discussed various family problems and I asked him to find me more land to cultivate as the children were hungry. . . . After a while he took me roughly to sleep with him. . . . I was very worried and thought I and the children would die as my husband did not look after us. . . . Then I thought I would kill my husband, and call the elders in the morning and they would hang me or return me to my father's house if they found my husband had been neglecting me. I picked up an axe and killed my husband by striking him on the neck with it.

In the end, Nyakihinyo's death sentence was reduced to one year's imprisonment.[57]

Polygyny was also a significant source of tension, whereby unequal treatment of and jealousy between the wives could result in violent, even lethal, conflict.[58] In 1953, the young Samburu woman Nderunye daughter of Lan-galte was convicted of the murder of Dubeya, her senior co-wife, during a quarrel in which Dubeya was slashed several times across the head with a panga (machete). Although their husband maintained that he treated both his wives equally, and they were on the best of terms, the magistrate for the North-ern Frontier District who tried the case, Mr. N. Kennedy, was convinced that the Nderunye was "a very unhappy young woman and habitually bullied and persecuted by the deceased and her husband."[59] Women, however, could also be violent in their own right, and in their own self-interest, as when their hus-bands persistently failed to fulfill their marital duties.[60] Chengawani killed her husband in Nyasaland 1931, after a quarrel about his failure to provide her with clothes.[61] In Kenya, Gando daughter of Kithongo, murdered her husband dur-ing a quarrel after he refused to get medicine for her.[62] Both represented their actions as rational and justifiable in the circumstances.

Unlike some of the men who beat their wives to death, it was perfectly clear that these women had intended to kill their husbands. Perhaps due to their lesser physical strength or socialized restraint of aggressive impulses, women often waited after a quarrel and then determinedly killed their spouse, often in his sleep.[63] Whereas men tended to strike at the body of their victims, there was a definite tendency among female killers to strike at the head and neck of their victims, reflecting a gendered nature of anatomical assault.

THE PREHISTORY OF CRIME:
PUTTING DOMESTIC MURDERS IN CONTEXT

A recognition that the full story behind a murder often did not emerge from the trial narrative led colonial states and legal systems to further interrogate what turned African subjects into murderers. Such knowledge-gathering meant that more was known about such people than almost any other set of African subjects. In an attempt to properly contextualize spousal murders, reports were furnished by district officers detailing (where such information was available) the treatment of previous spouses by the convicted person, and relationships with their families and their spouse's families. James Kamwezi, convicted of the murder of his wife near Ntondwe, Nyasaland, in 1945, was reported as having been divorced by his previous wife on the grounds of cruelty. She claimed he had beaten her almost daily, and her father stated, "James would have killed her if she had not run away."[64] In another case, in Kilifi, Kenya, DC Power brought it to the governor's attention that Ngutu, son of Mungyoki, convicted of brutally murdering his wife, had a reputation locally for violence and several previous assaults on women. He had been previously expelled from Kwale and made to promise to behave at a public *baraza*, but was known to continually ill-treat his wife.[65] Information such as this became crucial in mercy decisions.

The collection of such information required closer interaction between the colonial state and African communities in discourses of domestic murder, and, as such, by the 1930s local opinions became more influential in deciding the final disposition of such cases, although their influence never matched that of the judge or executive council. DO Wickham, reporting on the case of Mangulenji Phiri convicted of murdering his wife in Kota Kota, stated that local opinion believed that "For what he has done he thoroughly deserves to pay the penalty of death. Everyone is glad to know that the death sentence has been passed on him, and that he will therefore pay that penalty. They go so far as to say that had the case come before their court he would already have paid."[66] In Nyasaland there appears to have been a hardening of attitudes among African populations toward spousal murders throughout the colonial period, although it is difficult to determine whether this is a direct result of the spread of colonial rule and criminal justice, Christianity, or the changing social status of women.[67] In 1950s Kenya, customary law relating to domestic murders was taken increasingly into consideration. District officers would inform the executive council of native custom, such as that for the Nandi murder was a serious offense and "usually brought the retribution of a life for a life, although payment of blood money was acceptable if a second death could be avoided."[68]

As colonial states never established a full monopoly of violence in either Kenya or Nyasaland, however, localized strategies for punishing domestic abuse and murder outside the colonial legal arenas persisted throughout the period. Elders or local communities often judged and punished offenders according to their own practices, including public pledges to good behavior, compensation, or exile. In the 1940s and 1950s in Nyasaland a number of men appear to have committed suicide after killing their wives, possibly due to feelings of guilt and to preempt sanctions from local elders.[69] Despite apparent shifts in the expression of colonial, local, and "customary" attitudes toward domestic violence and murder over the period, the underlying trend was of continuity: domestic murders kept occurring, and the private sphere was where colonial and African authorities proved least able to eradicate violence and disorder.

INFURIATING FAMILIES AND THE FAILURE OF CONFLICT-RESOLUTION STRATEGIES

The question remains, though: Why did these murders occur when and where they did? What caused a pattern of domestic violence to escalate from petty recrimination and chastisement to lethal violence? Most households had constant access to tools such as pangas and axes, so potentially lethal instruments were almost universally available and thus cannot explain the patterns of murder. Individual pathology is difficult to quantify and assess historically from the available sources. However, what does seem apparent from trial narratives and judgments is that many domestic murders were a result of the failure of prior strategies of conflict resolution and strains in wider family networks.

Tensions in the relationships with a spouse's family could easily be a factor in spousal murder. Julius, a catechist from the South African General Mission in Port Herald, murdered his wife, Malita, in 1946 because of her father's constant aggravation about Julius and Malita living as Christians.[70] Other men killed their wives after the wife's family tried to take the woman away from her husband and back to their village.[71] In the case of Yakobe, who in 1923 murdered his mother-in-law, Ziyisa, Magistrate Brackenbury noted that he would be inclined to give a light sentence "because mothers-in-law are often irritating enough to civilized persons, but to savages they must be unbearable when they try to inveigle their daughters back, usually in order to give them to another man."[72] Others could kill family members in order to protect themselves, their children, and other relatives. As Luongo has argued in another chapter, witchcraft-related crimes can be read as incidences of domestic violence, and in both Kenya and Nyasaland many murders occurring within homesteads or communal spaces between family members were narrated around the tropes of witchcraft threats and accusations.[73] Weyulo Kankozi was convicted of stabbing her father-in-law to death, and claimed she did so after he threatened to bewitch her children, and one of them died.[74] In other cases, men and women were killed because of their intervention in a domestic quarrel between others.[75]

The killing of children by a man was usually undertaken from revenge or rage as a result of a quarrel with his wife, the child's mother.[76] This particularly occurred where the wife was suspected of infidelity, the outraged husband viewing the child as a symbol of his cuckoldry. In one Nyasaland case described by Lockhart-Smith as "the cruelest of my whole experience," Kamatowola Bokos killed Diaysi, his wife's young child, in revenge for the wife's adultery, strangling the child and eating her flesh.[77] In Kenya, Jeremiah Mwangi was convicted of murdering his three children after his wife, their mother, tried to divorce him at a native tribunal.[78]

Many people killed their spouses after earlier complaints to families, elders, or native tribunals had gone unanswered. In Nyasaland in 1945, Sanato Jesitara claimed that "it was rather the fact that his complaints had not been listened to that caused him to kill his wife," not her adultery in itself.[79] Women particularly seem to have found their complaints against abusive husbands or family members ignored. Kabon, wife of Kirop, was a Kamasia woman convicted of murdering her husband in Kipchorwa, Kenya, in 1946. Although she was convicted of a premeditated murder because she waited for her husband to fall asleep and then struck him with an axe several times, Judge Horne reported that "throughout her marriage there had been quarrels between her and her husband, and complaints by her of insufficient food for herself and her children, and that her relatives did not regard these complaints with sufficient seriousness, with the result that she felt it necessary to kill her husband." During Kabon's trial her father, Chepkeitan arap Chebiegon, affirmed: "It is true that she used to come home to complain very frequently. I used to talk to her and advise her to be patient but she said that she was troubled very much by her husband." It was after being repeatedly sent home by her father that Kabon killed her husband.[80]

It is difficult to determine exactly why domestic violence erupted into murder. It would seem though that although cultures of patriarchy and normative uses of physical discipline, combined with the socioeconomic changes and dislocations of colonial rule in some areas created the general background to the high levels of domestic violence experienced in Nyasaland and Kenya, what led to fatal attacks in many cases were perceived slights against the individual's honor or challenges to their position within that society. For men it was often a direct threat to their control over a household and its inhabitants that provoked a lethal reaction, or a slur against their masculinity, in the form of verbal insult or adultery. Women, on the contrary, seem to have resorted to lethal violence in despair or depression more than anger. It was the failure to fulfill marital bargains—to provide food, land, and clothing—that led to quarrels in these households, especially where many children had to be provided for. Frequently, women determined to kill their husbands as a result of long-term physical abuse, often shortly after a severe beating or marital rape. The failure of conflict resolution strategies was therefore crucial in the escalation of violence. What this suggests in relation to our wider understanding of domestic violence in Kenya and Nyasaland is that increasing tensions in the relationship between individual and families' lives, and "public" or community mediation of "private" conflicts need to be investigated to fully understand the escalation of patterns of abuse into domestic murder. It also suggests that gendered constructions of masculinity and "womanhood" are critical to these killings.

⌐

Domestic violence was a significant factor in murder cases in both Kenya and Nyasaland during the colonial period. Spousal killings and other domestic murders, committed by both men and women, illustrate that gender, racial, and ethnic stereotypes had a substantial impact on sentencing in colonial courts. The evidence from capital trial records illustrates that domestic killings were usually not isolated eruptions of violence—although defense narratives often sought to present them as such—but were rather part of a wider pattern of domestic violence and gendered social inequalities. Domestic murders also highlighted marked divergences and contests between colonial and African attitudes toward domestic violence and crimes that challenged social hierarchies: the difficulty for the colonial state lay in reconciling these attitudes to achieve an acceptable form of "justice." These cases involved extreme flash points of tensions and strains within households, but by reading through the lens they grant us on patterns of domestic violence, we can illustrate what made systemic violence both unacceptable and unbearable for communities in Kenya and Nyasaland. Although some level of "domestic abuse" may have been regarded as normative in many communities, what transitioned this abuse into lethal assault was often a threat or insult to a person's gendered and social identity. But it was the failure of conflict-resolution strategies within communities that played an important role in driving domestic tensions to a level where such acts of exceptional, extreme violence occurred.

NOTES

Research for this chapter was generously supported by the Arts and Humanities Research Council of Britain, alongside the Beit Fund and the African Studies Centre at the University of Oxford. This paper has benefited from the comments and generous advice offered by colleagues at the "Domestic Violence in Africa" symposium at Stanford University and the African History Seminar at the University of Cambridge. I am also indebted to Richard Waller, Jan-Georg Deutsch, David Anderson, and Megan Vaughan for their suggestions.

1. *Tabule d/o [daughter of] Kipkiget w/o [wife of] Kipruto arap Soi*, CC212/47, MLA/1/281, Kenyan National Archives, Nairobi (hereafter KNA).

2. Katherine Luongo, "Domestic Dramas and Occult Acts: Witchcraft and Violence in the Arena of the Intimate," this volume.

3. See Henry F. Morris and James S. Read, *Indirect Rule and the Search for Justice: Essays in East African Legal History* (Oxford: Clarendon, 1972).

4. See Stacey Hynd, "Imperial Gallows: Capital Punishment, Violence and Colonial Rule in Britain's African Territories, c. 1908–68" (DPhil, University of Oxford, 2007), 96–97.

5. Martin Wiener, "Judges v. Jurors: Courtroom Tensions and the Law of Criminal Responsibility in Nineteenth-Century England," *Law and History Review* 17, no. 3 (1999): 470.

6. Hynd, "Imperial Gallows," chap. 2.

7. That both series of evidence are drawn from different time periods adds difficulty to drawing direct comparisons between Kenya and Nyasaland.

8. Sir Charles Belcher, Reminiscences, 93, MSS. Brit. Emp s. 347, Rhodes House Library, Oxford (hereafter RHL).

9. Useful texts include Brett Shadle, *"Girl Cases": Marriage and Colonialism in Gusiiland, Kenya, 1890–1970* (Portsmouth, NH: Heinemann, 2006); Tabitha Kanogo, *African Womanhood in Colonial Kenya, 1900–50* (Oxford: James Currey; Athens: Ohio University Press, 2005); Megan Vaughan, *The Story of an African Famine: Gender and Famine in Twentieth-Century Malawi* (Cambridge: Cambridge University Press, 1987).

10. See Great Britain, *Royal Commission on Capital Punishment 1949–53: Report Presented to Parliament by Command of Her Majesty, September 1953* (London: HMSO, 1953), 26 for figures.

11. Renée Heberle, "Law's Violence and the Challenge of the Feminine," in *Studies in Law, Society and Politics,* ed. Austin Sarat and Patricia Ewick (Greenwich, CT: JAI Press, 2001), 51.

12. Elizabeth Rapaport, "The Death Penalty and Gender Discrimination," *Law and Society Review* 25, no. 2 (1991): 381.

13. These are the only years for which consistent, standardized information on sentencing exists in MLA/1/1–1356, KNA.

14. Roger Chadwick, *Bureaucratic Mercy: The Home Office and the Treatment of Capital Cases in Victorian Britain* (London: Garland, 1992), 393; Martin Wiener, *Men of Blood: Violence, Manliness and Criminal Justice in Victorian England* (Cambridge: Cambridge University Press, 2004).

15. Giorgio Agamben, *Homo Sacer: Sovereign Power and Bare Life,* trans. Daniel Heller-Roazen (Stanford, CA: Stanford University Press, 1998), 19.

16. *Rex v. Ngahotoka,* Judge Griffin, J5/12/7, National Archives of Malawi (hereafter NAM).

17. *Rex v. Chengawani,* CC14/31, J5/5/35, NAM.

18. *Ukutayi Shifushi,* CC60/40, Judge Thacker, 20 November 1940, MLA/1/66, KNA.

19. See *Kimanua s/o [son of] Kitori,* CC82/41; *Segenge s/o Ngege,* CC61/44, MLA/1/108, KNA; *Omodin s/o Simame,* CC71/46, MLA/1/249; *Kaleli Mwikyamwoko,* CC89/48, MLA/1/291; *Wambete s/o Namasani,* CC121/51, MLA/1/418; *Chamon arap Towet,* CC190/55, MLA/1/133.

20. See *Munasa Mukabore,* CC131/41, MLA/1/124, KNA; *Sulemani Sindano s/o Maraki,* C184/42, MLA/1/170; *Robert Owiti Obiero,* CC34/49, MLA/1/323.

21. See *Chege s/o Karigo,* MLA/1/21, KNA; *Kadhami s/o Madhanjuku,* C72/45, MLA/1/220; Criminal Cases 1952–55; *R. v. Kuria s/o Mbathia,* CC244/51, DC/MUR/3/10/11; *Mbwana Ali,* CC26/54, MLA/1/1219.

22. Scott London, "Constructing Law, Contesting Violence," this volume. See also Darlene Rude, "Reasonable Men and Provocative Women: A Gendered Analysis of Domestic Homicide in Zambia," *Journal of Southern African Studies* 29, no. 1 (1999): 7–27.

23. Many thanks to David Anderson and Richard Waller for this information.

24. Ann Laura Stoler, "'In Cold Blood': Hierarchies of Credibility and the Politics of Colonial Narratives," *Representations* 37 (Winter 1992): 152–54.

25. *Wamutitio Kathega,* C250/49, MLA/1/354, KNA; *James Robert Omolo s/o Stefano Olembo,* CC186/52, MLA/1/448.

26. Confidential Reports of Persons Convicted of Murder and Sentenced to Death, *R. v. Bendulo Kachimanga* 1945, *R. v. James Kamwezi,* CC22/45, PCC/1/16/2, NAM; *Kipsangut arap Reremoi,* CC229/44, MLA/1/220, KNA; *Gando d/o Kithongo,* CC85/45, MLA/1/223.

27. Confidential Reports on the Prerogative of Mercy, DC Lilongwe, Bedulo Kachimanga, 12 April 1945, NAM.

28. Much more research needs to be conducted in both Kenya and Malawi to properly establish both the relationship between socioeconomic pressure and incidences of domestic murder, and between these murders and wider manifestations of domestic violence.

29. See, e.g., *Rex v. Tabalika alias Magombo* 1928, S/1/773/28, NAM; *Rex v. Tom* 1921, S1/1244/21; *Kipruto arap Tanui*, CC169/55, MLA/1/1315, KNA.

30. *Rex v. John Seremani* 1922, Confession by John Seremani, 27 November 1922, S1/2627, NAM.

31. *Gitai Mabiria*, CC69/45, MLA/1/230, NAM.

32. *Manghachini s/o Nachame*, CC220/45, MLA/1/237, KNA.

33. *Rex v. Jeck Jezelani*, CC50/460, NAM, PCC/1/16/2; *Rex v. Kamoto* 1922, S1/189/36; *Hirbo Filsa*, MLA/1/255, KNA; *Wamutitio Kathega*, CC250/49, MLA/1/354.

34. *Rex v. Chiseka Mateyo Mvula*, ,CC17/38, S1/147/38, NAM; *Rex v. Daniel alias Tewesa* 1938, S1/239/38; *Itubula Chemasi*, CC47/49, MLA/1/326, KNA.

35. *Rex v. Sanato Jesitara*, CC4/45, PCC/1/16/2, NAM; *Rex v. Ndyanyama*, CC25/38, S1/240/38; *Kalume wa Tuku Saidi*, CC26/53, MLA/1/568, KNA.

36. Judge and Attorney-General Correspondence, DC Blantyre, 1914, NBB/1/3/2, NAM. This held for only legally recognized marriages, however, and did not include cohabiting couples.

37. *Rex v. Bwezani*, Acting Judge Belcher, 7 April 1921, J5/12/16, NAM.

38. *Rex v. Mbalati* 1924, Judge Belcher, S/1/1915/24, NAM.

39. *James Robert Omolo s/o Stefano Olembo*, CC186/52, MLA/1/448, KNA.

40. *Rex v. Diamon* 1930, J5/12/28, NAM; *Kipsangut arap Reremoi*, CC229/44, MLA/1/220, KNA.

41. *Rex v. Table Cholo*, CC76/31, DC Philips, J5/12/30, NAM.

42. *Rex v. Mjepa*, CC34/47, Acting Chief Justice Lockhart-Smith, J5/5/101a, NAM.

43. Mumbi Machera, "Domestic Violence in Kenya: A Study of Newspaper Reports," in *Men, Women, and Violence: A Collection of Papers from CODESRIA Gender Institute 1997*, ed. F. Oyekanmi (Dakar, Senegal: CODESRIA, 1997), 27–52.

44. *Rex v. Viaji*, CC7/38, Judge Morgan, 26 February 1938, NAM, J5/5/62.

45. Robert Paul Wolff, "On Violence," in *Violence and Its Alternatives: An Interdisciplinary Reader*, ed. Manfred B. Steger and Nancy S. Lind (Basingstoke: Macmillan, 1999), 12–22.

46. One interesting question that needs further study is what the impact of Christian morality and disciplinary violence was on incidences of domestic violence in African communities.

47. *Rex v. Bester*, Judge Belcher, 12 May 1935, S1/954/25, NAM.

48. *Rex v. Sanato Jesitara*, CC4/45, Petition by prisoner, PCC/1/16/2, NAM.

49. *Kerubo w/o Ayienda*, CC176/51, MLA/1/431, KNA.

50. A high level of acceptance of wife-beating was still evident in Malawi's traditional courts after independence. See Paul Brietzke, "Murder and Manslaughter in Malawi's Traditional Courts," *Journal of African Law* 18, no. 1 (1974): 45.

51. *Omodin s/o Simame*, CC71/46, Judge Horne, 7 August 1948, MLA/1/249, KNA.

52. *Rex v. Mkwapatila*, CC37/28, Judge Hanagin, 12 May 1928, J5/12/25, NAM.

53. *Rex v. Majawa* 1910, J5/12/7, NAM.

54. *Rex v. Beston alias Moforo*, CC10/38, J5/5/64, NAM.

55. For another interesting discussion of female offenders see Tapiwa B. Zimudzi, "African Women, Violent Crime and the Criminal Law in Colonial Zimbabwe 1900–1952," *Journal of Southern African Studies* 30, no. 3 (2004): 499–517.

56. *Kabon w/o Kirop*, CC66/46, MLA/1/248, KNA. The case records for females convicted on capital charges contain significantly more detailed transcripts and evidence than many cases involving men, due to British officials' cultural reluctance to convict women on such charges.

57. *Nyakihinyo w/o Wiathenyi*, CC209/49, DC Fort Hall, 12 December 1949, MLA/1/350, KNA.

58. *Rex v. Usale*, CC1/32, NAM, J5/12/31; *Nyakihinyo w/o Waithenyi*, CC209/49, MLA/1/350, KNA; *Kerubo w/o Ayienda*, CC176/51, MLA/1/431; *Tapchelong w/o Buyot*, C292/52, MLA/1/458.

59. *Nderunye d/o Langalte*, MLA/1/637, KNA.

60. Miranda Davies, *Women and Violence: Realities and Responses Worldwide* (London: Zed Books, 1994).

61. *Rex v. Chengawani*, CC14/31, J5/5/35, NAM.

62. *Gando d/o Kithongo*, CC85/45, MLA/1/223, KNA.

63. Leonore Walker, *The Battered Woman Syndrome* (New York: Springer, 1984).

64. *Rex v. James Kamwezi*, CC22/45, P. O'Riordan, 15 September 1945, PCC/1/16/2, NAM.

65. *Ngutu s/o Mungyoki*, CC226/49, MLA/1/344, KNA.

66. *R. v. Mangulenji Phiri*, confidential reports, CC58/43, report by B. Wickham, 23 February 1944, PCC 1/16/1, NAM.

67. *Rex v. Namoni s/o Kliyaza*, confidential reports, CC24/58, DC Lilongwe, NAM.

68. *Kipruto arap Tanui*, CC169/55, DC Brown, 12 December 1955, MLA/1/1315, KNA.

69. Many thanks to Megan Vaughan for this information.

70. *Rex v. Julius*, CC44/46, PCC/1/16/2, NAM.

71. *Rex v. Frank Mwale*, 1936, J5/12/36, NAM.

72. *Rex v. Yakobe*, 1924, Magistrate Brackenbury, 1 January 1924, J5/12/21, NAM.

73. Luongo, "Domestic Dramas and Occult Acts."

74. *Weyulo Kankozi*, CC111/41, MLA/1/119, KNA. The relationship between witchcraft belief and domestic violence is one that deserves extensive further attention.

75. *Rex v. Sikisi* CC8/36, S1/198/36, NAM; *Francis Okumu s/o Muluka* CC59/51, MLA/1/396, KNA.

76. *Rex v. Table Cholo*, CC76/31, J5/12/30 NAM; *R. v. Amos alias Fewst Eber*, CC9/35, S1/235/35; *R. v. Kipsany arap Tembor*, Commutation of Death Sentences,

1925–40, AG/52/139, KNA; *Kipkirumi arap Chuma*, CC142/49, MLA/1/339; *R. v. Kipsang arap Tembor*, MLA/1/502.

77. *Rex v. Kamatowola Bokos*, CC49/47, Chief Justice Lockhart Smith, J5/5/102, NAM.

78. *Jeremiah Mwangi*, CC310a/51, MLA/1/402, KNA.

79. *Rex v. Sanato Jesitara*, EACA judgment, 11 September 1945, CC4/45, PCC/1/16/2, NAM.

80. *Kabon w/o Kirop*, CC66/46, MLA/1/248, KNA. See also *Sagamo w/o Kinsop*, CC216/49, MLA/1/347.

8 ⤳ Domestic Dramas and Occult Acts

Witchcraft and Violence in the Arena of the Intimate

KATHERINE LUONGO

FOCUSING ON COLONIAL KENYA, I consider "witchcraft"-related violence as a space in which to explore the wider meanings of "domestic violence" and the broader scope of state interventions into intimate relations.[1] Cases of witchcraft-driven violence can be read as being as much about domestic dramas as they are about occult actions. Focusing on such crimes opens avenues to further analyze and historicize violence as well as domesticity and intimacy. Reading witchcraft-related crimes as incidences of "domestic violence" suggests that "witchcraft" was one of the few tropes available in colonial legal settings for talking about domestic violence in Kenya. It indicates that state authorities regarded disciplining witchcraft not simply as a matter of law but as yet another arena in which to (tacitly) intervene in Africans' intimate affairs.

Witch-driven murders offer a wider view of the domestic, figuring it not simply as contained within the bounds of the individual homestead but also including communal spaces where activities related to the community's social reproduction occurred. Reading witchcraft-related crimes as domestic violence broadens the scope of the term *domestic violence*. Witchcraft-related domestic violence includes actions perpetrated by alleged witches and encompasses an alleged witch's lethal speech and deadly thoughts as well as the epistemological violence of the witchcraft accusation, a speech act often leading to retributive physical violence and even to the witch's death.

Reading witchcraft-related crimes within the context of domestic violence complicates issues of power. It demonstrates that domestic violence is not necessarily or even primarily an issue of male power directed against a female intimate partner. Male and female witches are equally alleged to be the initial instigators of violence against intimate partners such as spouses or lovers,

179

but also against assorted kin—especially children—and close associates. The epistemological violence of accusations of witchcraft and the retributive violence directed against witches are also wielded equally by women and men.[2] Witchcraft-driven domestic violence foregrounds the affective states underlying the will to power tied up in domestic violence.

State documents pertaining to witchcraft-related violence demonstrate that officials recognized that the circumstances of such crimes were rife with intimate abuse and domestic conflict. Reading such records with an eye for the intimate reveals how colonial authorities approached cases of witchcraft-driven domestic violence as an additional space to intrude upon Africans' interpersonal conduct, suggesting what sorts of attitudes and affective states were legally recognizable and "reasonable."

Colonial court transcripts in witch-murder cases give narrative form to the domestic dramas underlying occult actions and subsequent violence. Judicial opinions turned primarily on legal questions of "malice aforethought" and "grave and sudden provocation." These principles hinged on the affect and intent underlying the domestic dramas driving witchcraft-related violence. More subtly, antiwitchcraft legislation suggested the state's recognition of the affective states wrapped up in witchcraft practices (and accusations) and in resulting episodes of domestic violence.

As Stacey Hynd notes in this volume, "In colonial Africa, murder trials were an arena where notions of 'violence' and socially acceptable behavior clashed and were contested, where private lives became the subject of public discourses."[3] This chapter offers a case study of a witch-murder trial, *Rex versus Ali Mwinyi*, in which domestic dramas underlay (alleged) occult acts and violence.[4] Out of numerous witch-murder dossiers accessible in the Ministry of Legal Affairs case files, I have chosen to focus on *Ali Mwinyi* because it entails exceptional elements of intimacy buried within broader judicial narratives.[5]

In 1953, Ali Mwinyi, a Digo teenager from Kwale District, was tried in the Supreme Court of Kenya for killing Juma Ali, the father of a close friend of the accused. The defense argued that Ali Mwinyi had been justified in killing Juma Ali after experiencing years of escalating bewitchment at his hands. Juma Ali, the defense asserted, had initiated his serial pattern of witchcraft against the accused late one night as Ali Mwinyi and Juma Ali's son slept in the son's space.[6]

Yet, neither the defense nor the prosecution raised the issue that the "funny things" Ali Mwinyi had vaguely described in various legal settings as marking the initial act of bewitchment also included an incidence of male rape. *Ali Mwinyi* indicates how colonial jurisprudence regarded the African "household as an imaginary space" in which "violence occur[red] as both normalcy and criminality."[7] It foregrounds how "witchcraft" was one of the few available categories for talking about intimate violence among close associates in domestic spaces. Witchcraft was a much more available category than either rape, the only legal classification overtly addressing violence in the arena of the intimate, or "unnatural offences," the primary legal classification for dealing with sex (consensual or otherwise) between men.[8]

THEORIES AND CONTEXT

While "violence" operated as a central rubric of state discourse (and practice), its meanings and uses were strongly contested in colonial Kenya. A facile understanding of "violence" is that of injurious physical force directed against the body of one person by another in pursuit of the perpetrator's aims.[9] This "instrumental" conception elides "interactions in which physical hurt is either absent or not readily apparent, even if it may have been intended" and is the sort most readily apprehended and employed by state actors in colonial legal settings.[10] The evidentiary-based legal systems of most modern states have necessarily demanded operational categories that are readily discernible, neatly bounded, and subject to stable definition.[11]

In colonies like Kenya, governmentality in the criminal sphere centered on the state's claim to a monopoly on the legitimate exercise of violence.[12] Authorities reinforced this claim discursively, consistently juxtaposing the "rationality" of modern, state-centered legal systems with the "repugnancy" of backward, local "customary" laws.[13] The state took an instrumental view of violence when assessing its subjects' behaviors and wielded instrumental violence through punishments such as flogging and hanging. Both routinized and ad hoc state violence also took a mundane variety of forms.[14]

Ali Mwinyi suggests that the ambiguities over the legitimate exercise of violence in colonial settings were created in part by the courts' focus on instrumental violence. Where the state sought to create categories of "punishable people" and to discipline them via confinement and/or violence, most local juridical systems in Kenya sought to identify and punish, sometimes through juridical violence, "categories of dangerous persons" apt to perpetrate violence against bodies, spirits, and psyche.[15] Yet, many of the sorts of social malefactors, such as witches, who fell into "categories of dangerous persons" identified by local communities often did *not* qualify as practically punishable in the eyes of the state. In the legal interstices created by the state's emphasis on instrumental violence, local forms of juridical violence often superseded the state's dictates.

This trend was evident in *Ali Mwinyi*. Juma Ali's "funny things," stipulated as "witchcraft" by Ali Mwinyi, would not have rendered Juma Ali a punishable person in the perspective of the colonial legal system. Though the state in Kenya recognized the dangers surrounding "witchcraft" and enacted antiwitchcraft laws, it also demanded a strict standard of tangible evidence in prosecuting an inherently invisible crime. Ali Mwinyi, having slain Juma Ali with a panga in front of witnesses, was clearly classifiable as a perpetrator of instrumental violence, as a punishable person according to state legal standards.

Ambiguities arose with Ali Mwinyi's casting of Juma Ali as a "witch," as a "dangerous person" who was *not* practically punishable within the state system. As the state failed to offer him protection, and as both state and local codes regarded "witchcraft" as dangerous, Ali Mwinyi, or so the defense argued, was justified in taking matters into his own hands; stepping into the space created by the state's untenable evidentiary demands and its instrumentalist view of violence to exercise violence against a dangerous person in protection of his own body and psyche. This argument was directed at mitigating the colonial state's necessary categorization of Ali Mwinyi as a punishable person.

Colonial-era Digo conceptions of violence are much more elusive than the state's neat categories. Available ethnography and *Ali Mwinyi* suggest that for Digo people "violence" entailed important elements of performance and self-fashioning. Sources suggest that understandings of what constituted violence were not limited to discernible moments of physical aggression but entailed behavior deliberately producing psychic and affective damage. Describing a moment of violent performance remarkably similar to the behaviors enacted by Ali Mwinyi, Roger Gomm writes,

> Digo men are known to be violent. They will seize a panga and rush from the house to avenge an insult. Usually they are stopped by well-wishers before they can perpetrate a seriously violent act, but their displays of violence and aggression are credited with meaning . . . even if they make as if to strike their friends . . . it is assumed that they have some good reason for behaving as they do.[16]

In Digo spaces, violence was both produced by and productive of social relations. Relations entangled in various sorts of affective states generated aggressive acts involving bodies, psyches, and sentiments. In certain circumstances, violence was used as a means to discipline violence. State categorizations of violence, in contrast, classed violence as harm done to bodies. Acts of aggression toward the body evidenced a contravention of social order that demanded state intervention. Colonial and Digo estimations shared the notion that violence could be as much a restoration as a rupture. They differed over who could legitimately wield violence as a corrective.

If the state was prepared to recognize bodily harm as violence, the question arises again of why Ali Mwinyi centered his defense on "witchcraft" rather than intimate abuse. By problematizing "the domestic," "the intimate," and "rape" in colonial contexts, the logics undergirding his legal strategy emerge.

Whether it be the violence of "witchcraft" that Ali Mwinyi repeatedly referenced or the violence of sodomy that was raised and then abruptly dropped, in both instances the violence affecting Ali Mwinyi was of an intimate nature and occurred in domestic spaces. Parsing Ali Mwinyi's claims about the violence in which he was involved opens a space to consider the notion of domestic violence in colonial African contexts. The violence in *Ali Mwinyi*—physical and psychic destruction exchanged between associates—raises the issue of how to delineate the bounds of "domestic/domesticity" and the nuances of "intimate/intimacy" in social situations in colonial Africa.[17] The case indicates that the scholar's gaze needs to be retrained on Africans' notions of space and of self-fashioning; discerning both a microhistorical view of why particular actors thought and behaved as they did and adding ethnographic texture to the oft-flattened legal landscape of the state.

In communities such as Ali Mwinyi's, wide webs of affinity—from polygamous marriages to clan ties—joined people.[18] The idea of domestic space thus needs to be expanded beyond the discrete, individualized dwelling to overlapping homesteads, from single-family homes to communal hearths. Spaces of broad belonging constituted "the domestic." "Domesticity" in such settings is best figured as the variety of pursuits undertaken at the homestead and around the hearth necessary to reproduce wider webs of affinity.

Ali Mwinyi further suggests an expansion of "intimate/intimacy." The arena of the "intimate" is the close, interpersonal relationship, and "intimacy" refers to the conditions—physical, psychic, and sentimental—tied up in the "intimate." European constructions took the marital relationship as the primary locus of "domestic/domesticity" and attendant "intimate/intimacy."[19] In communities like Ali Mwinyi's, in contrast, more fluid boundaries of space and sociability produced varieties of "domestic/domesticity" and "intimate/intimacy" without necessarily taking the marital dyad as central.

Thinking through these categories with fresh frameworks helps problematize domestic violence. Much literature on domestic violence naturalizes the marital relationship as the taken-for-granted nexus of abuse, the marital home as the central space of attack, and women as the exclusive victims of maltreatment.[20] *Ali Mwinyi* troubles the dominant narrative, suggesting how domestic violence might be mobilized as a category taking in "any violation where the victim and the perpetrator have some sort of personal or family relationship or where they have had a relationship in the past."[21]

Yet, although a wider understanding of domestic violence casts Ali Mwinyi as a victim of intimate aggressions occurring in domestic arenas, it also figures him as a perpetrator of domestic violence. "Witchcraft," affective, psychic, and bodily destruction most often deployed against a close associate and occurring in the arena of the intimate, was itself a permutation of domestic violence. But witchcraft *accusations* of the sort leveled by Ali Mwinyi, speech acts implying intimate knowledge of their objects, also did discursive violence within the domain of domestic relations by injuring the reputations of the accused and their own security of self. Such speech acts often resulted in bodily or even deadly damage to the accused witch, carried out by the accuser or by local juridical authorities.

Analyzing typologies of violence and categories of domesticity and intimacy in *Ali Mwinyi* raises the following questions: If Ali Mwinyi experienced sodomy, an instrumental (and intimate) form of violence, and himself carried out a panga attack, an instrumental (and highly personal) form of violence, why did he couch all the violence done to bodies in the arena of the intimate in terms of witchcraft? Why were state actors willing to accept and to engage with the witchcraft frame in dealing with an incidence of domestic violence? Attending to the legally available languages for talking about domestic violence begins to offer answers.

A complex of ideas about gender and age informed legal approaches to sexuality in colonial Africa. Colonial states drew distinctions between licit/legal and illicit/illegal sexual acts and relationships. These distinctions were subject to various degrees of policing and enforcement.

Under colonial legal regimes in Africa, rape was simultaneously a clear-cut and a fraught offense. Legislation clearly articulated what actions constituted rape, but imposed a heavy burden of proof on the alleged victim. It treated rape as an obviously gendered violence, exclusively a crime of male perpetrators and female victims.

Such was the case in colonial Kenya, where the Kenya Legislative Council elevated rape to a capital crime in 1926 thus rendering the Kenya High Court the sole provenance for prosecuting rape. This elevation did not necessarily imply that colonial authorities thought Africans took rape (or other sexual offenses) seriously.[22] Rather, rape was elevated to a capital crime in response to the "black peril" of 1926.[23]

While rape's elevation evidenced colonial concerns with African men's allegedly rampant sexuality, the Kenyan law conformed to gendered colonial notions of rape. The law contra rape stipulated, "Carnal knowledge means sexual intercourse. The offence committed is the penetration of the female organ by the male organ."[24] Although Ali Mwinyi experienced intimate, sexual violence, the colonial code disqualified him from being able to argue rape since the forcible sex act criminalized by antirape legislation was vaginal penetration.

"Indecent assault" constituted another diffuse, gendered legal category through which less serious sexualized crimes could be hashed out. Colonial legal language constructed "indecent assault" first as a crime perpetrated by men against women.[25] Legislation and case law focused less on a man's actions and more on the motivations that underlay them. Further, the law asserted syllogistically that in order to be considered indecent assault rather than assault per se "any assault must be accompanied by acts of indecency. Even a kiss can amount to indecent assault," while related case law attended to how the act of indecency was not always indecent.[26]

While indecent assault legislation was gendered, it did have a section under which males could seek redress. The law noted, "Indecent assault of a boy under the age of fourteen years is also a felony with a liability to imprisonment for seven years, with or without corporal punishment (section 164)."[27] The law constructed "indecent assault" as a sexualized crime perpetrated by men against women or boys. It offered no provision for an assault of an "indecent" nature being perpetrated on one adult male by another.

Even had Ali Mwinyi been able to cast Juma Ali's sodomy as an indecent assault, he would have been disqualified from seeking redress as the medical examiner's form noted him to be around eighteen years old at the time of the trial. Had he come forward four years earlier after the initial assault occurred, he might have been able to bring a case against Juma Ali under indecent assault legislation.

Certain sexual acts were criminalized in Kenya under legislation pertaining to "Unnatural Offences," which made it illegal for anyone to "consent to carnal knowledge that is against the order of nature."[28] Exploiting the fluidity of this legislation, Ali Mwinyi might have had success in bringing Juma Ali to court for perpetrating an "unnatural offence." Yet, in demonstrating that he had been *forcibly* subjected to an "unnatural act," Ali Mwinyi would have faced a double burden in proving that the unnatural act had occurred and that it been due to violation, not volition. Indeed, the failure to bring the case to the attention of the colonial authorities might well have been construed as consent by state agents.

The shame entailed by having been sodomized also could have contributed to Ali Mwinyi's reticence. Writing on homosexual rapes cases in colonial Zimbabwe, Mark Epprecht notes, "Court records also understate the relevance of nonconsensual relationships. As with heterosexual rape, shame and fear of retribution were powerful constraints upon victims coming forward."[29] Such sentiments might have produced a reluctance even more pronounced in Ali Mwinyi's case as Juma Ali was an elder, not a peer. Bewitchment, in contrast, was an almost quotidian experience that invited sympathy, not shame, for the victim.

Practically speaking, while colonial law contained a developed body of case law for adjudicating witch-murder cases, nothing comparable existed for dealing with cases of intimate violence or, more important, for dealing with the intimate violence perpetrated by the deceased being levied as a mitigating element of provocation. The corpus of witch-murder cases was replete with (moderately successful) claims by defendants that the deceaseds' witchcraft was a mitigating factor.

It is possible too that Ali Mwinyi viewed the intimate abuse perpetrated by Juma Ali as a type of "witchcraft."[30] The circumstances under which Juma Ali's assault occurred and the conditions that it produced in Ali Mwinyi could have contributed to something of a conflation of intimate violence and witchcraft. Similar to Juma Ali's actions, witchcraft was practiced in secret, often at night, and produced languishing in body, psyche, and sentiment. Beyond simple sodomy, the acts Juma Ali was alleged to have perpetrated mirrored a standard witchcraft repertoire.

INITIATING ACTS?
"WITCHCRAFT" IN KENYA AND IN KWALE DISTRICT

Notions about witchcraft in play in *Ali Mwinyi* illuminate clashing state and local perspectives on what sort of witchcraft-related violence should be adjudicated. From Ali Mwinyi's viewpoint, the witchcraft practiced by Juma Ali was the initiating act of domestic violence in the case and the act demanding discipline. From the colonial standpoint, Ali Mwinyi's witchcraft accusations against and subsequent attack on Juma Ali constituted the violence that initiated state legal actions. Both perspectives show witchcraft acts, witchcraft accusations, and antiwitchcraft attacks to be violent domestic dramas occurring in the arenas of the intimate.

Colonial Conceptions

In colonial Kenya, witchcraft operated as a way of knowing and a means of telling about the disruption of sociopolitical order and about individual distress. Ideas of witchcraft shared the notion of "magical harm"—damage done through the management of malevolent magic.[31] The 1925 Witchcraft Ordinance, in force during *Ali Mwinyi*, defined witchcraft widely, as discursive and material, entailing speech, acts, and substances.[32] Judicial opinions on witchcraft cases shared these broad conceptualizations. Indeed, the imprecision of "witchcraft" as a category within colonial discourse and experience enabled it to stand in for domestic violence in *Ali Mwinyi*.[33]

Witchcraft in Kwale District

Each tribe in Kenya also retained particular permutations of "magical harm." Historiography about Digo people is regrettably thin, making it hard to know where *Ali Mwinyi* fits in the genealogy of Digo witchcraft or in the history of Digo sociopolitical situations more generally. The more abundant ethnography, though still limited, offers a means to contextualize witchcraft discourses present in *Ali Mwinyi*. H. T. M. Kayamba's 1947 article, "Notes on the Wa-digo," and Diane Ciekawy's chapter on witchcraft among the Mijikenda, the broader ethnic umbrella under which the Digo are included, offer a lens into the general contours of witchcraft in Ali Mwinyi's community.[34]

Kayamba's article for the anthro-administrative journal *Tanganyika Notes and Records* outlines the shape of Digo witchcraft.[35] Digo witchcraft relied on substances, violated the victim's domestic space while upsetting his sensibilities, took place at night, and was gendered male. The description of witchcraft offered by Ali Mwinyi in many ways accorded with Kayamba's explanation. Ali Mwinyi asserted that he had been bewitched with a mixture of harmful substances and toxic looks, that the initiating act had happened in the dark, at home at night, and had involved nudity. The "funny things" ascribed to Juma Ali had disturbed his sleep and his sensibility.

Kayamba also addressed Digo juridical procedures for dealing with witchcraft, steps that resulted ultimately in cleansing the falsely accused witch's reputation or in the judicial killing of a guilty witch. Kayamaba detailed the deliberated nature of Digo judicial processes for dealing with witches, procedures for which Ali Mwinyi substituted ad hoc justice in killing Juma Ali.[36] Substituting vigilante justice for local juridical mechanisms in witchcraft cases was unexceptional in colonial Kenya as antiwitchcraft legislation criminalized witchcraft accusations—step one in Digo judicial procedures—and entailed a heavy evidentiary burden that made prosecuting witchcraft in colonial courts nearly impossible.

Writing on "magical harm" in Mijikenda communities, Ciekawy attends to issues of affect, agency, and aim tied up in witchcraft. Like other forms of domestic violence, witchcraft causes psychical, psychic, and emotional suffering in its victims, and is something for which the victim is not to be blamed—although perpetrators assert otherwise.[37] Mirroring other forms of intimate abuse, witchcraft is produced by negative sentiments in perpetrators, most often a sentimental matrix of envy and resentment called *wivu* by Mijikenda people. *Wivu* is enhanced by literal and figurative proximity, and like other modes of domestic abuse, it is turned largely against intimates with whom the witch has "ongoing face-to-face encounters."[38]

Ali Mwinyi's detailing of his afflictions accords with the above descriptions. Juma Ali, the father of a friend whom Ali Mwinyi saw regularly, bewitched him out of jealousy over Ali Mwinyi's academic success. Bewitchment produced via negative emotions stripped Ali Mwinyi's health, causing physical, psychological, and affective suffering. Ali Mwinyi foregrounded how witchcraft was done *to* him, hinting again at how intimate abuse and witchcraft could be conflated because both types of violence imply a victim who "had been used."[39] And, the contours of Digo witchcraft could have likely led Ali Mwinyi to conflate two forms of domestic violence—witchcraft and intimate abuse.

In cases such as *Ali Mwinyi*, witchcraft emerged from courtroom narratives as squarely in the domestic, productive of violence between close associates, practiced intimately and affectively, with the results visible in the spaces of home and hearth. Witchcraft explained the background to the violence perpetrated by the accused, suggesting that its subtle violence demanded the sort of spectacular violence that the accused was alleged to have perpetrated. The statements of the accused added important layers of meaning to witchcraft and spoke to the strength and scope of the deceased's witchcraft-driven violence.

Ali Mwinyi described passing Juma Ali's house in the early evening of 9 June 1953 and seeing Juma Ali make a face at him. Ali Mwinyi explained that he was so "angered" by Juma Ali's behavior that he went to the verandah of Juma Ali's house and hit him with a panga without having "intended" to do so. He stated that Juma Ali had "bewitched" him four years earlier in the course of a sleepover with Juma Ali's son at Juma Ali's house. During the night a "naked" Juma Ali "did funny things" to Ali Mwinyi, blew black powder at him, and professed that he wished for Ali Mwinyi's death because Ali Mwinyi had attained more education than had Juma Ali's son.[40]

Ali Mwinyi's assertion that Juma Ali had bewitched him on a regularly recurring basis because of Juma Ali's jealous grudge against him was characteristic of defenses in witch-murder cases. His elaboration that incidences of illness led him to believe that witchcraft had been practiced against him and that witnessing witchcraft practices or apprehending threats of witchcraft directed against him had caused him to believe "magical harm" had been perpetrated and was again imminent was also a regular feature of the accused's testimony in witch-murder cases.

Emphasizing the recidivist nature of the deceased's witchcraft, the facts of cases and related testimony in similar cases point to lack of immediate temporal proximity between the incidences of witchcraft and witch-killings. Varying degrees of lag time generally exist between incidences or threats of witchcraft and the witch-killings. Ali Mwinyi believed himself continually bewitched, commencing with an incident four years previous to Juma Ali's killing.

In *Ali Mwinyi*, witchcraft served simultaneously to draw out and to relegate to the background exceptional elements of the intimate tied up in the case. Ali Mwinyi's relationship to Juma Ali seems to have been not simply one of neighbor-to-neighbor, but one of minor victim to adult sexual abuser. Along with "mental confusion caused on suspicion of witchcraft," the report of the district commissioner, Kwale, also cited "alleged sodomy by the deceased" on the list of "extenuating circumstances and/or provocation."[41] Although raised by the district commissioner, the issue of sodomy was never addressed in any court and neither party attended to Ali Mwinyi's claims about Juma Ali's nudity or the "funny things" he did.

Taken solely as a case of witch-murder, *Ali Mwinyi* was quite straightforward from both the defense's and the state's perspectives. Precedent in witch-murder cases provided avenues for the defense to argue for mitigation, for the prosecution to convict, and for the high courts to recommend clemency.[42] Introducing the complicated (and legally unspeakable) issue of homosexual rape into the stew of circumstances surrounding Juma Ali's killing would have been futile as ready jurisprudence for managing such an incidence of domestic violence simply did not exist. Witchcraft was the least ambivalent and most accessible category of domestic violence for all parties enmeshed in the case.

AFFECT AND ADJUDICATION

"Witchcraft" offered a broadly situated and readily available category for dealing with domestic violence in the space of the courts. State authorities had regularly mobilized witchcraft as a heuristic to explain (and to substitute for) all sorts of disorder from the mundane to the masochistic. Consequently, a well-developed body of jurisprudence about witchcraft and capital violence was easily accessible to the players in *Ali Mwinyi*.

As Scott London notes in this volume, domestic violence is a deeply "entangled" category, subject to competing claims in legal settings.[43] This section parses the entangled claims made about witchcraft and domestic violence tied up in *Ali Mwinyi*, attending to how judicial tenets shaped their production. It traces how the courts drew on precedent in order to assess whether the witchcraft of the deceased—and the domestic violence imbricated in it—added up to mitigation.

In Ali Mwinyi's initial testimony, violence emerged as undeniably intimate and squarely situated within domestic spaces and relations of domesticity. It is worth quoting this testimony at length.

> On 9.6.53, I went to the verandah of the deceased's house at 6 p.m. and struck him with a panga. I did this because . . . he looked at me and made a face at me, opening his mouth. This *angered* me very much, *so unexpectedly, without having intended it,* I cut him with a panga.
>
> Deceased had bewitched me . . . about 4 years ago. One night his son asked me to spend the night with him (the son) in his house. . . . I lay down to go to sleep, deceased approached me, naked. *He then did funny things to me.* He had *black powder* in his left hand, and *he blew it at me,* into my ears and nose and face, saying, "I don't want to see you because I find that *you are becoming more educated than my son.* I want

you to die because I don't want to see you in this world." There was a lamp burning at the time. . . . When I caught deceased's arm he threw the powder down on the floor. When deceased blew powder into my eyes and nose I was *afraid* of him. I felt that he was *bewitching* me.

From then on, *I felt a physical change in myself.* I felt my head was becoming weak, and my blood was decreasing. And I didn't sleep as well as I had . . . I don't feel any better even now.

During the four years between my *bewitching* and my killing deceased, I met deceased often. . . . I would run away from him because I was *angry* with him because he had *bewitched* me.[44]

Considering this testimony more closely, one can see how the accused's approach to narrating witchcraft-related domestic violence was typically an "experiential" one in which violence was treated as "subjective" and ascribed meaning "mainly through an individual's perception of a violent situation."[45]

The violence that Ali Mwinyi experienced and perpetrated was intimate, and it was natural that he should speak about it in subjective and affective terms, attending strongly to the effects that Juma Ali's "witchcraft" and his own actions ultimately had on his sentiments and sensibilities. He made multiple mentions of *anger* and *fear*, explaining that Juma Ali's expression (leveled just before Ali Mwinyi killed him) had "angered" him very much and that he had run from Juma Ali's presence four years earlier, "angry with him because he had bewitched me." He said that when Juma Ali "blew powder into my eyes and nose, I was afraid of him."

This testimony shows how an "experiential" approach worked also to reference *legal* languages of affect. The particular terms employed worked to (re)formulate Ali Mwinyi's experience to adhere to key judicial categories of mitigation, "grave and sudden provocation" and "malice aforethought." Opinions in a triad of witch-murder trials that included buried elements of domestic violence, heard in East Africa's highest courts from the early 1930s to the early 1950s, established these terms.[46]

In the 1931 case, *Rex v. Kumwaka s/o [son of] Mulumbi and 69 Others*, sixty Wakamba men were tried in Kenya's High Court for murdering a neighbor woman, Mwaiki, whom they alleged had bewitched the wife of one of their number.[47] The defense argued that in killing Mwaiki the men had been practicing an old form of Kamba justice to protect the community at large from the violence of a recidivist witch. Extant jurisprudence left the High Court no alternative but to hand down death sentences on all accused with recommendations to the governor-in-council for clemency.[48]

The case was appealed in the High Court of Appeal for Eastern Africa on the grounds that the witchcraft of the deceased had constituted "grave and sudden provocation," a legally mitigating condition capable of reducing sentences of murder to ones of manslaughter.[49] The justices concluded that the facts of the case did *not* add up to "grave and sudden provocation." *Kumwaka* became the benchmark for adjudicating cases such as *Ali Mwinyi*.

Appellants in the 1941 case, *Fabiano Kinene s/o Mukye, Seperiano Kiwanuka s/o Kintu, Albert Iseja s/o Kintu,* who had argued that the witchcraft of the deceased had driven them to kill him after finding the deceased crawling naked around their compound, achieved a different result.[50] The conviction was reduced from murder to manslaughter, relying in part on *Kumwaka* to reach the decision that "grave and sudden provocation" *was* held proved. The *Fabiano* decision's complex analysis was cited in almost all subsequent witchcraft-related murder cases, including *Ali Mwinyi.* Addressing "grave and sudden provocation," the decision also focused on questions of "malice aforethought," on the truthfulness and reasonableness of the appellants' witchcraft beliefs, and on "native mentalité."

The appeals court concurred with the High Court of Uganda that Fabiano and his cohort demonstrated that they had killed the deceased with "malice aforethought" and concluded that the appellants did hold a "real but mistaken belief" in the deceased's witchcraft.[51] Drawing on *Kumwaka,* the courts concluded that the appellants' belief in witchcraft while introducing the *possibility* of a defense of "grave and sudden provocation," did not alone constitute sufficient grounds to prove "grave and sudden provocation."[52] *Fabiano* critiqued the notion of "fear" and added that witchcraft could also be regarded as inducement to the sort of anger that in turn constituted an element of the "heat of passion" phrasing in the Uganda Penal Code section dealing with "provocation."[53]

The opinion wove together two important ideas, arguing first that an additional affective state, "anger," was sufficient to induce the immediate and overwhelming passion that was an ineluctable constituent part of "provocation." Second, the opinion attended to "native mentalité" regarding witchcraft, identifying a standard of reasonableness taking in local mind-sets and mores, but also designating witchcraft as it was extrapolated in *colonial* law.[54]

Eria Galikuwa v. Rex, a 1951 case cited in *Ali Mwinyi,* refined and reemphasized many of the aforementioned principles. Eria Galikuwa, the appellant, claimed that the deceased, a witch doctor, had threatened to kill him unless he paid an exorbitant fee. Unable to pay, Galikuwa instead killed the deceased. *Eria Galikuwa* critiqued and revised *Fabiano,* asserting that states of anger *and* fear both had to be present in the mind of the accused in order to constitute the "passion" which was an essential element of "grave and sudden provocation."[55] The decision also emphasized that the "provocative" act of witchcraft needed to be "overt," that is, "physical," "visible," or "audible," and had to constitute witchcraft according to antiwitchcraft legislation. It also expanded the time frame for "provocation."[56]

The appeals court found that the conditions for "provocation" were not satisfied because Galikuwa had shown himself to be motivated by "fear alone" and had acted in "despair" rather than in the "heat of passion." The decision added that the appellant's actions resulted from deliberated intention, not from being "suddenly deprived of his self-control." The court found the appellant had not availed himself of the legal options available for dealing with the deceased's threats and "chose deliberately to take the law into his own hands."[57]

The courts were constrained by the law from dealing directly with the elements of intimacy and domesticity tied up in the violence at hand. Yet even when drawing on the notion of witchcraft to negotiate an array of domestic dramas and occult acts in intimate arenas, the courts were still limited to considering witchcraft as a defense only when attaching another legal category to it. Nonetheless, attention to witchcraft enabled the courts to distinguish killings in retribution for witchcraft from killings for more mundane reasons.

Accordingly, Ali Mwinyi's initial testimony referenced "fear" and "anger" and spoke to standards for "grave and sudden provocation." Testimony on cross and redirect reinforced and expanded his earlier claims.

He explained,

> The night of the bewitching was not the only time I thought he was bewitching me. I thought so again the night of the killing, when I passed his house; this was just because of the way he looked at me. He was not just yawning. I had my panga in my hand already. So I struck him with it. I felt both anger and fear on this occasion. When he pulled that face at me . . . he was eating his evening meal. . . . He glared at me too. . . .
>
> When the deceased pulled the face at me, I was so *angry* that I was determined to kill him. . . . He had pulled similar faces at me, during those 4 years, and I used to run away. I didn't run away on 9th June 1953, when pulled that face, because I got very *angry* with him. On the other occasions when he pulled faces at me he had not made me so angry. He made a worse face at me on this occasion than on the previous occasions. I could have run away, but I got very *angry* and found myself cutting him.

He added on redirect, "The face he pulled this time was a frightful one."[58]

This testimony emphasized the exceptional nature of Juma Ali's expression on the night he was killed, thus constituting the expression, rather than the "funny things" of years previous, as the immediate provocative act. As above, Ali Mwinyi's "anger and fear" again pointed to "provocation."

This testimony referenced "malice aforethought," a legal condition that the Kenya Penal Code stipulated had to be present in the mind of the accused for an action to constitute murder. Explaining, "I had my panga in my hand already," and " . . . I found myself cutting him," Ali Mwinyi aimed to (re)emphasize the suddenness of his actions, made in response to an immediate "provocation," and to disable the element of consideration of one's actions as including "malice aforethought."

Subsequent testimony posed strategic claims about the witchcraft of the deceased. Causing "fear, annoyance or injury" through purporting to have supernatural power was an offense under the 1925 Witchcraft Ordinance.[59] Describing his fear in response to Juma Ali's (alleged occult) actions, Ali Mwinyi cast Juma Ali as a witchcraft practitioner.

Attention to Juma Ali's "face-pulling" over a period of years suggests a *recidivist* pattern of witchcraft. Under local codes, serial practice of witchcraft legitimized judicial witch-killings. The courts considered arguments about local codes as part of a broader assessment of the accused's witchcraft *mentalité*.

Testimony in *Ali Mwinyi* and the circumstances surrounding the cases used to adjudicate it demonstrated the degree to which domestic violence permeated witch-murders. The nuanced nature of Ali Mwinyi's testimony raises the question of how effective his claims about domestic violence, cast as witchcraft, ultimately were.

Judgments in *Ali Mwinyi* followed a relatively standardized structure, and as witchcraft constituted a key element of the defense, the judgments also attended to it.[60] Justice R. Windham, writing for the Kenya High Court, assessed Ali Mwinyi's claims according to legal protocols and precedents.[61] For the courts, the key question was whether "grave and sudden provocation" had been present in a case of "prima facie murder," thus reducing the murder charge to manslaughter. The courts accepted Ali Mwinyi's assertions about Juma Ali's witchcraft and about the affective states that Juma Ali's actions had produced within Ali Mwinyi.[62]

It would seem at first that Ali Mwinyi's defense succeeded. However, drawing on extant jurisprudence, the courts exercised their own subtle analysis of Ali Mwinyi's deliberately structured narrative. While accepting that Ali Mwinyi sincerely believed he had been bewitched, the opinion subsequently assessed whether Juma Ali's actions *legally* constituted witchcraft and whether Ali Mwinyi's belief in Juma Ali's witchcraft achieved a standard of "reasonableness." For a defense of "grave and sudden provocation" motivated by the witchcraft of the deceased to work, the act of witchcraft had to conform to the legal standard set out by the 1925 Witchcraft Ordinance or to a standard of "reasonable belief" within the community in question.[63]

Citing *Fabiano* and *Eria Galikuwa*, the courts concluded that Juma Ali's actions *did not* constitute "grave and sudden provocation.[64] As noted above, both decisions attended strongly to the issue of ordinary local mentalités vis-à-vis witchcraft. Justice Windham adduced,

But even to an ordinary African to whom the power of witchcraft is a very real thing I cannot hold that the mere pulling of a face by another person, however frightful the face, would be a grave enough provocation to deprive him of his power of self-control so as to make him in the heat of passion kill that other person. That the accused in this case did in fact lose his self-control there can be no doubt. . . . But I cannot hold that the act of the deceased in pulling the face . . . was of such a nature as to be likely, if done to an ordinary African believing it to be an act of witchcraft, to make such an African lose his self-control and kill the other.

According to the standards established in preceding cases, Ali Mwinyi had failed to make the case that his experience of domestic violence, couched in witchcraft claims, was sufficient for reducing a charge of murder to manslaughter.[65] The failure of his arguments, particularly when read in conversation with case law, pointed to the difficulty in meeting legal standards. Ali Mwinyi was convicted of murder.

CONCLUSIONS OF CONFLICTS

Ali Mwinyi concluded with the courts' recommendations and the accused's appeals to the clemency of Kenya's governor-in-council. While dossiers concerning the case do not contain records of whether or not the governor commuted the death sentence, a survey of similar cases indicates that in cases where the accused's "real but mistaken belief" in the deceased's witchcraft was held proved, death sentences were commuted.[66] Given the readiness with which the courts accepted the claims about Ali Mwinyi's firm beliefs that he had been bewitched, it is likely that his sentence was commuted too.

Cases such as *Ali Mwinyi* offer a lens into broad understandings of violence and demonstrate how conflicts are produced by differing perceptions not only of mediation but also by varying perceptions of what constitutes conflict at all. From the accused's perspective, the central conflict in *Ali Mwinyi* was between the victim of domestic violence and the abuser that he killed. The primary form of violence at issue was the intimate abuses wrought by the deceased's "witchcraft." The violence of the accused was of secondary concern, driven by his personal experiences of violence exercised through witchcraft in intimate arenas.

No matter how violence was cast, the conflict concerning the state the most was that over who retained the right to legitimately wield violence. Although such cases exposed the limits of state power, they opened spaces for the state to delve into the toolbox of *lawfare*, the use of law as a weapon of domination, in order to (re)assert hegemony over the use of violence.[67] The state asserted itself by first providing the accused in cases such as *Ali Mwinyi* with avenues to argue mitigation and then systematically shutting these arguments down. *Ali Mwinyi* illustrates how witchcraft offered ways of addressing violent domestic dramas carried out in arenas of the intimate.

NOTES

1. It is well known and widely articulated inside and outside the academy that "witchcraft" is inadequate to cover the nuances, subtleties, and differences among the various practices and beliefs that are often subsumed under the rubric "witch-craft/la sorcerllerie." My point is not to trace the particulars of specific practices and beliefs that could be broadly termed "witchcraft," but instead to attend to some of the ways that "witchcraft" as a catchall category can do and has done a variety of work. Generally speaking, from the colonial-era to the present day, people in Kenya have broadly explained "witchcraft" as an embodied power or a bought substance, each of which is used to do malevolent "magic" in order to harm the person, psyche, property, or kin of another.

2. I use the present tense because of the persistence of such crimes into the present day. Walter Menya and Angwenyi Gichana, "Kisii's Night of Deadly Witch-Hunt," *Daily Nation*, 28 May 2008.

3. Stacey Hynd, "Fatal Families," this volume.

4. *Regina v. Ali s/o Mwinyi*, Nairobi, 1953, MLA 1/567, Kenya National Archives (hereafter KNA).

5. *Ali Mwinyi* is discussed in Richard Waller's foundational article, "Witchcraft and Colonial Law in Kenya," *Past and Present* 180, no. 1 (2003): 241–75. I am grateful to Richard for sharing his work with me.

6. *Regina v. Ali s/o Mwinyi*, Nairobi, 1953, MLA 1/567, KNA. The night in question was not the only occasion on which Ali Mwinyi had slept over at Juma Ali's home, but it was the only occasion on which abuse was alleged.

7. Rosalind C. Morris, "The Mute and the Unspeakable: Political Subjectivity, Violent Crime, and the 'Sexual Thing' in a South African Mining Community," in *Law and Disorder in the Postcolony*, ed. Jean Comaroff and John L. Comaroff (Chicago: University of Chicago Press, 2006), 87.

8. The author surveyed more than one hundred Ministry of Legal Affairs (MLA) files on capital cases tried in the High Court of Kenya between 1939 and 1941. In seventeen of these cases, the "witchcraft" of the deceased was offered by the defense as a mitigating circumstance. Unfortunately, a fire in the secretariat in 1939 destroyed all trial transcripts up to 1939. "Witch-murder" cases were also identified through the author's more limited survey of MLA files on cases with multiple defendants.

9. Carole Nagengast, "Violence, Terror, and the Crisis of the State," *Annual Review of Anthropology* 23 (1994): 111.

10. Ibid.

11. Lauren Benton, "Colonial Law and Cultural Difference: Jurisdictional Politics and the Formation of the Colonial State," *Comparative Studies in Society and History* 41, no. 3 (1999): 563–88.

12. John L. Comaroff and Jean Comaroff, "Law and Disorder in the Postcolony: An Introduction," in *Law and Disorder in the Postcolony*, ed. Jean Comaroff and John L. Comaroff (Chicago: University of Chicago Press, 2006), 30–31.

13. Colonial officials were somewhat prepared to negotiate with issues of "custom" in the civil arena. See H. F. Morris and James S. Read, *Indirect Rule and the Search for Justice* (Oxford: Clarendon Press, 1972); Sally Falk Moore, "Treating Law as Knowledge: Telling Colonial Officers What to Say to Africans about Running 'Their Own' Native Courts," *Journal of History and Society* 26, no. 2 (1992): 11–46. Falk Moore focuses on the administration of justice in the civil arena as a function of the colonial imaginary. However, discourses about crime and justice expressed by colonial authorities in documents pertaining to the administration of justice in criminal matters can be profitably theorized as products of the colonial imaginary as well.

14. See especially Steven Pierce and Anupama Rao, eds., *Discipline and the Other Body: Correction, Corporeality, Colonialism* (Durham, NC: Duke University Press, 2006), and Michel Foucault, *Discipline and Punish: The Birth of the Prison* (New York: Vintage Books, 1995). As Foucault reminds us, "modern" states moved away from didactically employing spectacles of violent discipline toward regimes of correction and coercion predicated on more subtle (often discursive) forms of violence directed toward easily reproducible objects. The sorts of spectacular violence as described in the opening pages of Foucault's *Discipline and Punish* were not seen in Kenya until the Mau Mau when state officials and functionaries sought to discipline known or suspected Mau Mau adherents through various forms of torture. On Mau Mau, see Caroline Elkins, *Imperial Reckoning: The Untold Story of Britain's Gulag in Kenya* (New York: Henry Holt, 2005).

15. Nagengast, "Violence, Terror, and the Crisis of the State," 122. Suzette Heald, *Controlling Anger: The Anthropology of Gisu Violence* (Oxford: James Currey, 1998).

16. Roger Gomm, "Bargaining from Weakness: Spirit Possession on the South Kenya Coast," *Man*, new series, 10, no. 4 (1975): 535.

17. Karen Tranberg Hansen, Introduction to *African Encounters with Domesticity*, ed. Karen Tranberg Hansen (New Brunswick, NJ: Rutgers University Press, 1992), 1–33; John L. Comaroff and Jean Comaroff, Introduction to *Of Revelation and Revolution*, vol. 2: *The Dialectics of Modernity on a South African Frontier*, ed. Jean Comaroff and John L. Comaroff (Chicago: University of Chicago Press, 1997), 1–62. See also Steven Feierman, "The Comaroffs and the Practice of Historical Ethnography," *Interventions: International Journal of Postcolonial Studies* 3, no. 1 (2001): 24–36, and Nancy Rose Hunt, A *Colonial Lexicon of Birth Ritual, Medicalization, and Mobility in the Congo* (Durham, NC: Duke University Press, 1999).

18. H. M. T. Kayamba, "Notes on the Wadigo," *Tanganyika Notes and Records* 23 (June 1947): 80–87.

19. Madelaine Adelman, "Review Article: Domestic Violence and Difference," *American Anthropologist* 31, no. 1 (2004): 131–41.

20. Wilhelmina J. Kalu, "Violence against Women in Africa: Impact of Culture on Womanhood," in *International Perspectives on Violence*, ed. Leonore Loeb Adler and Florence L. Denmark (Westport, CT: Praeger, 2004), 190–92. Kalu offers a critique of this literature.

21. Mumbi Machera, "Domestic Violence in Kenya: A Survey of Newspaper Reports," in *Men, Women, and Violence: A Collection of Papers from CODESRIA Gender Institute 1997*, ed. Felicia Oyekanmi (Dakar, Senegal: CODESRIA, 2000), 27–28.

22. Brett Shadle, "Rape in the Courts of Gusiiland, Kenya, 1940s–1960s," *African Studies Review* 51, no. 2 (2008): 3–45. I am grateful to Brett Shadle for sharing his writing and research on this subject with me.

23. Shadle, "Rape in the Courts of Gusiiland, Kenya," 15.

24. Tudor Jackson, *The Law of Kenya: An Introduction* (Nairobi, Kenya: East Africa Literature Bureau, 1970), 106.

25. Ibid., 107. The law explained, "Any person who unlawfully and indecently assaults any woman or girl is guilty of a felony and is liable to imprisonment for five years, with or without corporeal punishment (Penal Code, section 144 [1])."

26. Jackson, *The Law of Kenya*, 107. Case law suggested, "[I]f a young man kisses a young woman against her will and with feeling of carnal passion and with a view to gratifying his passion or to excite hers, that would be indecent assault. There are, of course, many ways in which a kiss is not indecent. A father's kisses are holy, the kisses of young people in seasons of universal gaiety are not indecent."

27. Ibid.

28. Laws of Kenya (in force as of 1/1/24). I am grateful to Brett Shadle for sharing this information with me. The Indian Penal Code noted that "unnatural offences" were punishable by exile to a Penal Colony for life or ten years in prison and a fine. This code was adopted into the Kenya Penal Code with very few substantive changes in 1930, and the law about "unnatural offences" was retained. Patricia Kameri-Mbote, "Violence against Women in Kenya: An Analysis of Law, Policy and Institutions," International Environmental Law Research Centre (Geneva: IELRC, 2001), 10.

29. Marc Epprecht, "'Good God Almighty, What's This!' Homosexual 'Crime' in Early Colonial Zimbabwe," in *Boy-Wives and Female Husbands: Studies of African Homosexualities*, ed. Stephen O. Murray and Will Roscoe (New York: St. Martin's Press, 1998), 203–4; Ross G. Forman, "Randy on the Rand: Portuguese African Labor and the Discourse on 'Unnatural Vice' in the Transvaal in the Early Twentieth Century," *Journal of the History of Sexuality* 11, no. 4 (2002): 570–609.

30. As Epprecht notes, many Shona people cast homosexuality as a mode of witchcraft, as "an other inexplicable exception to the normal moral order" (Epprecht, "Good God Almighty, What's This!" 202).

31. George Clement Bond and Diane Ciekawy, introduction to *Witchcraft Dialogues: Anthropological and Philosophical Exchanges*, ed. George Clement Bond and Diane Ciekawy (Athens: Ohio University Center for International Studies, 2003). 26. Diane Ciekawy, "Witchcraft in Statecraft: Five Technologies of Power

in Colonial and Postcolonial Coastal Kenya," *African Studies Review* 41, no. 3 (1998): 119–42.

32. In Kenya, the first witchcraft ordinance was instituted in 1909. The initial goal of the bill was "to make provision for the punishment of persons practicing or making use of so called witchcraft" (East Africa Protectorate Legislative Council Minutes, meetings held 1 March 1909, 18 May 1909, and 5 July 1909, CO 544/2, Public Record Office [hereafter PRO]; Official Gazettes of the East Africa Protectorate, Special Issue: An Ordinance to Consolidate and Amend the Law Relating to Witchcraft, 1925, CO 542/19, 1131, PRO).

33. Peter Probst, Jan-Georg Deutsch, and Heike Schmidt have argued in a similar vein for problematizing ambivalence within the catchall category of "African Modernities" (Peter Probst, Jan-Georg Deutsch, and Heike Schmidt, "Cherished Visions and Entangled Meanings," in *African Modernities*, ed. Peter Probst, Jan-Georg Deutsch, and Heike Schmidt [Oxford: James Currey, 2002], 1–17).

34. Kayamba, "Notes on the Wadigo," 85–86; Diane Ciekawy, "Utasi as Ethical Discourse: A Critique of Power from the Mijikenda in Coastal Kenya," in Bond and Ciekawy, *Witchcraft Dialogues*, 58–89.

35. Kayamba, "Notes on the Wadigo," 85. He wrote, "Witchcraft in the Digo country consists of poison which a wizard puts in food and gives to the person whom he intends to kill. He also goes in the night to his enemy's house and dances nude outside it. The effect of his magic dance disturbs the inmate of the house and makes him babble in his sleep."

36. Ibid. Kayamaba wrote, "If an Mdigo is suspected of witchcraft, the person who suspects him, reports him to the elders of the village. The elders call together all the elders of the neighboring villages and two elders of each village go to a diviner. The diviner tells them to sit down in a circle or half-circle. The diviner then snuffs his medicine, and holding the tail of an ox or buffalo circles round them. If one of them (elder's relations) is a wizard, the diviner drops the tail on his (the elder's) hips and tells him that one of his relations is a wizard and identifies him. The elders then return and arrest him as the wizard who was responsible for the deceased's death. If he denies they take him to a blacksmith to take the oath. The blacksmith places a hot iron on the palm of his hand and he (the suspected man) recites: 'If I am a wizard let this hot iron burn my palm, if I am not it shall not burn me.' If the hot iron does not burn him the process is repeated three times. . . . The man who accused him of witchcraft is then fined three cattle (two cows and one ox). Two cows are paid to the suspected person and the ox is killed and eaten by the villagers. The three cattle killed are called *Mkomola usawi*, i.e., 'Remove the witchcraft from the falsely accused person.' But if the accused's palm is burnt by the hot iron, he is beaten to death."

37. Ciekawy, "Utasi as Ethical Discourse," 180.

38. Ibid., 170–71. "Envy of the features or qualities of another person's life," Ciekawy elucidates, can lead to the desire to end or diminish that which the other enjoys."

39. Ciekawy explains, "The most common euphemism for being affected by utasi is 'to be done to' (*-fanyiwa*). . . . [P]eople remarked that it indicated that the afflicted 'did not choose it,' 'did not agree,' and 'had been used'" (ibid., 181).

40. *Regina v. Ali s/o Mwinyi*, Nairobi, 1953, MLA 1/567, KNA.

41. *Regina v. Ali s/o Mwinyi*, Nairobi, 1953, MLA 1/567, KNA.

42. Legal precedent in witch-murder cases is discussed in greater detail later in this paper.

43. Scott London, "Constructing Law, Contesting Violence," this volume.

44. *Regina v. Ali s/o Mwinyi*, Nairobi, 1953, MLA 1/567, KNA. My emphasis.

45. Bettina E. Schmidt and Ingo W. Schröder, introduction to *Anthropology of Violence and Confict*, ed. Schmidt and Schröder (London: Routledge, 2007), 17.

46. Katherine Luongo, "Motive Rather Than Means: Legal Genealogies of Witch-Killing Cases," *Cahiers d'Études Africaines* 48, no. 1–2 (2008): 35–57.

47. *Rex v. Kumwaka s/o Mulumbi and 69 others*, Nairobi, 1932, 14 Law Reports of Kenya (hereafter LRK).

48. Katherine Luongo, "Contested Codes and Conflicting Justice: Witchcraft and the State in Kenya" (PhD diss., University of Michigan, 2006).

49. *Rex v. Kumwaka s/o Mulumbi and 69 others*, Nairobi, 1932, 14 LRK.

50. *Rex v. Fabiano Kinene s/o Mukye, Seperiano Kiwanuka s/o Kintu, Albert Iseja s/o Kintu*, Nairobi, 1941, 8 East Africa Court of Appeal (hereafter EACA).

51. *Rex v. Fabiano Kinene s/o Mukye, Seperiano Kiwanuka s/o Kintu, Albert Iseja s/o Kintu*, Nairobi, 1941, 8 EACA.

52. *Rex v. Kimutai arap Mursoi*, Nairobi, 1939, 6 EACA. *Rex v. Mawalawa bin Nyangweza*, Nairobi, 1949, 7 EACA.

53. *Rex v. Fabiano Kinene s/o Mukye, Seperiano Kiwanuka s/o Kintu, Albert Iseja s/o Kintu, Nairobi*, 1941, 8 EACA. The justice explained the principle generally and in regard to the circumstances of *Fabiano*. He wrote, "In our opinion the principle in those cases [*Kumwaka, etc.*] is stated somewhat too narrowly and perhaps not altogether accurately, in that the words 'in the heat of passion' used in s. 198 of the Penal Code (Uganda) are more properly referable to the emotion of anger than to that of fear. We think that if the facts proved establish that the victim was performing in the actual presence of the accused some act which the accused did genuinely believe, and which an ordinary person of the community to which the accused belongs would genuinely believe, to be an act of witchcraft against him or another person under his immediate care (which would be a criminal offence under the Criminal Law [witchcraft] Ordinance of Uganda and similar legislation in other East African territories) he might be angered to such an extent as to be deprived of the power of self-control and induced to assault the person doing the act of witchcraft. And if this be the case a defence of grave and sudden provocation is open to him. It must always be a question of fact as to whether he is in all the circumstances of the particular case acting in the heat of passion caused by grave and sudden provocation and of course on such an issue he must be given the benefit of any reasonable doubt. We think it not unreasonable to say that in the present case the accused persons, when they seized the deceased in the compound and proceeded to kill him, may have been so acting."

54. *Rex v. Fabiano Kinene s/o Mukye, Seperiano Kiwanuka s/o Kintu, Albert Iseja s/o Kintu*, Nairobi, 1941, 8 EACA. Nevertheless, the justices concluded by reiterating that despite the decision in *Fabiano*, they "in no way mean[t] to suggest that we believe witchcraft per se will constitute a circumstance of excuse of

mitigation for killing a person believed to be a witch or wizard when there is no immediate provocative act."

55. *Rex v. Eria Galikuwa*, Nairobi, 1951, 18 EACA.

56. *Rex v. Eria Galikuwa*, Nairobi, 1951, 18 EACA. *Rex v. Petero Wabwire*, Nairobi, 1949, 16 EACA. The decision explained, "The Penal Code does not say that the unlawful act or insult done to or in the presence of another person must be one entailing immediate consequences of a wrongful nature, and there might be upon occasion a wrongful act which was indicative of a future intention on the part of the doer and which therefore might be of such a nature as to come within the legal definition of provocation."

57. *Rex v. Eria Galikuwa*, Nairobi, 1951, 18 EACA.

58. *Regina v. Ali s/o Mwinyi*, Nairobi, 1953, MLA 1/567, KNA.

59. Official Gazettes of the East Africa Protectorate, Special Issue: An Ordinance to Consolidate and Amend the Law Relating to Witchcraft 1925, CO 542/19, 1131, PRO.

60. Judgments portrayed violence more cognitively, as "culturally constructed, as a representation of cultural values" rather than as primarily contingent individuated imperatives. Schmidt and Schröder, "Introduction," 17.

61. *Regina v. Ali s/o Mwinyi*, Nairobi, 1953, MLA 1/567, KNA.

62. *Regina v. Ali s/o Mwinyi*, Nairobi, 1953, MLA 1/567, KNA. Windham explained, "[A]s regards the reason he [Ali Mwinyi] advances for why he killed the deceased I believe him. I also believe his story . . . regarding an act of witchcraft or attempted witchcraft practiced upon him by the deceased four years ago. . . . This made the accused so angry, and also so fearful (although not of any immediate danger to his life) that he lost control of himself and killed the deceased with his panga."

63. *Rex v. Kelementi Maganga s/o of Ochieng, Zadoki Omoiti s/o Okechi*, Nairobi, 1942 20 LRK, Part II, 1942. *Rex v. Kajuna s/o of Mbake*, Nairobi, 1945, 12 EACA. The judgment queried, "But did the deceased's act in pulling that face from him at the verandah, even taking into account the cumulative resentment and fear conjured up in the accused's mind by the deceased's act of four years ago and his subsequent face-pullings, constitute a grave and sudden provocation such as the law would recognize as sufficient to reduce his offence from murder to manslaughter?"

64. *Regina v. Ali s/o Mwinyi*, Nairobi, 1953, MLA 1/567, KNA. The opinion read, "Upon a careful study of the principles enunciated by the East Africa Court of Appeal in witchcraft cases such as this, in *Rex v. Fabiano and others* (1941), 96, EACA, and *Eria Galikuwa* (1951) 18, 175, EACA. I am of the opinion that the act of the deceased did not constitute grave and sudden provocation."

65. *Regina v. Ali s/o Mwinyi*, Nairobi, 1953, MLA 1/567, KNA.

66. Luongo, "Motive Rather Than Means."

67. Comaroff and Comaroff, "Law and Disorder in the Postcolony," 30–31.

PART III

Domestic Violence,

Conjugal Relationships,

and the Politics of the State

in Postcolonial Africa

THE ANALYSES OF contemporary debates about domestic violence found in the third part of this book are attuned to the lasting consequences of institutions and viewpoints forged during colonialism. As Saida Hodžić and Benedetta Faedi both note, the battles over the definition of *custom* continue to have a significant impact on the ability of organizations working to combat domestic violence to effect legislative changes. However, as Scott London's analysis of domestic violence cases in Senegal reveals, the power of the state to control local practice—even within its own bureaucracy and even if it had the political will to do so—is limited by the persistence of alternative moral economies. The ineffectiveness of international human rights conventions and much national legislation leads Codou Bop to conclude that activists must work to change the cultural and religious norms that make domestic violence acceptable to large parts of the population. All of these analyses—and indeed, the problem of domestic violence in contemporary Africa—make most sense in the light of our knowledge of the historical dynamic that has shaped them.

9 ꙩ "I killed her because she disobeyed me in wearing this new hairstyle . . ."

Gender-Based Violence, Laws, and Impunity in Senegal

CODOU BOP

DOKI NIASS, a thirty-year-old woman, was beaten to death by her husband in 1993. She was beaten to death because she was sick during Ramadan, the mandatory Muslim fasting period, and was unable to cook dinner for his guests. It took two years of protest from women's and human rights groups for the murderer to finally get arrested. Nonetheless he spent only three months in jail. The case was dismissed on the grounds that the forensic evidence did not prove that the beating was the cause of her death.[1]

In 1999, an eight-year-old girl was raped by a sixty-six-year-old man, an important political and religious leader who had four wives and twenty-two children. Again women's groups got involved in the case, gained media attention, and actively protested. Unlike in the previous case, the law on violence against women was applied, and the man was sentenced to the maximum sentence of ten years in prison and a fine.

In August 2002 in the northern region of Senegal, a twelve-year-old girl bled to death after her first and coerced intercourse with her husband. She had been forced into the marriage by her uncle. After the trial, the girl's husband and uncle were each sentenced to only two months in jail, an extremely lenient sentence given that the legal age of marriage in Senegal is sixteen for girls and that the law forbids forced marriages. Specific provisions of the penal code are in place supposedly to protect minors.[2] This judgment was a setback for the Senegalese women's movement and for Senegal's adherence to international and national laws prohibiting violence against women.

In July 2006, in a town in southern Senegal, a twelve-year-old girl who had been forced into a marriage was sentenced to six months in jail and fined 50,000 CFA francs (roughly US$100). She was charged with abandonment of the conjugal home after running away from physical and psychological abuse. In court, however, the girl reported that it was not the violence that led her to flee. She stated that she would have stayed except for the fact that her in-laws were trying to force her into having sex with her husband's younger brother. Once again women's groups intensively protested and fought for the case. They were able to secure the girl's release after twelve days imprisonment.

Chosen among hundreds, these cases show a common pattern with respect to gender-based violence in Senegal. This chapter highlights the disconnect between Senegal's willingness to sign all the major international and African conventions committing the nation to ending violence and discrimination against women and both the persistence of gender-based violence in Senegal and the state's failure to address the problem forcefully. In the first section of the chapter, I define violence against women and examine the scope and forms of violence that apply to Senegalese women. Some forms of violence apply to women everywhere; other forms of violence are shaped by cultural and social factors specific to the Senegalese society. The second section examines the body of domestic laws and the ways in which the Senegalese legal system actually contributes to violence against women through its complexity and its repressive character. In the third section, I analyze the various influences on the Senegalese legal system and how those influences lead to tensions between customary laws, social norms, modern laws, and the international conventions ratified by Senegal. Those tensions play an important role in determining why a Senegalese husband is able to get away with murdering his wife over a meal not cooked or a hairstyle not liked. In the final section I focus on the struggles of Senegalese women to end such violence—whether at an individual level or a collective level—through the action of women's groups.

DEFINITION, SCOPE, AND FORMS OF GENDER-BASED VIOLENCE IN SENEGAL

I prefer the concept of "gender-based violence" rather than "violence against women" because I believe that violence is a gendered phenomenon that is linked to power relations within a given society and that it is used to control women. In my preference, I follow the United Nations Commission on Human Rights (UNCHR), which defines gender-based violence as "a means of control and oppression that can include emotional, social, or economic force, coercion, or pressure, as well as physical harm. It can be overt, in the form of physical assault or threat with a weapon; it can also be covert, in the form of intimidation, threats, persecution, deception, or other forms of psychological or social pressure. The person targeted by this kind of violence is compelled to behave as expected or to act against her will out of fear."[3] The UNCHR definition goes on as follows: "an incident of violence is an act or a series of harmful acts by a perpetrator or a group of perpetrators against a person or a group of individuals. It may involve multiple types of and repeated acts of violence over a period of time, with variable durations. It can take minutes, hours, days or a lifetime."

Considering violence that a woman may experience during her lifetime as a gendered phenomenon helps to bring violence out of the domestic sphere and forces society and the state to take responsibility for its pervasiveness and permanence. What we know about cases of violence against women in Senegal is more likely to come from the media than from published studies. The local press regularly reports violent attacks against women, murders, rape cases (often involving children), incest, and sexual harassment. To date, there are very few research studies on violence against women in Senegal. This is in due in part to the fact that despite internationally recognized definitions of and prohibitions against gender violence, such as the United Nations Declaration on the Elimination of Violence against Women[4] and the African Union's Protocol on the Rights of Women in Africa,[5] there is no specific definition of violence against women in Senegal pertinent to the national context.

In 2001, the Groupe de Recherche sur les Femmes et les Lois au Sénégal (GREFELS) conducted one of the first studies on violence against women in Senegal. The study's main findings are the three following points:

- Gender-based violence is pervasive and can occur at home, in public schools, in Qur'anic schools, in the street, or at the market.
- Wife and child beating are generally accepted in public opinion and considered "normal"—women themselves consider it as a given part of their lives.
- Local authorities such as the state, religious, and traditional authorities are passive about the issue.

A study conducted by the Canadian Centre for International Studies and Cooperation (CECI) in two provinces in 2000 found additional support for those findings. Studies by Wildaf[6] and Amsatou Sow Sidibé[7] addressed gender-based violence, but they focused primarily on the legal aspects. Research has also been conducted on female genital mutilation. Little data exists on Senegalese women's attitudes to gender-based violence; what data we have come from the national health and demographic surveys. To my knowledge the Senegalese government has not conducted any studies on this topic. Due to the scarcity of published reports, systematic data on the prevalence of gender-based violence, the profile of the victims, or its consequences are few. Senegalese women are victims of the full range of gender-based violence discussed in the introduction to this volume. In addition, Senegalese women are subject to other forms of violence that have a cultural basis. These include unequal inheritance rights between men and women following the Islamic law; female genital mutilation; forced and early marriage; polygyny; trafficking for forced begging; harsh divorce practices (while repudiation is not legal in Senegal under the Family Code, it is still widely practiced by men who are not aware of, or choose not to be aware of, Senegalese Family Code provisions); and harsh widowhood practices.

SENEGALESE LAWS REGARDING GENDER-BASED VIOLENCE AND ITS INTERNATIONAL COMMITMENTS

The sources of laws in Senegal are both domestic and international. All national laws have been influenced both by the French and Muslim legal systems. When Senegal was a French colony, it had a plural legal system in which its legislation was derived from French metropolitan law, customary law, and Islamic laws. Even after the country became independent in 1960, its laws reflected this colonial inheritance. As far as Islam is concerned, its presence in Senegal dates back to the eleventh century. Ninety-four percent of Senegalese are Muslims. Although the country is a secular republic, Islamic law has a profound influence on society. Customary laws remain influential in marriages. Recognition of the importance of customs is a key feature of Senegalese family law, which acknowledges custom as a determinant of the law. Modern and customary laws thus have legal standing as far as marriage is concerned.

The first major effort to reform the colonial inheritance regarding family law was a compromise reached by President Léopold Sédar Senghor in 1972. The 1972 family code thus drew on the French metropolitan model and on Islam (following the Maliki legal school).[8] In addition to state law, Senegal has signed and ratified all international and regional treaties protecting human rights and more specifically women's and children's rights. In this vein, Senegal has passed several laws expressly designed to protect women from gender-based violence.[9] Thus, both state law and international legal instruments provide the legal foundation for efforts to protect women from violence.

All legal conditions concerning the family (marriage, divorce, child custody, inheritance, etc.) are contained in the family code issued in 1972. These conditions apply to every Senegalese person regardless of sex, origin, or religion. In particular, article 300 states that the legal age of marriage is sixteen, and consent to the marriage is the first condition for its validity. Legally, no one can be forced into marriage. This article was an assault on some forms of traditional marriage. Henceforth, whoever under the framework of a traditional marriage attempts to have sex with a female child under thirteen is subject to two to five years' imprisonment. If serious injuries, infirmity (even if only temporary), or death result from the forced intercourse, or if the intercourse was performed with violence, the sentence can range from five to ten years. As Scott London describes elsewhere in this volume, the 1972 family code was a compromise reached between competing ideologies regarding the legal protections afforded to women and was thus deeply flawed.

The next major effort to refine and clarify protections for women from gender-based violence took place in the reform of the penal code. Enacted in 19 January 1999 by the National Assembly, law no. 05–99 amended the penal code bans on domestic violence, pedophilia, sexual harassment, rape, incest, and female genital mutilation. Within this law, several articles address specific types of violence. Article 297, section 2 punishes domestic violence with a jail sentence of one to five years and a fine ranging from 50,000 CFA francs (US$100) to 500,000 CFA francs (US$1,000) if an illness or complete inability to work for more than twenty days results from the violence. Article 299 bis (i.e., section 2) of the penal code prohibits female genital mutilation. The article states that "whosoever violates or attempts to violate the integrity of the genital organs of a female person by total or partial ablation of one or several of the organ's parts, by infibulation, by desensitization, or by any other means, will be punished with an imprisonment of six months to five years." In addition, the article identifies who is liable to be punished. "The maximum penalty will be imposed when these sexual mutilations are performed or abetted by a member of the medical or paramedical corps. . . . When they result in death, the penalty shall be forced labor for life. . . . Any person who, through gifts, promises, influences, threats, intimidation, abuse of authority or of power, provokes these sexual mutilations or gives instructions for their commission shall be punished with the same penalties." Sexual harassment is also outlawed by the new penal code. Article 319 bis punishes sexual harassment and sets forth fines and prison terms for offenders.

Rape is addressed specifically by article 320 of the penal code, which defines it as "any act of sexual penetration, of any nature whatsoever, which has been perpetrated against another person by means of violence, force, threat, or surprise." Those guilty of rape are subject to five to ten years of imprisonment. If rape results in mutilation or permanent injury, or if the rape was committed by sequestration or by a group of people, the sentence will be ten to twenty years of imprisonment. If rape results in death, the perpetrators may be tried for murder. If the rape was committed against a child under the age of thirteen, or against a person who is particularly vulnerable because of her pregnancy, age, or health, the perpetrator will receive the maximum sentence. If the rape is committed by a child's older relatives, teachers, or paid servants, or by officials or ministers of a religion, the sentence will be ten years' imprisonment. The penal code contains no articles and no definition regarding spousal rape. Incest is not identified directly, but article 319 states that "any act of indecent assault, which has been committed by a child's relatives, or by any person who exercises authority over the victim, even if the child is over the age of 13, will carry the maximum sentence." In contrast, pedophilia is specifically addressed in article 320 bis, which punishes pedophilia and the holding of meetings of a sexual nature involving a minor.

Article 346 of the penal code addresses the issue of kidnapping or abducting a minor. The article states, "[W]hoever, by fraud or violence, kidnaps or abducts minors . . . will be liable to forced labor. If the kidnapped or abducted minor is under the age of 15, the perpetrator will be liable for forced labor for life. . . . The abduction will carry the death penalty if the minor is found dead." The same article, however, contains a provision that minimizes the crime of kidnapping or abducting if the act results in marriage. "If a perpetrator subsequently marries a minor after kidnapping or abducting her, he can only be brought to court by persons who would be authorized to request the annulment of the marriage. The perpetrator can be found guilty only after the marriage has been annulled."

Most recently, Senegal has enacted legislation prohibiting trafficking of persons and protecting its victims. Article 1 of law no. 05, 2005 on trafficking in persons, assimilated practices and protection of victims provides that "those who recruit, transport, transfer, or harbor persons, whether by means of violence, fraud, abuse of authority, or otherwise for the purposes of sexual exploitation, labor, forced servitude, or slavery are subject to imprisonment of five to 10 years and a fine of 5 to 20 million CFA Francs [US$10,000 to US$40,000]." Penalties go up when torture is used or when a child is involved.

Despite the number of state laws and Senegal's ratification of regional and international instruments regarding violence against women, gender-based violence is still very common in the country. According to the "shadow report"[10] compiled by the Center for Reproductive Law and Policy (CRLP) and GREFELS, "domestic violence, both physical and mental, is a common occurrence. . . . [I]t is not only prevalent, but is accepted as normal behavior."[11] In 2006, the Bureau of Democracy, Human Rights, and Labor of the U.S. State Department issued a *Report on Human Rights in Senegal*, which stated, "domestic violence, including spousal abuse, was a widespread problem. Several women's groups and the local NGO Committee to Combat Violence against Women (CLVF) reported a rise in cases of violence against women during the year."[12]

The main barrier to the reduction in gender-based violence in Senegal stems from the mismatch between available laws and actual legal practices. The court system is extremely complex and difficult to navigate. The most serious barrier remains the lack of genuine political will from the state to enforce the laws or to honor the international conventions it signed. This lack of political will and the tensions and influences of the different sources of laws in the Senegalese legal system contribute to the problem of gender-based violence.

LAW AND THE PERSISTENCE OF GENDER-BASED VIOLENCE IN SENEGAL

As stated, spousal rape and sex with a minor are two major forms of sexual violence in Senegal. Spousal rape is not addressed at all in the Senegalese penal code and incest only obliquely and with conditions that lessen punishment. The penal code does not recognize the prevalence of these forms of abuse within families, with the result that the offenders go unpunished. Under the influence of traditional marriage practices, the abductor of a child can escape punishment if he marries the child. Only if the marriage is annulled will the abductor face punishment. Otherwise, the crime is lessened to the status of "a negotiable conflict." Since the definition of rape is penile-vaginal penetration, other forms of penetration are likely to be considered lesser crimes. Thus, the very weakness of the law contributes to violence against women because some violations go unpunished.

The very complexity of legal procedure contributes to the persistence of the problem. According to the law, enforcement officers are allowed in a private home only between 8 a.m. and 9 p.m., except when a claim is made by someone who lives in the house.[13] These restrictions contribute to the persistence of gender-based violence because most domestic violence happens at night, when men are most often at home. Moreover, officials prefer to have family members (usually in-laws) intervene and provide advice toward reconciliation in the case of domestic violence.

Victims of gender-based violence also face a high burden of proof. According to the law, any perpetrator of violence against women is presumed innocent until proven guilty. Under Senegalese procedure, a judge may request investigators to provide evidence of the accusations and seek advice from experts who examine the findings. Yet the judge is neither obliged to request an investigation nor bound by the conclusions of the experts. Except when the victim is a child, the burden of the proof falls on the victim. In the law against trafficking of women, for example, the adult victim is required to provide proof that she has truly been trafficked or exploited according to the legal definitions. Injuries or deaths are considered meaningful evidence. Claims by victims who bear no physical traces of harm are often dismissed. Evidence provided by neighbors or members of the family can be considered as proof, but these people are often reluctant to testify. The 2006 U.S. State Department report points out that "it was nearly impossible for victims to provide judges with sufficient proof to merit convictions. Some groups felt that the harsh sentences under the law caused judges to require higher burdens of proof before finding potential offenders guilty, resulting in fewer total convictions for domestic violence."[14]

Article 297 of the penal code requires the victim to provide medical evidence of the seriousness of physical injuries to assist the judge in determining the appropriate sentence. However, acquiring this evidence poses problems. Because medical consultations can be quite expensive, many victims cannot afford them. Health care facilities are often scarce in rural areas, which makes obtaining medical statements difficult.

Women seeking to pursue cases of domestic violence face additional hurdles in dealing with the legal system. Judges and policemen are not immune from the widespread belief that women who are victims of gender-based violence somehow deserve the violence they received either because they misbehaved or because they "tempted" the perpetrator with indecent clothes or behavior. When presented with cases of domestic violence, judges have full authority on the verdict of the cases. According to Sow-Sidibé, in cases where the victim dies, judges often classify cases of murder as manslaughter, which is a lesser offense.[15] Such a context leads offenders to believe that they will never be arrested and punished, which in turn perpetuates violence against women. Women are hesitant to report abuse because they are aware how difficult it is to be believed and for the abuser to be punished. These attitudes contribute to an institutionalized acceptance of gender-based violence.

GENDER AND VIOLENCE IN SENEGAL

Understanding how violence is shaped by gender necessitates an examination of the cultural and religious contexts within which this violence occurs. We must also bear in mind that culture is alive and undergoes transformations caused by internal and external forces, including colonization and globalization, changes in local economy and politics, as well as social gains and backlash from class and gender struggles.

Senegal is generally perceived as a democratic country. The constitution declares equality between men and women. However, formal laws on violence against women and other legislation such as the family code reveal deep contradictions between the constitutional principle of gender equality and reality. While modern laws formally promote women's social position, customary and religious norms construct women as powerless, thus making them vulnerable to violence.

Gender-based violence in Senegal is rooted in social construction of the woman as a submissive being whose body and sexuality need to be controlled. Early marriage, female genital mutilation, polygyny, and limited access to economic and political resources as well as education are the means to control them. These forms of control are legitimated by religion and customs.

Islamic law that affirms authority of men over women[16] provides a basis for the principle in the 1972 family code that men are the heads of the family. The Senegalese Family Code was also influenced by the Napoleonic Code, first promulgated in 1804, which affirmed the total legal incapacity of married women and gave husbands full authority over their wives.

Such conceptions of male superiority, rooted in religion and custom, help explain the inability of the Senegalese legal system to imagine the possibility of spousal rape. Article 149 of the family code, which deals with cohabitation, states that spouses have an obligation to provide sexual services and that failure to do so may be a cause for divorce. According to Islamic law, a husband may refuse his wife sexual relations for three months as a punishment for her disobedience. If he continues beyond this period, his wife may seek divorce. However, for a wife the only acceptable reasons for refusal of sex are religious: obligatory fasting or menstruation. One often cited hadith states, "[A]mong things most hated by Allah, is the wife who constantly answers to her husband that she is sick or has her periods. Such a wife is cursed by angels the whole night." Given the religiously sanctioned obligation to provide sexual services to her husband, it is therefore understandable that spousal rape is not considered by the law as a form of gender-based violence.

Another important cause of gender-based violence is the perception that women are minors and that men may punish their misbehavior. Wives are supposed to submit to their husband's will and endure his punishment. According to Surah 3:34, "[T]he righteous women are devoutly obedient, and guard in (the husband's) absence what Allah would have them guard. As those women on whose part ye fear disloyalty and ill-conduct, admonish them (first), (next) refuse to share their beds, (And last) beat them; but if they return to obedience, seek not against them means (of annoyance): for Allah is the most High, (above you all)." Many men feel it is their right to beat their wives if, for instance, she burns a meal, leaves the home without husband's or in-laws' authorization, or refuses sex. Many women also share this perception, as revealed in the information provided in the health and demographic surveys on women's opinions about domestic violence.[17]

Forced marriages are among the most common forms of gender-based violence in Senegal. As Elke Stockreiter describes in her chapter in this volume, the issues of the age of puberty and of consent from young girls have been discussed in Muslim societies for centuries. Islamic law does not specify the age at which a girl is considered to have reached puberty but allows marriages once puberty has been reached. According to the Convention on the Rights of the Child (1989), a child is any person under eighteen.[18] Thus in setting the minimum age at which a girl can be married at sixteen, the family code violates this international convention ratified by the Senegalese state. Worse, it does not prosecute guardians and husbands who condone marriages of girls even younger than sixteen; intercourse with an underage wife is punishable only if she is below the age of thirteen. As far as consent is concerned, most ulamas' response is as unsatisfactory as their conception of puberty. According to them, if a girl remains silent when asked whether or not she approves of a marriage, she is considered to have consented.

Due to their physical and sexual immaturity, children who are forced into marriages are at a greater risk of experiencing pregnancy and childbirth-related health problems including vesico-vaginal fistula and death.[19] According to the 2005 Senegalese Health and Demographic Survey (hereafter HDS), every year 401 women out of 100,000 live births die from pregnancy-related illnesses. Among them, 27 percent are younger than nineteen years of age.[20] Moreover, gendered power imbalances within marriage are worsened by the fact that children who are forced into marriages cannot negotiate intercourse with their husbands, not to mention contraception or sexual pleasure. Despite all these reproductive health and rights violations and the strong element of coercion contained in marriages involving young girls, the Senegalese Family Code authorizes them. According to HDS (2005), 15 percent of Senegalese women younger than fifteen and 48 percent younger than eighteen are already married; 19 percent of them have one or several children.[21]

The 2005 HDS also indicates that 28 percent of Senegalese women have undergone some form of genital mutilation. Arguments in support of female genital mutilation (FGM) in Senegal include the prevention of promiscuity, preservation of virginity, enhancement of fertility, and religious cleanliness. In a society that values a girl's virginity, FGM and early marriages are means to control women's sexuality. Despite decades of sensitization campaigns about their harmful consequences to women's health, life, and sexuality, and the passing of laws prohibiting this practice, these customs are still widely practiced.

ARE SENEGALESE WOMEN ENTITLED TO HUMAN RIGHTS?

Senegal has signed and ratified *all* regional and international laws regarding women's human rights and therefore recognizes violence as a human-rights abuse and accepts the responsibility of preventing and punishing it. But Senegal does not respect its international commitments. This is the main problem with human rights conventions: no matter how thorough they are in asserting human rights, their enforcement depends on the state's political will, and no mechanism exists to oblige states to implement them (see the chapter by Benedetta Faedi in this volume).

To understand the attitude of the Senegalese toward women's human rights, we need to reflect on the views held in Senegalese society on whether or not women should have rights. In Africa and more specifically in Senegal, the discussion about women as rights bearers is a never-ending one. People are eager to discuss political, human, cultural, or economic rights of the whole, but they are reluctant to discuss women's rights and will quickly invoke culture or religion to justify limitations on those rights. A study of Islam and women's reproductive health and rights showed that more than 83 percent of respondents believed that religion and culture oppose women's reproductive rights.[22] A UNICEF/Senegal report (2002) revealed that

> women generally do not exercise their human rights, and the non-application of texts and practices to address discrimination in daily life, explains, in part, the lack of a true culture of human rights in Senegal. This fact is characterized by the low popular awareness of the existence of fundamental rights, leading to the existence of social practices that deny rights, with women being considered more frequently as objects, rather than subjects, of rights.[23]

Such blindness to women's rights as human rights explains the widespread ignorance of these rights and has implications for gender-based violence. In addition, human rights as defined by international treaties may seem quite remote from the lives of ordinary women. I am not suggesting that the international discourse on women's human rights is not useful. On the contrary, it has provided women's groups with tools to demand legal reforms and to pressure the government into respecting its international commitments. The challenges are in translating human rights rhetoric into local contexts and in providing regionally based enforcement regimes, as Benedetta Faedi describes in her chapter.

GENDER-BASED VIOLENCE AND SENEGALESE WOMEN'S AGENCY

In this section, I draw on Naila Kabeer, who defines agency as "power within," which encompasses "a much wider range of purposive actions, including bargaining, negotiation, manipulation, subversion, resistance and protest as well as the more intangible, cognitive processes of reflection and analysis. Agency also encompasses collective as well as individual reflections and action."[24] I link agency with choice, power, and capacity to make decisions informed by one's understanding of possibilities offered by one's social and economic situation.

The ways in which Senegalese women respond to gender-based violence at the individual and collective levels are shaped by the history of their society and the evolution of their social status. In the precolonial period, most ethnic groups in Senegal were matrilineal, with women enjoying more power at the family and social levels. Yet decision making, the economy, and ideology were controlled by men. Even in traditional Senegalese matrilineal societies the idea that women, regardless of their social class, ought to be considered minors, remained strong. Relationships between husband and wife were characterized by domination by the husband and submission of the wife. This domination did not have the Marxist connotation of exploitation but should be understood as one of a senior to a junior. Women's status improved dramatically with age because elderly women were highly respected and honored.

A new configuration of the Senegalese family emerged first in the colonial context of the 1920s and was organized around the husband to whom social authority and monetary employment were transferred. French and Islamic values reinforced during the colonial period strengthened forms of patriarchal control and deprived women of their traditional rights under customary laws. Marginalized by the colonizers, women were defined as housekeepers and subsistence farmers. As a result, new power relations, including new forms of economic dependence, emerged, generating more constraints and demands for submission, thereby contributing to the context in which violence against women occurred and was sanctioned.

The rise in gender-based violence can also be linked to the economic situation in Senegal. Living conditions have worsened, and poverty has increased since the 1980s. These conditions make it harder for men to be the sole breadwinners; that difficulty can be perceived as a threat to their authority in the family, especially as women are increasingly able to bring income to the family. Women may face violence from husbands eager to reassert their authority. Moreover, traditional social systems that used to provide support and solidarity have weakened.

Most Senegalese women are unable or unwilling to adopt a style of agency characterized by overt collective resistance, radicalism, or rupture. At the individual level, instead, women bargain and negotiate strategically. A doctor interviewed by GREFELS for its study on violence against women summed up how many battered women proceed with a suit:

> When a victim feels that the battering is too much, she may decide to take action. On her way to the market (to shop for food), she'd stop here at the health care center where we check on her and give her a medical statement about injuries she suffered and the number of days she will be unable to work as a result of the beating. Then she'd proceed to the police station to file a complaint against her husband. Thanks to the medical statement her claim is usually taken into consideration and the police will summon the husband to the station and eventually arrest him. For a man in these communities, being arrested, detained, or appearing before the court are considered very shameful. Therefore before the trial, the husband manages to call for

reconciliation with parents or elders in the community. He will recognize his torts and give a present to his wife. Women usually accept the present and stay with the violent man . . . until the next time.[25]

Such a strategy suggests that Senegalese women adopt a mixture of tradition (complying with social norms of reconciliation) and modernity (attempting to use the law prohibiting violence against them). However, these strategies emerge from the failures of the state to provide effective protection to victims of gender-based violence. Because there are no shelters or other state-funded structures for abused women and because most women are too poor to support themselves, many women settle for reconciliation and return to the homes where they are abused again. In this context, strategies of bargaining and negotiating should not be seen as passivity or resignation; instead, within the dialectic of power and control over a woman's life, they should be considered a mature analysis of one's individual situation and what one could gain or lose depending on the choice one makes. Better-educated or wealthier women are much more likely to go to court and obtain a divorce.

However, Senegalese women are not alone in their struggles against domestic violence. The vibrancy and diversity of women's groups in Senegal are widely recognized, and they exist in both rural and urban areas. Women's groups are also organized for particular purposes, such as income-generating activities, the promotion of reproductive and sexual health and rights, education reform, environment, law reform, political leadership, and so on. It was only with the shock resulting from the murder of Doki Niasse in 1993 that campaigns to bring the issue of gender-based violence to public attention increased. The type of initiatives that were implemented can be broadly divided into the following categories: (1) services to women and girls who experience gender-based violence; (2) activities designed to prevent or reduce gender-based violence; and (3) encouragement to families to press charges of sexual abuse. The strategies are aimed mostly at improving the legal framework and at getting the state to enforce the laws that already exist. In accordance with the socioeconomic and religious context, they involved campaigns to educate the public on the phenomenon, including talks in women's groups at grassroots levels, health centers, and schools, and on radio and television programs. Legal and psychological assistance was provided to the victims of violence with lawsuits or reconciliation of spouses where it was possible.

Parallel to these actions, protests were held when particularly odious acts of gender-based violence were perpetrated or during special occasions such as the annual "16 days' protest to end violence against women," Pan-African Women's Day (July 31), or International Women's Day (March 8). Women's groups organized other protests and petition-signing campaigns to increase pressure on the government to pass laws or enforce them. Women's groups also lobbied special groups, which by their profession or social standing could influence the punishment of gender-based violence. The targets of the lobbying efforts are always carefully defined: religious and customary leaders, trade unions, lawyers, magistrates, and other law enforcement officials. Because they play a crucial social role in the Senegalese society, customary and religious leaders are powerful allies. They may also act as referees in conflicts arising within the community and may be called to advise judges. Most of them are illiterate and might be unaware that violence against women is unlawful. Doctors are also important allies. They advise judges in medical matters and also provide victims with the medical statements testifying to the seriousness of the violence.

Currently the main effort by women's groups is to pressure the government to enact legislation that will permit these groups to bring suits on behalf of victims. These strategies continue to confront the lack of political will in Senegal to enforce the laws already in place that prohibit gender-based violence. Reforming legislation is not enough. The social system as a whole sanctions gender-based violence. On the one hand, it presents gender-based violence as a matter concerning women only; on the other hand, it presents it as a private or domestic issue. Such a position depoliticizes gender-based violence and alleviates the state's responsibility to protect women's rights.

The important task for the Senegalese women's movement and for human rights activists is to expose the gendered dimension of domestic violence.[26] This allows them to highlight the indivisibility of women's human rights and facilitates the integration of the struggle to end gender-based violence with other struggles to end discrimination and inequalities. Analyzing the gendered roots of gender-based violence also means bringing men into the picture, not only as perpetrators of violence but also as the other social component and as the bearer of social power. Such a perspective also challenges the social construction of masculinity and aggressiveness.

↩

The complexity of the Senegalese legal process, the high number of dismissed cases by judges, and the apathy of concerned authorities, including the minister of justice and the associations of lawyers or of magistrates, indicate the lack of political will to address and punish gender-based violence. The state's response to gender-based violence has mostly been to enact laws, but enforcement is generally lacking. The government has not funded research to help understand the magnitude of the phenomenon and to implement relevant programs to address it. Except for a national plan of action on female genital mutilation, gender-based violence has not been integrated into reproductive health or economic programs targeting women. There are no shelters for battered women in

Senegal, no prevention programs, and no state-funded training for police officers, lawyers, judges, or others who encounter cases of abuse. Nongovernmental organizations that deal with gender-based violence are typically underfunded.

All the laws relating to gender-based violence are about punishment, which reflects the fact that the state understands the problem as a penal issue rather than a social problem. The strategy of the Senegalese women's movement is to push the state and other actors to view gender-based violence as inextricably related to other gender inequalities. This approach reveals that the state's current failure to comprehend that the imbalance of power between women and men, the way in which gender roles are articulated through customary norms, and the interpretation of Islamic texts are major obstacles to women's full enjoyment of their formal rights.

Laws are not neutral institutions. They support social and gender relations that structure any given society. Violence is gender-based because it is rooted in the inequalities between sexes and classes. Looking into the structural aspects of gender-based violence reveals how it is encompassed in a range of social, cultural, economic, legal, and political institutions that sustain inequality. This is why in Senegal the modern laws—even if originating from progressive international and regional treaties and from Senegalese women's individual and collective efforts to end gender-based violence—are still insufficient to change the conservative customary and religious norms, which are considered valid sources of laws but which contribute to the pervasiveness of violence and to the impunity it is granted. A stronger political discourse as well as activism that presents gender-based violence as a public social issue requiring change in the construction of masculinity and femininity is urgently needed to make decisive steps toward ending gender-based violence.

NOTES

1. The title of this chapter comes from an event on 16 December 2007, at the moment when this paper was being completed. A radio news program broke the news that a man had murdered his wife in anger at the new hairstyle she was wearing for the celebration of the Eid El Kebir, the most important Muslim feast, which commemorates the sacrifice of Abraham and the end of the hajj, the pilgrimage to Mecca. On these celebrations, Muslims are urged to dress and eat well, make their children and family happy, and foster peace in the community.

2. Senegalese Family Code, 1972.

3. Coordination of Humanitarian Affairs, United Nations High Commissioner for Refugees, *Sexual and Gender-Based Violence against Refugees, Returnees and Internally Displaced Persons* (Geneva: Office of the United Nations High Commissioner for Refugees, 2003).

4. United Nations, Convention on Elimination of All Forms of Discrimination against Women, 1979; Senegalese law no. 99–06 on violence against women.

5. African Union, Protocol to the African Charter on Human and Peoples' Rights on the Rights of Women in Africa (Maputo, Mozambique, 2003).

6. Women in Law and Development in Africa, *Pour une société sans violence au Sénégal*; Women in Law and Development in Africa, *Femmes, droit et développement en Afrique* (Dakar, Senegal: Women in Law and Development/Senegal, 2002).

7. A. Sow Sidibé, *Etude technique sur les violences infligées aux femmes au Sénégal* (Dakar, Senegal: Fondation Friedrich Ebert and Collectif des Femmes Parlementaires, 1997).

8. The Mazhabs or Muslim schools of thought were formed through the personal allegiance of groups of jurists to a founder-member from whom they derived their names. They are the Hanafis (named after founder Abu Hanifah [d. 767]), the Malikis (named after founder Malik [b. Anas, d. 795]), the Shafi'i (named after Abou 'Abd Allah Mohamed Ben Idris [d. 820]), and the Hanbali (named after Ahmad Ben Hanbal [d. 855]).

9. *Journal Officiel de la République du Sénégal*, 27 February 1999: Law 99–06 of 20 January 1999, which modified certain provisions of the Code of Criminal Procedure.

10. "Shadow reports" are presented to UN bodies by nongovernmental organizations (NGOs) in order to provide the UN with credible, reliable, and independent information about the legal status of women and their real-life situations as well as about the efforts governments have made to comply with their international commitments in signed conventions. It is one way of putting pressure on governments to promulgate or implement necessary legal and political changes. On shadow reports relating to the CEDAW, see Sally Engle Merry, *Human Rights and Gender Violence: Translating International Law into Local Justice* (Chicago: University of Chicago Press, 2006), 86.

11. The Center for Reproductive Law and Policy and Le Groupe de Recherche sur les Femmes et les Lois au Sénégal, *Women's Reproductive Rights in Senegal: A Shadow Report* (Dakar, Senegal: GREFELS, 2001).

12. U.S. Department of State, Bureau of Democracy, Human Rights, and Labor, *Senegal Country Reports on Human Rights* (Washington, DC: State Department, 2006).

13. Sow Sidibé, *Étude technique sur les violences infligées aux femmes au Sénégal.*

14. U.S. Department of State, Bureau of Democracy, Human Rights, and Labor, *Senegal Country Reports on Human Rights* (Washington, DC: State Department, 2007).

15. Sow Sidibé, *Etude technique sur les violences infligées aux femmes au Sénégal.*

16. Surah 4:34 reads: "Men have guardianship and authority over women, because Allah has made one superior to the other, and because of the advantage they have over them and because they spend their property in supporting them."

17. Salif Ndiaye et Mohamed Ayad, *Enquête démographique et de santé au Sénégal 2005* (Dakar, Senegal: Centre de Recherche pour le Développement Humain, 2006).

18. United Nations, Convention on the Rights of the Child, adopted and opened for signature, ratification, and accession by General Assembly resolution 44/25 of 20 November 1989.

19. World Health Organization, *La santé des femmes à travers les âges* (Geneva: WHO, 1999).

20. Salif Ndiaye and Mohamed Ayad, *Enquête démographique et de Santé: Sénégal 2005* (Dakar, Senegal: Ministère de la Santé et de la Prévention Médicale and Centre de Recherche pour le Développement Humain, 2005). http://www.measuredhs.com/pubs/pub_details.cfm?ID=583&ctry_id=36&SrchTp=ctry.

21. Ndiaye and Ayad, *Enquête démographique et de Santé.*

22. Codou Bop, *Islam and Women's Reproductive and Sexual Health and Rights in Senegal* (Atlanta: Religion and Human Rights Project, Emory University School of Law, 2003).

23. C. I. Niang and P. Quarles van Ufford, *Impacts socio-économiques du VIH/SIDA sur les enfants: Le cas du Sénégal* (Paris: UNICEF, 2002).

24. Naila Kabeer, "Reflections on the Measurement of Women's Empowerment," in *Discussing Women's Empowerment: Theory and Practice*, Sida Studies, no. 3 (Stockholm: Swedish International Development Agency, 2001).

25. Coudou Bop, *Les violences contre les femmes au Sénégal* (Dakar, Senegal: Groupe de Recherche sur les Femmes et les Lois au Sénégal [GREFELS], 1998).

26. Groupe Citoyens et Justice, *Les violences intra familiales: Etat des lieux et perspectives de développement des interventions socio-judiciaires* (Paris: GCJVIF, 2005).

10 ⏤ The Logics of Controversy

*Gender Violence as a Site of Frictions in
Ghanaian Advocacy*

SAIDA HODŽIĆ

IF ONE AIM of anthropology and history is to particularize knowledge claims and write against globalist ideologies, a conceptual method we rely on is analyzing controversies in places where many see only flat surfaces. The cracks, fissures, and fault lines that disrupt the presumed global order reveal themselves in specific contexts, speaking against the universalizing tendencies of globalization itself and its theorists. Controversies erupt in surprising locations and remain buried in others.

For many activists, institutions, and scholars, violence against women, or gender violence—as well as advocacy against it—is flat and universal. "Violence against women" is spoken of in the singular, and female genital cutting, female infanticide, dowry murders, and so on are named in one breath as "types" that belong to this larger, unifying category.[1] According to Margaret Keck and Kathryn Sikkink, the universality of violence against women had such a hold on imagination of activists and government representatives from both the global North and South at the 1985 United Nations conference in Nairobi that it allowed them to agree that this was a key human rights violation.[2]

While the taxonomy that subsumes different phenomena to the larger category of "violence against women" may make the gendered and universal aspects of violence visible, it also obscures crucial differences. I argue against the globalist portrayal of "violence against women" as a singular and consensus-leading human rights violation. Cultural difference, postcolonial legacies, and the politics of location all bring "a creative friction to global connections."[3] Ghanaian campaigns to criminalize female genital cutting and domestic violence reveal what Tsing calls "zones of awkward engagement"—"where words mean something different across a divide even as people agree to speak."[4]

Whereas the category "violence against women" may have been easy to agree on at UN conferences, it did not lend itself to a unified consensus in much of Africa. The trajectories of efforts to criminalize cutting and domestic violence reveal that frictions emerge in surprising places. In Ghana, and elsewhere in sub-Saharan Africa, the attempts to criminalize domestic violence and marital rape have provoked moral panics and unprecedented struggles between activists and governments since the 1990s. Governments campaigned against the proposed laws; media propagated masculinist discourses; and women parliamentarians walked out of parliament sessions in protest against the discriminatory remarks of their colleagues. In contrast, criminalization of female genital cutting was rather tame, and cutting was outlawed in most countries that introduced such laws.

This chapter examines the logics that determine when controversies erupt and when advocacy is tamed and laws are embraced. My ethnography offers a situated account of debates in the Ghanaian public sphere, revealing a complex web of conditions that structured the faiths of the two laws. I seek to uncover the cultural logics and politics that shape both taming and controversy. I ask: Why do governments fiercely resist some forms of activism but embrace others? What makes laws controversial in particular places? How does female genital cutting become tame while domestic violence engenders disagreement? The logics of taming and controversy, I argue, are shaped by both global and local forces and by the shifting dynamics of culture and power—the configurations of class, ethnicity, gender, and sexuality, the discourses of rights and modernity, as well relations between nongovernmental organizations (NGOs) and the state.

TAMING CUTTING, PASSING LAWS

Although in particular historical moments, legislation against female genital cutting inspired anticolonial revolts, in much of contemporary sub-Saharan Africa, it receives salutatory headlines. Countries that have criminalized female genital cutting since the mid-1990s include both those in which the practice is prevalent (Benin, Burkina Faso, Chad, Djibouti, Egypt, Eritrea, Ethiopia, Ghana, Guinea, Ivory Coast, Kenya, Niger, Senegal, Tanzania, Togo) and those in which it is not (Madagascar, South Africa).[5] Given that legislation is largely considered a government's domain, these laws are often interpreted as governments' deeds. However, governments have not been the main force behind these laws, but rather side actors. African women's NGOs have been the primary advocates for criminalization of cutting. Their legal advocacy was not met with strong government or popular resistance, except, notably, in Kenya, Sierra Leone, Egypt, and Guinea-Bissau.[6]

Criminalizing female genital cutting did not cause a *public* controversy in Ghana. I emphasize the "public" to draw attention to the specific context this chapter addresses. Although the effects of criminalization did create tensions and conflicts in communities where cutting is practiced, these tensions did not reverberate widely and had no effect on the course of national politics.[7]

The general lack of contention about criminalization of female genital cutting is surprising, as history tells us that outlawing female genital cutting can become highly contentious. Female genital cutting was one of the explosive sites that made women's bodies into a site of resistance against colonial rule.[8] Historians have also shown that banning female genital cutting in the late colonial period produced acts of popular resistance. When the local council in Kenya's Meru district outlawed cutting in 1956, "adolescent girls defied the ban, attempting to excise each other."[9] This was not a small number of girls—more than 2,400 persons were eventually prosecuted for defying the ban.

The lack of controversy around the criminalization of cutting also speaks against Africanist and anthropological intuitions and intentions. As Bettina Shell-Duncan and Ylva Hernlund write, "[T]he practices of female genital cutting appear to—more than almost any other issue—capture the popular imagination, trigger emotional responses, and reduce the complex to the non-negotiable absolute."[10] Anthropologists write against this packaging of female genital cutting, hoping "to illustrate that it is impossible to offer simplistic solutions or pat answers."[11] As scholars, we intend to reveal the frictions and controversies in order to problematize and complicate the sensationalist and simplistic accounts.

Yet controversies are neither timeless nor universal. In Ghana, female genital cutting has become a tame issue—an issue that can be discussed without subverting the order of things. This realization took me by surprise during fieldwork in the summer of 2002, when a group discussion on "women's issues" at a conference on reproductive health in Accra revealed that the question of cutting was far from contentious.

The "Sociocultural Dimensions of Reproductive Health and Human Development" conference, sponsored by the United Nations Development Program and held at the University of Ghana, Legon, was structured in a mix of the academic and development cultures. Formal presentations and challenging debates were followed by tea breaks and group discussions during which the participants created lists of issues that researchers should focus on. Presenters gave talks about women's workloads and impact on health, HIV/AIDS and vulnerable populations, contraceptive use, maternal mortality, the role of traditional birth attendants, cultural norms, and nutrition.

The group discussion on key issues for future research took place on the last day of the conference. I was in a group of students and professors at the University of Ghana, among them a nurse, a geographer, and a sociologist.

Before much discussion took place, the chair of the group whom I had met earlier introduced me as "doing research on FGM." This caught the attention of the group members.

"Yes, FGM is a key issue," one of them motioned.

"Please do not mention this issue just because I am in the group," I objected. The group rejoined:

"No, *we* think it is very important."

"More research on FGM is necessary."

"We are not saying it because of you. This is a problem for Ghanaian women."

"You see, there is a law against it, but they are now taking girls across the border to Burkina and doing it there."

A chorus of voices silenced my objection. I was embarrassed. I had come to listen and learn, but now my interest was being cast as an important "issue." It did not seem that these researchers actually thought that female genital cutting was an important topic, as none of over thirty presentations had addressed it. Yet, the members of my group declared it one of the most important issues to be studied. What was going on? I took their declaration as a sign of the group's politeness and an attempt to include the guest in their world. But I had taken myself too seriously.

Over the next several years, in and out of fieldwork in Accra and in the Upper East region of Ghana, I found that "FGM" was a common and safe topic. It was raised as a "women's issue" par excellence at conferences, seminars, and workshops that I observed, regardless of their contents. These included everything from a high-profile health summit between the Ghanaian government and its donors, to NGO workshops on women in politics and girl-child education. In other words, cutting was a favorite topic that topped the list of women's issues whether it seemed directly relevant to the workshop purpose or not.

Moreover, the extent of conversations about cutting was disproportionate to actual projects related to it. While the number of NGOs and researchers that worked on cutting was small, the practice was discussed frequently. It seems that the harmfulness of cutting was one issue that Ghanaian social engineers—development workers, government officials, journalists, activists, and others—could always agree on. When group discussions meandered or got heated, the topic of FGM was brought up as a measure of relief. In other words, FGM had become a tame issue that everyone could talk about and agree that it was a harmful traditional practice that needed to be abandoned.

THE SCOPE OF FEMALE GENITAL CUTTING IN GHANA

Although female genital cutting is a frequent topic of discussion, Ghana is one of many West African countries in which cutting is practiced only in a few regions: by ethnic groups living in the northern part of the country—the

Upper East, Upper West, and parts of the Northern region—and by largely dis-enfranchised migrants from these regions and neighboring countries. People from northern Ghana are constructed as the modern nation's ethnic "others," and cutting is one issue that marks them as such. Due to complex historical reasons that range from economic patterns of trade to warfare and colonial policies, these regions have been marginalized—culturally, economically, and politically.[12] Ghana's culturally and politically dominant groups, such as the Akan, do not circumcise girls.

It is not known just how many Ghanaian women have been cut. To establish that cutting was indeed prevalent in Ghana, the NGO Ghanian Association for Women's Welfare (GAWW) commissioned a research study in the 1980s, and other researchers have followed suit. Nevertheless, the epidemiological data on cutting—asserted authoritatively on international websites and in publications—are scarce and unreliable.[13] National studies cite an incidence of 15 percent,[14] 12 percent,[15] and 9 percent.[16] Various forms of cutting exist in Ghana, but the excision and clitoridectomy are most common.[17]

LEGISLATION AND ACTIVISM

Despite the fact that female genital cutting is confined to specific pockets of the country, interventions against cutting have a social life of their own. At once exotic and familiar, the question of cutting strikes a chord with many Ghanaians. The history of activism against female genital cutting in Ghana is rich and complex. In ethnographic interviews, I was told that various individuals—from Christian nuns to community leaders—have been trying to bring the practice to a halt for decades. Organized activism began in the early 1980s. Two main sets of institutions have carried our virtually all interventions since: Ghanaian NGOs and, to a much lesser extent, the government's National Council on Women and Development (NCWD). The list of NGO activities aimed at stopping cutting is long and includes legal advocacy, community mobilizing, public health projects, and "sensitization" of various stakeholders.

The discursive taming of cutting enabled its criminalization. NGOs frame cutting as a health hazard and, less commonly, a human rights violation, staying away from discussions of gender and sexuality. In the public sphere, however, the notion of cutting as a "backward" practice that impedes development and modernization is the most resonant frame for its understanding. This resonance seems common across the continent. Although campaigns against cutting differ from country to country, many African organizations rely on the dominant notion that female genital cutting is a "harmful traditional practice" that stands in the way of development and modernity. The largest umbrella of African organizations working to stop cutting is in fact called "The Inter-African Committee on Traditional Practices Affecting the Health of Women and Children." The framing of cutting as harmful for health grounds most interventions in Ghana and elsewhere in Africa, including calls for legislation.

Ghana has two laws against cutting. In 1994, Ghana became the first independent African country to criminalize cutting. The second law was enacted in 2007. Ghanaian NGOs created both pieces of legislation, advocated for their passage to law, and then lobbied the government for their enforcement.

"IT WAS ALL LANGUAGE"

Both laws have been passed without political controversy. The first law amended the country's Criminal Code, inserting a new section:

> Whoever excises, infibulates or otherwise mutilates the whole or any part of the labia minora, labia majora and the clitoris of another person commits an offence and shall be guilty of a second degree felony and liable on conviction to imprisonment of not less than three years.[18]

The GAWW was the main organization advocating for this law.[19] Set up in 1984, this is the first and most active Ghanaian NGO dedicated specifically to the issue of stopping cutting. GAWW collaborated with the centralized government, sharing a legal project grant with the National Council on Women and Development, then the highest government body regarding women. The director of the Center for Muslim Families, a community-based NGO that also claims some authorship over the law, told me about the character of this collaboration. According to Mr. Yahaya, the two NGOs set the political stage for passing the law by involving the government at all stages:

> We worked through the National Council on Women and Development. They actually did the lobbying. They used the few women in the Parliament to actually speak for them. And *we* got the community involved.

Mr. Yahaya believes that the character of the practice of cutting was so horrendous that there could be no controversy about it. According to him, it wasn't difficult to convince the Parliament to pass the law. In his rendering, the sheer visual representation of the pain of cutting convinced the legislators:

> We took the movie to the Parliament and the members of Parliament watched it. After that, there wasn't much argument. They said, "[W]e have to pass that law." Some of them actually could not bear sitting down to watch it; they went out. [They said] that it was too brutal, very brutal.

Gender Violence as a Site of Frictions in Ghanaian Advocacy ⇝ 225

Another NGO director—a lawyer by profession and a leader in Ghana's women's rights movement—explained that there was little controversy about this law: "It was an exciting moment for us. It didn't attract the hullabaloo that other Bills of this nature had attracted but it was still comforting to know that Ghana had criminalized it."

In the late 1990s, the law was enforced in the Upper East region, where a circumciser was arrested and convicted. Other cases soon followed. Nevertheless, GAWW found the legislation insufficient, as it punished only the circumcisers but not the families who requested their services. Intent on reforming the law, GAWW sought and received funding to draft new legislation with support from women's rights lawyers. I asked one of these lawyers about the kinds of discussions the committee had had in their meetings. The making of this law was not contentious, she said: "We were pretty much agreed on many things, it was all language, you know. There were very few disagreements, to tell you the truth. In fact, what I saw us doing was trying to fine-tune the language."

I observed the last of the GAWW legal workshops, at which they presented the draft of the law and the memorandum justifying its necessity to NGO and government representatives, journalists, lawyers, and donors. Like many other NGO workshops, this one was ceremonial and ritualistic. During the first half of the day, participants listened to opening speeches and watched a movie about cutting. After the coffee break, the lawyers explained the bill's provisions and its necessity. In the discussion period, the participants commented on the best language for the memorandum and debated the length of sentences. They enthusiastically agreed that the law should refer to the practice as "mutilation" rather than as circumcision or cutting. The consensus was that both the language of the law and the sentences provided by it should reflect the severity of the offense of cutting.

Moreover, women who consent to cutting should not be exempt from prosecution, they argued. "Suicide is also a crime," one participant pointed out. This argument erased any possibility of a woman's agency and consent to cutting. The bill that was eventually presented to the Parliament does not address this question specifically, leaving room for the interpretation that consent to cutting is in fact impossible and that nobody is exempt from prosecution.[20] In addition, the bill prescribed a *minimal* four-year sentence for circumcisers and provided punishment for anybody "concerned with the procedure."[21] The bill extended culpability to a wide range of persons, including whole families, neighbors, and healers who attend to wounds. If pushed to its limits, the law would make it possible to arrest much of a village.

Despite its historically radical content, the law passed without much debate or controversy. Between 2002, when the bill was submitted to the attorney general, and 2007, when it was passed, the government voiced no objections.

The media and the general public also remained silent. The bill made its way through the annals of bureaucracy and reached the Parliament in wording close to the original NGO-proposed draft, altered only little by governmental intervention. Moreover, when the members of the Parliament discussed the bill in 2006 and 2007, they did not question *whether* or not to pass it—the passing seemed a given. The only debate that took place was *how much* the sentences should be increased and whether or not the circumcisers should be treated "humanely":

> The passage of the Bill had been preceded by lengthy and vigorous debate following disagreements over whether to deal humanely or otherwise with practitioners of FGM. . . . Some members called for a minimum of five and maximum of 10 years jail sentence for offenders, while others said the degrading cultural practice could result in death and proposed a minimum of 10 years and maximum of 25 years to deter practitioners and accomplices of FGM.[22]

For the Ghanaian Parliament, then, widening the scope of the law was not a contested question. The larger public sphere also welcomed the revisions to the Criminal Code.[23] Newspapers celebrated the law's passage, sending "kudos to parliament on female genital mutilation amendment."[24]

ADVOCACY FOR DOMESTIC VIOLENCE LEGISLATION IN GHANA

In contrast, Ghana is one of the many African countries that have passed laws against domestic violence only after protracted and heated debates. Contrary to scholarly assertions of international "convergence around the issue of violence against women,"[25] the process of criminalizing domestic violence has been tumultuous. While many laws have been passed, others have been stalled, shred to pieces, or passed only in reduced form.[26] Campaigns for these laws have produced explosive debates, encountering resistance from politicians across the continent. The issue of criminalizing marital rape has been most controversial, generating a moral panic that traveled across the continent. The Ugandan Parliament tried to declare the Sexual Offences Act "not urgent" enough to be discussed.[27] In Malawi, a Supreme Court judge declared that he opposed making marital rape a criminal offense.[28] In Swaziland, a senator opposed a bill that he thought would allow a woman to "have the legal right to deny her husband sex when and as she felt so inclined."[29] In Zimbabwe, Kenya, and Ghana, women parliamentarians protested against the overt chauvinism of their colleagues by walking out of the parliaments.

Ghana passed the Domestic Violence Bill (hereafter referred to as the DVB) after five years of state opposition and only after deletion of the clause explicitly criminalizing marital rape. The DVB was proposed by a coalition of Ghanaian activists and supported by a wide range of NGOs, unions, other civil society organizations, and some government officials. The advocacy for the DVB emerged out of the newly constructed international women's rights framework that explicitly condemned violence against women as well as out of local perceptions about the increase of violence against women in Ghana.[30] The proponents of the DVB drew on research that showed the large extent of violence in the country, finding that one in three women had experienced physical violence and that one in four had been forced to have sex.[31] The relationship between gender norms, violence against women, and state politics was also revealed. According to the study, victims rarely reported having been subjected to violence, and when they did turn to the police and the courts, they found no support: "Police at Sefsi Wiafso in the Western Region for example blamed the PNDC Law 111 for making women wicked and killing their husbands so they can inherit property. . . . A Judge in the Gonja West district blamed inappropriate dressing on the part of the women as the cause of violence against them."[32] Ghanaian academics and activists drew on these findings to argue that state institutions contributed to the perpetuation of violence—"the research opened the floodgates for advocacy."[33] Activists built on the research to claim that "governments fail to provide the logistical support and political climate that can effect change."[34]

For the DVB's proponents, power relations across the private and public spheres were directly related to domestic violence. An analysis of power was central to the arguments about rape and domestic violence, I was often told by women's rights activists. One NGO explains:

> The problem of VAW [violence against women] lies in the inequality of status between men and women in society. Positions of power in politics, economics and religion are still dominated by men even though women make up more than half the population. Our culture and most religions put women at an unequal position—their social status, quality of living and economic well-being are often dependent on or controlled by men. Women's subordinate positions make them more vulnerable to violence. VAW is an expression of the power of men over women.[35]

In other words, NGOs argued that violence against women can only be understood in relation to gendered power structures. Their critiques of gender relations were not restricted to the home or the realm of tradition, but encompassed inequality across the social spectrum, highlighting that the structures that contribute to violence eclipse the realm of the domestic.

The legislation was an attempt to rearticulate the relationship between the state and the "domestic" setting. The rationale for focusing on the "domestic" was that neither the previously existing laws nor the ways in which they were enforced protected women from the most ubiquitous form of violence—the domestic (or the intimate/private) kind. The DVB—much like the introduction to this volume—defined the domestic relationship broadly, as a "family or family-like relationship, or a relationship in a domestic situation that exists or has existed between people."[36] While the DVB criminalized rape and violence in marriage, its definition of violence was quite extensive. It included "any threats or acts of physical or sexual harm; economic, verbal, or psychological abuse; or harassment that takes place within the context of a previous or existing domestic relationship."[37] The DVB also instituted a new set of mechanisms for addressing violence.[38] Distinguishing the DVB from the existing "limited, blunt instrument of the Criminal Code," the new legislation introduced a range of dispute resolutions such as mediation, arbitration, and counseling, and instituted protection orders.[39] Given that "sending a husband to court," as Ghanaians put it, is unpopular, the coalition hoped that the emphasis on alternative dispute resolution would be more appealing. According to the memorandum—the rationale-providing document accompanying the draft bill—"Custodial sentences after protracted court processes often do not provide the victims with the redress they need."[40] Moreover, the DVB required that the police respond to all cases reported to them and secured free medical treatment to victims of violence.

GOVERNMENT RESISTANCE AND THE MAKING OF A CONTROVERSY

The opposition to the DVB, which erupted in 2004, did not involve a large coalition of organizations, but it included powerful political actors. The president and the cabinet opposed the legislation and charged the minister of women's and children's affairs, Gladys Asmah, with the task of undermining it.[41] The government launched an unprecedented public campaign against the DVB. Advocating against the DVB became the minister's full-time job during the second half of her tenure. In keeping with the media's general focus on the voice of authorities, newspapers also amplified Asmah's voice by largely restricting their reporting to stylized repetitions of her statements.[42]

In the course of 2004, Minister Asmah held press conferences, gave speeches, and, most effectively, toured much of the country advocating against the proposed law. I observed her campaign when she came to Bolgatanga. This was Asmah's first visit to this region in her four years as minister. Her arrival meant that the government was willing to go far out of its way to oppose this legislation.

In Bolgatanga, the minister delivered a speech against the DVB. She declared the bill a threat to Ghanaian families, singling out the marital rape clause: "in the countries that have this particular clause, we are told that about 65% of marriages break down." At this and other occasions, the minister claimed that this clause was a threat not only to the family but also to the nation. "We are first and foremost Ghanaians, and so we must first of all find home brewed solutions to our problems."[43] In her speech, Asmah framed the DVB as a foreign imposition and the government as a defender of Ghanaian culture and nation, casting women's rights advocacy as a threat to the nation. Finally, she also cast women's sexuality in marriage as a private matter that men, not women, should have a say over: "And if you, my brothers, say, 'She's my wife, I married her. What does the government want to do in my bedroom,' let's discuss this and see what we can do about that particular clause."

The government's campaign had the unintended effect of rejuvenating activism. NGOs mobilized in defense of the DVB and formed a coalition that included members of Parliament, local and other national government officials, teachers, nurses, union representatives, academics, and others.[44] The coalition mobilized support not only from women but also from members of groups that were thought to be opposed to the DVB, such as religious clerics and chiefs—Christian, Muslim, and traditional. Over the course of several years, NGOs from the capital toured the country and worked with local NGOs to persuade Ghanaians that the DVB was in their interest. The DVB was eventually passed due to NGO activism and Ghana's desire to safeguard its international image as a "gender-progressive country," but only after the government expunged the marital rape clause.

THE LOGICS OF CONTROVERSY

> Ethnographic fragments ask us to pay attention to details. The travels
> that inspire global connection turn out to be less controllable than
> those at the top imply.[45]

This ethnography shows that we cannot presume a coherent movement around the question of "violence against women." By paying close attention to the two Ghanaian campaigns, I have shown that controversies erupt in surprising places and quietly percolate in others. Why was the domestic violence legislation contested whereas the criminalization of cutting was tame? The following analysis is an attempt to sketch out preliminary conclusions about the reasons that guided the differing logics. Controversies, I argue, are products of competing discourses and power struggles between women's NGOs and the state.

The discrepancy between the two campaigns is guided by their different articulations of culture, power, modernity, and rights. The criminalization of cutting was facilitated by a framework that understands cutting as a "harmful traditional practice," rooted in an "outdated" tradition. In Ghana, cutting is often understood as being "clearly outmoded."[46] Although we may see this as problematic from a scholarly perspective, the discourse that posits that the path to "development" and modernity is obstructed by "harmful traditions" is dominant in the Ghanaian public sphere. The idea of modernity that promises a "global status and a political-economic condition . . . of being 'first class'" enchants Ghanaians despite the postcolonial frustrations with development.[47] This promise of modernity is grounded in a rejection of traditions and a teleological understanding of culture according to which the "backward" evolves and becomes "modern." While not everybody subscribes to it, the discourse of tradition as an obstacle to development is a dominant one. Packaging cutting as a "harmful traditional practice" proved successful for Ghanaian activists because it resonated with the discourse of modernity, taming the issue of cutting and making NGO advocacy more palatable.

The target of the DVB campaign, however, was not culture, but power. The DVB advocacy was grounded in a subversive framework that critiqued the gendered power relations in both the private and public spheres. The DVB's proponents continually emphasized the fact that domestic violence is universal and not limited to the traditional. They articulated gender inequality as a structural problem that underlies violence. Their critique of power relations did not target the "domestic" realm only, but charged the state with being responsible for perpetuating gendered inequality. Unlike advocacy for female genital cutting legislation, DVB advocacy addressed and challenged power relations at all levels of the state-demanding social, cultural, and political transformations of gender relations. For the government, this kind of advocacy presented an explicit challenge; there was nothing "tame" about it.

The challenge posed by the DVB was manifested at the discursive level by the coalition's deployment of the women's rights discourse. The coalition mobilized notions of internationally and domestically guaranteed human rights, making demands for women's citizenship and empowerment. In contrast, the articulation of women's rights was largely absent from the advocacy for criminalization of cutting. While the rights discourse is not inherently subversive, it certainly challenges the state more than the discourse of harmful traditions. Ghanaian articulations of the rights discourse included demands that women be treated not only as subjects that the state should protect but also as citizens with full rights, whereas the criminalization of cutting in Ghana asked the state to protect women from their tradition and from themselves.

CLASS, GENDER, AND ETHNICITY

The logics of controversy and taming are also informed by the intersecting axes of class, gender, and ethnicity. Whether or not laws are passed is not just a matter of strategies and discourses—the identities of those who become reconfigured as the law's subjects and citizens also matter. The subjects of the two laws are marked by different configurations of class, ethnicity, and gender. Whose practices are criminalized? is the crucial question here.

The subjects regulated by the criminalization of cutting in Ghana are marginalized women and men. As I mentioned earlier, cutting is practiced by disenfranchised migrants and by dwellers from the North, most of whom are rural. In other words, the subjects of criminalization are Ghana's ethnic and classed others who live on the geographical and symbolic fringes of the state. Thus, it was easy for the government to criminalize cutting because this legislation had no consequences for most Ghanaian citizens who matter in the cultural and political sense. In other words, this law punishes bodies that the state already considers marginal. Moreover, this law was understood as gender-neutral, as Ghanaian circumcisers are both women and men.

In contrast, the DVB was understood as singling out male perpetrators. Domestic violence is spread across urban and rural areas and affects those rich and poor, with or without formal education. The subjects who feared being regulated by this law included professional and powerful men, men otherwise protected by laws, not punished by them. As I explained above, the resistance to the DVB began with the president and the cabinet—men at the top of the state's structure of authority. The opponents cast the bill as singling out men arbitrarily and without due process. Given the discrepancy in reception of the two laws, we are left with the question if the state was less willing to regulate and criminalize domestic violence because of the gender of the state itself.[48]

NGO-STATE RELATIONS

Finally, the logics of controversy and taming are also shaped by NGO-state relations. A closer look at the character of the main actors leading the campaigns and their relationships to the state may help explain why the controversy about the DVB spiraled out of control while the criminalization of cutting was tame. Class relations play a role here again, as the backgrounds of the laws' advocates shaped their participation in the public sphere. NGO leaders who advocated for the legislation on cutting are solidly middle-class: nurses, librarians, journalists, and social workers. In contrast, many DVB advocates studied abroad and hold degrees from foreign universities such as Georgetown. They are upper-class professionals; some are lawyers, others academics or aspiring politicians. This background has enabled them to participate in the larger public sphere and be politically visible. The proponents of the DVB included the movers and shakers of Ghana's women's movement and civil society, people whose views matter.

Another crucial difference in the trajectories of the two laws is the extent to which they mobilized civil society, threatening the state. The DVB campaign encompassed a broad coalition. The DVB coalition had a generative function in that it mobilized large swaths of Ghanaians and fomented their engagement within the larger women's movement, a movement that has been critical of the government. In contrast, NGOs that advocated for criminalization of cutting—GAWW being the main one—are single-issue organizations focused on one goal: abandonment of cutting. They do not play a larger role in Ghana's women's movement or the public sphere since their work and their advocacy have a less extensive reach and they are less threatening to the state.

GAWW not only closely collaborates with the government's central authority on women, but it also, in many ways, depends on the state. Its main staff members are in fact state employees, on "secondment" (in theory, a temporary reassignment) to the NGO, and their salaries were at times paid by the government. This NGO's proximity to the government is also visible in the physical space that it occupies: the office was built on government-donated land, within the Ghana National Commission on Children compound. The DVB coalition, in contrast, is independent of the government, has looser ties to it, and is less governable. The size and character of the coalition posed a threat to the state. Theirs was an ad hoc assemblage of NGOs, other organizations, and activists. They were neither registered with the state nor financially or otherwise dependent on it. Thus, both the discursive framework of their advocacy, as well as the form of their organizing, posed a challenge to the state, which responded by mobilizing a powerful opposition to the DVB.

CONCLUSION AND THEORETICAL IMPLICATIONS

In conclusion, I address some methodological and theoretical implications of my analysis. This ethnography shows why it is necessary to dig beneath and around the categories of violence against women, gender violence, and women's rights. Dominant scholarly frameworks would represent the Ghanaian campaigns against female genital cutting and domestic violence as examples of women's rights advocacy against gender violence. Yet, the contours of these campaigns and the opposition they generated reveal more differences than similarities. The campaigns mobilized dramatically different notions of violence as well as discrete ideas about whether and how these laws would promote women's rights.

Scholars examining the global proliferation of gender violence campaigns have emphasized their similarities, and Merry's argument that a global template of advocacy for gender violence laws becomes "localized" worldwide in a hegemonic fashion has been particularly influential.[49] NGOs come to rely on the same template of strategies, she argues: they use survey research to highlight the extent of the problem, provide services for communities and individuals, educate the public, and push for legislation.[50] At first glance, it appears that the Ghanaian strategies correspond to this model, as both campaigns have combined research, service provision, education, and legal advocacy. Yet these similarities belie the striking differences in the trajectories of the two campaigns: the advocacy is identical only from a bird's-eye perspective. I have shown that this model of gender violence advocacy cannot account for the divergent trajectories of the two campaigns or explain why the DVB became controversial while female genital cutting was criminalized swiftly.

This chapter has argued for a different scale of analysis, showing that the logics that guide the emergence of controversies are rooted in a larger set of global power relations as well as in more specific national dynamics. Criminalization of cutting was unchallenged in Ghana due to the local politics of class and ethnicity and the hegemonic discourses of development and modernity—global discourses which have gained local traction. In contrast, the opposition to the Domestic Violence Bill was motivated by the government's desire to have a say over the shifting configurations of gender and sexuality and by its struggle to maintain sovereignty in the age of neoliberalism.

Building on this analysis, I would like to suggest some methodological implications for studying gender violence advocacy in transnational perspective. The dominant model of analysis focuses on how rights are constructed at the United Nations and then travel to nation-states.[51] Yet this model overestimates the significance of the universal category violence against women and the importance of the UN system for understanding the transnational connections in gender-related advocacy. By equating the global with the UN, this model misses crucial connections and border crossings of gender-related advocacy and discourses mobilized to oppose it. The Ghanaian logics of controversy and taming show why it is important to examine specific forms of advocacy at the country level, while the similarities of campaigns and opposition strategies across sub-Saharan Africa invite us to adopt a wider angle of analysis. The political deployment of virtually the same discourses in opposition to rights-based domestic violence and sexual offenses campaigns across the continent suggests that the travel of these discourses is an important site for understanding the transnational aspect of gender-related advocacy.

Finally, my ethnography raises questions about the theoretical concepts that guide our analysis of power and hegemony in gender violence advocacy.

If we are interested in answering the important questions of which power relations are transformed by advocacy, and which reinscribed, the proposed notion of "localization" understood as adaptation of rights to "fully indigenous terms" cannot suffice.[52]

My analysis of the Ghanaian advocacy reveals that discourses that resonate locally are not purely local, and that the concept of the local does not guarantee the freedom from hegemonic discourses. I have shown that the notion of "harmful traditional practices" resonated in Ghana because it is embedded in discourses of development and modernity. As products of colonial encounters and global inequities that shape the lives of Ghanaians, these discourses are at once global and local, in the sense that they are familiar and pervasive. In other words, the "local" is already globalized. Although the local resonance of these discourses made advocacy against cutting work—the government passed the law without contesting it and no controversy erupted—it did not make it "fully indigenous" or less hegemonic. For me, this means that the proximity of NGO discourses to the culturally resonant notions has a pragmatic, not a moral or a political, value.

I therefore argue that the concept of localization that explores whether discourses are foreign or fully localized is an insufficient tool for analyzing whether and how advocacy transforms power relations. Rather than trying to locate origins of advocacy, we may ask whose interests it serves, protects, and shapes. Hence, rather than asking, Are women's rights laws a Western product? and Is this advocacy local enough? it might be more useful to inquire: Who benefits from articulations and productions of gender-related advocacy? Whose interests are served by new laws? Which cultural logics shape who can be the subjects and who the citizens of the state?

NOTES

1. Jutta M. Joachim, *Agenda Setting, the UN, and NGOs: Gender Violence and Reproductive Rights* (Washington, DC: Georgetown University Press, 2007), 103.

2. Margaret Keck and Kathryn Sikkink, *Activists beyond Borders: Advocacy Networks in International Politics* (Ithaca, NY: Cornell University Press, 1998), 170.

3. Anna L. Tsing, *Friction: An Ethnography of Global Connection* (Princeton, NJ: Princeton University Press, 2005), x.

4. Ibid., xi.

5. A comprehensive report on legislation against cutting in Africa can be found on http://www.homeoffice.gov.uk/rds/pdfs08/africa-fgm-080708.doc. Due to transnational politics of migration, and asylum claims on the basis of cutting in particular, immigration authorities such as the UK Border Agency compile such reports, revealing how knowledge and governmental power are tied together.

6. Kenya and Guinea-Bissau have passed modified legislation (when cutting pertains to children under sixteen, or has led to death, respectively). The Sierra

Leonean public and many politicians actively support cutting, which makes NGO anticutting initiatives highly contentious. See *IRIN News*, 1 March 2005. *IRIN News* is a project of the UN Office for the Coordination of Humanitarian Affairs, available at http://www.irinnews.org/Report.aspx?ReportId=62473.

7. I analyze community-level controversies as well as the intended and unintended effects of the legislation in my other work, "Of Rebels, Spirits, and Social Engineers: The Problems with Ending Female Genital Cutting" (manuscript in progress).

8. See Tabitha Kanogo, *African Womanhood in Colonial Kenya, 1900–1950* (Athens: Ohio University Press, 2005).

9. Lynn Thomas, "*Ngaitana*—I Will Circumcise Myself: Lessons from Colonial Campaigns to Ban Excision in Mery, Kenya," in *Female "Circumcision" in Africa: Culture, Controversy, and Change*, ed. Bettina Shell-Duncan and Ylva Hernlund (Boulder, CO: Lynne Rienner, 2000), 129.

10. Bettina Shell-Duncan and Ylva Hernlund, "Female 'Circumcision' in Africa: Dimensions of the Practice and Debates," in Shell-Duncan and Hernlund, *Female "Circumcision" in Africa*, 38.

11. Ibid., 38.

12. The North is on the margins of the state's economic priorities, and average per capita incomes that are two to four times lower than elsewhere in the country reflect that. See Andrew Shepherd et al., "Bridging the North South Divide in Ghana? Draft Background Paper for the 2005 World Development Report," *Equity and Development, World Development Report*, 2004 (Washington, DC: World Bank, 2004).

13. The Navrongo Health Research Center found that the data on cutting are inconsistent and misleading, as women interviewed about cutting in 1995 gave different responses in 2000, after cutting had been criminalized. See Elizabeth F. Jackson et al., "Inconsistent Reporting of Female Genital Cutting Status in Northern Ghana: Explanatory Factors and Analytical Consequences," *Studies in Family Planning* 34, no. 3 (2003): 200–210.

14. Marilyn Aniwa, "Prevalence," in *Breaking the Silence and Challenging the Myths of Violence against Women and Children in Ghana: Report of a National Study on Violence*, ed. Dorcas Coker Appiah and Kathy Cusack (Accra, Ghana: Gender Studies and Human Rights Documentation Centre, 1999), 71.

15. Elizabeth Ardayfio-Schandorf, "Violence against Women: The Ghanaian Case," expert paper presented at the meeting "Violence against Women: A Statistical Overview, Challenges and Gaps in Data Collection and Methodology and Approaches for Overcoming Them," UN Division for the Advancement of Women, Geneva, Switzerland, 11–14 April 2005, 10.

16. Kwasi Odoi-Agyarko, "Evaluation of Five Years of Implementation of Regional Plan of Action for Accelerating the Elimination of Female Genital Mutilation (FGM) in Africa: The Situation in Ghana," report submitted to the World Health Organization, Ghana, 15 October 2003.

17. In the widely used, universalized language of the World Health Organization, the various practices of cutting are divided into "types." Type 1 stands for "excision of the prepuce, with or without excision of part or all of the clitoris"; type 2 stands for "excision of the clitoris, with partial or total excision of the labia

minora"; and infibulation or type 3 stands for "excision of part or all of the external genitalia, and stitching/narrowing of the vaginal opening" (World Health Organization, *Factsheet 241* [Geneva: WHO, 2000]).

18. Act 484, the Criminal Code (Amendment) Act, 1994, Ghana Publishing Corporation Printing Division, A&O, A619/800/7/94.

19. Except for GAWW, who chose to be references by their proper name, names of the NGOs I studied ethnographically are pseudonyms.

20. Criminal Code (Amendment) Bill, GPC/Assembly Press, Accra, GPCI AIJ 4/300/2/2006.

21. Ibid.

22. *Accra Mail*, 15 June 2007.

23. There was one notable voice of objection: an editorial that compared "FGM" to "FSM" and "FHM"—the author's neologisms for skin bleaching ("female skin mutilation") and hair straightening ("female hair mutilation") (*The Mirror*, 30 June 2007).

24. *Public Agenda*, 11 June 2007.

25. Keck and Sikkink, *Activists beyond Borders*, 170.

26. Countries that have passed domestic violence laws include South Africa, Ghana, Zimbabwe, some Nigerian states, Namibia, Mauritius, Malawi, and the Seychelles. Other countries, including Botswana, Lesotho, Tanzania, and Kenya, have passed sexual offenses laws, which criminalize rape and other forms of violence related to sexuality.

27. Mari Kimani, "Taking on Violence against Women in Africa," *Africa Renewal* 21, no. 2 (July 2007). For an analysis of the controversy about Uganda's domestic relations bill, see Sylvia Tamale, "The Right to Culture and the Culture of Rights: A Critical Perspective on Women's Sexual Rights in Africa," *Feminist Legal Studies* 16, no. 1 (2008): 47–69.

28. *BBC News*, 26 December 2001.

29. Sari Wastell, "Being Swazi, Being Human: Custom, Constitutionalism, and Human Rights in an African Polity," in *The Practice of Human Rights: Tracking Law between the Global and the Local*, ed. Mark Goodale and Sally E. Merry (Cambridge: Cambridge University Press, 2007), 336.

30. According to Tamale, the women's rights framework is also one of the hallmarks of African feminism (Tamale, "Right to Culture," 54).

31. Dorcas Coker Appiah and Kathy Cusack, eds., *Breaking the Silence and Challenging the Myths of Violence against Women and Children in Ghana: Report of a National Study on Violence* (Accra, Ghana: Gender Studies and Human Rights Documentation Centre, 1999).

32. Mansah Prah, "Outcomes of Women's and Children's Responses," in Appiah and Cusack, *Breaking the Silence and Challenging the Myths*, 110.

33. Bernice Sam, "Domestic Violence Act 2007 of Ghana," paper presented at the workshop organized by Women in Law and Development in Africa, New York, 1 March 2007, 2.

34. Akosua Adomako-Ampofo, Esi Awotwi, and Angela Dwamena-Aboagye, "How the Perpetrators of Violence against Women and Children Escape," in

Women and Violence in Africa (Dakar, Senegal: Association of African Women in Research and Development, 2005), 223.

35. "Myths about Violence," pamphlet produced by the Gender Studies and Human Rights Documentation Centre, Accra, Ghana.

36. Coalition on Domestic Violence Legislation in Ghana, *A Guide to Ghana's Domestic Violence Bill* (author's library), 1.

37. Ibid.

38. For a legal argument explaining the DVB in detail, see Nancy Kaymar Stafford, "Permission for Domestic Violence: Marital Rape in Ghanaian Marriages," *Women's Rights Law Reporter* 29, no. 2–3 (2008): 63–76.

39. Coalition on Domestic Violence Legislation in Ghana, *A Guide to Ghana's Domestic Violence Bill*, 1.

40. Domestic Violence Bill Memorandum (author's library), 1.

41. Parliament of Ghana, Department of Official Reports, Parliamentary Debates, *Official Report*, 1 February 2005, vol. 49 (Accra, Ghana: Parliament House), 222.

42. Jennifer Hasty, *The Press and Political Culture in Ghana* (Bloomington: Indiana University Press, 2005).

43. *Public Agenda*, 3 June 2003.

44. Ghanaian academics were also involved in advocacy efforts, and some have written about the DVB. See Margaret Ivy Amoakohene, "Violence against Women in Ghana: A Look at Women's Perceptions and Review of Policy and Social Responses," *Social Science and Medicine* 59, no. 11 (2004): 2373–85; Takyiwaa Manuh, "Doing Gender Work in Ghana," in *Africa after Gender*, ed. Catherine M. Cole, Takyiwaa Manuh, and Stephan Miescher (Bloomington: Indiana University Press, 2007), 125–49; Rose Mary Amenga-Etego, "Violence against Women in Contemporary Ghanaian Society," *Theology and Sexuality* 13, no. 1 (2006): 23–46.

45. Tsing, *Friction*, 271.

46. This representation of cutting is shared across sub-Saharan Africa and globally. As Merry writes in her ethnography of the United Nations, female genital cutting "is the poster child" for the understanding of culture as tradition (ibid., 12).

47. James Ferguson, *Global Shadows: Africa in the Neoliberal World Order* (Durham, NC: Duke University Press, 2006), 187.

48. Wendy Brown, "Finding the Man in the State," *Feminist Studies* 18, no. 1 (1992): 7–34.

49. See also Joachim, *Agenda Setting, the UN, and NGOs*, 103.

50. Sally Engle Merry, *Human Rights and Gender Violence: Translating International Law into Local Justice* (Chicago: University of Chicago Press, 2006), 139.

51. See Keck and Sikkink, *Activists beyond Borders*; Joachim, *Agenda Setting, the UN and NGOs*; and Merry, *Human Rights and Gender Violence*.

52. Merry, *Human Rights and Gender Violence*, 222. She explains that localizing rights means tailoring them to the local context and making them resonant with the local cultural framework (ibid., 221).

11 ⇽ Constructing Law, Contesting Violence

The Senegalese Family Code and Narratives of Domestic Abuse

SCOTT LONDON

AFRICAN FAMILY LAW has emerged in the postcolonial era as a reflection of competing claims about tradition and modernity, cultural authenticity and religious fidelity. Gender relations reside at the heart of these claims, and efforts to regulate them through law generate controversies with which the postcolonial state and society must contend. Issues such as domestic violence are deeply entangled with these controversies, and battered women hoping to make use of the law to end or escape violence must negotiate not only the legal system, but the competing claims that surround it. In Senegal, the Family Code[1] represents an attempt in the years following independence in 1960 to blend aspects of French, Muslim, and African laws and norms. The result is a legal text in which all constituencies—Westernized urban elites, women's rights activists, leaders of the Muslim brotherhoods—can find something to embrace, as well as something to loathe.

While the Family Code establishes many protections for women, its reach and effectiveness are limited in three ways. First, knowledge of the law and access to the courts are limited outside urban areas. Second, the marabouts who lead the major Muslim brotherhoods encourage "passive noncompliance"[2] among followers. Third, my research indicates that the Family Code is not applied consistently within the legal process, as disputants in family cases wend their way through open court and the closed, mandatory mediation sessions that often impose a conventional gender ideology that thwarts full application of the law.

Cases involving domestic violence are particularly complex because the issue only enters formally into the Family Code as a justification for divorce, whereas violence is an important—though often marginalized—element of a wide range of cases. The last part of the chapter examines two case studies that demonstrate how the power dynamics in mandatory family mediation sessions tend to privilege a gender ideology that references Islam and African identity, while marginalizing implicit or explicit claims of abuse. The first case highlights the way in which violence explicitly noted in the dispute narrative is sidelined in exchanges between disputants and the judge. The second case demonstrates how implied violence remains hidden and suppressed as the mediation process unfolds. These two cases unfolded in the Departmental and Regional Family Tribunals of Saint-Louis, Senegal, in 1997. They were among about three hundred family cases reviewed during the period 1994–1997 (consisting mostly of divorce, maintenance, and custody disputes).

By comparing dispute narratives from a variety of sources—correspondence with judges, judges' notes, police reports, clerk's case summaries, and my own observational notes and recordings—I have been able to identify patterns in the transformation of women's narrative accounts. Complaints about unjust conditions and mistreatment are turned into morality tales by husbands and judges in which women's own behavior is at fault. Women's behavior is particularly vulnerable to criticism in reference to being a "good" Muslim wife and mother, determined by the degree of "submission and obedience" to her husband.

SENEGALESE FAMILY LAW

Beginning in the mid-nineteenth century, the French set up a network of tribunals overseen by local leaders selected and controlled by French colonial administrators. The appeals courts were headed by a French military commander, assisted by two European and two indigenous assessors (judicial advisors).[3] In areas where Islam had already taken firm hold of cultural and political life, the French successfully co-opted and restructured local qadis' (imams') courts, although they were unable to uphold the standard that qadis be literate in the French language.[4] By the time of independence in 1960, an elaborate network of French-mandated Islamic courts existed in the expanding areas dominated by Islam. These courts heard mostly civil and minor criminal cases. Serious cases and those heard on appeal still went before the colonial administrative courts. The latter were to be transformed after independence into the French-style state civil and criminal courts, divided geographically by department and region, that are familiar today. The former Muslim tribunals were kept "on the books" in the early postcolonial years as an adjunct to the secular state civil courts, but were slowly phased out.

The Family Code of Senegal was the inspiration of Léopold Sénghor, the Catholic, French-educated poet and father of independent Senegal. The Family Code was at the heart of Senghor's vision of a unified, stable, and postcolonial nation. The goal of the new Western-style code was the formulation of a single body of law that would supersede the ethnic, regional, and religious differences that had characterized family law under colonialism. It was also intended to placate a range of audiences. Senghor wanted to please urban elites who saw Western standards of gender equality as progressive and democratic. He wanted to impress France, the former colonial power, and other potential Western donors with the new country's eagerness to "Westernize."

But Senghor also knew that he could only test the patience of the powerful Muslim brotherhoods so far. With over 90 percent of the population Muslim, and most of these identifying with one of three Sufi Muslim brotherhoods, the leaders held enormous sway. Authority over gender relations and family life was, and remains, a hotly contested issue in Senegal. In the interests of stability and legitimacy of the new state, Senghor opted for a grand "compromise" in the formation of the Family Code, which developed into a patchwork of French, Islamic, and African law intended to satisfy all constituencies.

THE FAMILY CODE:
CONSTITUENCIES AND PERSPECTIVES

Senghor's determination to see the code come into effect reflected his conviction that the country needed a unified body of law in order to "modernize."[5] In this respect, he represented the Western-educated urban elites, who though predominantly Muslim, shared Senghor's vision of a secular state. Senghor's view also harmonized with women's rights activists and feminists who believed that key French civil law provisions in the code would protect women's interests in the family. But these affinities did not stop Senghor from both reaching out to Muslim leaders and attempting to play them off each other when they opposed his proposals. In the end, none of the primary constituencies—urban elites, feminists, the Muslim brotherhoods, Islamic reformers—obtained more than pieces of its desired outcome. The debates that shaped the passage of the code at its inception affect ongoing efforts to reform the law. And these same debates affect the way the law is applied inside the courthouse.

Women activists and feminists associated with the Dakar-based organization *Yewwu Yewwi* ("Raise Consciousness for Liberation") applauded the establishment of an age of consent to marriage, the right of women to alimony and child support, the abolition of repudiation (the unilateral male authority to impose a divorce), and the requirement that divorce be awarded in the state civil courts.[6] But the gains were mixed with losses, and other discriminatory elements of the law remained, such as the husband's status as sole head of the family.[7]

The aspects of the law that most disappointed the feminists were intended to placate the marabouts who led the Muslim brotherhoods. Instead, the code was broadly dismissed by the marabouts and their followers as insufficient in its embrace of shari'a and biased in favor of women and Western norms.[8] The

Islamic High Council of Senegal convened to condemn the Family Code in unambiguous language:

> [B]y virtue of the obligations that result from the roles assigned to us by our religious positions, we must necessarily remove any ambiguity about our position by solemnly reaffirming our unshakable conviction to *categorically reject any measure, even an official one, which does not respect the sacred principles of our religion.*[9]

Islamist (or "fundamentalist") reformers who criticized the marabouts and the brotherhoods in other contexts, joined with them now to denounce the code as an attack on Islam and an intrusion by outsiders.[10] At the same time, educated Muslim men who were not broadly sympathetic to the Islamists shared their concern that the code would threaten traditional values and prompt women to take their husbands to court.[11]

There is a marked diversity of ideological positions on how Islam pertains to gender relations in Senegal. But despite this diversity, a majority of men, along with many women, view the Family Code as being at odds with Islam, as well as indigenous culture and tradition. Derided as "The Woman's Code," the law is caricatured as a misfit Western import, despite the fact that many key elements derive directly from Islamic law. This caricature of the code is closely linked with the social stigma surrounding going to court. Women who do file for divorce are perceived as directly challenging the system of hierarchical gender relations, and risk ridicule, ostracism, and difficulty remarrying. Leading clerics have instructed followers to engage in passive noncompliance with the code, opting to marry or divorce in the mosque and disregard state requirements. Many men value this behavior as an act of defiance against a secular government.

The fact that the Family Code was passed despite these strong objections is a testament to Senghor's determination and political acumen, and to the limits of the marabouts' ability to challenge the state. Leonardo Villalon argues, however, that this victory "was more apparent than real,"[12] and suggests that the marabouts effectively practiced a form of legal "isolation" as a means of limiting state authority, instructing followers to ignore legal requirements regarding marriage, divorce, and inheritance. Senghor, in turn, in the interests of pragmatism, turned a blind eye to this lack of compliance.[13] While the picture has been more complex in urban centers, in rural areas compliance with the family code has been the exception and not the rule. This helps explain why the brotherhoods have been more muted in their criticisms of the code in recent years, while the Islamists continue to call for its replacement with a system based on shari'a.[14]

Despite these limitations, a significant minority of Senegalese people throughout Senegal use the civil family court structure based on the Family Code. Assessing the effectiveness of the code requires examining the law in action in this setting, not just the historical context and public controversies that surround it. This is particularly true in the case of domestic violence, which the law addresses explicitly only in very limited ways. The issue of domestic violence emerges directly and indirectly in a range of marital dispute cases that involve divorce, maintenance, choice of residence, abandonment, inheritance, and related areas of conflict.

The cases reviewed below are based on ethnographic observations of mandatory mediation sessions conducted by civil court judges. The findings suggest that women tend not to fare well in cases involving disputes between husbands and wives, particularly in high-stakes cases involving complaints that challenge male authority in the family, such as domestic violence claims. In these instances the Family Code does not function simply as a list of rules and obligations to be enforced, but as a broad set of legally plural principles that are actively interpreted and negotiated among judges and disputants. Moreover, the code assigns the judge broad latitude in family mediation sessions to discharge his "social role" by encouraging troubled couples (including those actively seeking divorce) to resolve conflicts and remain together. This role is often exercised in an authoritarian style that privileges a patriarchal discourse and thwarts women's efforts to exercise rights delineated by the code.

A comparison with another African context that exhibits a different pattern of case outcomes helps highlight the factors that shape Senegalese family law. In her primarily linguistic study of the qadi's courts used by Swahili Muslims in coastal Kenya, Susan Hirsch[15] discovers that women often obtain favorable outcomes in family disputes, notwithstanding the religious and cultural edict that they quietly "persevere" in the face of conflict (Hirsch also notes that enforcement of these outcomes is uneven).[16] Hirsch examines the gendered nature of competing discourses at play in the mediation sessions conducted by qadis and argues that the legal process does not always unfold along expected lines. Although Islamic legal discourse privileges men in key ways, qadis frequently remind men of their spousal obligations under Islamic law (regarding a range of issues from domestic violence[17] to maintenance[18]). Moreover, although women more commonly rely on other gendered discourses (what Hirsch terms discourses of "Swahili ethics" and "spiritual health"), their agency in court sometimes does encompass demanding their rights under Islamic law.[19] In assessing the qadi's courts as a source of women's empowerment, Hirsch gives credit to women who persist in taking their disputes to the qadi's court. She also credits qadis who treat women's narratives of perseverance with sympathy[20] and push back against men whom they perceive to challenge their authority.[21] Finally, the Kenyan state's oversight of the qadi's courts has made them more amenable to women's interests, although the motive is one of control, not women's legal empowerment.[22]

One of the chief contributions of Hirsch's analysis is her reflection on the qadi's courts as sites of resistance to patriarchal family relations and social norms.[23] Hirsch argues that both women who use the court successfully and the qadis themselves view their outcomes as individual remedies, and not as part of a larger effort to extend legal rights or foster social change. Hirsch notes, however, that the fact that women go to court and leave with favorable outcomes changes legal consciousness and expectations of dispute outcomes that may indirectly empower women.[24] Careful not to overstate the implications of her findings, Hirsch argues convincingly for the possibility of women's agency in the context of African legal pluralism and Islamic law.

The Kenyan and Senegalese contexts share several attributes. In both cases the intermediary (a qadi in one case, a civil judge in the other) conducts a semistructured mediation session that accommodates open-ended exchanges with the disputants. Both illustrate instances of postcolonial African legal pluralism that includes Islamic law. In the two instances Islamic legal discourse serves as one of several complex cultural and legal resources on which the intermediary and disputants draw. In Kenyan and Senegalese mediations the intermediary exercises broad authority to control the exchange. But differences abound. Kenya's qadi-run Islamic courts coexist with civil and criminal courts as a separate but integral part of the state legal system serving Muslims with family disputes. In contrast, Senegal's Islamic courts were phased out in the postcolonial period. Senegalese Muslims (and everyone else) with family disputes enter a secular civil family court system[25] rooted in the legally plural Family Code. Although Senegalese women do sometimes frame complaints in reference to lapses in behaviors prescribed by Islamic law (regarding the husband's obligation to provide materially for the family, for example), and judges do sometimes verbally admonish men in these instances, case outcomes do not typically turn on these moments. Moreover, while Hirsch makes clear that Islamic law is only one of four distinct discourses at play in the mediations she observes, the qadi's courts appear to be more explicitly and broadly grounded in Islamic law than the Senegalese family courts rooted in the Family Code. As Hirsch points out, her case study challenges the common assumption that Islamic law always has a primarily patriarchal effect, especially if we look beyond legal texts to the complex ways in which Muslim women exercise agency within legal settings.[26] This is not to argue that Muslim women would be better off legally if Senegal had kept its Islamic courts. Indeed, the comparison suggests that the specific nature of the available legal discourses is only one factor to consider, and that the power dynamics in the legal arena is what steers the negotiation among those discourses in one direction or another. The most salient difference between the two case studies may be that the Senegalese judges are generally less sympathetic to women and less inclined to check male authority than the Kenyan qadis for complex cultural reasons that would require further study to reveal.

MANDATORY MEDIATION SESSIONS OF FAMILY DISPUTES

Most disputes that come to the family court are initiated by a letter from one or both parties to the judge, followed by a preliminary public hearing at which time most cases are scheduled for mediation. Mediation sessions are a formal component of the judicial process that the Family Code requires for most family disputes, including divorces. Mediations typically take place in the judge's chambers in a closed session that includes disputants, the judge, and a clerk. Witnesses and family members are brought in only rarely. In describing the "social role" that the judge plays in this instance (in contrast to his "judicial role"), the Family Code instructs judges to take up to three mediation sessions spread over up to one year before granting a divorce, though in practice most cases end after the first session. Emphasis is placed on reconciliation and encouraging the couple to stay together. In fact, the Family Code does little to regulate how judges conduct mediations beyond imposing this mandate. Neither the code nor the judges I have interviewed view domestic violence situations as an exception to this mandate.[27] Getting a divorce in Senegal is generally characterized as relatively easy,[28] and in the end anyone with the will and the means can obtain one. But a woman using divorce to escape violence may be compelled by the judge to stay put for up to a year. In the sessions, violence, if it's addressed at all, becomes one more problem to be worked out in an effort to preserve the marriage.

CASE STUDIES

The following two case studies illuminate different moments in the process of bringing such a case to family court in Senegal. Each case illustrates dispute transformations that take place as the preliminary narrative accounts produced by the women—in the form of letters to the judge initiating the case—are recast to highlight the woman's failure to live up to gendered norms. The first case concerns a dispute between Fatima and her husband, Mamadou, in which Fatima complains that her husband's marabout—a cleric and local representative of one of the large Sufi Muslim brotherhoods—has raped her and beaten her children. In this case, I examine the transformation of dispute narratives contained in court documents by comparing the woman's letter and police report with the husband's police report and written decisions by the first judge to hear the case and the second judge who repealed it on appeal.

The second case involves a dispute between Hadi and her husband, Abdoulaye, in which Hadi alludes to possible violence and complains about living with her husband's parents, his unlawful repudiation of her, and his efforts to prevent her from working. Hadi has asked the judge to grant the couple a divorce, which Abdoulaye opposes. In the presentation of this case, I emphasize how dispute narratives are transformed through dialogue with the judge during a mandatory mediation session. As Hadi works to sustain a narrative of complaint, the judge continually derails her, so that her concerns remain vague and fragmented. Instead, he repeatedly compels her to answer for her perceived recalcitrance, framing her as a suspect wife and a reluctant problem-solver. Although Hadi implies that she may have been a victim of violence, she is never allowed — much less encouraged — to describe fully the anguish to which she alludes.

FIRST CASE: FATIMA AND MAMADOU

In this case, Fatima makes clear accusations that her husband has left her and their children in the care of a neglectful and violent marabout, and that Mamadou took no action to prevent further harm after Fatima brought the problem to his attention. Five years earlier, Mamadou, a police officer, had been transferred from the town of Diourbel to the town of Saint-Louis and soon brought Fatima and the children to live in the house of his marabout while he resided in a nearby police barracks. But after Mamadou was transferred back to Diourbel, he elected to leave his family with the marabout in Saint-Louis. In her letter to the judge initiating the case, Fatima describes the violence and neglect that led her to flee the situation and asks the judge to force her husband to take the children away from the marabout and return them to her.

> I encountered too many threats and problems in this house. This marabout hit me, insulted me with my children. We were treated like slaves. . . . [H]e tortured my one-year-old son. . . .
>
> [D]uring the five years that I spent at the home of the marabout, my husband spent all his salary on [the marabout]. I had no clothing. I left behind my five children. . . . I ask for my children.

After Fatima files her letter with the courts, she and Mamadou must each make a statement to the police. In her statement, Fatima implies that the marabout had an inappropriate hold on Mamadou, exacerbating the family's predicament.

> [M]y husband, . . . had been entranced by a marabout. . . . [W]e left our apartment to go live near him. . . . [M]y husband, who had

completely changed, abandoned us to the will of the marabout. . . .
[A]t the end of every month [my husband] gave . . . all of his salary to
[the marabout].

Fatima also takes the opportunity to add that the marabout's violence and
neglect were directed at her as well as the children.

> During the absence of my husband, this marabout mistreated me sav-
> agely. Sometimes he even allowed himself to make me do services,
> this while hitting me with a belt or a wire. . . .
> [T]he conditions at the marabout's home were disastrous. . . .
> I had a disease of the eyes that, according to the specialists, is due to
> malnutrition.

In Mamadou's police statement he directly refutes Fatima's characterization
of the situation.

> [M]y wife lived in very good conditions in Saint-Louis. Therefore, I
> am very surprised that she has spoken to the contrary.
> At no time was my wife mistreated during her stay [at the
> marabout's home]. What's more, she had never been beaten by the
> marabout.

Mamadou recasts her departure from the marabout's home not as an effort
to escape danger and seek help but as defiance of male authority by leaving
without authorization.

> I received a visit from my wife at my residence in the police barracks.
> At my request, she made it known to me that she had come back from
> Saint-Louis without any permission.

He goes on to describe her flight as an "abandonment" of the family and, by
extension, of her proper role as an obedient wife and mother.

> I request if it pleases the court that my wife returns as soon as pos-
> sible to the residence in Saint-Louis . . . that she had abandoned
> without any consent. She has taken this action of her own will with
> no valid motive.

The case is reviewed first by the judge in the departmental courts, whose narrative reads like a synopsis of Mamadou's.

> [Mamadou] has refuted the declarations of his wife who claims that the children are living in bad conditions in Saint-Louis. . . . He maintains that [Fatima] left the residence without his authorization.

While the judge appears to take Mamadou at his word, he dismisses Fatima's claims based on lack of evidence

> [N]o proof has been given of the existence of dangers and bad treatment invoked by [Fatima].

In addition to giving greater credence to Mamadou's account, the judge's own narrative includes a legal justification for denying Fatima's request and fulfilling Mamadou's.

> [According to] the terms of Article 153 of the Family Code, the choice of residence belongs to the husband so that the wife is bound to live there with him.

Finally, the judge concludes that Fatima's requests are unfounded and rules that "it pleases the court to order his wife to return to him at the conjugal residence in Saint-Louis."

Over the course of one year, as these documents were added one by one to the case file, Fatima's fears for herself and her children were transformed into a criticism of her behavior and a court ruling ordering her back into a dangerous home. At this stage in the process, Fatima's agency appears to be brutally constrained. She took bold action to use the courts to protect herself and her children from harm, yet the dominant patriarchal norms of the society in which the courts are embedded trumped her efforts.

But Fatima took the rare action of appealing the case to the higher regional courts, where the case was heard by a different judge. This judge took Fatima's description of the danger to the children seriously, ruling that further investigation was necessary.

> There is cause to investigate the security of the residence in Saint-Louis where the children are living, because even if the choice of the family residence belongs to the father of the family, it must be noted that the choice can be modified at the request of the mother in the event that she perceives physical or moral danger to those who must reside there. It is therefore necessary to open an investigation into the place of residence chosen by [Mamadou].

The judge does not directly affirm Fatima's rape claim, but he does provide an alternative legal narrative that validates her role in protecting her family as an adjunct to her husband's primary authority to decide where the family will live. The legal empowerment this judge offers is still couched in a gendered framework that defines Fatima as a mother (though in this case as a "good" mother looking out for her children) as opposed to an adult with rights to self-determination and protection from violence. But Fatima's case demonstrates that women's agency is possible under some circumstances.

SECOND CASE: HADI AND ABDOULAYE

In this second case study I review the transcript of and quote excerpts from a mandatory mediation session between Hadi and Abdoulaye, a couple in their early thirties. I focus here on two rhetorical strategies commonly employed by judges in response to women's dispute narratives: first, trivializing or ignoring the elements of the woman's narrative that highlight or legitimate her sense of mistreatment or injustice; and second, challenging the content and emphasis of the woman's dispute narrative in reference to an idealized notion of an African or Muslim woman who readily subordinates herself to the men in her family. Hadi has little chance to give full voice to her concerns in the face of these strategies. Rather than probing for a complete description of the problem she faces, the judge puts Hadi on the defensive and makes it very difficult for her to specify the details of her anguish. If violence is present in her story, there is no clear path to making it explicit within the context of the mediation.

Hadi has moved away from her husband and wants a divorce, which Abdoulaye says he does not want to give her. As in many civil divorce cases, it is the wife who makes the initial request in a letter to the judge. In the letter, Hadi raises four issues to explain why she wants to divorce Abdoulaye.

First, Hadi states painfully but vaguely in her letter, "I have been through things so terrible that I cannot even mention them here," suggesting, perhaps, violence or abuse. Second, she explains that Abdoulaye would not allow her to work. In fact, since a reform of the Family Code in 1989, a man can no longer legally bar his wife from seeking and holding employment. The third complaint is that Abdoulaye had repudiated her. Islamic law allows a husband to take unilateral action to divorce his wife, but the state does not recognize repudiations, and they are, in fact, illegal and punishable as a civil offense. Fourth, Abdoulaye has insisted they live in his parents' overcrowded house, a living arrangement that is not at all uncommon, though not always popular with younger couples.

During the course of the mediation Abdoulaye admits to having repudiated Hadi but claims he did not know that it was illegal to do so. He also complains of Hadi looking for work behind his back. As for the living arrangements, Abdoulaye explains that he cannot afford a residence separate from his parents because he has spent too much of his income on a television and other luxury goods for the family.

Of Hadi's four concerns, the judge repeatedly sidesteps all but one, her refusal to live with his parents. As for the possible indirect allusion to violence or ill-treatment in Hadi's letter, clear grounds for divorce under the Family Code, the judge neglects to inquire into what unspeakable things Hadi has experienced. In response to Hadi's complaint that Abdoulaye will not let her work, the judge simply changes the subject to that of her moving back in with his parents.

> Hadi: I have my principles. . . . I am working. I don't want to be a housewife—[pause]—I have my goals.

> Judge: Hadi, now, give me your decision—[pause]—Are you ready to go live there? [at his parents' house?]

Hadi's description of Abdoulaye's illegal repudiation is first ignored by the judge.

> Judge: If he were willing to change his ways, would you reconsider?
> Hadi: No, it is he who has repudiated me.
> Judge: What I have before me are two people linked by marriage.

Toward the end of the mediation when Hadi once again brings up the repudiation, the judge acknowledges the issue while marginalizing its importance

> Judge: Yes, he repudiated you, but on a civil level, it does not count.

In contrast, the judge devotes a good part of the mediation to Hadi's fourth complaint, Abdoulaye's insistence that they live in his parent's overcrowded house. The prolonged debate between Hadi and the judge illustrates the second rhetorical strategy used by this judge, that of reframing her dispute narrative to focus on the woman's behavioral shortcomings. This strategy permeates many mediations, and it is notably common in cases involving battering, in which the woman's behavior leading up to the husband's attack is scrutinized, and the violence itself usually sidelined.

In the debate between Hadi and the judge, the latter uses the weight of his authority, and an authoritarian tone, to try to overpower Hadi, who becomes visibly distraught. At one point in the exchange, the judge engages Abdoulaye, who readily affirms that Hadi has undermined his authority over her as her husband. Hadi begins the exchange by describing the uncomfortable conditions in the house, and reads off a long list of extended family members who live there.

Judge: In Africa, we are all victims of that. That has nothing to do with you in your role as a couple. Me, I think it's the best solution [that the two reunite]. We are Africans, we are all the same . . . African families.

Hadi: I cannot live with his parents. That is not a solution. I accept everything but to go to his parents' house.

Judge: [addressing Abdoulaye and expressing dismay at Hadi's intransigence]: What can we do now?

Abdoulaye: I have lost my authority as head of the household.

Hadi: For me, I have made an effort.

Judge: We are in Africa–[pause]–There are solutions, but you don't want solutions.

Hadi: What keeps him from renting a house?

Judge: Me, I have no solution [left] at all. And nevertheless, there are solutions. The husband, it is he who is the head of the household; it is up to him to decide where to live. He has the right to choose where to live.

At this point in the mediation, Hadi, who has been remarkably persistent during an unusually long session, begins to give in. Three of her four complaints have been ignored or trivialized, and the fourth has been reframed to make her appear to be the one preventing a reasonable solution. Moreover, she seems intimidated by the judge, who has been berating her in exasperated tones for over an hour. Finally, Hadi gives in and agrees to drop the divorce and return to the home of her in-laws.

By failing to maintain the legitimacy of her narrative account in the judge's eyes, Hadi appears convinced that she has "lost" in her effort to divorce her husband and gives up. In fact, from a legal standpoint, Hadi is not obliged to convince the judge that her account is accurate but simply to declare at the end of the mediation phase of the divorce process that she wants a divorce, which the judge is then legally obligated to grant. But Hadi, like many women seeking a divorce in the cases I observed, does not appear to know this, and the judge does not inform her. In this case the rule of law broke down in favor of the law of the more powerful storyteller.[29]

~

In the legal arena, storytelling is an activity with profound implications for self-determination, personal safety, and the type and degree of state intervention in everyday life. Women seeking legal empowerment—whether to obtain a divorce, secure child support, or to escape violence—enter a narrative mine-field as soon as they write to the judge, inviting his scrutiny. The subsequent transformation of disputes results in unpredictable outcomes, as the two cases demonstrate. As narrative accounts are reinterpreted by different actors at different stages, standards of legitimation are rooted primarily in patriarchal social norms. Because these norms tend to dictate the interpretation of women's stories by judges, as well as judges' interpretation of the law, women begin at a disadvantage. As Hadi's case implies, expanding women's legal knowledge may have an impact; had she known that the judge lacked the authority to decide the case based on his reinterpretation of her account, she might have continued to insist on divorce. It is not clear in Fatima's case why she took the initiative to appeal the decision when so few women appear to have the knowledge or wherewithal to pursue this option. But the desperation of her situation, and the judge's potentially dangerous retelling of her story, may have emboldened her to insist on legal legitimation of her narrative.

Ultimately, Fatima's case may have gone better because she convinced the judge on appeal that hers was the story of a "good" Muslim wife and mother whose husband was failing in his role. Hadi demonstrates the potential peril facing women whose stories draw instead on a discourse of women's self-determination that contradicts patriarchal norms. But if the ongoing movement in Senegal to expand women's legal knowledge is successful, these norms may be transformed.

POSTSCRIPT

The debates surrounding the Family Code have continued into the present, and the ongoing tug-of-war among constituencies has given way to some notable changes, though without leaving any group satisfied with women's legal and social status. Yet some of these formal changes in the law (including reforms to the Penal Code as well as the Family Code) have been substantive from the perspective of expansion of women's rights. The 1989 reform of the Family Code repeals a husband's authority to prevent his wife from working, replaces unitary paternal authority over children with parental authority shared by the wife and husband, ensures the wife's access to legal documents pertaining to the marriage, and expands the husband's maintenance obligation upon divorce.[30]

Proponents of the reforms based their arguments in part on human rights discourse and Senegal's obligations under international law. The ratification of the Convention on the Elimination of All Forms of Discrimination against Women (CEDAW) and other international human rights accords formally committing Senegal to the protection of women's rights have provided a benchmark for activists, as well as the government.[31] Indeed, Senegal's 1994 report to the United Nations' Committee on the Elimination of Discrimination against Women touts the 1989 reforms as a marker of Senegal's successful efforts to comply with the Convention and international legal norms.

The Senegalese government has also heralded the 1999 reform of the Penal Code (Law 99–05) as a necessary and positive integration of the precepts of CEDAW into domestic law.[32] The change brings Senegalese law into harmony with CEDAW by prohibiting a broad range of forms of gender-based violence, including female excision, child molestation, domestic violence, and rape.[33] It also provides a newly invigorated avenue for victims of violence, who may now find more remedies in the criminal arena than the civil arena.

While these changes reflect efforts by women's rights advocates, critics note that these reforms come up short in three ways. First, the Family Code revisions have not gone far enough in complying with CEDAW and with feminist expectations because article 152 continues to define the husband as the head of the family (*chef de la famille*). Second, there is a broad (though not universal) consensus among commentators that the Family Code and Penal Code revisions are, at best, applied inconsistently and remain of little value to the majority of Senegalese women who might benefit in theory.[34] This problem exists on two levels: the widespread noncompliance with the law noted above (that is, most people do not go to court) and the nonenforcement of the law (that is, the courts do not apply the law consistently). Third, the existence of potentially helpful laws and the possibility that norms of noncompliance might change are undermined by limited public awareness (of both the content of the law and how to access the legal system).

At the same time, these observations raise challenging questions about how to assess the value of law in the context of gender, violence, and human rights. The explicit criminalization of gender-based violence is an accomplishment in its own right, the use of law to make an authoritative normative statement challenging gendered forms of tyranny and torture in everyday life. This is a success whole and apart from how that statement is subsequently engaged by different constituencies within the society. Moreover, it is easy to oversimplify the nature of that engagement and to mischaracterize it as static. Issues of compliance, enforcement, and awareness are always potentially in flux as legal reforms roil hegemonic discourses and controversies ignite public debate. As awareness shifts, people carry new expectations into court that may shift the ground of negotiations over meaning and justice. New research is needed in the light of these recent legal reforms and their impact on how people are addressing issues of violence, gender, and law.

NOTES

1. The Senegalese Family Code was voted into law in 1972 and revised significantly in 1989.

2. Leonardo Villalon, *Islamic Society and State Power in Senegal: Disciples and Citizens in Fatick* (Cambridge: Cambridge University Press, 1995), 107.

3. Michael Crowder, "The White Chiefs of Tropical Africa," in Crowder, *Colonial West Africa: Collected Essays* (London: Frank Cass, 1978), 141.

4. Martin Klein, *Islam and Imperialism in Senegal: Sine-Saloum, 1847–1914* (Stanford, CA: Stanford University Press, 1968), 199.

5. Villalon, *Islamic Society and State Power in Senegal*, 98.

6. Moriba Magassouba, *Islam au Senegal: Demain les mollahs?* (Paris: Karthala, 1985); Fatou Sow, "Fundamentalisms, Globalisation and Women's Human Rights in Senegal," *Gender and Development* 11, no. 1 (2003): 72.

7. Lucy Creevey, "Islam, Women and the Role of the State in Senegal," *Journal of Religion in Africa* 26, no. 3 (1996): 298–99; Sow, "Fundamentalisms, Globalisation and Women's Human Rights in Senegal," 72.

8. Creevey, "Islam, Women and the Role of the State in Senegal," 297; Sow, "Fundamentalisms, Globalisation and Women's Human Rights in Senegal," 72.

9. Quoted in Villalon, *Islamic Society and State Power in Senegal*, 228.

10. Creevey, "Islam, Women and the Role of the State in Senegal," 300; Sow, "Fundamentalisms, Globalisation and Women's Human Rights in Senegal," 74.

11. Creevey, "Islam, Women and the Role of the State in Senegal," 300.

12. Villalon, *Islamic Society and State Power in Senegal*, 228.

13. Creevey, "Islam, Women and the Role of the State in Senegal," 298.

14. Codou Bop, "Islam and Women's Sexual Health and Rights in Senegal," *Muslim World Journal of Human Rights* 2, no. 1 (2005): 9.

15. Susan Hirsch, *Pronouncing and Persevering: Gender and the Discourses of Disputing in an African Islamic Court* (Chicago: University of Chicago Press, 1998).

16. Susan F. Hirsch, "Kadhi's Courts as Complex Sites of Resistance: The State, Islam, and Gender in Postcolonial Kenya," in *Contested States: Law, Hegemony and Resistance*, ed. Mindie Lazarus-Black and Susan F. Hirsch (New York: Routledge, 1994), 218.

17. Hirsch, *Pronouncing and Persevering*, 91.

18. Ibid., 86, 109.

19. Ibid., 109.

20. Ibid., 243–44.

21. Hirsch, "Kadhi's Courts," 218.

22. Ibid., 219.

23. Hirsch, *Pronouncing and Persevering*, 136–37.

24. Ibid.,137.

25. Marabouts in villages and urban neighborhoods also provide informal dispute resolution based on Islamic legal principles.

26. Hirsch, *Pronouncing and Persevering*, 244.

27. Scott London, "Conciliation and Domestic Violence in Senegal, West Africa," *Political and Legal Anthropology Review* 20, no. 2 (1997): 83–91.

28. Barbara Callaway and Lucy Creevey, *The Heritage of Islam: Women, Religion, and Politics in West Africa* (Boulder, CO: Lynne Rienner, 1994).

29. Hadi has been treated like a defendant compelled to argue in her own defense. In reality, under the "irreconcilable differences" clause in the Family Code, even if only one spouse insists on a divorce, the judge must grant it. The limit of the judge's formal power is that he can prolong the mediation phase for up to a year. But the judge here is exploiting Hadi's lack of knowledge of the law to sustain a fiction that he is in fact adjudicating rather than mediating the dispute—a distinction that does not appear to be clear to most disputants in family court—and that she must submit to his decree if she fails to "win" this contest.

30. Callaway and Creevey, *The Heritage of Islam*; Amsatou Sow Sidibé, "Senegal's Evolving Family Law," *Journal of Family Law* 32, no. 2 (1993–94): 421–29.

31. Adel Arab, "Senegal: Civil Society Suggests a Review of the Bill Modifying the Family Code," *Women's Global Network for Reproductive Rights Newsletter* 75 (April 2002); Aminata Diouf Ndiaye, "Violences à l'égard des femmes: Situation au Sénégal," report of the Ministère de la Femme, de la Famille et du Développement Social, 2006; Sow, "Fundamentalisms, Globalisation and Women's Human Rights in Senegal."

32. Ndiaye, "Violences à l'égard des femmes."

33. Bop, "Islam and Women's Sexual Health and Rights in Senegal."

34. Fatou Camara, "Women and the Law: A Critique of Senegalese Family Law," *Social Identities* 13, no. 6 (2007): 787–800; Sow Sidibé, "Senegal's Evolving Family Law"; U.S. Department of State, "Senegal," *Country Reports on Human Rights Practices—2006*. Camara argues that the fundamental weakness of Senegal's Family Code resides not in its insufficient embrace of international human rights or Western legal precepts, but in its abandonment of indigenous norms and practices that in the past effectively conferred rights and protections on Senegalese women.

12 ⮑ Domestic Violence as a Human Rights Violation

The Challenges of a Regional Human Rights Approach in Africa

BENEDETTA FAEDI

INTERNATIONAL LEGAL DISCOURSE has since the 1990s defined human rights to include rights to equality, security, and dignity and the enjoyment of fundamental freedoms. In this framework, domestic violence constitutes one of the most pervasive human rights violations.[1] Analyzed as a historical manifestation of unequal power relationships between men and women, gender-based violence fosters practices of domination over and discrimination against women that leads to the failure of women to advance and fully participate in a society.

The estimated number of victims varies from 15 percent to 71 percent among countries.[2] The prevalence of domestic violence reveals that, contrary to popularly held belief, the home is often not the safest place to be. Instead, intimate abuse may occur most often within family relationships. Because of the emotional breakdown of values and trust that women endure within the home, incidents of domestic violence are highly underreported by victims fearing retaliation or secretly bearing the shame of the aggression.

In contrast, historical biases and strategies of convenience shape states' policies of noninterference and nonintervention in family matters, ignoring the fact that tolerance of such crimes and claims of extraneousness already entail complicity in the violence inflicted. In the words of Rosa Brooks, "[W]idespread domestic violence is possible only when state structures encourage, tolerate, or consistently fail to remedy it."[3] Particularly in Africa, where local governments counterpose cultural and religious diversity claims to international standards, the human rights debate on domestic violence seeks a balance between traditions and modernity, customary practices and fundamental rights.

By interpreting domestic violence as a violation of women's human rights, this chapter aims to provide a general legal appreciation of intimate abuse in its formulation under the international treaties devoted to women's rights. The analysis of domestic violence as an international human rights issue reveals the limitations of this approach in facing the deep disjuncture between international law benchmarks and local realities. By examining international human rights instruments for women's rights, on the one hand, and, on the other, signatories' resistance to comply with their obligations and adequately implement treaties' provisions in domestic legal systems, the chapter sheds light on the gap between international law aspirations and human rights outrages. It also acknowledges the continuing tension between universal standards and grassroots arrangements. As an alternative approach, the chapter proposes insights into strengthening the key role that regional human rights institutions may play in leading a constructive dialogue on strategies for change among diverse actors and, hence, responding adequately to practices of abuse in the private space. Specific references to and instances of the distinctiveness and challenges of the African system follow throughout the chapter.

DOMESTIC VIOLENCE AS A HUMAN RIGHTS VIOLATION

Domestic violence has been generally understood as a private issue, on the grounds of an idealized image of the home as a place of safety and security away from government involvement.[4] However, research has revealed that "far from being a place of safety, the family can be [a] cradle of violence and that much of this violence is directed at the female members of the family."[5] A 2005 study by the World Health Organization (WHO) reported that intimate partner abuse is the most prevalent yet relatively hidden and ignored form of violence in women's lives.[6] Although comprehensive statistics are hard to come by, the proportion of victims ranged from 15 percent to 71 percent with most countries falling between 29 percent and 62 percent.

In spite of the systematic and widespread domestic violence affecting women, it was only since the 1990s and after considerable efforts, that the international community came to focus on human rights for women, classifying intimate partner abuse as a pervasive and specific form of violence, constituting a human rights violation. The first international instrument espousing gender equality as its focus and acknowledging women as victims of unique human rights violations was the Convention on the Elimination of All Forms of Discrimination against Women (hereafter the Convention). Adopted in 1979 by the United Nations General Assembly, the Convention defined the term *discrimination against women* to encompass any distinction, exclusion, or restriction made on the basis of sex that has the effect or purpose of impairing or nullifying the recognition, enjoyment, or exercise by women of human rights and fundamental freedoms.[7] Moreover, states parties[8] of the Convention committed themselves to condemning discrimination against women in all its forms and agreed to adopt all the appropriate measures, including legislation, to modify or abolish existing laws, customs, and social and cultural patterns that are based on the idea of inferiority or superiority of either of the sexes or on stereotypical roles for men and women.[9]

In order to achieve the Convention's stated goals, article 17 established a Committee on the Elimination of Discrimination against Women (hereafter the CEDAW committee), a supervisory body responsible for monitoring members' efforts to meet their obligations through a review of periodic reports submitted for consideration by states parties.[10] The CEDAW committee also drafted general recommendations aimed at interpreting the treaty on issues beyond the discrimination framework as well as ensuring its application to serious violations against women.[11] Although the general recommendations are not legally binding in the same terms as the Convention, they served the purpose of clarifying states parties' obligations when they are not mentioned or adequately explained in the text.

In the case of violence against women, the silence of the Convention was subsequently replaced by two general recommendations on the topic. The first one, General Recommendation no. 12, issued by the monitoring body in 1989, acknowledged states parties' obligation to protect women against violence of any kind occurring within the family or in any other area of social life. General Recommendation no. 19, promulgated in January 1992, developed the issue further, asserting that the definition of discrimination against women also includes any practice of gender-based violence, that is, violence directed against a woman because she is a woman or that affects women disproportionately.[12] It pointed out that cultural norms that regard women as inferior to men perpetuate a structure of subordination and generate patterns of gender-based violence, which ultimately impairs or nullifies women's enjoyment of human rights and fundamental freedoms.[13]

Provisions included in General Recommendation no. 19 became the first basis for the preparation of another international initiative in the area, the Declaration on the Elimination of Violence against Women (hereafter the Declaration), adopted by the United Nations General Assembly in 1993. The Declaration defined violence against women to include any act of gender-based violence that results in, or is likely to result in, physical, sexual, or psychological harm or suffering to women, whether in public or in private life.[14] The terms of the Declaration specifically include in the category of violence against women, any physical, sexual, and psychological violence occurring in the family, including battering, the sexual abuse of female children in the household, dowry-related violence, marital rape, female genital mutilation, and other traditional practices harmful to women.[15]

One of the most significant endeavors of the international community to eradicate practices of violence affecting women worldwide, the Declaration also encouraged data collection and compilation of statistics concerning intimate abuse and the prevalence of different forms of violence against women. Its most significant legacy has been in the form of studies on the causes, nature, gravity, and consequences of practices of abuse against women as well as the evaluation of the effectiveness of measures and strategies implemented to prevent and redress violence against women.[16]

LIMITS OF AN INTERNATIONAL HUMAN RIGHTS APPROACH TO DOMESTIC VIOLENCE

The categorization of domestic violence as a human rights issue has important and critical consequences. Acknowledging violence against women as a violation of human rights conveys binding obligations on states parties to prevent, eliminate, and prosecute practices of abuse against women as well as holding states accountable if they fail to comply with such commitments. Thus, claims on states parties to take all appropriate measures to combat inequality and protect and promote human rights for women shift from the sphere of discretion, becoming, on the one hand, legal entitlements for citizens and, on the other, obligations for states.[17]

The concept of state responsibility has traditionally been understood under international law on human rights violations as arising only when acts of violence against women can be imputed to the state or any of its agents. Because intimate abuse involves private individuals, domestic violence crimes have long been deemed outside the scope of state accountability. Since the 1990s, however, the concept of state responsibility has been expanded to include not only state actions but also omissions and the failure to take appropriate measures to protect and promote women's rights. Accordingly, in addition to refraining from committing violence against women through their own agents, states must also fulfill the obligation to prevent human rights violations by private individuals by investigating relevant allegations, prosecuting the perpetrators, and providing adequate remedies for victims. States can therefore be held accountable for domestic violence because "although the state does not actually commit the primary abuse, its failure to prosecute the abuse amounts to complicity in it."[18]

In theory, then, states have a duty to protect women from violence and can be held accountable if they fail to comply with those undertakings. The standard of due diligence required has been articulated in General Recommendation no. 19, setting forth the fact that states parties "may also be responsible for private acts if they fail to act with due diligence to prevent violations of rights or to investigate and punish acts of violence, and for providing compensation."[19]

States' liability, therefore, should be construed on a case-by-case basis, through the criterion of reasonableness, based on the general principles of nondiscrimination and good faith.[20] Yet, the standard of due diligence requires states parties to use any appropriate measures at their disposal to address both individual acts of violence against women and structural causes so as to prevent future violations and punish wrongdoers.

Further procedures to enhance state accountability for violence against women are contained in the Optional Protocol to the Convention on the Elimination of All Forms of Discrimination against Women (hereafter the Optional Protocol). In force since 22 December 2000, the Optional Protocol includes a complaints procedure enabling individuals to petition for or to complain about violations of rights and an inquiry procedure allowing the CEDAW committee to conduct inquiries into serious and systematic abuses of women's human rights occurring within the states parties to the Optional Protocol.[21] Under the complaints procedure the CEDAW committee is able to focus on individual cases and develop jurisprudence for any particular matter; through the inquiry procedure the CEDAW committee can investigate substantial abuses in which individual communications and complaints have failed, address a broad range of critical issues in a particular country, and release specific recommendations on the structural causes of violence. The lack of a judicial enforcement mechanism to enact the provisions of the Convention implies that the primary tool of compliance relies on the judiciary of states parties responsible for recasting domestic law to conform to the treaty.

Despite the effort to overcome states' timidity to intervene in the private realm and take positive actions against intimate abuse, the figures mentioned in the first section of this chapter regarding the perpetration of domestic violence suggest the shortcomings of the system and the inadequacy of the responses. To date 185 countries, including 52 African states, have either ratified or acceded to the Convention, meaning that over 90 percent of the members of the United Nations agreed to be parties to the treaty.[22] However, only 88 countries, including 24 African states, assented to be parties to the Optional Protocol and to be bound by its improved and additional enforcement mechanisms for women's human rights.[23] Yet, despite the fact that the Convention is one of the most broadly ratified international human rights instruments, it also has the highest number of reservations[24] by its states parties.

States may, indeed, ratify the treaty with reservations about specific items by declaring themselves not to be bound by certain provisions. However, in article 28, paragraph 2, the Convention borrows the provision from the Vienna Convention on the Law of Treaties, clarifying the fact that a state party may make a reservation unless it is incompatible with the object and purpose of the treaty itself.[25] A recent study reveals that the Convention counts 123 reservations, declarations, and interpretative statements, which are, in substance, reservations as well.[26] Three-quarters of these (76 percent) refer to essential parts of the text itself rather than to its application procedures.[27] To date, 57 countries, which represent approximately 31 percent of states parties, have entered the treaty with reservations.[28]

Some of those reservations clearly undermine core portions of the Convention, subverting its ultimate goals. In Africa, states that have declared such reservations include Algeria, Morocco, Egypt, and Lesotho. Algeria, for instance, agreed to apply the provisions of article 2, which condemns discrimination against women and calls for an appropriate eradication policy, on condition that they do not conflict with the provisions of the Algerian Family Code. Algeria also declared that "the provisions of Article 16 concerning equal rights for men and women in all matters relating to marriage, both during marriage and at its dissolution, should not contradict the provisions of the Algerian Family Code."[29] The government of Morocco entered a more precise reservation to article 2, explaining that "certain of the provisions contained in the Moroccan Code of Personal Status according women rights that differ from the rights conferred on men may not be infringed upon or abrogated because they derive primarily from the Islamic Shariah, which strives, among its other objectives, to strike a balance between spouses in order to preserve the coherence of family life."[30] Furthermore, Morocco argued that the equality of the kind expressed in article 16 is considered "incompatible with the Islamic Shariah, which guarantees to each of the spouses rights and responsibilities within a framework of equilibrium and complementarity in order to preserve the sacred bond of matrimony."[31] Similarly, Egypt entered a reservation to article 16, declaring that equal rights and responsibilities on entry into and at dissolution of marriage among men and women is "out of respect for the sacrosanct nature of the firm religious beliefs which govern marital relations in Egypt and which may not be called in question and in view of the fact that one of the most important bases of these relations is an equivalency of rights and duties so as to ensure complementarity, which guarantees true equality between the spouses."[32] As an example of an African country that is not predominantly Muslim, the government of Lesotho declared itself not to be bound by article 2 "to the extent that it conflicts with Lesotho's constitutional stipulations relative to succession to the throne of the Kingdom of Lesotho and law relating to succession to chieftainship."[33]

Anne Bayefsky reports that article 2 elicited five general reservations, eight normative general declarations and interpretative statements, and twelve more specific reservations, whereas article 16 has reached a total of twenty-five reservations.[34] Several states parties objected to these reservations based on the fact that they are incompatible with the object and purpose of the

Convention and, therefore, are prohibited by virtue of its article 28, paragraph 2.[35] However, tolerance has been recommended by the CEDAW committee on the ground of securing extensive participation in the treaty; the CEDAW committee is also reluctant to invalidate a state party's ratification because of its reservations.[36] Compliance with the obligation to submit national reports at least every four years on the status of the measures undertaken for the application of the treaty is also lacking. Countries that have delayed submission of states parties' periodic reports exceed twenty-nine, including twelve African states that have never delivered a report since the ratification, utterly disregarding their commitments.[37]

States parties' incentives for entering international human rights treaties arise from their wish for recognition within the international community and the desire to benefit from the trade relations and foreign aid or investments that such recognition may imply. Experts have emphasized that ratification often facilitates bilateral aid among countries as well as aid from the European Union and UN agencies.[38] But Bayefsky emphasizes another reason: states might enter into a treaty for the sole purpose of the ratification itself, believing that the relatively harmless monitoring system and timid enforcement mechanisms will not affect national positions.[39] Oona Hathaway, in her study on human rights treaty compliance, explains that due to the weak monitoring and enforcement procedures of human rights instruments, states can benefit from the positive appreciation they acquire in the international arena from ratification and, hence, the simultaneous decreased pressure for improvements, without bearing significant costs or collateral consequences.[40]

In addition to these structural limitations, a number of practical problems exist. The crucial argument for state responsibility for widespread intimate abuse and patterns of impunity collides with the lack of accurate reporting. Inadequate documentation and unreliable statistics are common problems with regard to human rights abuses against women and even more so when such abuses are perpetrated in private settings. The lack of reliable and regular data impedes a longitudinal understanding of domestic violence, a meaningful comparison of existing information, and a sensitive evaluation of the impact and effectiveness of extant measures addressing intimate abuse.[41] Moreover, without detailed data and information on the incidence of domestic violence and the failure of criminal justice responses it becomes difficult to file a case against states to hold them accountable or to promote political intervention and effective policies in the respective countries.

Another limitation of the international human rights approach is its focus on acts of violence and crimes rather than on their structural causes. Practices of discrimination and violence against women are rooted in systemic imbalances in gender relationships. Disparities in intimate liaisons are simply a dismal reflection of broader social and economic inequalities. The prosecution of perpetrators is only a first step in addressing domestic violence and surely not a permanent solution unless such prosecution is combined with positive state measures concerning, inter alia, education, economic development, health policy, and other basic services. The international human rights system already faces a critical task in confronting states' gender bias in the application of the law. It would be even more challenging to direct states to intervene in the discriminatory features of a society in order to pursue social programs for change.[42]

FINDING A NEW WAY: A REGIONAL HUMAN RIGHTS APPROACH TO DOMESTIC VIOLENCE

In an attempt to promote international peace and security, chapter 8 of the Charter of the United Nations provides for regional arrangements or agencies devoted to the maintenance of mutual order among states, the development of peaceful settlements, and enforcement action under the authorization of the Security Council.[43] Nevertheless, the treaty does not mention any human rights cooperation at the regional level, revealing the UN's concern that regionalism could have been the "expression of a breakaway movement, calling the universality of human rights into question."[44] It was only in 1977 that the General Assembly endorsed a new approach toward regional human rights instruments, urging states parties to enter into agreements with one another, "with a view to the establishment within their respective regions of suitable regional machinery for the promotion and protection of human rights."[45]

Despite the UN's ambivalence with respect to regionalism and its suitability for addressing human rights violations and promoting adequate responses, regional arrangements and agencies have sprung up since after the adoption of the Charter of the United Nations in Europe, Latin America, and Africa. The first comprehensive treaty in this field was the European Convention for the Protection of Human Rights and Fundamental Freedoms (hereafter the European Convention), adopted by the Council of Europe in 1950 and entered into force in 1953. Arising in response to the atrocities committed in Europe during the Second World War, the European Convention established the first enforcement mechanism for the obligations of its member states articulated in a complaints procedure and an international court for the adjudication of human rights cases. A further significant evolution of the two institutions entrusted with such duties, the European Commission of Human Rights and the European Court of Human Rights (hereafter the European Court), established in 1954 and 1959, respectively, included the adoption of a procedure for hearing individual complaints against member states in 1998.[46] The most judicially developed of all the regional human rights instruments, the European Court currently exercises extensive jurisdiction over the forty-seven member states of the Council of Europe.

Unlike the European system, the impetus for the establishment of the inter-American human rights system in Latin America came from the states of emergency and ruthlessness of military and authoritarian regimes, the failure and corruption of the domestic judiciary, and the widespread practices of torture, disappearance, and executions of political opponents. Established in 1948 at the Inter-American Conference in Bogotá, Colombia, with a view "to strengthen the peace and security of the continent [and] promote and consolidate representative democracy,"[47] immediately after its constitution, the Organization of American States adopted the American Declaration of the Rights and Duties of Man.

The hostility and reluctance of governments toward the development of a specific human rights treaty and effective monitoring machinery in the region delayed the creation of the Inter-American Commission on Human Rights (hereafter the Inter-American Commission) until 1959 and the adoption and entrance into force of the American Convention on Human Rights (hereafter the American Convention) until 1969 and 1978, respectively. Ratified by twenty-five nation-states to date, the American Convention, inter alia, establishes the Inter-American Court of Human Rights (hereafter the Inter-American Court) in its chapter 8. Unlike in the European Convention, only states parties and the Inter-American Commission have the right to submit a case to the Inter-American Court, excluding any individual recourse.[48]

On the subject of discrimination against women, the European Convention includes a nondiscriminatory provision on the basis of sex for the enjoyment of the rights and freedoms set forth in the treaty. But the American Convention only urges states parties to ensure the equality of rights and the adequate balancing of responsibilities of the spouses during marriage and in the event of its dissolution.[49] Further recommendations issued by the Council of Europe emphasize the extent, seriousness, and negative consequences of domestic violence, encouraging states parties to take social and emergency measures for the protection of victims and the prevention of similar incidents.[50]

In contrast to the nontreaty status of the Council of Europe's recommendations, the 1994 Inter-American Convention on the Prevention, Punishment and Eradication of Violence against Women sets forth binding obligations for (currently) thirty-two states parties and declares that violence against women shall be understood as any physical, sexual, and psychological act of violence that occurs, inter alia, within the family or domestic unit, including rape, battery, and sexual abuse. It acknowledges that violence against women is an offense against human dignity and a manifestation of the historically unequal power relationships between women and men.[51]

An increasing body of jurisprudence concerning violence against women has recently been produced by the European and inter-American human rights systems, representing an important set of precedents for the applicability of international human rights law to state and individual responsibility for practices of abuse against women. References to some of these decisions dealing specifically with domestic violence will serve as a source of comparison and insight for the purpose of the subsequent analysis of the African human rights system.

THE REGIONAL HUMAN RIGHTS SYSTEM FOR WOMEN IN AFRICA

The most recent, controversial, and least developed among the regional human rights regimes is the African system, established in 1981 with the adoption of the African Charter on Human Rights and Peoples' Rights (hereafter the African Charter) by the Assembly of the Heads of States and Government of the Organization of African Unity (hereafter the OAU). Inspired by the anticolonial endeavors of the late 1950s, the OAU moved from its initial focus on eradicating colonialism in the region to the subsequent goal of promoting "the unity and solidarity of African states, as well as defense of their territorial integrity and independence."[52] Despite the intention of facilitating internal relations and forging a regional approach toward external powers, the OAU was hampered by the legacy of colonialism in Africa. Anticolonial struggles themselves had created a commitment to the inviolability of territorial borders and noninterference in the internal affairs of member states that ultimately hindered the development of a human rights system.

Although the constitution of the OAU goes back to 1963, a regional human rights treaty was not established until the adoption of the African Charter in 1981, which entered into force only in 1986. Reaffirming the pledge to eradicate all forms of colonialism from the continent, the African Charter urges member states to coordinate and intensify their collaboration and efforts to achieve a better life for the peoples of Africa as well as to promote international cooperation with respect to the Charter of the United Nations and the Universal Declaration of Human Rights.[53] It establishes an African Commission on Human and Peoples' Rights (hereafter the African Commission) as a measure of safeguard for the terms of the treaty as well as the promotion and protection of the human and peoples' rights in the region.[54] Similar to the European and inter-American regimes for human rights, the African Charter encompasses monitoring and enforcement mechanisms for member states' obligations, including a complaints procedure by a state party concerning another state party as well as a procedure for complaints by individuals and national or international institutions that have exhausted local remedies.[55]

A breakthrough for the African human rights system was the 1998 adoption of the Protocol to the African Charter on Human and Peoples' Rights on the Establishment of an African Court on Human and Peoples' Rights (hereafter the African Court). The African Court entered into force only in 2004, and its judges were finally elected in 2006. It is intended to be an organ of the African Union (which came into being in 2001 out of a merger of the OAU and the African Economic Community) and to complement and reinforce the protective mandate of the African Commission.[56] Among other things, it provides that states parties, the African Commission, and African intergovernmental organizations are entitled to submit complaints against a member state. However, unlike in the case of the European Court, individuals and nongovernmental organizations are unable to invoke its jurisdiction unless provided otherwise at its sole discretion and by the apposite declaration duly signed by the respective state.[57] This double obstacle not only precludes the direct access of individuals to the court but also impedes the functional growth of its jurisprudence. The consequences of such barriers will be particularly important for cases involving domestic violence, because of states' reluctance to intervene in those matters primarily because of their concern about being held accountable.

The general provision contained in the African Charter for the elimination of discrimination against women and the protection of women's rights should be read together with the duty of states to protect the physical health and morals of the family as well as the duty of individuals to preserve the harmonious development of the family and work for the cohesion and respect of the family relationship.[58] Commentators contended, however, that the solely nondiscriminatory provision on women's rights under the African Charter was inadequate, particularly in the face of discourses that equate traditional culture with male dominance.[59] The evident lack of consideration of human rights violations specific to women under the African Charter was finally addressed in the extended process of drafting conducted by the African Commission in view of the auspicious Protocol on the Rights of Women in Africa (hereafter the African Protocol), adopted in 2003 by the African Union.

The African Protocol goes further than the Convention in its content, embracing basic rights for women, such as education, health, employment, food security, and housing, together with explicit prohibitions of harmful practices and inequity in marriage.[60] Emphasis is placed on the elimination of gender-based violence, first, by defining violence against women as any act that causes or may cause them physical, sexual, psychological, or economic harm, including the threat to endure such aggression or to undertake the imposition of arbitrary restrictions on or deprivation of fundamental freedoms in private or public life; second, by requiring states parties to enact and enforce laws to prohibit all forms of violence against women, including unwanted or forcible sex, whether the violence takes place in private or public settings; and, finally, by soliciting states parties to ensure the protection of every woman's right to be respected in her dignity and protected against all forms of violence either sexual or verbal.

The African Protocol requires that states parties ensure the adoption of its provisions in their respective domestic legal systems and that they periodically report "the legislative and other measures undertaken for the full realization of the rights [t]herein recognized."[61] States parties are also required to provide for appropriate judicial, administrative, or legislative remedies to any woman whose rights or freedoms have been violated.[62] As is the case for other human rights treaties, however, the African Protocol does not provide enforcement mechanisms. In this scenario, the delay in the establishment and full operation of the African Court has contributed to creating a vacuum in the actual effectiveness of the treaty and the evolution of an African human rights system for women. Commentators might question the usefulness of a human rights instrument in the first place. It is relevant to counter that even the smallest impact that human rights mechanisms may have is still worth the effort when it comes to gender rights. Furthermore, the key role of human rights treaties in devising international benchmarks for domestic legal systems and raising awareness of women's rights and needs cannot be ignored.

THE CHALLENGES OF A REGIONAL HUMAN RIGHTS APPROACH TO DOMESTIC VIOLENCE IN AFRICA

Resistance to regionalism in the human rights regime has gradually been overcome by the appreciation of the world's heterogeneity as well as the conclusion that "only within limited segments of the globe can we find the cultural foundations of common loyalties, the objective similarity of national problems, and the potential awareness of common interests which are necessary for the effective functioning of multilateral institutions."[63] The diversity and complexity of the world, embracing cultural, economic, physical, and religious disparities, are hardly capable of being channeled into the higher level of common involvement and joint commitment that an international human rights scrutiny implies. Applications of the principle of universality typically face the defensive hostility of those countries still haunted by colonial memories and yet struggling to find a balance between customary laws and traditions, on the one hand, and international standards and Western models, on the other.

In contrast, a regional interpretation of international solutions to local problems might be a more advantageous and practical pursuit. After all, responsibility and compliance are easily achieved in the first place and more likely to endure in the long term when they emerge from a spontaneous awareness of cohesion and mutuality, rather than unpopular impositions or antagonistic sanctions. It is worth mentioning, however, that the suitability of a regional approach to human rights primarily depends on the nature of the issue to be addressed. Because of their global scale, some problems may actually need to be treated solely by global agencies, whereas others could be more successfully resolved through the cooperation with an intermediate body more receptive to local identities and needs.

Regional human rights instruments can serve the purposes of attaining a better understanding of social patterns and popular perceptions of human rights issues; appreciating the extent of the violations and their potential causes; portraying a reliable scenario of on-the-ground conditions; envisaging effective and practical responses; and translating international treaty provisions into people's lives locally.[64] This is equally true for women's human rights in the private domain, intimately intertwined with traditional practices, patriarchal values, and social dynamics and, hence, requiring local interpretations of universal texts.

Like other regional human rights regimes, the relatively new African system confronts the challenge of crafting the general principles contained in the paramount international human rights mechanisms to specific situations. It faces the critical task of filling the gap between transnational human rights standards, on the one hand, and local culture and traditional claims on the other. Tailoring provisions of the Convention and its Optional Protocol to practical formulations applicable in local contexts serves to support women's rights activists in their struggle against abuse.[65] When such activists question traditional practices and impugn patterns of domestic violence, they should rely not only on the transnational prohibitions but also on the intermediate regional instruments pressuring governments to comply with international obligations as well as promoting local arrangements for human rights and social justice.

The deep gulf between international law aspirations and human rights violations mirrors the ongoing tension between universal principles and grassroots initiatives and ultimately impels regional human rights regimes to lead a constructive dialogue on strategies for the protection of women. Giving local groups a voice and space in global settings through the mediation of regional institutions facilitates nation-states' assimilation of international standards and specifically raises consciousness in local cultures of international human rights benchmarks. Particularly in Africa, where the anticolonialist heritage still rebuffs transnational interference in internal matters and hampers improvement in women's conditions in favor of tradition and cultural relativism, a regional human rights approach to domestic violence can be a valuable tool in conciliating external pressure and local resentment in order to provide adequate protective strategies.

Following the example of international human rights monitoring bodies, regional mechanisms contribute to enhancing state accountability with respect to violence against women and to producing relevant jurisprudence in the field to serve as precedents for future cases. For instance, in the *AT v. Hungary* decision, the CEDAW committee remarked that the lack of specific legislation addressing domestic violence itself constitutes a violation of human rights and fundamental freedoms for women.[66] In the *AT v. Hungary* case, the victim lamented that she had been subjected to regular severe domestic violence and death threats by her husband for four years. She stated that she was not able to visit a shelter because no shelter in Hungary was equipped to provide assistance to a mother and her two children, one of whom was brain-damaged. She also denounced the fact that no protection or restraining orders were available at the time under Hungarian law. In response to her complaint, the CEDAW committee expressed its concern for the lack of specific legislation and measures to combat domestic violence in the country, including protection or exclusion orders and shelters for victims. The CEDAW committee declared that the state party's failure to comply with its obligations constituted a violation of the victim's human rights and, particularly, her right to security of person. In its capacity as monitoring body of the Convention, the CEDAW committee recommended that the state party provide the victim and her family with immediate and effective assistance, including a safe home, psychological and legal support, and "reparation proportionate to the physical and mental harm undergone and to the gravity of the violation of her rights."[67]

Other decisions with respect to domestic violence issued by the CEDAW committee include the *Şahide Goekce v. Austria* and *Fatma Yildirim v. Austria* cases. In both decisions, the CEDAW committee reaffirmed that under international law states parties may also be held accountable "for private acts if they fail to act with due diligence to prevent violations of rights or to investigate and punish acts of violence."[68] In both cases, the CEDAW committee noted that the state party was in breach of its due diligence obligation to protect the victims and promptly investigate and prosecute the batterers. In the case of *Maria da Penha Maia Fernandes v. Brazil*, the Inter-American Commission declared that the state party's failure to prosecute and punish a perpetrator of domestic violence after more than fifteen years of investigation "form[ed] a pattern of discrimination evidenced by the condoning of domestic violence against women in Brazil through ineffective judicial action."[69] It also stated that the state party's violation contravened the member state's international commitments and eventually revealed its tolerance and complicity in the violence inflicted.

It is still too early to assess the work of the newly completed African Court, but we can hope that it will pursue a similar course in addressing violations of women's human rights occurring in the private domain. Mindful of the African nations' struggle for independence and their distinctive customs, the African Court will be better placed than any international monitoring body to demarcate the threshold between gender, religion, cultural diversity claims, and harmful practices.[70] Disaggregating culture from a specific practice and distinguishing it from a gross violation of the human right to bodily integrity will be a critical challenge for the institution but also one of its key functions. Equally difficult will be producing substantive jurisprudence on domestic violence, given the dual barriers which preclude individuals and nongovernmental organizations from submitting direct complaints to the African Court unless provided otherwise at its sole discretion and by the apposite declaration duly signed by the respective state.[71] Under the current framework, governments that resist engaging in positive measures to prevent intimate abuse will find it relatively simple to avoid having to defend their actions before the African Court.

Another practical limitation of the international human rights approach to the matter, the lack of reliable data on the incidence and pervasiveness of domestic violence cases, can be better monitored and addressed by the regional alter ego of the UN Rapporteur on the Rights of Women in Africa. Appointed by the African Commission in 1999, the mandate for the Special Rapporteur on the Rights of Women in Africa includes serving as a focal point for the promotion and protection of the rights of women in the region; assisting African governments in the development and implementation of their relevant policies as well as with the domestication of the African Protocol; undertaking fact-finding missions and comparative studies for the investigation and reporting on the situation of women's rights in the various African countries; and finally designing guidelines for nation-states to ensure adequate responses to violence against women in cooperation with the other actors responsible within both the international and regional human rights arenas.[72] Under the terms of the mandate, the Special Rapporteur on the Rights of Women in Africa can entreat national institutions to collect accurate statistics on domestic violence crimes for the purpose of raising awareness of the issue and promoting political responses. She or he can pursue informative and constructive dialogues with nongovernmental organizations dealing on-the-ground with violence against women in the various African countries; and, furthermore, she or he can become an institutional interlocutor for local initiatives advocating strategies for the eradication of domestic violence and alternative responses of social justice.

A regional strategy for addressing domestic violence should promote the active involvement of the civil society in pressuring local governments to fulfill their reporting obligations with the African commission on legislative and practical measures that have been undertaken to combat intimate abuse. For instance, the mandate of the Special Rapporteur on the Rights of Women in Africa should be expanded to include monitoring and reporting on the status of the implementation of the African Protocol. Advocacy with national institutions should be pursued to raise awareness of the incidence and pervasiveness of violations as well as of the content and resources of the African Protocol and the human rights system for women in the region. An effective adaptation of the treaty's provisions for local contexts and social justice requires the improvement of communication among diverse institutional actors to overcome political reluctance and to encourage new policy recommendations, legal reforms, and financial resources, as well as judiciary, implementation, and reporting mechanisms for the African Protocol.[73] Legislative intervention must remove dichotomies and antagonistic tensions between international instruments and domestic constitutions. Coordinating civil society organizations' efforts to combat domestic violence is also essential to strengthening their voice and action in the national and international arena. Partnership and cooperation between media and local institutions and regional human rights bodies can facilitate accurate disclosure of data and information regarding intimate abuse in order to sensitize public opinion, governments, and the international community to domestic violence. Furthermore, women's advocates and activists should advance their agenda to promote gender capacity-building in national and regional institutions, including the African Court.

In Africa, the intermediate function of regional human rights institutions represents an important tool for translating universal rights into the daily struggles of African women who face domestic violence. However, the most critical limitation on an effective application of international human rights law to domestic violence remains the broader spectrum of social and economic inequalities affecting women in both the public and the private domain, which often translate into practices of gender-based violence. Effective responses and long-term solutions for such structural and institutional gaps require the engaged efforts and commitment of both transnational and national agents. Regional human rights instruments focusing on women's rights certainly represent key players, pursuing the preeminent task of mediating between cultural diversity claims and international human rights standards as well as directing international cooperation and national policies toward the implementation of adequate measures to combat gender inequality and domestic abuse.

～

The pervasiveness of domestic violence worldwide calls for a multilayered approach and strategies for change. Historically and socially understood as products of unequal gender relationships, patterns of abuse perpetrated in the domestic space came recently to be recognized as human rights violations.

Women's activists advanced their agenda to raise awareness on the issue in the international arena. Their efforts gained momentum and led to the adoption of the Convention on the Elimination of All Forms of Discrimination against Women in 1979 and of other international human rights instruments equally devoted to women's rights and their need of protection. The international human rights approach to domestic violence employs overarching benchmarks that serve the dual purpose of pressuring governments to take appropriate measures to address and prosecute domestic violence crimes and supporting local activists in their struggle against states' inertia.

Despite the value of an international human rights response to intimate abuse, the chapter revealed also its structural and methodological limitations. Lack of accurate data and enforcement mechanisms as well as state parties' overuse of treaty reservations eventually undermine the effectiveness of the international human rights machinery to combat domestic violence. In other words, particularly by entering the treaty with reservations incompatible with its object and purpose, "too many nations give lip service to the international human rights system while actual progress at the nation-state level on substantive legal and administrative reforms stagnates."[74] Given the flaws of the international human rights approach to domestic violence, the chapter suggests an alternative: regional human rights institutions may have the power to interpret the incentives and rationale for governments' noncompliance and recast treaty provisions into domestic legal systems. Particularly in Africa, where international standards are still perceived as an ongoing reminder of colonialist imperialism, a regional human rights approach to domestic violence can contribute to loosening the tension between international law aspirations and local claims and, ultimately, crafting adequate responses to domestic violence.

NOTES

1. "Domestic Violence against Women and Girls," *UNICEF—Innocenti Digest* 6 (June 2000): 1–31.

2. See WHO, *Multi-country Study on Women's Health and Domestic Violence against Women* (Geneva: World Health Organization, 2005).

3. Rosa Ehrenreich Brooks, "Feminist Justice, at Home and Abroad: Feminism and International Law: An Opportunity for Transformation," *Yale Journal of Law and Feminism* 14, no. 2 (2002): 349.

4. Martha R. Mahoney, "Legal Images of Battered Women: Redefining the Issue of Separation," *Michigan Law Review* 90, no. 1 (1991): 38; Elizabeth M. Schneider, "The Violence of Privacy," *Connecticut Law Review* 23, no. 4 (1991): 983–85; See also Martha Minow, "Words and the Door to the Land of Change: Law, Language, and Family Violence," *Vanderbilt Law Review* 43, no. 6 (1990): 1665–99.

5. Jane Francis Connors, *Violence against Women in the Family* (New York: United Nations, 1989), 14.

6. See generally WHO, *Multi-country Study on Women's Health and Domestic Violence against Women.*

7. Convention on Elimination of All Forms of Discrimination against Women, 18 December 1979, opened for signature 1 March 1980, 19 I.L.M. 33 (1980), art 1 [hereafter CEDAW].

8. "States parties" are the states that have ratified the treaty, and, therefore, they are bound by the relevant provisions.

9. CEDAW, arts. 2 and 5.

10. CEDAW, arts. 17–21.

11. Andrew Byrnes, "The Committee on the Elimination of Discrimination against Women," *Yale Journal of International Law* 14, no. 1 (1989): 2–67.

12. See General Recommendation no. 19, Committee on the Elimination of Discrimination against Women, UN Doc A/47/38 (1992).

13. Specifically, paragraph 23 of General Recommendation no. 19 provides that "[f]amily violence is one of the most insidious forms of violence against women. It is prevalent in all societies. Within family relationships women of all ages are subjected to violence of all kinds, including battering, rape, other forms of sexual assault, mental and other forms of violence, which are perpetuated by traditional attitudes. Lack of economic independence forces many women to stay in violent relationships . . . These forms of violence put women's health at risk and impair their ability to participate in family life and public life on a basis of equality."

14. See Declaration on the Elimination of Violence against Women, adopted 20 December 1993, G.A. Res. 48/104, UN GAOR, 48th Sess., 85th plen. mtg., UN Doc. A/RES/48/104 (1993), art. 1.

15. Ibid., art. 2(a).

16. Ibid., art. 4.

17. United Nations, *Advancement of Women, In-Depth Study on All Forms of Violence against Women,* Report of the Secretary-General, 18 (6 July 2006).

18. Dorothy Q. Thomas and Michele E. Beasley, "Domestic Violence as a Human Rights Issue," *Human Rights Quarterly* 15, no. 1 (1993): 41.

19. See General Recommendation no. 19.

20. UN, *Advancement of Women, In-Depth Study on All Forms of Violence against Women,* 74.

21. See the Optional Protocol to the Convention on the Elimination of All Forms of Discrimination against Women, 22 December 2000.

22. See Ratifications and Accessions to CEDAW.

23. See Ratifications and Accessions to the Optional Protocol to CEDAW.

24. According to art. 2 (d) of the Vienna Convention on the Law of Treaties adopted in 1969 the term *reservation* "means a unilateral statement, however phrased or named, made by a State, when signing, ratifying, accepting, approving or acceding to a treaty, whereby it purports to exclude or to modify the legal effect of certain provisions of the treaty in their application to that State."

25. See art. 28 (2) of the CEDAW and art. 19 of the Vienna Convention on the Law of Treaties.

26. Sally Engle Merry, *Human Rights and Gender Violence: Translating International Law into Local Justice* (Chicago: University of Chicago Press, 2006), 81.

27. Anne F. Bayefsky, *The UN Human Rights Treaty System: Universality at the Crossroads* (Ardsley, NY: Transnational, 2001).

28. See declarations, reservations, objections, and notifications of withdrawal of reservations relating to the Convention on the Elimination of All Forms of Discrimination against Women, CEDAW/SP/2006/2.

29. See Algeria's reservations to arts. 2 and 16 of CEDAW.

30. See Morocco's reservations to art. 2 of CEDAW.

31. See Morocco's reservations to art. 16 of CEDAW.

32. See Egypt's reservations to art. 16 of CEDAW.

33. See Lesotho's reservation to art. 2 of CEDAW.

34. Bayefsky, *The UN Human Rights Treaty System*, 69.

35. See art. 28 (2) of the CEDAW, which states that reservations that are incompatible with the object and purpose of the treaty shall not be permitted.

36. Henry J. Steiner and Philip Alston, *International Human Rights in Context* (Oxford: Oxford University Press, 2000), 441.

37. See Country Reports to the Convention on the Elimination of All Forms of Discrimination against Women.

38. Merry, *Human Rights and Gender Violence*, 79.

39. Bayefsky, *The UN Human Rights Treaty System*, 7.

40. Oona A. Hathaway, "Do Human Rights Treaties Make a Difference?" *Yale Law Journal* 111, no. 8 (2002): 1935–2042.

41. UN, *Advancement of Women, In-Depth Study on All Forms of Violence against Women*, 56.

42. Thomas and Beasley, "Domestic Violence as a Human Rights Issue," 59.

43. Charter of the United Nations, chap. 8, arts. 52 and 53.

44. Karel Vasak and Philip Alston, eds., *The International Dimension of Human Rights* (Westport, CT: Greenwood Press, 1982), 2:451.

45. General Assembly Resolution 32/127 (1977).

46. See Protocol no. 11 to the European Convention for the Protection of Human Rights and Fundamental Freedoms.

47. *Annual Report of the Inter-American Commission on Human Rights* (1994), 347.

48. See art. 61 of the American Convention on Human Rights (1969).

49. See art. 14 of the European Convention for the Protection of Human Rights and Fundamental Freedoms (1950); and art. 17 of the American Convention on Human Rights (1969).

50. See generally Recommendation no. R (85) 4 on Violence in the Family (1985); Recommendation no. R (85) 11 on the Position of the Victim in the Framework of Criminal Law and Procedure; Recommendation no. R (90) 2 on Social Measures concerning Violence within the Family (1990); Recommendation no. R (91) 9 on Emergency Measures in Family Matters (1991); Recommendation no. R (1450) on Violence against Women in Europe (2000); Recommendation no. R (5) of the Committee of Ministers to Member States on the Protection of Women against Violence (2002).

51. See Preamble and art. 2 of the Inter-American Convention on the Prevention, Punishment and Eradication of Violence against Women (1994).

52. See The Constitutive Act of the African Union adopted by the thirty-sixth ordinary session of the Assembly of Heads of State and Government (11 July 2000).

53. See Preamble of the African Charter on Human Rights and Peoples' Rights (1981).

54. See art. 33 of the African Charter on Human Rights and Peoples' Rights.

55. See arts. 47 and 56 of the African Charter on Human Rights and Peoples' Rights.

56. See art. 2 of the Protocol to the African Charter on Human and Peoples' Rights on the Establishment of an African Court on Human and Peoples' Rights (1998).

57. See arts. 5 (3) and 34 (6) of the Protocol to the African Charter on Human and Peoples' Rights on the Establishment of an African Court on Human and Peoples' Rights stating that "at the time of the ratification of [the African] . . . Protocol or any time thereafter, the State shall make a declaration accepting the competence of the [African] Court to receive cases under article 5 (3) of [the African] . . . Protocol. The [African] Court shall not receive any petition under article 5 (3) involving a State Party which has not made such a declaration." According to art. 5 (3) "[t]he [African] Court may entitle relevant Non Governmental organizations (NGOs) with observer status before the [African] Commission, and individuals to institute cases directly before it, in accordance with article 34 (6) of this Protocol."

58. See arts. 18 and 29 (1) of the African Charter on Human Rights and Peoples' Rights.

59. For instance, according to the terms of Nigeria's initial report to the CEDAW committee: "[T]he authority in the home is the monopoly of the man. . . . Any attack on discrimination against women must honestly attack cultural and inhibitive factors inherent in the primary unit. . . . In traditional society, a woman is treated as chattel, to be bought and sold, discarded at will, inherited and disposed of with other property upon the death of her husband and without consent. . . . True there are no provisions discriminatory of women in our statute books, but it is equally true that there are no enforceable laws that offer her succor when she is discriminated against by customs, administrative directives and discriminative religious practices. . . . There are still no enforceable laws that protect against traditions, attitudes, customs, religion and illiteracy," as reported by Vincent O. Orlu Nmehielle, *The African Human Rights System* (Leiden, the Netherlands: Martinus Nijhoff, 2001), 134.

60. See Protocol on the Rights of Women in Africa (2003).

61. Ibid., art. 26.

62. Ibid., art. 25.

63. Inis Claude, *Swords into Plowshares: The Problems and Progress of International Organization* (New York: Random House, 1982), 102.

64. See Helen Stacy, *Human Rights for the Twenty-first Century* (Stanford, CA: Stanford University Press, 2009).

65. Merry, *Human Rights and Gender Violence*, 104.

66. *AT v. Hungary*, Human Rights Committee (2005).

67. Ibid.

68. *Şahide Goekce v. Austria*, Human Rights Committee (2005), and *Fatma Yildirim v. Austria*, Human Rights Committee (2005).

69. *Maria da Penha Maia Fernandes v. Brazil*, Inter-American Commission on Human Rights, Case 12.051 (2002).

70. Stacy, *Human Rights for the Twenty-first Century*.

71. See arts. 5 and 34 of the Protocol to the African Charter on Human and Peoples' Rights on the Establishment of an African Court on Human and Peoples' Rights.

72. See Mandate of the Special Rapporteur on the Rights of Women in Africa adopted by the African Commission resolution ACHPR/res.38 (XXV) 99 on the occasion of its 25th Ordinary Session held in Bujumbura, Burundi, from 26 April to 5 May 1999.

73. Mary Wandia, "Institutionalizing Strategies for the Protocol," in *Breathing Life into the African Union Protocol on Women's Rights in Africa*, ed. Roselynn Musa, Faiza Jama Mohammed, and Firoze Manji (Oxford: African Books Collective, 2006), 34–37.

74. Stacy, "Regional Jurisprudence and Women's Human Rights," 490.

Finding Gendered Justice in the Age of Human Rights

PAMELA SCULLY

THIS VOLUME IS so important in that it creates a field for placing domestic violence and human rights within historical and political contexts of the colonial and the postcolonial. History and historical consciousness are crucially important to contemporary engagements around issues relating to domestic violence. This volume combines a number of literatures and fields that do not often come together: that of historical work on domestic violence, colonial African history, and contemporary human rights. While each of these literatures is fairly well developed in and of itself, placing domestic violence within African colonial history is innovative, as is the conversation developed, if implicitly, in this book between colonial history and contemporary human rights activism. History tends to play a relatively small role in theorizing human rights and gender.[1] One of the central challenges facing local women's rights activists working within the international human rights frame is how to navigate the tensions arising from local conditions deeply informed by colonial histories of violence and subjugation, and a transnational human rights agenda, which denies its own relationship to the colonial project. In fact, the conversation between colonial African history, women's history, and international human rights is crucial if women's rights are indeed going to be integrated into societal transformations in the twenty-first century. Such a dialogue is by and large implicit rather than explicit in the volume. This afterword explicitly makes the case for the importance of historical conceptualization to foster a better understanding of the complicity of the West in creating the very sites of violence against women that now travel under the sign of "local" culture. I argue that historical consciousness is crucial for developing ethical collaborative relationships between transnational elites and local activists around women's issues.

International human rights discourse gives up on women's rights, even as it ostensibly advances them. The focus on the integrity and rights of the state reproduces a neglect of women's rights, particularly around the issue of protection from male violence. One result of this respect for state rights over those of women is that even the United Nations resolutions and conventions drawn up to elucidate and protect women's rights, such as CEDAW, have also allowed states to opt out of those articles that would most revolutionize gender relations.

In *Human Rights and Gender Violence*, Sally Engle Merry powerfully argues that cultural claims help push women's rights off the international stage. The international human rights community surrenders women's rights, albeit reluctantly, in the face of demands made both in the human rights community and in local societies, that indigenous rural cultures be respected, legacies preserved, even if this means ignoring men's violence against women. As Merry suggests, the understanding of culture that has been operational in transnational circles is one that understands indigenous (and this is often elided with rural) cultures as static and ahistorical.[2]

Thus, when presumed representatives of a group argue that men's authority over women in all things is natural in their community, and that imposition of international norms supporting women's education, or raising the age of marriage, for example, will violate the community's cultural heritage, international actors, especially in the wake of the controversial female genital cutting campaigns of the 1980s, generally genuflect in respect and back off. Merry suggests that international actors rather ought to educate themselves about the extent to which claims to culture are claims to power. She advocates the use of a nuanced, flexible definition of culture alert to the multiple constituencies in any community.[3] Such an understanding would enable international activists to be allies of those individuals at the local level who assert different views of women's rights than what might be currently hegemonic in their society.

It is precisely at this juncture of the global and the local around the issue of culture and domestic violence against women that makes historical consciousness so necessary. While notions of culture now traveling under the sign of the local, originated in part from European ideas of nationalism and culture elaborated in the nineteenth century, it is the mobilization of such ideas through European rule in Africa that consolidated the notion of Africa as a place without history, a place, rather, of fetishized cultural practices.

As Achebe's famous novel *Things Fall Apart* shows, the idea of "tribes" with essential atavistic cultural traits arose in part through European officials' and missionaries' encounters with societies they had difficulty interpreting. The claims to authenticity and unchanging tradition that different groups mobilize to either deny women's rights or explain why they have to be denied, are part of modernity and arise from shared, although certainly unequal, colonial entanglements from the late nineteenth century.[4] Ironically, the idea of indigenous cultures as tied immutably to some ancient and unchanging tradition, which a variety of actors so often invoke to skirt the issue of women's rights, is in fact relatively new.

This history then matters as it suggests the realities of transformation. As Merry argues, no society is immune from change, and practices are always up for grabs. In addition, I would argue, and I think the chapters in this book demonstrate, that knowledge of the histories of European imperialism and colonialism in Africa is also crucial in helping international activists recognize their own entanglement in categories of modernity and tradition that so often register as separate.

As many chapters in this book show, a discussion of domestic violence demonstrates the importance of putting gender-based violence on the historical agenda, a topic all too often neglected in African history.[5] Different chapters elaborate the usefulness of the term domestic violence to discuss the abuse of women and children within the broader family or domestic sphere, but also point to the limitations of such a term. The term *domestic violence* turns our attention to the family, and assumes that the domestic space and tranquility are not automatic partners. In this sense, the term has great utility in calling forth an analysis of struggle within the household in ways that the usual conventions of African historical categories such as resistance and nation can obscure.[6]

On the other hand, the very term *domestic violence* assumes a division between private and public spheres, which does not always travel transhistorically or transculturally.[7] The chapters point to the possible larger usefulness of the category of the household and of sexual violence as terms that travel further and wider than *domestic violence*. As Thornberry suggests in her chapter, for example, in nineteenth-century Xhosaland familial relationships constituted politics in a way that makes irrelevant the notion of the public/private divide normally invoked by domestic violence studies. What does this mean for our use of the term *domestic violence?* If the family itself is not purely domestic, do we need to turn to a different term: *household violence?* Such a term has some utility in moving beyond the idea of the nuclear family, which sustains much of the literature on domestic violence. Given the American and British origins of the term *domestic violence* the notion that one is talking of violence within a nuclear family is embedded historically in the terminology, even if the nuclear family is not the necessary precondition for using the category of domestic violence. Talking of household violence might thus allow for more flexibility in historical analysis. However, given the complex resonance and limitations of that term itself in African studies, using the concept of the household is unlikely to solve the analytic problems.[8]

I would argue that gender-based violence (GBV) works better as a category of analysis than household violence or domestic violence.[9] Domestic violence is violence visited on women precisely because they are women. In that regard, a man's abuse of his daughter, wife, niece, for example, shares much with the larger patterns of gender violence experienced by women every day outside of the household. The term *gender-based violence* forces us to question the divides that theory and law make between private and public spaces. As the term *domestic violence* has helped us turn our attention to the violence that often constitutes household and family, so the term *gender-based violence* undoes the very notion that violence in the family needs special forms of analysis. Gender-based violence turns our attention both practically, as a matter of historical and contemporary investigation, and theoretically to the fact that the violence experienced by women from men is almost a constitutive part of a woman's experiencing herself as a woman. It is the gender assumptions about women's availability to men, rather than a private/public divide, that continue to underlie the pervasiveness of violence against women. The term *gender-based violence* captures this dynamic.

Gender-based violence is a concept that now has much traction in international humanitarian work and postconflict reconstruction. In the wake of the Yugoslavian rape camps, the sexualized genocide of Rwanda, and contemporary terrors of sexual violence, the international human rights community has increasingly turned its attention to combating gender-based violence, particularly in times of war. We see evidence of this in Security Council Resolution 1325 of 2000, which was the first resolution ever to talk about women, peace, and international security. It focuses particular attention on the experiences of women and girls in conflict and urges that women be involved in the peace-making and peace-keeping processes. Security Council Resolution 1820, of 2008, made sexual violence against women and girls in times of conflict a matter of international peace and security, thus committing the UN to protect women and girls against sexual assault in times of conflict. There is also an array of GBV programming being done by UNIFEM, the International Rescue Committee, and the Reproductive Health Refugee Consortium.

Much of the current work on GBV is premised on conceptions of violence and solutions emanating from Europe and the United States of America.[10] Very little attention is paid to local understandings of violence and sexuality or to the histories of colonialism, all of which, as these chapters have so eloquently demonstrated, are crucial to figuring out solutions to domestic violence. Historical work as evidenced in this book on gender-based violence in Liberia, Sierra Leone, the Democratic Republic of Congo, for example, as well as knowledge of the history of the state, of disciplinary practices, of various legal forms of rule from local councils of elders to other mechanisms, will help create nuanced understandings of how to combat violence against women. It is precisely because the authors of the various chapters in this volume take history so seriously that I think this book has much to contribute to the growing humanitarian work on gender-based violence in Africa.

The term *gender-based violence* has the potential to widen the frame of understanding and reference for how we write and understand violence in general. Gender-based violence is a more capacious term than domestic violence and one I would advocate for use in the future. However, as is seen above, organizations tend to use it narrowly as a shorthand to describe various forms of intimate partner violence by men against women. The UN Committee on the Elimination of Discrimination against Women (CEDAW), for example, defines GBV as "violence that is directed against a woman because she is a woman or that affects women disproportionately."[11] The term *gender-based violence* refers to various forms of assault or coercion that are directed at individuals *because of their gender*. As the International Center for Transitional Justice notes, various groups suffer from gender-based violence, including men, boys, and sexual minorities.[12] The term could be expanded as a way of thinking about the structural violence that men are subjected to also because of their gender; for example, the killing of men in war because they are men, or the susceptibility of young boys to being made child soldiers.[13]

Indeed many of the chapters in this book are concerned with gender alliances between men, and demonstrate how deep structures of gendered power help maintain domestic and other forms of violence. This is both one of the most important and perhaps one of the more implicit contributions of this volume. The assumption of women's subordinate status in African households was a pillar of colonial rule under both the French and the British. As chapters by Hynd, Rodet, and others indicate, colonial officials and African elder men's views of women's subordination cohered in ways that made it very difficult for women and girls to find redress in the colonial court systems. However, the work of other scholars suggests that women were also able to navigate the colonial courts in ways that could result in greater freedoms, often through making successful alliances with male lawyers.[14]

The creation of two legal orders, one operating in the frame of the West, and the other, named as customary law, ostensibly located in "traditional" rules, is perhaps the most salient historical phenomenon bearing on international human rights and women's rights today. As a number of chapters show, the separation of customary and other legal systems created and then affirmed women's inferiority, and thus vulnerability to male violence. The invention of women's new subordination under customary law was masked precisely by the discourse on custom and tradition.[15] The authors in this volume working on French West Africa demonstrate the extent to which the colonial state and

African men then invoked customary law to justify the abuse and control of women in periods of great instability. The state operated primarily within the legal system created by the West around rights and punishment, but relinquished women's rights, be it access to land or protection from male violence, to customary law, where masculine power was encoded.

A discussion of legal systems across Africa in terms of Western legal systems, shari'a, and customary law has enormous implications for women's human rights in the twenty-first century. The trend in which states and the international community absolve their support of women's rights in the face of claims by local actors to be protecting local traditions in fact reifies the very colonial laws and spheres of influence created under colonial rule. As London's chapter on Senegal suggests, the postcolonial African state offers many competing ideas of religion, state allegiance, and culture. Gender relations are at the center of all these sites of identity and power.

The very architecture of international rights discourse affirms its own centrality to debates about equality, while also inscribing the understanding that some societies are more available to transformation and access to equality than others. The UN might be seen less as a break with European imperialism than a continuation of its reach in a new register. The international human rights community arose in the wake of World War II, but many of the premises on which the concept of human rights has engaged with the Third World are deeply informed by the colonial era. This is not to deny the importance of the discourse of human rights to the international arena. It is to say that this discourse is a very complicated one in which the intent of individual agents can sometimes be subverted by the difficult genesis of the notion of an international political agenda for change. As historians of Africa well know, the laudable campaigns to end the trans-Atlantic slave trade also fed, in complicated ways, the calls for European intervention in Africa from the mid-nineteenth century. The claim of absolute and uncontestable moral authority to intervene in the lives of others continues to resonate in complicated ways.[16]

International human rights is pulled in different directions: by respect for the local, by respect for the autonomy of the state, but also by the belief in absolute moral authority generated by the discourse of human rights that is premised on the notion that intervention on behalf of the suffering and the right-less is a universal good. The idea that some societies were sufficiently advanced to exercise rights as opposed to so-called uncivilized societies who could not, was braided into the very architecture of the League of Nations, which was started after World War I to prevent international disputes from erupting into armed conflict. Territories seen as insufficiently developed to rule themselves were handed over to colonial powers or settler colonies such as South Africa in the case of German South West Africa. As we know, the

United Nations, begun after World War II, inherited the mantle of the earlier League of Nations.

It is germane that two of the leading architects of the League of Nations were men deeply invested in the colonial enterprise. Lord Frederick Lugard, ex-governor of Nigeria, had a long history of ruling in Africa, and Jan Smuts was a former Boer general and later prime minister of white-ruled South Africa. Lugard in particular helped shape the policy of mandated territories according to quasi social-Darwinian notions of rule he had practiced in colonial Nigeria. As many readers of this book know, under Lugard's policy of indirect rule, the Muslim city-states of Northern Nigeria were given authority to rule through their institutions. In contrast, Lugard established chiefs over the stateless societies of the south, which he saw as lacking the capacities of civilization, since they had did not have a centralized leadership structure or a monotheistic religion.[17]

The idea that human rights are available to everyone but that not all societies are equally advanced lingers to this day. It is precisely the demand emanating from the international community that a country needs to demonstrate its commitment to international principles of justice and law in order to get funding through the International Monetary Fund (IMF) and other international bodies that persuades countries around the world to sign such conventions as CEDAW. And yet, paradoxically, it is precisely an assumption that some countries either are in their entirety captured by tradition, or contain societies that are "traditional" and incapable of change, that drives the UN and other actors to let certain countries off the hook. It is again precisely around women's rights that this tension often arises and is deflected.

In this context, and indeed in this book, the role of culture and of the law in combating gender-based violence remains a matter of debate. Merry posits that a shared transnational, if locally rooted, understanding of rights and culture exists. Culture has to be reclaimed at the local level in a way that moves the terrain beyond rights discourse into a much more dynamic and historically constituted site of language and activism.

Indeed, a number of chapters in this book demonstrate the great elasticity of human rights frames, and they raise questions as to the role of the law. On the one hand, London's chapter on Senegal in the 1990s suggests the need to reform the legal system to help create the conditions for combating domestic violence. On the other hand, Bop's chapter on Senegal suggests that a sole focus on the law negates the important work that local actors need to undertake in order to combat gender-based violence. The Senegalese state fails to truly combat gender violence precisely because it relies so much on the legal frame. Bop argues rather for efforts to create social networks that will sustain women fighting for gender justice both in the legal arena and, importantly, in the household. Given the inability of the law to render justice or transform consciousness, one wonders at the apparent dominance of legal solutions and the reliance on the state that governs so much of the solutions offered in manuals regarding the implementation of gender-based violence programs.

We see ongoing tensions in places as diverse as South Africa and Liberia, between feminist constitutions and national laws regarding rape and the rights of women, and the abrogation of rights and the difficulty of implementing these principles at the local level. In South Africa, which has one of the most progressive constitutions in the world regarding women's rights and sexual orientation, a rape culture tied to extreme acts of violence against women inside and outside of households continues to be pervasive. In addition, the passing of laws relating to land rights and chiefly authorities has undermined women's access to land and to the rights secured in the constitution at the national level.

Women thus fall out of various categories that are absolutely essential to human rights discourse and the focus on legal mechanisms to redress historic inequalities. The state bias within international law makes it difficult to address women's rights through a frame of international human rights, and as chapters in this book show, that bias has its own colonial legacy within Africa. As Faedi points out in her compelling chapter, domestic violence remains one of the most persistent human rights violations today, across different families, nations, and continents. A continuing focus on state actors and on the state as the mechanism through which human rights should be secured ignores significant sites where women's rights are curtailed: in familial settings, in household arenas, in religious institutions.[18] Further, as we have seen, in Africa, the presence of multiple forms of legal practice and constituencies competing for power often take place around issues relating to women's access to rural land, to legal rights under customary law, to the implementation of national constitutional principles.[19]

Given the challenges facing women's rights activists, what is the way forward? Bop's argument that the state's tendency to see domestic violence as a criminal issue rather than as a pervasive "social problem" is highly germane. Domestic violence is also an index of the larger social problem of men's authority over women, and the belief that such authority is inherently justified. It is important that we find new political and indeed legal languages to theorize domestic violence as an integral part of politics, of claims to power and authority both at the national and the local level.

The chapters in this book go quite a long way in helping put these matters of colonial history and domestic violence into a frame which makes clear the complexities of human rights law and practice when it comes to women's lives. The histories of local struggles over meaning, of the variety of interpretations of violence, and women's relations to the law are central to understanding the pervasiveness of domestic violence and sexual violence in the contemporary era and the challenges facing those who wish to consign such violence to the past.

NOTES

I am grateful to Durba Mitra, the editors, and the external readers for their comments on earlier versions of this chapter.

1. For an exception, see Joan Scott, *The Politics of the Veil* (Princeton, NJ: Princeton University Press, 2004).

2. By such transnational actors, Merry includes both people at the level of the UN and local activists employing human rights discourse in their work. Sally Engle Merry, *Human Rights and Gender Violence: Translating International Law into Local Justice* (Chicago: University of Chicago Press, 2006).

3. For discussion of aspects of this question see Merry, *Human Rights and Gender Violence*. On FGC see Elizabeth Heger Boyle, *Female Genital Cutting: Cultural Conflict in the Global Community* (Baltimore: Johns Hopkins University Press, 2002).

4. The literature on tribe in African history is vast. For a very helpful discussion of the idea of tribe see Chris Lowe, "Talking about 'Tribe': Moving from Stereotypes to Analysis," Background Paper, Africa Policy Information Center, November 1997. The classic is Terence Ranger, "The Invention of Tradition in Colonial Africa," in *The Invention of Tradition*, ed. Eric Hobsbawm and Terence Ranger (Cambridge: Cambridge University Press, 1983).

5. For early discussions see Pamela Scully, *Liberating the Family? Gender and British Slave Emancipation in the Rural Western Cape, South Africa, 1823–1853* (Portsmouth, NH: Heinemann, 1997), and Pamela Scully, "Rape, Race and Colonial Culture: The Sexual Politics of Identity in the Nineteenth-Century Cape Colony, South Africa," *American Historical Review* 100, no. 2 (1995): 335–59.

6. For a discussion of the need to move beyond the household when discussing rights, see Martha Nussbaum, *Women and Human Development: The Capabilities Approach* (Cambridge: Cambridge University Press, 2000).

7. See Carole Pateman, *The Disorder of Women: Democracy, Theory and Political Theory* (Stanford, CA: Stanford University Press, 1989).

8. Jane Guyer, "Household and Community in African Studies," *African Studies Review* 24, no. 2/3, Social Science and Humanistic Research on Africa: An Assessment (1981): 87–137.

9. Margareth Etienne, "Addressing Gender-Based Violence in an International Context," *Harvard Women's Law Journal* 18 (1995): 139. See also Geraldine Terry and Joanna Hoare, eds., *Gender-Based Violence*, Working in Gender and Development Series (Oxford: Oxfam, 2007).

10. See, for example, the interesting tensions in an otherwise very thorough report: Beth Vann, *Gender-Based Violence: Emerging Issues in Programs Serving Displaced Populations* (New York: Reproductive Health for Refugees Consortium, 2002).

11. Humanitarian News and Analysis, "In-Depth: Our Bodies—Their Battle Ground: Gender-based Violence in Conflict Zones" (New York: UN Office for the Coordination of Humanitarian Affairs, 2004). http://www.irinnews.org/IndepthMain.aspx?IndepthId=20&ReportId=62814.

12. Vesuki Nesiah et al., *Truth Commissions and Gender: Principles, Policies, and Procedures*, Gender Justice Series (New York: International Center for Transitional Justice, 2006).

13. Adam Jones, *Gendercide and Genocide* (Nashville, TN: Vanderbilt University Press, 2004).

14. Judith Byfield, *The Bluest Hands: A Social and Economic History of Women Dyers in Abeokuta (Nigeria), 1890–1940* (Portsmouth, NH: Heinemann, 2002); Martin Klein and Richard Roberts, "Gender and Emancipation in French West Africa," in *Gender and Slave Emancipation in the Atlantic World*, ed. Pamela Scully and Diana Paton (Durham, NC: Duke University Press, 2005), 162–80; Jane Parpart, "Sexuality and Power on the Zambian Copperbelt, 1926–1924," in *Patriarchy and Class: African Women in the Home and the Workforce*, ed. Sharon Stichter and Jane Parpart (Boulder, CO: Westview Press, 1988).

15. Martin Chanock, *Law, Custom, and Social Order: The Colonial Experience in Malawi and Zambia* (Cambridge: Cambridge University Press, 1985).

16. Jack Donnelly, "Human Rights, A New Standard of Civilization?" *International Affairs* (Royal Institute of International Affairs 1944–) 74, no. 1 (1998): 1–23. The campaigns against female genital cutting exemplify the challenges of operating with this kind of confidence. See Boyle, *Female Genital Cutting*. The conference titled Intervening in Africa, held at Emory University in March 2007, organized by the Institute of Comparative and International Studies, highlighted the ongoing paradoxes of such intervention. Representatives from Doctors without Borders, Human Rights Watch, and other organizations made eloquent contributions to the discussion.

17. See Frederick Lugard's famous *The Dual Mandate in British Tropical Africa*, 2d ed. (Edinburgh: W. Blackwood and Sons, 1923).

18. See particularly Karen Knop, "Why Rethinking the Sovereign State Is Important for Women's Human Rights Law," in *Human Rights of Women: National and International Perspectives*, ed. Rebecca Cook (Philadelphia: University of Pennsylvania Press, 1994), 153–64.

19. Fareda Banda, *Women, Rights and Human Law in Africa: An African Perspective* (Portland, OR: Hart, 2005).

Selected Bibiliography

This is a consolidated list of recommended readings drawn from the chapters in this volume. We urge readers to consult the more extensive notes for each chapter.

Agamben, Giorgio. *Homo Sacer: Sovereign Power and Bare Life.* Translated by Daniel Heller-Roazen. Stanford, CA: Stanford University Press, 1998.

Allman, Jean, and Victoria Tashjian. *"I Will Not Eat Stone": A Women's History of Colonial Asante.* Portsmouth, NH: Heinemann, 2000.

Andall, Jacqueline, and Derek Duncan, eds. *Italian Colonialism: Legacy and Memory.* Bern/Oxford: Peter Lang, 2005.

Anderson, J. N. D. *Islamic Law in Africa.* New impression with preface. London: Frank Cass, 1970.

Appiah, Dorcas Coker, and Kathy Cusack, eds. *Breaking the Silence and Challenging the Myths of Violence against Women and Children in Ghana: Report of a National Study on Violence.* Accra, Ghana: Gender Studies and Human Rights Documentation Centre, 1999.

Arab, Adel. "Senegal: Civil Society Suggests a Review of the Bill Modifying the Family Code." *Women's Global Network for Reproductive Rights Newsletter* 75 (2002).

Bang, Anne K. *Sufis and Scholars of the Sea: Family Networks in East Africa, 1860–1925.* London: RoutledgeCurzon, 2003.

Barrera, Giulia. "Colonial Affairs: Italian Men, Eritrean Women, and the Construction of Racial Hierarchies in Colonial Eritrea." PhD diss., Northwestern University, 2002.

Bayefsky, Anne F. *The UN Human Rights Treaty System: Universality at the Crossroads.* Ardsley, NY: Transnational, 2001.

Ben-Ghiat, Ruth, and Mia Fuller, eds. *Italian Colonialism.* New York: Palgrave Macmillan, 2005.

Benton, Lauren. "Colonial Law and Cultural Difference: Jurisdictional Politics and the Formation of the Colonial State," *Comparative Studies in Society and History* 41, no. 3 (1999): 563–88

———. *Law and Colonial Cultures: Legal Regimes in World History, 1400–1900.* New York: Cambridge University Press, 2002.

Bernault, Florence, ed. *Enfermement, prison et châtiments.* Paris: Karthala, 1999.

Bledsoe, Caroline, "'No Success without Struggle': Social Mobility and Hardship for Foster Children in Sierra Leone." *Man* 25, no. 1 (1990): 70–88.

Bop, Codou. *Islam and Women's Reproductive and Sexual Health and Rights in Senegal.* Atlanta: Religion and Human Rights Project, Emory University School of Law, 2003.

———. "Islam and Women's Sexual Health and Rights in Senegal." *Muslim World Journal of Human Rights* 2, no. 1 (2005): 1–30.

Brietzke, Paul, "Murder and Manslaughter in Malawi's Traditional Courts." *Journal of African Law* 18, no. 1 (1974): 37–56.

Brooks, Rosa Ehrenreich. "Feminist Justice, at Home and Abroad: Feminism and International Law: An Opportunity for Transformation." *Yale Journal of Law and Feminism* 14, no. 2 (2002): 345–61.

Brown, Wendy. "Finding the Man in the State." *Feminist Studies* 18, no. 1 (1992): 7–34.

Burdett, Charles. *Journeys through Fascism: Italian Travel Writing between the Wars.* New York: Berghan Books, 2007.

Burrill, Emily. "Disputing Wife Abuse: Tribunal Narratives of the Corporal Punishment of Wives in Colonial Sikasso, 1930s." *Cahiers d'Études Africaines* 47, no. 3–4 (2007): 603–22.

Byfield, Judith. "Women, Marriage, Divorce and the Emerging Colonial State in Abeokuta (Nigeria) 1892–1904." In *"Wicked" Women and the Reconfiguration of Gender in Africa*, edited by Dorothy L. Hodgson and Sheryl A. McCurdy, 27–46. Portsmouth, NH: Heinemann, 2001.

Camara, Fatou. "Women and the Law: A Critique of Senegalese Family Law." *Social Identities* 13, no. 6 (2007): 787–800.

Carsten, Janet. *The Heat of the Hearth: The Process of Kinship in a Malay Fishing Community.* Oxford: Clarendon Press, 1997.

Center for Reproductive Law and Policy and Le Groupe de Recherche sur les Femmes et les Lois au Senegal. *Women of the World: Laws and Policies Affecting Their Reproductive Lives: Francophone Africa.* New York: Center for Reproductive Law and Policy, 1999.

———. *Women's Reproductive Rights in Senegal: A Shadow Report.* New York and Dakar: Center for Reproductive Rights and GREFELS, 2001.

Chadwick, Roger. *Bureaucratic Mercy: The Home Office and the Treatment of Capital Cases in Victorian Britain.* London: Garland, 1992.

Chanock, Martin. *Law, Custom, and Social Order: The Colonial Experience in Malawi and Zambia.* Cambridge: Cambridge University Press, 1985.

Ciekawy, Diane. "Witchcraft in Statecraft: Five Technologies of Power in Colonial and Postcolonial Coastal Kenya." *African Studies Review* 41, no. 3 (1998): 119–42.

Clark, Anna. *Women's Silence, Men's Violence: Sexual Assault in England, 1770–1845.* New York: Pandora, 1987.

Comaroff, John L., and Jean Comaroff. "Law and Disorder in the Postcolony: An Introduction." In *Law and Disorder in the Postcolony*, edited by Jean Comaroff and John L. Comaroff, 1–56. Chicago: University of Chicago Press, 2006.

Creevey, Lucy. "Islam, Women and the Role of the State in Senegal." *Journal of Religion in Africa* 26, no. 3 (1996): 293–301.

Crowder, Michael. "The White Chiefs of Tropical Africa." In *Colonial West Africa: Collected Essays*, 122–50. London: Frank Cass, 1978.

Del Boca, Angelo. *Gli italiani in Africa Orientale*. 4 vols. Rome-Bari: Laterza, 1976–1987.

Donnelly, Jack. "Human Rights, A New Standard of Civilization?" *International Affairs* 74, no. 1 (1998): 1–23.

Epprecht, Marc. "'Good God Almighty, What's This!' Homosexual 'Crime' in Early Colonial Zimbabwe." In *Boy-Wives and Female Husbands: Studies of African Homosexualities*, edited by Stephen O. Murray and Will Roscoe, 197–221. New York: St. Martin's Press, 1998.

Erlank, Natasha. "Sexual Misconduct and Church Power on Scottish Mission Stations in Xhosaland, South Africa, in the 1840s." *Gender and History* 15, no. 1 (2003): 69–84.

Fallers, Lloyd A. *Law without Precedent: Legal Ideas in Action in the Courts of Colonial Basoga*. Chicago: University of Chicago Press, 1969.

Ferguson, James. *Global Shadows: Africa in the Neoliberal World Order*. Durham, NC: Duke University Press, 2006.

Goodale, Mark, and Sally Engle Merry, eds. *The Practice of Human Rights: Tracking Law between the Global and the Local*. Cambridge: Cambridge University Press, 2007.

Goody, Esther. *Parenthood and Social Reproduction: Fostering and Occupational Roles in West Africa*. Cambridge: Cambridge University Press, 1982.

Goody, Jack. "The Evolution of the Family." In *Household and Family in Past Time*, edited by Peter Laslett and Richard Wall, 103–24. Cambridge: Cambridge University Press, 1972.

———. *Production and Reproduction: A Comparative Study of the Domestic Domain*. Cambridge: Cambridge University Press, 1976.

Gordon, Linda. *Heroes of Their Own Lives: The Politics and History of Family Violence, Boston 1880–1960*. New York: Viking, 1988.

Haenger, Peter. *Slaves and Slave Holders on the Gold Coast: Towards an Understanding of Social Bondage in West Africa*. Basel: P. Schlettwein, 2000.

Hansen, Karen Tranberg. Introduction to *African Encounters with Domesticity*, edited by Karen Tranberg Hansen, 1–33. New Brunswick, NJ: Rutgers University Press, 1992.

Hasty, Jennifer. *The Press and Political Culture in Ghana*. Bloomington: Indiana University Press, 2005.

Hathaway, Oona A. "Do Human Rights Treaties Make a Difference?" *Yale Law Journal* 111, no. 8 (2002): 1935–2042.

Heald, Suzette. *Controlling Anger: The Anthropology of Gisu Violence*. Oxford: James Currey, 1998.

Heberle, Renée. "Law's Violence and the Challenge of the Feminine." In *Studies in Law, Society and Politics*, edited by Austin Sarat and Patricia Ewick. Greenwich, CT: JAI Press, 2001.

Hemedi, Ali bin. *Nikahi: A Handbook of the Law of Marriage in Islam*. Translated into English by J. W. T. Allen. N.p., [1934].

Hirsch, Susan F. *Pronouncing and Persevering: Gender and the Discourses of Disputing in an African Islamic Court*. Chicago: University of Chicago Press, 1998.

Hobsbawm, Eric J., and Terence Ranger, eds. *The Invention of Tradition*. Cambridge: Cambridge University Press, 1983.

Hynd, Stacey. "Imperial Gallows: Capital Punishment, Violence and Colonial Rule in Britain's African Territories, c. 1908–68." DPhil, University of Oxford, 2007.

Jackson, Elizabeth F., et al. "Inconsistent Reporting of Female Genital Cutting Status in Northern Ghana: Explanatory Factors and Analytical Consequences." *Studies in Family Planning* 34, no. 3 (2003).

Jeater, Diana. *Marriage, Perversion, and Power: The Construction of Moral Discourse in Southern Rhodesia*. Oxford: Clarendon Press, 1994.

Kabeer, N. "Reflections on the Measurement of Women's Empowerment." In *Discussing Women's Empowerment-Theory and Practice*, edited by Sida Studies. Swedish International Development Agency, No. 3, 2001, http://www.sida.se/sida/jsp/sida.jsp?d=118&a=2080&language=en_US

Kanogo, Tabitha. *African Womanhood in Colonial Kenya, 1900–50*. Oxford: James Currey; Athens: Ohio University Press, 2005.

Keck, Margaret, and Kathryn Sikkink. *Activists beyond Borders: Advocacy Networks in International Politics*. Ithaca, NY: Cornell University Press, 1998.

Kelly, Kristen A. *Domestic Violence and the Politics of Privacy*. Ithaca, NY: Cornell University Press, 2003.

King, Peter. "Punishing Assault: The Transformation of Attitudes in the English Courts." *Journal of Interdisciplinary History* 27, no. 1 (1996): 43–74.

Klein, Martin. *Slavery and Colonial Rule in French West Africa*. New York: Cambridge University Press, 1998.

Knop, Karen. "Why Rethinking the Sovereign State Is Important for Women's Human Rights Law." In *Human Rights of Women: National and International Perspectives*, edited by Rebecca Cook. Philadelphia: University of Pennsylvania Press, 1994.

Labanca, Nicola. *Oltremare. Storia dell'espansione coloniale italiana*. Bologna: il Mulino, 2002.

Lallemand, Suzanne. *La circulation des enfants en société traditionelle: Prêt, don, échange*. Paris: Editions L'Harmattan, 1993.

Lonsdale, John. "The Moral Economy of Mau Mau: Wealth, Poverty and Civic Virtue in Kikuyu Political Thought." In *Unhappy Valley: Conflict in Kenya and Africa*, book 2: *Violence and Ethnicity*, by Bruce Berman and John Lonsdale. Athens: Ohio University Press, 1992.

Loue, Sana. *Intimate Partner Violence: Societal, Medical, Legal, and Individual Responses*. New York: Kluwer Academic/Plenum, 2001.

Luongo, Katherine. "Motive Rather Than Means: Legal Genealogies of Witch-Killing Cases." *Cahiers d'Études Africaines* 48, no. 1–2 (2008): 35–57.

Machera, Mumbi. "Domestic Violence in Kenya: A Survey of Newspaper Reports." In *Men, Women, and Violence: A Collection of Papers from CODESRIA Gender Institute 1997*, edited by F. Oyekanmi. Dakar, Senegal: CODESRIA, 2000.

Mackie, Gerry. "Female Genital Cutting: The Beginning of the End." In *Female"Circumcision" in Africa: Culture, Controversy, and Change*, edited by Bettina Shell-Duncan and Ylva Herlund. Boulder, CO: Lynne Rienner, 2000.

MacLean, John, ed. *Compendium of Kafir Life and Customs: Including Genealogical Tables of Kafir Chiefs and Various Local Census Returns.* 1858. Reprint, London: F. Cass, 1968.

Mahoney, Martha R. "Legal Images of Battered Women: Redefining the Issue of Separation." *Michigan Law Review* 90, no. 1 (1991): 1–94.

Mama, Amina. "Sheroes and Villains: Conceptualizing Colonial and Contemporary Violence against Women in Africa." In *Feminist Genealogies, Colonial Legacies, Democratic Futures,* edited by M. Jacqui Alexander and Chandra Mohanty. London: Routledge, 1998.

Mann, Kristin, and Richard Roberts, eds. *Law in Colonial Africa.* Portsmouth, NH: Heinemann, 1991.

Marks, Shula, and Richard Rathbone. "The History of the Family in Africa: Introduction." *Journal of African History* 24, no. 2 (1983): 145–61.

Martone, Luciano. *Giustizia coloniale: Modelli e prassi penale per i sudditi d'Africa dall'età giolittiana al fascismo.* Naples: Jovene, 2002.

McClendon, Thomas. *Gender and Generations Apart: Labor Tenants and Customary Law in Segregation-Era South Africa.* Portsmouth, NH: Heinemann, 2002.

Merry, Sally Engle. "Anthropology, Law, and Transnational Processes." *Annual Review of Anthropology* 21 (1992): 357–79.

———. *Human Rights and Gender Violence: Translating International Law into Local Justice.* Chicago: University of Chicago Press, 2006.

Moens, B., V. Zeitlin, C. Bop, and R. Gaye. *Study on the Practice of Trafficking in Persons in Senegal.* Washington, DC: USAID, September 2004.

Morris, Henry F., and James S. Read. *Indirect Rule and the Search for Justice: Essays in East African Legal History.* Oxford: Clarendon Press, 1972.

Nagengast, Carole. "Violence, Terror, and the Crisis of the State." *Annual Review of Anthropology* 23 (1994).

Negash, Tekeste. *Italian Colonialism in Eritrea, 1882–1941: Policies, Praxis and Impact.* Uppsala, Sweden: Uppsala University, 1987.

Nmehielle,Vincent O. Orlu. *The African Human Rights System.* Leiden, the Netherlands: Martinus Nijhoff, 2001.

Palumbo, Patrizia, ed. *A Place in the Sun: Africa in Italian Colonial Culture from Post-Unification to the Present.* Berkeley: University of California Press, 2003.

Pateman, Carole. *The Disorder of Women: Democracy, Theory and Political Theory.* Stanford, CA: Stanford University Press, 1989.

Pautrat, René. *La justice locale et la justice musulmane en A.O.F.* Rufisque: Imprimerie du Haut Commissariat de la République en Afrique occidentale française, 1957.

Phoofolo, Pule. "Female Extramarital Relationships and Their Regulation in Early Colonial Thembuland, South Africa, 1875–95." *Journal of Family History* 30, no. 1 (2005): 3–47.

Ranger, Terence. "The Invention of Tradition in Colonial Africa." In *The Invention of Tradition,* edited by Eric J. Hobsbawm and Terence Ranger, 211–62. Cambridge: Cambridge University Press, 1993.

Roberts, Richard. *Litigants and Households: African Disputes and Colonial Courts in the French Soudan, 1895–1912*. Portsmouth, NH: Heinemann, 2005.

Roberts, Richard, and Martin Klein, "The Banamba Slave Exodus of 1905 and the Decline of Slavery in the Western Sudan." *Journal of African History* 21, no. 3 (1980): 375–94.

Rodet, Marie. "Disrupting Masculinist Discourse on African Migration: The Study of Neglected Forms of Female Migration." In *Crossing Places: New Research in African Studies*, edited by Charlotte Baker and Zoë Norridge. Newcastle, UK: Cambridge Scholars Publishing, 2007.

———. "Genre, coutumes et droit colonial au Soudan français (1918–1939)." *Cahiers d'Études Africaines* 187–88 (2007): 583–602.

———. "Migrants in French Sudan: Gender Biases in the Historiography." In *Trans-Atlantic Migration: The Paradoxes of Exile*, edited by Toyin Falola and Niyi Afolabi. New York: Routledge, 2007.

Rude, Darlene. "Reasonable Men and Provocative Women: A Gendered Analysis of Domestic Homicide in Zambia." *Journal of Southern African Studies* 29, no. 1 (1999): 7–27.

Scott, James. *The Moral Economy of the Peasant: Rebellion and Subsistence in Southeast Asia*. New Haven, CT: Yale University Press, 1976.

Scott, Joan. *The Politics of the Veil*. Princeton, NJ: Princeton University Press, 2004.

Scully, Pamela. *Liberating the Family? Gender and British Slave Emancipation in the Rural Western Cape, South Africa, 1823–1853*. Portsmouth, NH: Heinemann, 1997.

———. "Rape, Race and Colonial Culture: The Sexual Politics of Identity in the Nineteenth-Century Cape Colony, South Africa." *American Historical Review* 100, no. 2 (1995): 335–59.

Shadle, Brett. *"Girl Cases": Marriage and Colonialism in Gusiiland, Kenya, 1890–1970*. Portsmouth, NH: Heinemann, 2006.

———. "Rape in the Courts of Gusiiland, Kenya, 1940s–1960s." *African Studies Review* 51, no. 2 (2008): 27–50.

Shaham, Ron. *Family and the Courts in Modern Egypt: A Study Based on Decisions by the Sharia Courts, 1900–1955*. Leiden: E. J. Brill, 1997.

Shell-Duncan, Bettina, and Ylva Hernlund, eds. *Female "Circumcision" in Africa: Culture, Controversy, and Change*. Boulder, CO: Lynne Rienner, 2000.

Smith, Mary. *Baba of Karo, a Woman of the Muslim Hausa*. New Haven, CT: Yale University Press, 1981.

Sòrgoni, Barbara. *Parole e corpi: Antropologia, discorso giuridico e politiche sessuali interrazziali nella colonia Eritrea, 1890–1941*. Naples: Liguori, 1998.

Sow, Fatou. "Fundamentalisms, Globalisation and Women's Human Rights in Senegal." *Gender and Development* 11, no. 1 (2003): 69–76.

Sow Sidibé, Amsatou. "Senegal's Evolving Family Law." *Journal of Family Law* 32, no. 2 (1993–94): 421–29.

Spear, Thomas. *Mountain Farmers: Moral Economies of Land and Agricultural Development in Arusha and Meru*. Berkeley: University of California Press, 1997.

Stacy, Helen. *Human Rights for the Twenty-first Century.* Stanford, CA: Stanford University Press, 2009.

Stafford, Nancy Kaymar. "Permission for Domestic Violence: Marital Rape in Ghanaian Marriages." *Women's Rights Law Reporter* 29, no. 2–3 (2008): 63–76.

Stockreiter, Elke E. "Tying and Untying the Knot: *Kadhi's* Courts and the Negotiation of Social Status in Zanzibar Town, 1900–1963." PhD diss., School of Oriental and African Studies, University of London, 2008.

Stoler, Ann Laura. "'In Cold Blood': Hierarchies of Credibility and the Politics of Colonial Narratives." *Representations* 37 (Winter 1992): 151–89.

Stowasser, Barbara. "Gender Issues and Contemporary Quran Interpretation." In *Islam, Gender, and Social Change*, edited by Yvonne Yazbeck Haddad and John L. Esposito, 30–44. Oxford: Oxford University Press, 1998.

Taddia, Irma. *L'Eritrea-colonia 1890–1952: Paesaggi, strutture, uomini del colonialismo.* Milan: Franco Angeli, 1986.

Thioub, Ibrahima. "Sénégal: La prison à l'époque coloniale: Significations, évitement et évasions." In *Enfermement, prison et châtiments*, edited by Florence Bernault, 285–303. Paris: Karthala, 1999.

Thomas, Dorothy Q., and Michele E. Beasley. "Domestic Violence as a Human Rights Issue." *Human Rights Quarterly* 15, no. 1 (1993): 36–62.

Thompson, E. P. "The Moral Economy of the English Crowd in the Eighteenth Century." *Past and Present* 50 (February 1971): 76–136.

Tsing, Anna L. *Friction: An Ethnography of Global Connection.* Princeton, NJ: Princeton University Press, 2005.

Vaughan, Megan. "Which Family? Problems in the Reconstruction of the History of the Family as an Economic and Cultural Unit." *Journal of African History* 24, no. 2 (1983): 275–83.

Villalon, Leonardo. *Islamic Society and State Power in Senegal: Disciples and Citizens in Fatick.* Cambridge: Cambridge University Press, 1995.

Walker, Leonore. *The Battered Woman Syndrome.* New York: Springer, 1984.

Waller, Richard. "Witchcraft and Colonial Law in Kenya." *Past and Present* 180, no. 1 (2003): 241–75.

Wandia, Mary. "Institutionalizing Strategies for the Protocol." In *Breathing Life into the African Union Protocol on Women's Rights in Africa*, edited by Roselynn Musa, Faiza Jama Mohammed, and Firoze Manji, 34–37. Oxford: African Books Collective, 2006.

Whitehead, Ann, "Men and Women, Kinship and Property: Some General Issues." In *Women and Property, Women as Property*, edited by Renée Hirschon, 176–92. London: Croom Helm, 1984.

Wiener, Martin. "Judges v. Jurors: Courtroom Tensions and the Law of Criminal Responsibility in Nineteenth-Century England." *Law and History Review* 17, no. 3 (1999): 467–506.

———. *Men of Blood: Violence, Manliness and Criminal Justice in Victorian England.* Cambridge: Cambridge University Press, 2004.

Wolf, Diane L. *Factory Daughters: Gender, Household Dynamics, and Industrialization in Java.* Berkeley: University of California Press, 1992.

Wolf, Margery. *Women and the Family in Rural Taiwan.* Stanford, CA: Stanford University Press, 1972.

World Health Organization. *Multi-country Study on Women's Health and Domestic Violence against Women.* Geneva, 2005.

Wright, Marcia. *Strategies of Slaves and Women: Life-Stories from East/Central Africa.* New York: Lilian Barber Press, 1993.

Contributors

CODOU BOP is a Senegalese freelance consultant and political activist. She coordinates the Groupe de Recherche sur les Femmes et les Lois au Sénégal (GREFELS), a women's human rights association active at the local and regional levels. She is also a research officer with International Planned Parenthood Federation, with the Population Council, and with the Association of African Women for Research and Development. She has been a Humphrey Fellow and a Fellow of the Religion and Human Rights program at Emory University.

EMILY BURRILL received her PhD in African history from Stanford University and is currently an assistant professor of women's studies and history at the University of North Carolina, Chapel Hill. Her research, conducted in Mali, examines changing gender roles and household relationships in the Sikasso region during the colonial and postcolonial periods. Her articles have appeared in *Slavery and Abolition, Cahiers d'Études Africaines,* and *Ultramarines: Revue de l'Association des Amis des Archives d'Outre-Mer.*

CATI COE is an associate professor of anthropology at Rutgers University, Camden. Her PhD in anthropology is from the University of Pennsylvania. She has published *Dilemmas of Culture in African Schools: Youth, Nationalism, and the Transformation of Knowledge* and several articles on the construction of tradition, narrative, and nation through schools in Ghana and elsewhere. Her current work focuses on child-fosterage arrangements among Ghanaian transnational families.

BENEDETTA FAEDI is a doctoral candidate at Stanford Law School, Stanford University. She received her LLB from the University of Rome, an MA in political science from the University of Florence, and an LLM from the London School of Economics and Political Science. Before joining Stanford, Benedetta practiced law in London, served as a research assistant to the School of Law at Queen Mary, University of London, and worked for the Child Protection Unit of the United Nations Stabilization Mission in Haiti. She specializes in international law, international human rights, and law and sexuality. Her article "The Double Weakness of Girls: Discrimination and Sexual Violence in Haiti" was awarded the 2007 Carle Mason Franklin Prize in International Law and was published in the *Stanford Journal of International Law.*

SAIDA HODŽIĆ is an assistant professor of women and gender studies at George Mason University. She received her PhD in medical anthropology at UC Berkeley and UC San Francisco. This chapter complements her articles on women's rights and the Ghanaian advocacy for the Domestic Violence Bill published in *Ethnos* and forthcoming in *Confronting Global Gender Justice: Women's Rights, Human Lives*. She is currently working on a manuscript titled *Of Rebels, Spirits, and Social Engineers: The Awkward Endings of Female Genital Cutting*, supported by a research and writing grant from the Harry Frank Guggenheim Foundation.

STACEY HYND is a lecturer in history at Exeter University. She received her DPhil in African history from Oxford University for her dissertation on capital punishment, violence, and British colonial rule in Africa. She has also taught at Cambridge University.

SCOTT LONDON received his PhD in cultural anthropology from the University of Arizona. He conducted fieldwork in Senegal in 1995–97. His research focuses on family law, gender, domestic violence, and sexual assault. He is currently an associate professor in the Department of Sociology and Anthropology at Randolph-Macon College in Ashland, Virginia.

KATHERINE LUONGO is an assistant professor of history at Northeastern University in Boston. In 2004, she was a Fulbright-Hays Fellow in Kenya, where she completed historical and ethnographic research for her dissertation on the intersections of the criminal legal system and Kamba witchcraft. She also worked as a research associate at the Institut Français de Recherche en Afrique in Nairobi in 2004. Her research and teaching interests include the occult, legal systems, and the intersection of anthropology and history.

RICHARD ROBERTS is the Frances and Charles Field Professor of History and director of the Center for African Studies, Stanford University. His PhD is from the University of Toronto. He has written widely on the social and legal history of West Africa, and his recent books include *Litigants and Households: African Disputes and Colonial Courts in the French Soudan, 1895–1912* and *Intermediaries, Interpreters, and Clerks: African Employees in the Making of Modern Africa*, edited with Benjamin N. Lawrance and Emily L. Osborn.

MARIE RODET is a Hertha-Firnberg Research Fellow and lecturer at the University of Vienna. She received her PhD from the University of Vienna in November 2006. Her research interests include migration history, gender studies, and legal history in West Africa. Her most recent publications include *Les migrantes ignorées du Haut-Sénégal (1900–1946)*.

MARTINA SALVANTE is a doctoral student at the European University Institute in Florence, Italy. Her thesis focuses on the figure of the paterfamilias under the Fascist regime in Italy (1922–43). As part of it, she has extensively researched the special legislation affecting interracial relations in the Italian colonies in Africa.

PAMELA SCULLY is a professor of women's studies and African studies at Emory University. She has her PhD from the University of Michigan. She is the author of books and articles concerning aspects of gender, sexuality, and slave emancipation. She is the coauthor, with Clifton Crais, of *Sara Baartman and the Hottentot Venus: A Ghost Story and a Biography*. Scully is now working on gender violence and gender justice in postconflict societies.

ELKE E. STOCKREITER obtained her PhD from the School of Oriental and African Studies, University of London, and is an assistant professor at the Department of History, University of Iowa. Her research engages with Muslim societies in sub-Saharan Africa, with a focus on gender, slavery, and Islamic law on the East African coast and in West Africa.

ELIZABETH THORNBERRY is a doctoral candidate in African history at Stanford University. Her research, supported by the Fulbright Institute for International Education, focuses on the history of sexual violence in the Eastern Cape in the nineteenth century.

Index

abandonment (of spouse or marital relationship), 41–44, 79, 203, 247; as grounds for divorce, 20. *See also* desertion of the marital home
abolition. *See* slavery: end of
Aburi, 58–59
Accra, 223
Achebe, Chinua, 278
Addis Ababa, 101, 106, 112
adultery, 86–87, 91–92, 122, 124, 129–32; as a motive in cases of domestic violence, 163–66, 172–73
African Charter on Human Rights and Peoples' Rights, 265, 266
African Commission, 270
African Court, 270–71
African Union, 266
Africa Orientala Italiana. *See* Italian East Africa
Afrique occidental français. *See* French West Africa
Akuapem, 57–66
alcohol, relation to domestic violence, 42, 162
Algeria, 261
Allman, Jean, 64
American Convention on Human Rights, 264
Amussen, Susan, 18
apprenticeship, 6, 54, 60, 66. *See also* fostering; servants
Asmah, Gladys, 229, 230
assessors in colonial courts, 16, 160, 163, 167–68, 240. *See also* colonial law

Bamako, 43, 84, 87
Banamba, 33–34, 36–39, 41, 43
Barrera, Giulia, 104
Basel Mission, Ghana, 57, 60, 64, 66
battered child syndrome, 11
battered wife syndrome, 11
Benson, Koni, 19
Bentham, Jeremy, 126
Berry, Sara, 16
Blackstone, William, 126
bridewealth, 10, 36, 42, 44–45, 47, 64–65, 78–80, 85, 120, 124, 145, 166. *See also* family; gender roles; household
British colonialism, 9, 16, 58, 118–25, 127–28, 131–32, 134, 138–39, 145, 160, 281. *See also* British Kaffraria; Kenya; Nyasaland; Zanzibar

British East Africa, 159–74. *See also* Kenya
British Kaffraria, 120–25
Brooks, Rosa, 256
Burdett, Charles, 97

Campassi, Gabriella, 105
Cape Colony, 117–32
capital punishment, 159–74
Chadya, Joyce, 19
Chanock, Martin, 125
chiefs. *See* custom; customary courts; traditional leaders
child abuse, 5, 35, 204
child custody, issue in divorce, 79
child fostering. *See* fostering
child marriage; British policy on, 145; consummation of, 146; in colonial Zanzibar, 139, 144–52; in contemporary Senegal, 203, 212; public opinion on, 147
child protection movement, 11
childraising, public debates about, Ghana, 66
children, appropriate behavior of, 62
Christelow, Allan, 146
Christianity, 7, 57–60, 66, 171–72; role in shaping sexual morality, 129
Ciekawy, Diane, 187
citizenship, 40, 86, 96–97, 231–32, 259
civilization, ideology of, 8, 16, 95, 122, 160, 282–83
civil law: distinction from criminal law, British thought, 126; customary law applied in civil cases, Cape Colony, 124–25; customary law applied in civil cases, French Soudan, 75
Clark, Anna, 121
cocoa, 57, 60–61, 63, 65, 68
Cohen, David, 7
colonial courts, 16, 33, 35, 39, 58, 75–76, 95, 118–19, 121, 124, 159,160, 164–66, 168, 173, 187, 281. *See also* colonial law; customary courts
colonialism, 9–10, 14, 277, 282.   *See also* British colonialism; French colonialism; Italian colonialism
colonial law, 14, 20, 40, 103, 282; Cape Colony, 118, 123, 129, 132; French Soudan, 74–87; Ghana, 58; Kenya, 162, 185, 191; Zanzibar, 145. *See also* customary law; shari'a
compensation payments, 46, 64, 79, 125–32, 142, 259

moral crisis, 84
moral economy, 18, 34, 39, 44, 45, 47, 166, 174
Morocco, 261
motherhood, 36, 42, 61–62. *See also* gender roles
motive, in cases of domestic violence, 162, 164–65
Moultrie, Ian Edward Ferguson, 146, 148–49
murder, 17, 159–74; of abusers by their victims, 168, 173; as domestic violence, 203; legal definition of, colonial Kenya, 190
Muslim brotherhoods, Senegal, 241, 245

native courts. *See* customary courts
native law. *See* customary law
Native Succession Ordinance (Cape Colony, 1864), 123
neoliberalism, 234
Niasse, Doki, 215
nongovernmental organizations (NGOs), 1, 14, 221; activities to combat domestic violence, Senegal, 215; relation to state, 232–33; work on women's issues, Ghana, 221–35
Nsawam, 54, 57–58, 61
Nyasaland (present-day Malawi), 125, 159–74

Optional Protocol to the Convention on the Elimination of All Forms of Discrimination against Women, 260
Organization of African Unity, 265

Pakro, 55, 57
patriarchal bargain, 18
patriarchy, 5, 8, 13, 17–18, 35, 41, 95, 108, 116, 123, 140, 173, 179, 221–47, 266, 281. *See also* masculinity
pawns, pawning, 55, 59, 60–62, 65–67. *See also* servants
Penal Code (Senegal), provisions on domestic violence, 253
physical abuse, 45, 46, 74; acceptable levels of, British East Africa, 166–67; as grounds for divorce, Cape Colony, 120; as grounds for divorce, French West Africa, 80–82; as proof of affection, 94, 101, 102; as reason for murder, 170. *See also* domestic violence
physical discipline, public acceptance of, Senegal, 211
Pickering, Chief Justice G. H., 140
police, policing, 57, 94–96, 99–103, 117, 148, 150, 210, 214, 217, 228–29, 246–47
Pollera, Alberto, 107
Pollet, Eric, 41
polygyny, 2, 6, 9, 119, 140, 162, 169, 206, 210. *See also* family; household
precolonial African history, 12
pregnancy, 80, 207, 212
private sphere, 118–19

property, 8–9, 125, 140, 228; women as, 166
protectorate, 14
Protocol on the Rights of Women in Africa, 266
psychological abuse, 4, 42–43, 75, 162, 187, 215, 229, 258, 264, 266, 269. *See also* emotional abuse
punishment, 2, 62, 123, 126–29, 181, 185; conception of domestic violence in terms of, 74, 211, 217; corporal, 16, 141; for domestic violence, 117, 131, 149, 162, 207, 209; for female genital cutting, 226, 232; for madamato, 98, 106
purdah, 140

qadi's courts, 16; French West Africa, 85; Kenya, 19, 243; Senegal, 240; Zanzibar, 138–44, 146–52. *See also* Islam; shari'a

race, racial ideology, racial purity, 16, 98, 100, 103–4
rape. *See* sexual assault
Rattray, R. S., 63
reasonableness, as legal standard, 180
regionalism, strategy for human rights enforcement, 267–68, 271
repugnancy clause, 16, 181
reservations, to international conventions/protocols on human rights, 260
Roberts, Richard, 146
Roman-Dutch law, 122–30
Rwanda, gender-based violence in 1994 genocide, 280

Saint-Louis, Senegal, 240
Scott, James, 34
seduction, offense in customary law, 128–32
Segu, 37, 44, 46
Senegal, 8, 13, 19, 41, 85, 203–17, 221, 239–53, 282–83. *See also* French West Africa
Senghor, Léopold Sédar, 206, 240
Senufo, 36
servants, 6, 54, 59–61, 95, 97, 102, 105–6, 207. *See also* fostering; pawns, pawning; slavery
sexual assault, 16, 55, 61, 63, 117, 121, 128, 129, 132, 183, 284; adjudication of cases, 124; law on, Cape Colony, 122; law on, Kenya, 183–84; law on, Senegal, 207; within marriage, 165, 166, 177, 204, 209; within marriage, Senegal, 204, 209; of minors, 203; South Africa, 284; in witchcraft allegations, 180. *See also* domestic violence, domestic abuse
sexual harassment, 207
sexuality (colonial perceptions of African), 103
Sexual Offences Acts (in Ghana, Kenya, Malawi, Swaziland, Uganda, Zimbabwe), 227
Shadle, Brett, 145
Shafi'i (Islamic school of law), 139–47, 150
shari'a, 14, 16, 19, 85, 88, 90, 138, 141, 206, 240–41, 282; British incorporation of, 139,